MW00790604

On the Front cover:

Page one of the United States Constitution

On the Back cover: (Hardcover Edition)

Page one of the United States Bill of Rights

On the Back cover: (Softcover Edition)

The Crusades

The Death of American Empire

Understanding How Unethical Geo-Politics, Fanatical World Religions and Economic Imperialism are Leading to World Crises in Health Care, Religious Conflict, Environmental Disaster and the Collapse of Civilization in the 21st Century

…and how to prepare for the next Age of Humankind…

SEMA INSTITUTE
P.O.Box 570459
Miami, Florida, 33257
(305) 378-6253 Fax: (305) 378-6253

The author is available for group lectures and individual counseling. For further information contact the publisher.

Ashby, Reginald Muata
The Death of American Empire
ISBN: 1-884564-45-3 (Hardcover), **ISBN:** 1-884564-25-9 (Softcover)

Library of Congress Cataloging in Publication Data

SEMA INSTITUTE

TABLE OF CONTENTS

Biography of Reginald Muata Ashby

Reginald Muata Ashby was born in New York City and in his later adolescent years grew up in the Caribbean before moving back to the United States to attend high school and college. His family is from Puerto Rico and Barbados. Displaying an early interest in ancient civilizations and the Humanities, he began to study these subjects while in college.

Mr. Ashby began studies in the area of religion and philosophy and achieved a doctorate degree and at the same time he began to collect his research into what would later become several books on the subject of World Religions, World history, African History, religion and ethics, world mythology, origins of Yoga Philosophy and practice in ancient Africa (Ancient Egypt/Nubia) and also the origins of Christianity in Ancient Egypt. He is an accomplished lecturer, musician, artist, poet, painter, screenwriter, playwright and author of over 30 books on yoga philosophy, religious philosophy and social philosophy based on ancient African principles.

Mr. Ashby holds a Doctor of Divinity Degree in Religion and Holistic Health and a Masters Degree in Liberal Arts and Religious Studies. He is also a Teacher of Yoga Philosophy and Discipline. Dr. Ashby received his Doctor of Divinity Degree from and is an adjunct faculty member of the American Institute of Holistic Theology. Dr. Ashby is a certified as a PREP Relationship Counselor.

Foreword

A word of encouragement.

I have written this book because I feel that the ancient Spiritual philosophy can bring insight into the problems of the world today. Many readers of this book, especially those who have read my previous books, some of which have dealt with ethical, political and economic issues in a limited way, may find this book intense because it almost exclusively concentrates on those social issues. It presents some themes and information that some may find to be shocking and maybe even frightening and or unbelievable but all readers should remember that the fear that they may feel from the proven and documented information that will be presented in this volume is reality based fear as opposed to imaginary fear, such as is presented in the media about an undetermined foe or disease, or that might be presented by religious fundamentalists or warmongering politicians. The reality based fear can be transformed into positive action to counteract the problem and in so doing a person should not feel paralyzed or depressed but rather invigorated and hopeful, that they will begin to discover the truth and will not be surprised when the changes of the future come about. Therefore, this book will attempt to provide insight from an ethical, philosophical and spiritual perspective about what has and is going on in the world and what we should expect in the future and how to meet the challenges that life will bring.

The information and evidences presented in this book are mostly derived from statements from the actual sources being discussed, encyclopedias and legitimate historical sources and non-traditional news sources, not controlled by the present day corporate owned and controlled mainstream media. Therefore, this is information that is well known to scholars and researchers and is freely available but not widely disseminated or talked about in regular political or economic discussions. However, after reading the book the reader will find that the few reports related to these subjects that are presented in the mainstream media will be noticed by them but having the background of this book they will be able to put together the meager bits of information into a coherent whole for proper understanding and then they will be able to take proper action.

This is not a political book, in the sense that I'm not advocating that the Democratic Party would be better if they come to power and would change things and solve the ills of society or that the Republican Party is better. I am trying to show that the flaws of the systems of government and the values of U.S.A. culture are in need of an ethical and spiritual reevaluation in order to understand where the problems are and then proceed to solve them. In fact it does not matter which party or form of government is used if it will be managed by unethical people because those people would corrupt the system. So this book should serve as a historical and ethical review of world history, showing how empires are created and how they die and how the malady of imperious desires are endemic in a segment of the human consciousness and how the society needs to be vigilant in order to reestablish balance so as to maintain and perpetuate civilization.

This work is a collection of essays relating to social and economic, leadership, and ethics, ecological and religious issues that are facing the world today in order to understand the course of history that has led humanity to its present condition and then arrive at positive solutions that will lead to better outcomes for all humanity. It surveys the development and decline of major empires throughout history and focuses on the creation of American Empire along with the social, political and economic policies that led to the prominence of the United States of America as a Superpower including the rise of the political control of the neo-con political philosophy including militarism and the military industrial complex in American politics and the rise of the religious right into and American Theocracy movement. This volume details, through historical and current events, the psychology behind the dominance of western culture in world politics through the *"Superpower Syndrome Mandatory Conflict Complex"* that drives the Superpower culture to establish itself above all others and then act hubristically to dominate world culture through legitimate influences as well as coercion, media censorship and misinformation leading to international hegemony and world conflict. This volume also details the financial policies that gave rise to American prominence in the global economy, especially after World War II, and promoted American preeminence over the world economy through Globalization as well as the environmental policies, including the oil economy, that are promoting degradation of the world ecology and contribute to the decline of America as an Empire culture. This volume finally explores the factors pointing to the decline of the American Empire economy and imperial power and what to expect in the aftermath of American prominence and how to survive the decline while at the same time promoting policies and social-economic-religious-political changes that are needed in order to promote the emergence of a beneficial and sustainable culture.

Many people scoff at those who criticize the U.S.A., pointing to the "greatness" and abundance and wealth of the country. They claim that those achievements, which may well be far ahead of any other culture in history, are proofs that the U.S.A. is the greatest country in the world and perhaps that ever was. Yet there are always flaws in any culture. However, when those flaws have major or even global implications it is important to examine those in order to discover and implement better solutions. Therefore, constructive criticism is important and necessary for the betterment of nations and for humanity as a whole.

There is no doubt that the U.S.A. has made grand achievements in science, technology and wealth creation but still there are many people who would like to go back to some mythic time "when America was great" and there was less crime and less malcontents, less homosexuals, less women talking back, etc. or at least they would like to imagine that it was like that at some point in the past. They claim that Americans should be proud and not criticize because Americans built this country with their own blood and sweat. The question is though, when was that time? And even if this period did exist at some point in the past does that mean that the social or economic policies should not be criticized?

The U.S.A. has been striving to control other countries and acquire territories since the time of its inception. The first acquisition was the land itself, which was usurped from the Native Americans. Americans did not create the U.S.A. if we consider that the European slave owners forced the Native Americans and Africans into slave labor and that free labor allowed the great profits that permitted the European power elite to build up the country. Today, the illusory wealth that most people in the middle and lower classes experience comes from being able to buy cheap goods. Those goods are cheap because other countries have been subjugated economically by their leaders or through neocolonial governments or through economic subjugation through loans from institutions like the IMF so that their populations are kept working for slave wages.

So while Americans can objectively enjoy modern conveniences and the capacity to purchase cheap goods those goods are in effect a source of sustaining the illusion of real American wealth since the real wealth goes to corporations and the power elite. Those same cheap goods are a cause for the commercialization of other countries and the enslavement and suffering of the populations of those countries. So, while there is reason to say that the U.S.A. leaders have been ingenious in wealth creation that wealth is not sustainable nor was it developed through legitimate commerce. Those sensitive people with sufficient conscience feel empathy with those who are suffering no matter where they are on earth and if they are Americans, would not want to perpetuate that suffering by supporting the consumer culture and imperial ideal. Therefore, the criticism of the U.S.A. is legitimate and needed to improve the situation for Americans and foreigners alike.

We may consider that in the tradition of Henry David Thoreau, social commentary and criticism are not only a right but a duty not only of American citizens but of anyone who considers him or her self as a citizen of the world, concerned for the well being of all human beings on earth.

PREFACE

American Empire?

im·pe·ri·al·ism (ĭm-pîr'ē-ə-lĭz'əm) *n.*

1. The policy of extending a nation's authority by territorial acquisition or by the establishment of economic and political hegemony over other nations.
2. The system, policies, or practices of such a government.

Prior to the 21st century, the open use of the term American Empire was resisted by many writers and commentators of the foreign policies of the United States of America [U.S.A.]. Nevertheless, terms such as American empire, American Hegemony, American Exeptionalism or American Imperialism have been used by people in the U.S.A. and in other countries to describe those U.S.A. policies related to territorial expansion or control of world markets or economies. American nationalism developed during and after the revolution as a concept of exeptionalism in which the people of the U.S.A. came to believe that they were doing something special and different that was better than anything else in human history. This disregarded the sources of the ideas that went into creating the new country that came from the Native Americans, and philosophers such as John Calvin and Thomas Hobbes, the upbringing of the Founding Fathers and from elsewhere. This idea also disregarded the ignoble actions that were not new and different but were indeed epitomizing the actions of previous societies to advance themselves including slavery, indentured service, devastation of native cultures, etc.

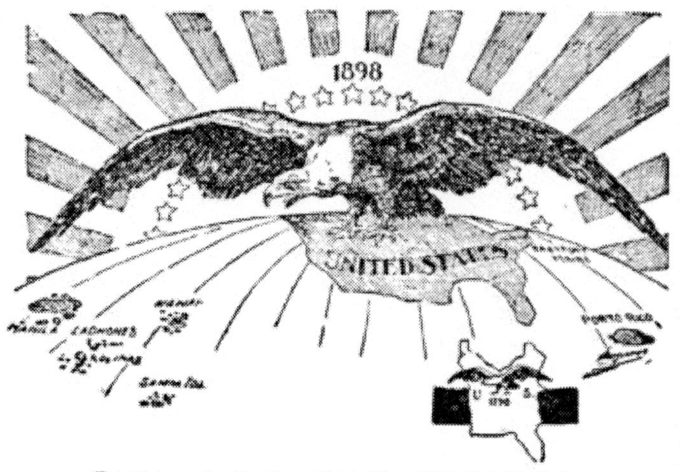

Ten thousand miles from tip to tip.—Philadelphia Press.

1898 political cartoon: "Ten Thousand Miles From Tip to Tip" meaning the extension of U.S. domination (symbolized by a bald eagle) from Puerto Rico to the Philippines. The cartoon contrasts this with a map of the smaller United States 100 years earlier in 1798.[1]

The concept of American exeptionalism as a particular and unique phenomenon was recognized in the 19th century by a French observer by the name of Alexis de Tocqueville. He said that the U.S.A. was *"proceeding along a path to which no limit can be perceived."*[2] Throughout U.S.A. history there have been several groups that have promoted an ideal of conservatism that includes American isolationism. Patrick Buchanan, a popular conservative of the country, makes a case that the contemporary United States policy towards empire is *"far from what the Founding Fathers had intended the young Republic to become."*[3] Sidney Lens, a historian, makes the case that *"the United States, from the time it gained its own independence, has used every available means -- political, economic, and military -- to dominate other nations."*[4] Lens considers the concept of American exeptionalism as a "myth," that is used by politicians and others to allow or excuse *"excesses and cruelties, though sometimes admitted, usually [to be] regarded as momentary aberrations."*[5] Noam Chomsky makes the case that propaganda, has been used as a systematic strategy, controlled and implemented by *"elite domination of the media";* that strategy allows them to *"fix the premises of discourse and interpretation, and the definition of what is newsworthy in the first place, and they explain the basis and operations of what amount to propaganda campaigns."*[6] Other groups have promoted expansionism but not until the post World War II era did the concept of world domination become a viable option to be considered. Yet the group now known as "Neo-conservatives" espouses just such a philosophy.

Charles Krauthammer, a Republican columnist said, *"People are now coming out of the closet on the word 'empire.'"* Writers such as Dinesh D'Souza and Mark Steyn and other political observers, operatives and scientists such as Zbigniew Brzezinski, and the historian Paul Johnson, have accepted the use of the term "American Empire."[7]

The following is a partial list of the United States interventions in other countries ["foreign interventions"[8]] that are referred to by critics as evidence of imperialism:

- Eradication policies against Native Americans involved in the establishment of the United States;
- Territorial conquests of Mexico;
- The Spanish-American War and the resulting occupation of Cuba, annexation of Puerto Rico, and Philippine-American War;
- Military intervention in Colombia to separate the department of Panama and build the Panama Canal.
- Intervention in the First World War and then subsequent invasion of Russia;
- Provocation of Japan prior to the Second World War;
- Division of the world with the Soviet Union into zones of control after the Second World War, as enforced for example by intervention in the Greek Civil War;
- Intervention in East Asian nations such as Korea, Cambodia, and (especially) Vietnam;
- Numerous interventions in Latin America justified by the Monroe Doctrine, for example the 1973 overthrow of Salvador Allende's government in Chile;
- Interference in the former Yugoslavia in the 1990's;
- Support for oppressive governments in the Middle East such as the Shah's Iran, Egypt after 1972, the monarchy in Saudi Arabia, Israel, and Saddam Hussein's Iraq prior to 1991 as well as the present occupation of that country.

In the three years following the invasion of Afghanistan and Iraq in 2001 and 2003 respectively, a certain critical mass was reached, just as the late 1990s critical mass was reached with the dot-com boom. At that time, almost overnight, every company had to have an internet presence and all of a sudden their web sites were advertised to the point that the public now knows that every company has one. In the same way, in the years 2005-2006 there appeared many new books talking about the empire of the U.S.A. and many commentators began to openly use the term "American Empire" although no one in the government openly speaks about the U.S.A. as an empire. Yet it became clear that that is what has been created through the network of military bases around the world, to enforce the will of the U.S.A. as well as through the extensive financial controls and the imposed use of the U.S.A. dollar as a world currency. The reality of the U.S.A. Empire prompted the writing of the book *The Sorrows of Empire: Militarism, Secrecy, and the End of the Republic,* by Chalmers Johnson.[9] He explained that *"American leaders now like to compare themselves to imperial Romans, even though they do not know much Roman history..."* Chalmers reflects that since September 11, 2001, the U.S.A. has *"undergone a transformation from republic to empire that may well prove irreversible..."*

Johnson was referring to the fact that before Rome became an Empire it had been previously a Republic, with an operating Senate. But that system of government was lost when they made the move towards imperial politics and economics. The U.S.A.'s imperial designs have definitely had an effect on the world economy and the world social relations. Yet most people in the U.S.A. itself are unaware of the worldwide impact of the U.S.A. which has been deleterious in most cases. In an interview on the program "Conversations with History" at the Institute of International Studies, with Harry Kreisler UC Berkeley, Chalmers Johnson further explored the issue of the U.S.A.'s similarities to the Roman Empire:

> What interests me here is that we're talking about a history that looks very much like the end of the Roman Republic, which was, in many ways, a model for our own republic -- and its conversion into a military

> dictatorship called the Roman Empire as the troops began to take over. The kind of figure that the Roman Republic began to look for in a military populist -- of course, the most obvious example is Julius Caesar, but after his assassination in 44 BC, the young Octavian who becomes the "god" Augustus Caesar was not unlike our boy emperor.

When we speak of America or American Empire we must clearly delineate what country we are speaking about. The term “America” properly does not refer to a particular country but a hemisphere. So when we speak of the American empire we are in reality not referring to Canada, Mexico, Argentina, Venezuela or Brazil which are countries located in the north and south American continents. It refers to the United States of America. The problem is that people from the United States of America have trouble referring to themselves in relation to other countries so they use the generic term “American” for themselves when it properly applies to all the people who reside from Canada in the northern tip of North America to Argentina in the southern tip of South America. But how would it sound to say “I am a United States of American” all the time? So most people in the Unites States of America have taken to calling themselves “American” but if one were to ask ordinary Canadians or Mexicans or Brazilians if they feel represented by or part of the “American Empire” they would say no and with good reason, because that is the truth. The term American has come to represent the U.S.A. and the marginalization of the rest of the people who live in the Americas and so it has become a hubristic term and a term that many residents of other countries in the Americas have come to regard as hegemonic. Yet the economic, political and military power that it represents is real in relative terms, and the effect it has on the world is far reaching. What kind of empire has the U.S.A. created and how does it compare to other empires of the past? Chalmers Johnson writes:

> "Empire is a physical reality with a distinct way of life, but also a network of economic and political interests tied in a thousand different ways to American corporations, universities, and communities, but kept separate from everyday life, that is, in the United States." And then you go on to say, "What is most fascinating and curious about the developing American form of empire, however, is that in its modern phase, it is solely an empire of bases, not of territories. And these bases now encircle the earth."

> "...The bases are the equivalent of what used to be colonies. They exist from Greenland to Australia, from Japan to Latin America."

An empire can express in different ways or in a combination of ways. The U.S.A. culture has expressed militarily but also there is an economic component. It can express as economic imperialism. It can also express as cultural imperialism.

Edward Said, who is regarded as a founder of the discipline of study of post-colonialism, makes the case that, *"So influential has been the discourse insisting on American specialness, altruism and opportunity, that imperialism in the United States as a word or ideology has turned up only rarely and recently in accounts of the United States culture, politics and history. But the connection between imperial politics and culture in North America, and in particular in the United States, is astonishingly direct."* Said describes the manner in which non-Americans, and especially non-Westerners, are typically considered in the U.S.A, as tacitly racist. It is done in a manner that permits imperialism and its attendant policies to be justified and operates through concepts like the White Man's Burden.[10]

The concept of the U.S.A. as being a "Superpower" is intimately related to the ideas of American imperialism. John Bellamy Foster, a Marxist sociologist scholar, noted that after the collapse of the Soviet Union as a superpower, the sole-superpower status the United States makes it the most dangerous world imperialist.[11] What is it that drives the Superpower country and in particular the United States of America? Is it a small group of people, a cabal, who direct and control the whole population or is it more complicated; are the masses complicit in the imperial pursuits and what would they have to gain by supporting an imperial agenda? John Bellamy Foster asked that question in a *National review* article.

> Numerous critics of the current expansion of the American empire—both on the U.S. left and in Europe—now argue that the United States under the administration of George W. Bush has been taken over by a neoconservative cabal, led by such figures as Paul Wolfowitz (deputy secretary of defense), Lewis Libby (the vice president's chief of staff), and Richard Perle (of the Defense Policy Board). This cabal is said to

> have the strong backing of Secretary of Defense Rumsfeld and Vice President Cheney, and, through them, President Bush.[12]

First we will explore some of the psychological aspects of the mentality that contributes to the justification for the persons who adopt the superpower concept as a viable and legitimate world view. Then we will explore the ethical and philosophical ramifications of the superpower and imperial viewpoint and strategy. Next we will explore the impact of the imperial form of philosophy on the world and the possible dangers to human civilizations that have arisen due to the imperial activities. Finally, we will explore how civilization can be perpetuated through ethical and sustainable social, economic and political policies.

The ultimate purpose of this book is to come to an understanding of the imperial form of thought because it is arguably the most influential force affecting human existence in the present; having recognized the neo-imperial philosophy, then it will be possible to realize how it affects every aspect of life, from ecology to what countries will be wealthy and which will be poor. Having understood the part that imperialism plays in the lives of human beings all over the world it will be possible to understand its deleterious effects and how to move towards a more balanced and equitable and sustainable form of social order that will allow humanity to continue in equilibrium instead of strife.

The self described economic hit-man, John Perkins, an avowed agent of the U.S.A. government and corporations, who facilitated the forcing of weaker countries into economic subjugation to the U.S.A. said,

> We economic hit men, during the last 30 or 40 years, have really created the world's first truly global empire, and we've done this primarily through economics, and the military only coming in as a last resort. Therefore, it's been done pretty much secretly. Most of the people in the United States have no idea that we've created this empire and, in fact, throughout the world it's been done very quietly, unlike old empires, where the army marched in; it was obvious.[13]

Part 1: The Importance of Questioning Reality and Evaluating Dissenting Opinions

John Stuart Mill

19th Century Wisdom on Questioning Reality, for Citizens of the New Millennium

Two important thinkers in Western culture during the 19th century were John Stuart Mill and Henry David Thoreau. Their writings are in many ways complementary and they speak to issues of continuing significance to citizens and modern professionals even today. It is interesting to realize how many parallels remain in modern culture to the experiences of Thoreau and Mill but it is not totally unexpected since the same system of government and social order that existed in the 19th century persists to this day. The writings of John Stuart Mill are highly philosophical as well as incisive with regard to the plight of not only the modern professional but also the citizen in general in dealing with the power of the state. Mill's main argument is that differences of opinion should be allowed because the challenge they present to the accepted ideas strengthens them by pointing out weaknesses or allows people to adopt new ideas that are better for society. Mill is particularly in opposition to the power that governments avail themselves of to coerce people.

> The power itself is illegitimate. The best government has no more title to it than the worst. It is as noxious, or more noxious, when exerted in accordance with public opinion, than when in opposition to it.
>
> - John Stuart Mill. *On Liberty* Chapter 2

In any society there may develop a general point of view in a majority of the population. That development may occur naturally by influence of some strong ideas, through discussion and consent of the individuals who make up the society. Mill puts for the noble idea that the human race is the loser when ideas are suppressed.

> But the peculiar evil of silencing the expression of an opinion is, that it is robbing the human race; posterity as well as the existing generation; those who dissent from the opinion, still more than those who hold it. If the opinion is right, they are deprived of the opportunity of exchanging error for truth: if wrong, they lose, what is almost as great a benefit, the

> clearer perception and livelier impression of truth, produced by its collision with error.
>
> - John Stuart Mill. *On Liberty* Chapter 2

One of Mill's central ideas is that stifling differences of opinion in public discourse is bad for society even if it's incorrect. This is because even the incorrect ideas force people to reexamine their "correct" ideas so that they might maintain a living presence in their minds with conscious understanding instead of becoming dogmas that are followed blindly and not understood but habitually practiced. That would presumably make people more susceptible to manipulation by unscrupulous politicians.

> We can never be sure that the opinion we are endeavoring to stifle is a false opinion; and if we were sure, stifling it would be an evil still.
>
> - John Stuart Mill. *On Liberty* Chapter 2

Mill importantly recognized the fallibility of people, which is no less visible in a government wherein the "authorities" seek to impose their opinion and quash dissenting ones.

> Those who desire to suppress it, of course deny its truth; but they are not infallible… All silencing of discussion is an assumption of infallibility.
>
> - John Stuart Mill. *On Liberty* Chapter 2

Mill specifically pointed out that Absolute Princes [rulers] and similar people who are accustomed to being accorded compliance by those who are acquiescent to their opinions are the ones who feel most confident of their opinions and presumably the error of others.

> Absolute princes, or others who are accustomed to unlimited deference, usually feel this complete confidence in their own opinions on nearly all subjects.
>
> - John Stuart Mill. *On Liberty* Chapter 2

This particular quality of a Prince or of others who are used to having their opinions accorded primacy if not exclusivity and the lack of listening to dissenting opinions is one of the primary prohibitions that Machiavelli presented in his book *The Prince:*

> A prince, therefore, ought always to take counsel, but only when he wishes and not when others wish; he ought rather to discourage every one from offering advice unless he asks it; but, however, he ought to be a constant inquirer, and afterwards a patient listener concerning the things of which he inquired; also, on learning that nay one, on any consideration, has not told him the truth, he should let his anger be felt. And if there are some who think that a prince who conveys an impression of his wisdom is not so through his own ability, but through the good advisers that he has around him, beyond doubt they are deceived, because this is an axiom which never fails: that a prince who is not wise himself will never take good advice, unless by chance he has yielded his affairs entirely to one person who happens to be a very prudent man. In this case indeed he may be well governed, but it would not be for long, because such a governor would in a short time take away his state from him.

However, unlike the ideal Prince of Machiavelli, Mill and Thoreau faced governmental regimes that actively sought to listen to their own council and they were not constant inquirers or patient listeners to the dissenting opinions of their time. To the contrary, pragmatists and business oriented people controlled the British government and the United States government who sought to impose their will on others for economic exploitation. Mill went on to describe those who are not used to having their opinions disputed and who hold strong beliefs when others share those opinions.

> People more happily situated, who sometimes hear their opinions disputed, and are not wholly unused to be set right when they are wrong, place the same unbounded reliance only on such of their opinions as are shared by all who surround them, or to whom they habitually defer: for in proportion to a man's want of confidence in his own solitary judgment, does he usually repose, with implicit trust, on the infallibility of "the world" in general.
>
> - John Stuart Mill. *On Liberty* Chapter 2

Mill went on to make the point that only those opinions that are tested by making them face refutation could provide anything resembling an assumption of being correct. That is unlike the usual preference of government which is to express an opinion and not have it contested.

> There is the greatest difference between presuming an opinion to be true, because, with every opportunity for contesting it, it has not been

> refuted, and assuming its truth for the purpose of not permitting its refutation.
>
> - John Stuart Mill. *On Liberty* Chapter 2

Thus, Mill's contention is that the often-unwritten rule of government, that there should be no dissent or even discussion of its policies is incorrect.

> There must be discussion, to show how experience is to be interpreted. Wrong opinions and practices gradually yield to fact and argument: but facts and arguments, to produce any effect on the mind, must be brought before it. Very few facts are able to tell their own story, without comments to bring out their meaning.
>
> - John Stuart Mill. *On Liberty* Chapter 2

However, Mill's contention that in order for the mind to be affected the arguments must be placed before it, does not always work. There are many who even after being confronted with well documented facts, refuse to even acknowledge those facts as legitimate, in order to maintain the policies that provide them with power or wealth or to maintain the notions they have been indoctrinated with. So in the case of the wealthy for example, they may not be adhering to policies that do contradict the facts of a given situation because they are weak-minded but rather because it serves their political or economic ends to do so. Mill points out, by highlighting contradictions in the logic of closely held beliefs, that those ideas were an accident of fate as it were. This contemplation would fly in the face of orthodox claims of holding absolute truth, that is, if people honestly reflected upon the nature of human existence.

> "...it never troubles him that mere accident has decided which of these numerous worlds is the object of his reliance, and that the same causes which make him a Churchman in London, would have made him a Buddhist or a Confucian in Pekin."
>
> - John Stuart Mill. *On Liberty* Chapter 2

Being phenomenological, mechanistic and materialistic in nature, unlike the East (India and China) and the South (Africa), Western culture tends to concretize and assign historicity to everything in its culture. This means that there is a tendency to allocate historicity even to religion, in order to garner authority by virtue of its reality, as opposed to the beliefs or religions of others which are mere myths, dreams or lesser people that need not be reckoned with, but which deserve to be at best ignored and subjugated or at worst eradicated. Nevertheless Mill went on to show that even an ethicist like Emperor Marcus Aurelius, who would otherwise appear to be as upstanding and righteous as Jesus, also took part in the persecution of Christians.

> This man (Emperor Marcus Aurelius), a better Christian in all but the dogmatic sense of the word, than almost any of the ostensibly Christian sovereigns who have since reigned, persecuted Christianity.
> - John Stuart Mill. *On Liberty* Chapter 2

So there is a problem here in that one would expect a person with a rational mind to uphold order, truth and righteousness, and if one supposes, as Mill did, that Jesus' moral code such as the one delivered in the Sermon on the Mount, is an example of order, truth and righteousness that it would be logically expected that Emperor Marcus Aurelius would agree with it and uphold it and not persecute the Christians. Yet the opposite was the case. In the same way, Mill knew in his own time, such men as Emperor Marcus Aurelius; men who would sacrifice good sense and righteous morals on the altar of expediency, greed and power.

Mill refuted one of the prominent rhetorical arguments of his time, namely that *"truth always triumphs over persecution."* In other words, the idea circulated that those who persecute would someday fail if they were wrong, so therefore, if they persist and continue to govern they must be correct. Thus, those people who tend to be compliant would take to further quiescence and thereby submit to the government. But that idea is contradicted by the truth as it is presented by history. History has demonstrated that even when governments have been wrong they most often seek to deny the evidence or place it in a context of non-culpability or non-responsibility so that the error or reality would not affect their rule.

> But, indeed, the dictum that truth always triumphs over persecution, is one of those pleasant falsehoods which men repeat after one another till they pass into commonplaces, but which all experience refutes. History teems with instances of truth put down by persecution...Reformation

> broke out at least twenty times before Luther, and was put down... Persecution has always succeeded, save where the heretics were too strong a party to be effectually persecuted.
>
> - John Stuart Mill. *On Liberty* Chapter 2

There are some arguments put forth by Mill in support of his main thesis about the need for dissent that seem to be contradictory to the ideal of freedom and expression in social life. Mill tried to use the example of Christianity as a dissenting opinion that was persecuted but which later rose to overtake other religions and philosophies.

> Christians were cast to the lions, but the Christian Church grew up a stately and spreading tree, overtopping the older and less vigorous growths, and stifling them by its shade.
>
> - John Stuart Mill. *On Liberty* Chapter 2

However, he apparently failed to realize that the rise of Christianity was accompanied by certain political needs of the ailing and decaying Roman Empire. Through adoption as a state religion and by means of church councils such as the Council at Nicea, the particular sect of orthodox Christians in Rome were able to use the power of what was left of the Roman Empire to persecute not only those who they called "pagans" but they also successfully persecuted those who upheld differing views of Christianity such as the Gnostics. So other religions were not stifled by the orthodox Christians, they were deliberately destroyed and converted by force of arms under the treat of execution. In other words, the emergence of Christianity as a dominant religion was not due to competition in a fair environment along with other competing religious philosophies in a way so that free debate could ensue and then the masses could make their choice freely about which religion they wanted to follow. An argument could be made that the sole reason why Christianity emerged from being one of many "cults" to the status of main and only religion was the deliberate repression of other religions and philosophies. So the persecuted became, in turn, the persecutors and the theme of persecuting non Christians has resounded throughout the history of Christianity which such notable instances as the Crusades, the inquisitions, the persecutions of Jews, the sanctioning of slavery and the destruction of Native American religions along with their cultures. One might easily draw the conclusion from the Christian example that even those who are persecuted will become persecutors, using the power of government to their own ends, if given a chance; an idea that Thoreau might vigorously agree with.

Mill went on to list simple but effective ways that the people in the government quash those protestors who were trying to uphold the truth. Legal or social penalties are used effectively especially on people who do not hold their convictions "zealously"; that is, willing to face the consequences of pushing forth their dissenting opinions.

> Men are not more zealous for truth than they often are for error, and a sufficient application of legal or even of social penalties will generally succeed in stopping the propagation of either.
>
> - John Stuart Mill. *On Liberty* Chapter 2

Nevertheless, history has also shown that while governments have been effective in suppressing dissent, there have also been people who have arisen throughout history to pick up the gauntlet as it were, to take the dissenting opinion up even in the next generation when conditions might be more conducive to its propagation throughout the masses.

> The real advantage which truth has, consists in this, that when an opinion is true, it may be extinguished once, twice, or many times, but in the course of ages there will generally be found persons to rediscover it, until some one of its reappearances falls on a time when from favourable circumstances it escapes persecution until it has made such head as to withstand all subsequent attempts to suppress it.
>
> - John Stuart Mill. *On Liberty* Chapter 2

Mill did try to give some credit to his society, England of the 19th century, by pointing out the advancement from the time of the inquisitions and the absolute power of the King and the state church and the government which by then was not executing heretics or applying sufficient force to completely destroy dissenting opinions. However, even though slavery ended in England in 1833, what about the oppression of the empire around the world and the atrocities committed by the British army and the East India

Company in putting down insurrections and depriving people of their freedom in the British colonies?

> It is true we no longer put heretics to death; and the amount of penal infliction which modern feeling would probably tolerate, even against the most obnoxious opinions, is not sufficient to extirpate them. But let us not flatter ourselves that we are yet free from the stain even of legal persecution. Penalties for opinion, or at least for its expression, still exist by law; and their enforcement is not, even in these times, so unexampled as to make it at all incredible that they may some day be revived in full force.
>
> - John Stuart Mill. *On Liberty* Chapter 2

Mill also alluded to the economic strings by which people are controlled and made compliant to the desires of the state. Those who are not independently wealthy have much to fear from the state because their very livelihood can be taken away. Therefore, economics are a perfect tool for obtaining compliance from people.

> "In respect to all persons but those whose pecuniary circumstances make them independent of the good will of other people, opinion, on this subject, is as efficacious as law; men might as well be imprisoned, as excluded from the means of earning their bread. Those whose bread is already secured, and who desire no favors from men in power, or from bodies of men, or from the public, have nothing to fear from the open avowal of any opinions, but to be ill-thought of and illspoken of, and this it ought not to require a very heroic mould to enable them to bear."
>
> - John Stuart Mill. *On Liberty* Chapter 2

Mill seemed to consent to an idea that was put forth by his opponents, that it was not necessary to have a populace that was disposed to study the opinions of *philosophers and theologians* and instead they only need to be *taught the obvious grounds of the truths* so that they only need to "trust" to some "authority" who is trained to resolve issues when they arise. This is the idea of top-down government wherein the people are to be dumbed down and made compliant to the rule of those who are capable to rule, presumably the aristocracy, oligarchy or plutocracy or as we see now in the early 21st century, the corporocracy and right wing theocracy.

> "...an enemy of free discussion may be supposed to say, that there is no necessity for mankind in general to know and understand all that can be said against or for their opinions by philosophers and theologians. That it is not needful for common men to be able to expose all the misstatements or fallacies of an ingenious opponent. That it is enough if there is always somebody capable of answering them, so that nothing likely to mislead uninstructed persons remains unrefuted. That simple minds, having been taught the obvious grounds of the truths inculcated on them, may trust to authority for the rest, and being aware that they have neither knowledge nor talent to resolve every difficulty which can be raised, may repose in the assurance that all those which have been raised have been or can be answered, by those who are specially trained to the task.
>
> Conceding to this view of the subject the utmost that can be claimed for it by those most easily satisfied with the amount of understanding of truth which ought to accompany the belief of it; even so, the argument for free discussion is no way weakened."
>
> - John Stuart Mill. *On Liberty* Chapter 2

This argument is uncannily similar to the conception of representative government in which legislative power is ceded to those who do not have any responsibility to the governed; who can act against the desires of those who voted for them with impunity, a perfect system of government for those who want to maintain power while giving the illusion to people that they are self-governed, a primary tenet of western democracies. This concept is also evident in orthodox religions that reject mystical philosophy because the orthodox practice promotes dependency on the religion through faith while the philosophical disciplines require critical thinking and independent action as opposed to dependency on and support of an organized religious institution that is primarily dedicated first and foremost to its own continued existence. This idea of ceding control over the decision making power by urging the populace not to pursue the depths of philosophy and theology for themselves, is prophetically evident in the present situation as was described by Charlotte Thomson Iserbyt, former Senior Policy Advisor in the U.S. Department of Education, who blew the whistle on government activities that withheld education from the public to promote an educational environment that did not seek to produce intelligent citizens but rather docile peasants.[14]

Further, it might be said also that this system of government in which people have been "dumbed down" as it were, purposely, has attained an unprecedented mode of compliance and acquiescence from the common people as evinced by the number of wars that have been engaged at the behest of the government, ignoring dissenting views, from the Mexican war to the war in Iraq through the means described by Mill but also now through the power of technology that has enabled an unprecedented powerful and effective propaganda system to emerge. That system encompasses but is not limited to the mass media which according to the U.S.A. Constitution was supposed to be free of government coercion. In our day, the press appears to be free from direct control by the government but in reality the media is controlled by corporations who themselves control the government through lobbying and political contributions. They control by forming a collusion of government policy and corporate interests through media support by promotion of the policies (through direct endorsements or by providing a mouthpiece to government officials without verifying their statements) or omission of contrary facts. Noam Chomsky wrote in *Manufacturing Consent* [(Pantheon, 1988)] that it's the primary function of the mass media in the United States to mobilize public support for the special interests that dominate the government and the private sector. What are those interests?

> CHOMSKY: Well, if you want to understand the way any society works, ours or any other, the first place to look is who is in a position to make the decisions that determine the way the society functions. Societies differ, but in ours, the major decisions over what happens in the society -- decisions over investment and production and distribution and so on -- are in the hands of a relatively concentrated network of major corporations and conglomerates and investment firms. They are also the ones who staff the major executive positions in the government. They're the ones who own the media and they're the ones who have to be in a position to make the decisions. They have an overwhelmingly dominant role in the way life happens. You know, what's done in the society. Within the economic system, by law and in principle, they dominate. The control over resources and the need to satisfy their interests imposes very sharp constraints on the political system and on the ideological system.

Mill went on to put forth his low opinion about people who "believe" in Christian morals but do not follow them or practice them, but merely follow and believe out of habit, tending instead to actually act out of "*The standard to which he does refer it, is the custom of his nation, his class, or his religious profession.*" Mill's impartiality is questioned, though, by his biased support of Christian morality as he states his belief that other ethics not derived from *Christian sources, must exist side by side with Christian ethics* so as to bring about an ethical renaissance of sorts. This kind of statement shows that even a person who has received above average education and has been exposed to other cultures would seek to impose his own arrogant ideal of morality on others based on the idea that Christian ethics are preeminent and essential to anyone who intends to have a system of ethics, disregarding other systems of ethics that came before and after Christianity; this idea implies that other systems of ethics are necessarily deficient without Christian ethics. Might he himself not be compared with others whom he himself has criticized, such as Emperor Marcus Aurelius?

> I believe that other ethics than any one which can be evolved from exclusively Christian sources, must exist side by side with Christian ethics to produce the moral regeneration of mankind; and that the Christian system is no exception to the rule that in an imperfect state of the human mind, the interests of truth require a diversity of opinions. It is not necessary that in ceasing to ignore the moral truths not contained in Christianity, men should ignore any of those which it does contain
>
> \- John Stuart Mill. *On Liberty* Chapter 2

The statement above can be construed as a kind of evidence of social arrogance and hubris that supports notions of superiority which lead to bigotry and the subjugation of other peoples, which would seem to be the opposite of what Mill is arguing for. To say that Christian ethics have value and can be consulted is perhaps a legitimate statement but to say that Christian values and morality *must* accompany any other form of ethics is to say that Christian ethics are superior to any other form of ethics and other forms of ethical doctrine are not complete or correct without it. Perhaps Mill was a victim of the deficiency he himself spoke about, namely that he lived in a world where Christian ethics was accepted by most or all as a standard and so perhaps he was never confronted by anyone who would question that idea, since it might appear as atheism or at least anti-Christian behavior. If that was the case Mill's argument about the necessity of having dissenting points of view would be proven correct.

Mills' statement would seem to be in contradiction with subsequent statements by Mill that specifically refute the right of one person to impose their beliefs on others: "*But neither one person, nor any number of persons, is warranted in saying to another human creature of ripe years, that he shall not do with his life for his own benefit what he chooses to do with it.*" (John Stuart Mill. *On Liberty* Chapter 4) This idea may be considered akin to the issue that Mill discusses later about the treatment of the religions of people under British control.

> The ravings of fanatics or charlatans from the pulpit may be unworthy of notice; but the heads of the Evangelical party have announced as their principle, for the government of Hindoos and Mahomedans, that no schools be supported by public money in which the Bible is not taught, and by necessary consequence that no public employment be given to any but real or pretended Christians. An Under-Secretary of State, in a speech delivered to his constituents on the 12th of November, 1857, is reported to have said: "Toleration of their faith" (the faith of a hundred millions of British subjects), **"the superstition which they called religion, by the British Government, had had the effect of retarding the ascendancy of the British name, and preventing the salutary growth of Christianity....** Toleration was the great corner-stone of the religious liberties of this country; but do not let them abuse that precious word toleration.
>
> - John Stuart Mill. *On Liberty* Chapter 2

Mill thus described a process by which there is recognition that there was too much tolerance in the British Empire and that the Empire should be say, more like the Spanish who imposed the Christian religion on the subjects of their own empire. The British were said to be too "tolerant" so in lieu of outright banning of other religions the Evangelical party set out to withdraw financial support from any schools that did not teach the Bible.

Even though Mill's thesis that dissent is necessary for a healthy society has been proven by him, there are other similarly troubling statements by Mill which show the difficulty of implementing it even by him. One such statement is included below wherein Mill tried to assert certain rights of the group ("We") over the acts of the individual.

> We have a right, also, in various ways, to act upon our unfavorable opinion of any one, not to the oppression of his individuality, but in the exercise of ours. We are not bound, for example, to seek his society; we have a right to avoid it (though not to parade the avoidance), for we have a right to choose the society most acceptable to us. We have a right, and it may be our duty, to caution others against him, if we think his example or conversation likely to have a pernicious effect on those with whom he associates. We may give others a preference over him in optional good offices, except those which tend to his improvement. In these various modes a person may suffer very severe penalties at the hands of others, for faults which directly concern only himself; but he suffers these penalties only in so far as they are the natural, and, as it were, the spontaneous consequences of the faults themselves, not because they are purposely inflicted on him for the sake of punishment.
>
> - John Stuart Mill. *On Liberty* Chapter 4

The statement above would seem to contain the same seed that gives rise to cliques and exclusive groups that then band together to take political power and segregate others and exclude them or enforce upon them the "majority" belief system. Who is the one to determine if another person's acts are or statements are pernicious? Mill, who obviously believed in Christian morality, would use that perspective in making his judgment, and if he did choose another society more acceptable to him would that not constitute closing off argument and dissent and he himself becoming part of the group of close-minded leaders of the society? In the following statement Mill would seem to have been adopting the form of coercion which he spoke out against. In the following statement Mill seemed to be trying to set up a logical basis for how to intervene when a person causes harm to self that affects society.

> But with regard to the merely contingent or, as it may be called, constructive injury which a person causes to society, by conduct which neither violates any specific duty to the public, nor occasions perceptible hurt to any assignable individual except himself; **the inconvenience is one which society can afford to bear**, for the sake of the greater good of human freedom. If grown persons are to be

> punished for not taking proper care of themselves, I would rather it were for their own sake, than under pretence of preventing them from impairing their capacity of rendering to society benefits which society does not pretend it has a right to exact.
>
> - John Stuart Mill. *On Liberty* Chapter 4

However, in the following statement Mill proposes the idea that society has a responsibility to bear the cost of what a deviant person has done to affect society adversely because society had the chance to mold the person in their youth.

> But I cannot consent to argue the point as if society had no means of bringing its weaker members up to its ordinary standard of rational conduct, except waiting till they do something irrational, and then punishing them, legally or morally, for it. Society has had absolute power over them during all the early portion of their existence: it has had the whole period of childhood and nonage in which to try whether it could make them capable of rational conduct in life.
>
> - John Stuart Mill. *On Liberty* Chapter 4

Can this idea be considered rational in the context of Mill's main thesis about the need for dissent? Is the society which is trying to allow freedom to an individual is going to intervene in their upbringing to condition them and what happens to the ability of those who are so conditioned to exercise freedom and practice democracy as critical individuals? Mill goes further in support of this idea by stating that his own generation had "mastered" the training and the design of the presumably social circumstances in which the following generation of people would exist and that the present generation has within its power the capacity to shape the coming generation.

> The existing generation is master both of the training and the entire circumstances of the generation to come; it cannot indeed make them perfectly wise and good, because it is itself so lamentably deficient in goodness and wisdom; and its best efforts are not always, in individual cases, its most successful ones; but it is perfectly well able to make the rising generation, as a whole, as good as, and a little better than, itself. If society lets any considerable number of its members grow up mere children, incapable of being acted on by rational consideration of distant motives, society has itself to blame for the consequences. Armed not only with all the powers of education, but with the ascendancy which the authority of a received opinion always exercises

> over the minds who are least fitted to judge for themselves; and aided by the natural penalties which cannot be prevented from falling on those who incur the distaste or the contempt *of those who know them*
> - John Stuart Mill. *On Liberty* Chapter 4

While Mill was trying to deal with one problem, namely, the emergence of negative personalities in the society, he created a contradiction with his own thesis which acknowledged the need for dissent. The statement above sounds like the same arrogant thinking of leaders who support the idea that society has amassed all the scientific knowledge to control the world and in this case educate a whole generation. Even if Mill's society, which at the time was the epitome of Western European hegemony over world cultures through colonialism, did possess the technological capability and the intellectual capacity, it would seem to have been atrophied by the same tendency of vanity or belief in their own superior philosophies, technologies and expediencies in the pursuit of greed and power that affected western culture from its inception with the Greek city states through wars and hostile competitions with other nations. Mill mentions what he calls the *ascendancy* of received ideas in the minds who can least judge for themselves as a tool for society to inculcate *prudence or temperance*. This idea could conceivably and many scholars such as Charlotte Thomson Iserbyt have asserted, be developed to include a dumping down component, in other words, if societies indoctrination or socialization process works best on those who are least able to "judge" as Mill says, "for themselves" then it follows logically that the society should want to promote policies that create conditions that produce people who are more impressionable, i.e. more susceptible to conditioning and indoctrination or programming through propaganda. Iserbyt's contention is that in effect the school system has become an integral part of that process. Thus, while it may be possible to say that there is some segment of the population that are naturally less able to "judge" it is also true that the educational system of a society has major influence in determining the level of learning a given group will have through such seemingly minor factors as teacher expectation, level of school overcrowding and the child's nutrition before coming to and during the school day.

In such a society, intolerance by the majority becomes the policy of government and even if as Mill said, those who are strong willed enough will reject the "yoke" that society has tried to place on them, those people who have refused the yoke, even if they have good intentions to benefit society through their opinions, will be marginalized because the society has the power of the purse through the taxation of weak minded people, who will not protest, as well as the power of their bodies which will be employed towards the end of supporting the government by their thoughts, words and deeds including the use of arms (police, army and national guard) to enforce the policies of the government.

Mill further elucidated on the difficulty of conducting discourse with those people who are offended by the opinions of others because they take those as personal affronts.

> There are many who consider as an injury to themselves any conduct which they have a distaste for, and resent it as an outrage to their feelings; as a religious bigot, when charged with disregarding the religious feelings of others, has been known to retort that they disregard his feelings, by persisting in their abominable worship or creed. But there is no parity between the feeling of a person for his own opinion, and the feeling of another who is offended at his holding it; no more than between the desire of a thief to take a purse, and the desire of the right owner to keep it... But where has there been seen a public which set any such limit to its censorship? or when does the public trouble itself about universal experience. In its interferences with personal conduct it is seldom thinking of anything but the enormity of acting or feeling differently from itself; and this standard of judgment, thinly disguised, is held up to mankind as the dictate of religion and philosophy, by nine tenths of all moralists and speculative writers. These teach that things are right because they are right; because we feel them to be so. They tell us to search in our own minds and hearts for laws of conduct binding on ourselves and on all others. What can the poor public do but apply these instructions, and make their own personal feelings of good and evil, if they are tolerably unanimous in them, obligatory on all the world?
>
> - John Stuart Mill. *On Liberty* Chapter 4

Thus, due to the inappropriate use or lack of use of logic, reason and sedate discourse on issues, society is rendered prejudiced and fanatical in holding and upholding baseless standards for judging the ideas of others. Those standards are based on pronouncements from religions or philosophies that are not proven but believed and sustained out of habit and not a living discourse, which implies being open to the possibility that one's ideas are incorrect or at least being humble enough to realize that one may gain something from the discourse. If the discourse lacks those features it is being carried out by closed minds that will not accept new information even if it is correct and they are wrong. Thereby, the populace is inevitably led to become the instrument of the bigotry that will act automatically even without direct behests from the government, to squelch dissenting views or the needs of the few in order to satisfy the desires of the majority or the power elite who are in control of the public opinion. In other words, once the opinion has been inculcated the person will act, based on it, even without outside direction.

Later in his book Mill presented the example of the Mormon community which has set itself up with doctrines that were objectionable to him and others. He cited another writer, whom he agrees with, who says that the Mormons should be stopped. Mill agrees with the writer but stops short of calling for violent action against them. Yet he did not denounce the actions of the British government which was actually doing the same thing to other cultures around the world.

> A recent writer, in some respects of considerable merit, proposes (to use his own words,) not a crusade, but a civilizade, against this polygamous community, to put an end to what seems to him a retrograde step in civilization. It also appears so to me, but I am not aware that any community has a right to force another to be civilized.
>
> - John Stuart Mill. *On Liberty* Chapter 4

Mill certainly made a good argument for the need to have dissenting points of view presented in the normal intercourse of human society. That discourse can be a kind of purifying force to lead society to better correct its ideas or to discard older less correct ones in favor of new ones. However, there can be a breakdown in that process if society is controlled by leaders who use sophistic statements and polemical arguments to shape the thought process of the masses to favorable opinions that will facilitate their plans which are not based in reality and or in the best interest of the public. So while Mill did not call for strong resistance in the form of civil disobedience to society, in principle he laid groundwork for the right of the dissenting views to exist and to be acknowledged by the society. Additionally, Mill constructed parameters for having confidence in opinions, beyond illogical or emotional or habitual reasons.

Part 2: The Struggle of Empires, Wealth, Power and the Plight of Humanity

Alexander, Caesar, Charlemagne, and I have founded empires. But on what did we rest the creation of our genius? Upon force.

~Napoleon

The Superpower Syndrome Mandatory Conflict Complex

INTRODUCTION to the *"Superpower Syndrome Mandatory Conflict Complex"*

In this essay we will explore the concept of the "superpower syndrome" and the components which produce a feeling in the leadership of countries to see themselves as having power over others, a condition that leads them to seek to control other countries and thereby necessarily leads them to conflict with other countries and their peoples. This essay will also explore the attending psychological complexes related to the particular form of hubris engendered by the self-concept as a "Superpower" country. This essay seeks to show that the course of action based on the Superpower Syndrome inevitably leads to a "Mental Complex" in the leadership of a superpower desirous country, and which is shared by enough of its population, that promotes notions of superiority and greed, that facilitate and compel the movement towards conflict and violence; it enables and even demands that leaders pursue postures and attitudes of aloofness, Messianic democracy,[15] delusion of superiority and finally war, which is the highest expression of killing. Firstly we will define the basis for this discussion in the context of humanitarian ethics. Since war can be seen as beneficial for one even as it is detrimental to another, by using humanitarian ethics we may establish a logical basis for this discussion from a more objective perspective. Next we will discern what a "superpower" is as well as what constitutes the "Superpower syndrome." Then we will define the *"Superpower Syndrome Mandatory Conflict Complex"* and next we will show how it manifests in foreign policy relationships and national politics.

This study could apply to the ancient Greeks especially under Pericles and Alexander, the Romans especially under the Emperors, the Spartans, the French Empire under Napoleon, the British Empire, German Nazis, Jewish Fundamentalism, Christian Fundamentalism, and Islamic Fundamentalism (and others) since those societies have acted in ways that could be considered as beset with the Superpower syndrome. However, the focus of this essay will be on the United States of America (U.S.A.) since that culture is presently having a strong effect on world culture and it finds itself in possession of unprecedented military power and sees itself as the controller of a world empire. Thus, it epitomizes the principles of a superpower culture and the imperialist ideal that the other nations throughout history sought but failed to achieve.

Humanitarian Ethics

It might be well justified to say that all human cultures, at some point in their history, have established what they believe to be moral (ethical) and principled standards for establishing and maintaining order in a society even if they apply it to their own society and selectively to others. The primary standard may be regarded as the injunction against harming others and the highest expression of that moral sanction is to refrain from killing. Therefore, from that highest of the humanitarian ethics we may accept the concept of non-killing as a universal canon or dictum that leads or at least should lead to peace and harmony in society. Consequently, we can say that policies and concepts that promote conflicts that directly or indirectly lead to social strife and killing are anti-humanitarian ethics or ethics of a purpose other than humanitarian conceptions, purposes or goals.

Pacifists believe that no war should ever be fought and that all wars are immoral. Mahatma Gandhi, the Indian leader, was a staunch supporter of this ideal. There is a school of belief that follows the idea that war is good. When World War I started, the writer Thomas Mann wrote, *"Is not peace an element of civil corruption and war a purification, a liberation, an enormous hope?"* Cultures like the ancient Spartans and the ancient Romans, also accepted the war ideal. After the loss of tens of millions of people, the vast destruction of Europe and the use of nuclear weapons during World War II, humanity [at least in Europe and Japan and some other places] seemed to have a reconsidered the war solution. With the emergence of the American and Soviet cold war and the continued development of the U.S.A. as an imperial power, corporatism appears to have taken over the most important position as motivator for war. One factor that usually facilitates the wars of convenience and conquest for profit is that the warmongers seldom pay any consequences in lost life or injury. Perhaps that factor as much as any number of contradictions in the philosophy of good war is the most important incongruity that negates the argument for war.

What is the "Super Power Syndrome"?

Robert Jay Lifton is a distinguished Professor of Psychology and Psychiatry at John Jay College and the Graduate Center of the City University of New York, and visiting psychiatry professor at Harvard Medical School. He defines the Superpower Syndrome as follows:

> "The American apocalyptic entity is less familiar to us. Even if its urges to power and domination seem historically recognizable, it nonetheless represents a new constellation of forces bound up with what I've come to think of as "superpower syndrome." By that term I mean a national mindset--put forward strongly by a tight-knit leadership group--that takes on a sense of omnipotence, of unique standing in the world that grants it the right to hold sway over all other nations. The American superpower status derives from our emergence from World War II as uniquely powerful in every respect, still more so as the only superpower from the end of the cold war in the early 1990s."[16]

> "Superpower syndrome really means an American sense of entitlement to rule the world because it's the strongest power in the world. Because one is militarily dominant one has the right to be a dominant superpower, and with that of course goes the unilateralism, the absence of mutuality, and the sense of really seeking to control history. Superpower syndrome, then, is the kind of overall rubric or way of understanding a lot of separate American policies, all of which shocked us, but putting them together as a consistent point of view, and stance in the world."[17]

The superpower syndrome is an imperative to move towards conquest that must have a validating philosophy (a sophisticated excuse or rationalization) or moral justification for promoting a self-image of entitlement that provides the superpower the right to lord over others. It is this imperative that necessarily requires the believer in such a concept to adopt peculiar psychological characteristics that lead to conflict. Primary among these characteristics are the self-given right to assign oneself the permission to control others, the arrogance to believe one is entitled to dominate others and condescend towards others by ignoring the needs, desires or protests of others. Just as taking over the possessions of others, ignoring their rights, imposing one's will on them and ignoring the desires of members of a family will quickly lead to conflicts such as domestic violence, child abuse, divorce, or even murder, so too in the family of nations the incapacity or unwillingness to communicate, live, share resources and otherwise cooperate with others in an equitable, just and benevolent manner inevitably leads to resentment, hatred and violence among nations.

The "Superpower Syndrome Mandatory Conflict Complex"

The *"Superpower Syndrome Mandatory Conflict Complex"* is therefore the psychological construct or mindset based on the superpower thought-process/belief-system that has the inevitable consequence of holding, accepting, agreeing with and acting based on the perspective of the Superpower Syndrome. The superpower syndrome is a way of thinking that inevitably leads to conflict because it necessitates one country's control over another or a person's control of another and since not all people like to be controlled they will fight against that control. The mental complex exhibits as an overpowering desire to control others beyond the personal distaste for that same control on oneself that overrides the personal concern and entitles itself to impose on others the very same condition one would not want to have imposed on oneself. In other words, those who hold to the Superpower Syndrome disregard the injustice they are perpetrating on others by thinking they are separate and above and thus entitled to impose it and that others are not entitled to impose it on them. Part of the complex is the acceptance of the violence or death that may occur as a result of the superpower policies as acceptable or even desirable. Therefore, they must also enter into conflict with others whom they are trying to control. The conflict rises beyond the desire for sex [physical pleasures or comforts] or money; it is dedicated to achieving power. This movement towards conflict is the result of the complex that arises in the personality of one who holds the Superpower Syndrome idea. In this context, the word "complex" is defined as:

> In psychology, "complex" is *a group of related, often repressed ideas and impulses that compel characteristic or habitual patterns of thought, feelings, and behavior.*[18]

If it is possible to regard the superpower mindset as an effect of a complex based on longstanding patterns of thinking, like Narcissism[1] that contradict ethics and the natural order of life but can be corrected and not as a manifestation of sociopathology,[2] we may examine the complex as a pattern that may be corrected in order to lead society towards social harmony instead of conflict by promoting a positive pattern of thought processes along with ethical regulations to insure the healthy behavior. The actions of a person who holds the Super Power conception should be thought of as a complex because there are several negative mental processes that have been taking place which have degraded the mind's capacity to rationalize how to work out the relationships in the world ethically, justly and equitably.

While it may rightly be ascertained that the leadership of governments is most culpable in leading the society to entertain ideations of superiority, hubris and delusions of invincibility, yet it is the public at large who also must accept the notions and ideas given to them by the leaders and offer their support to those leaders.

---

[1] A psychological condition characterized by self-preoccupation, lack of empathy, and unconscious deficits in self-esteem.; The attribute of the human psyche characterized by admiration of oneself but within normal limits.] Source: *The American Heritage® Stedman's Medical Dictionary*

[2] someone with a sociopathic personality; a person with an antisocial personality disorder (`psychopath' was once widely used but has now been superseded by `sociopath') [syn: psychopath] Source: *The American Heritage® Stedman's Medical Dictionary*

Granted, if the population has been dumbed down[19] through mis-education and or transformed into a bloodthirsty rabble through propaganda, there is some mitigation. Nevertheless, they will suffer the consequences of the actions of the nation most directly. There is a famous saying that goes: *People deserve the government they get and get the government they deserve* by Lester Lave. In this manner, it is understood that people allow themselves to be ruled by the kinds of people they admit to ruling positions and if they do not agree with them it is their responsibility to change their government leaders. If they do not they are tacitly accepting that government and the consequences of that government's actions. So this means that a nation's people are to some degree complicit in the actions of their government as long as they support the existence of the government. Yet, the leadership of a government is more responsible since they have the power of the office to lead and put forth propaganda that either educate or mis-educate the people.

A counterargument has been raised in reference to the aforesaid; that if people are mis-educated how can they be responsible? In this argument there is a valid point to the extent that people are ignorant but if they simply do not want to disrupt their lives through investigation of issues, holding their representatives accountable, even taking revolutionary action if necessary, the excuse does not fully apply. Furthermore, the leader(s) of the superpower count on the feelings of greed or acquiescence even in the face of exposed lies and impeachable offences. In the treatise by Noam Chomsky called *Manufacturing Consent* he spoke about the issues of the media giving people what they want; essentially presenting an image of life that goes along with their sentiments and therefore, they hide themselves from the truth. In such a case the society will have truth speakers but they will find no ears to listen to them and therefore no media to carry their message. Therefore, in such a society the leaders would not need to have an open dictatorship or a police state. The people are controlled by their own egoism, complacency, greed, or fear of change or blind faith in the superpower mentality or its leaders.

What, if anything, is different about the pre and post nuclear superpower? Various societies have come to power in human history and have adopted what could arguably be called megalomaniacal ideas of world domination, notably, Alexander the Great and Napoleon; some might add Hitler and Stalin to that list. While the Ancient Greeks, Romans, and others had, at one point, unsurpassed military power for their time, they have all faded into the winds of history. Part of the modern conception of a Superpower involves the capacity not only to overwhelm other military forces but also the capacity to destroy the world with weapons of mass destruction or control the world through financial markets and national bribery. The extent of that power is new in human history and having acquired that capacity the United States and the U.S.S.R {Soviet Union}, were now able to contemplate the idea of the superpower mentality that demands dominance and hegemony over all nations of the world as opposed to just being the preeminent power in their regions or in the manner of the older form of empires such as the British or Roman, which sought to extend their institutions in foreign lands. Now, by controlling the leadership of governments, through bribery and by intimidation, other governments could be controlled. So the Superpower mentality is the same in the pre and post nuclear weapon age even though the capacity of the superpower has been expanded in the post-nuclear age. The Neo-conservative idea that holds the directive of preeminence in the world is based in part on military superiority, and material wealth but also the idea that the United States will succeed in perpetuating its agenda of world domination where the other empires failed because of their capacity to coerce, buy or force nations into submission through the use of modern technologies such as global markets and manipulation of world economies as well as through indirect or direct military intervention if necessary.

The United States emerged from World War II with an enhanced capacity to finance a military industrial complex by having emerged from the war with the industrial sector virtually intact and having the capacity to export many goods needed around the world as a result of the devastation produced by the war. This turn of events allowed the United States to move ahead of all other nations in terms of economic development. Previous to the war the United States had ordinary imperialistic designs but after, with the power of nuclear weapons and its burgeoning economy, the United States was able to sustain unprecedented and unmatched military spending. So what is new in human history is not the superpower concept, since that idea has been around from ancient times, but rather that the megalomaniacal idea has been joined by the religious fundamentalism and also the technological capacity to destroy all human life on earth. This prospect even alarms many avowed conservatives [supporters of the president], as the following article demonstrates.

> "Just in the past few months," Bartlett said, "I think a light has gone off for people who've spent time up close to Bush: that this instinct he's always talking about is this sort of weird, Messianic idea of what he thinks God has told him to do." Bartlett, a 53-year-old columnist and self-described libertarian Republican who has lately been a champion for traditional Republicans concerned about Bush's governance, went on to say: "This is why George W. Bush is so clear-eyed about Al Qaeda and the Islamic fundamentalist enemy. He believes you have to kill them all. They can't be persuaded, that they're extremists, driven by a dark vision. He understands them, because he's just like them. . . .
>
> "This is why he dispenses with people who confront him with inconvenient facts," Bartlett went on to say. "He truly believes he's on a mission from God."[20]

There are four main sources of support that sustained president George W. Bush during his time as president of the United States, the corporations, the religious right-conservatives, political conservatives and the neo-conservatives. The corporations want to use the power of the government to promote worldwide conditions that allow them to control world markets and develop unlimited profits and economic power. The far right religious conservatives essentially want religious imperialism, to extend the practice of Christianity, as they see it, to the rest of the country [making it a theocracy] and ultimately of the world, supplanting all other practices. There have been political conservatives in the U.S.A.'s history since its inception. They promote policies such as financial responsibility, isolationism, individual privacy and "traditional values" [some conservative groups promote slavery, racism, and sexism] and U.S.A. preeminence in world affairs. The neoconservatives want world domination from the standpoint of imperialist control and subjugation of all other nations, to direct the course of world history, keep the U.S.A. as the only country controlling oil and other resources necessary for a country's advancement and the capacity to keep any other country from becoming a rival, that is, to become a superpower or in any way interfere with the desires of the power elite of the U.S.A. and by extension the power elite of Western Europe and a few other selected countries.

If the statement above is correct the neo-conservatives probably see the religiosity of President Bush and the religious right agenda as an effective cloak to obscure the true neo-con agenda of world domination and a means to secure an area of support to defeat the progressive movement. As concerns the president George W. Bush, while he is politically driven by the neo-cons, he is culturally driven by the religious right and his own conception about communing with God, that developed after his fall into depression and involvement with drugs (alcoholism) and subsequent "rediscovery" of himself by becoming a "born again" Christian, which ingratiates him to the fundamentalist religious right constituency. The concern has been raised even among notable personalities within the culture such as Studs Terkel, Burt Bacharach,[21] Robert Lifkin, and others who lived through the post World War II era, the Korean War, the protest movements of the 1960s, the Vietnam War and the last 35 years of undeclared wars and social strife as well as the conflicts with the U.S.S.R.; some remarked that they are more concerned for the future than at any other time in their lives.

The *Superpower Syndrome Mandatory Conflict Complex* has three main components. Firstly there is an illusion of superpower invincibility, which necessarily leads to the associated deluded ideals of entitlement to world mastery and the unilateral actions in pursuit of primacy. The second component is the leadership of the Superpower, which must by all means uphold the superpower myth. An individual heads the leadership of the superpower but it is actually composed of the president, king or Prince,[22] as Machiavelli would call it and the immediate advisors of the ruler, who actually represent the interests of the ruling class. In a republican form of government, the other component is the representatives or congresses who are supposed to represent the constituents of the government but who in reality operate as representatives of the power elite and accept legal bribes (political contributions) from them to take up their issues and concerns.

The superpower mental complex requires that all be bent on upholding the superpower myth, that the superpower is invincible, and entitled to dominate everyone else and that anyone who disagrees is a malcontent, or a traitor or an enemy to peace, democracy and or even God.

The need to uphold the complex of mental delusions can operate in dangerous ways when applied to foreign affairs policies. It is not unlike the practice in the east, of "saving face," that has been regarded by many westerners as ridiculous.[23] The concept of "losing face" almost brought the two post World War II superpowers into direct-armed conflict as evinced in the conflict known as the Cuban Missile Crisis, which was a conflict as much about missiles as reputation, and was decided by who can face the other one down instead of how to stop threatening the other and how to remove the danger to each other by doing away with missiles altogether. So, while the Chinese cultural practice of "face" is often denigrated by western society, in actuality, the *Superpower Syndrome Mandatory Conflict Complex* involves a primitive magnified and pathological[24] tendency towards apocalyptic brinkmanship with anyone who opposes its will, including the U.S.S.R., China (through the conflict in North Korea) and Iran.[25]

An important aspect of the superpower complex that leads to conflict is the incapacity to reverse itself or take a different course except under extraordinary political pressure from its own party leaders [republican or democrat], or constituents [only when the breakdown of social order is threatened; Ex.: the Great Depression, Civil rights movement], usually due to abject failure of a particular policy.

In 1991, when President Bush Sr. sent troops to the Middle East he could not withdraw them even if he wanted to (he could not go back on his words or change his course of action once stated or a posture taken) since doing so would have portrayed him as a weak leader and the United States as a second rate power; so that kind of "embarrassment" must be avoided even if it costs lives. Part of the complex is never repenting or admitting error no matter what the error is or how vast the blunder. That too would be seen as weakness.

The superpower mindset was perhaps best demonstrated by vice president George H. Bush in 1987. Before he became president Iran was locked in war with Iraq. Iran started to gain the advantage over Iraq, so the US forces were sent to decisively support Iraq [Saddam Hussein] so that Iran would not win and gain control of Iraq. President Ronald Reagan and vice president George H. Bush [of the republican party] sent a large US armada to the Persian Gulf to make sure that Iraq would receive weapons. A US gunship shot down an Iranian civilian airliner. They killed 290 passengers. In response to that tragedy and loss of civilian lives vice president Bush said:

> *"I will never apologize for America. I don't care what the facts are."*

The statement above denotes hubris but also a complex of superiority that devalues life in the pursuit of the superpower's goals and objectives and allows the personality to act callously to protect the superpower economy and hegemony at the cost of the lives of soldiers or civilians. To the superpower president the loss of human life is treated as a necessary part of maintaining the superpower supremacy. That loss of life is insignificant in the realm of superpower politics. In this way the mindset of Bush was not unlike the mindset of Madeline Albright [ambassador to the U.N. under president Bill Clinton-democratic party] who when asked about the U.S.A. policies that led to the deaths of "*half a million children*" in Iraq replied: *"I think this is a very hard choice, but the price -- we think the price is worth it."*

During the evolution of early Christianity, a fierce debate ensued about Papal infallibility, which can be seen also as a manifestation of the superpower syndrome complex that emerged in the church during its primacy of power, at the time when it controlled the religious and political affairs of most European nations.[26] In order to counter the rising liberalism and rationalism in society the Pope codified the principle of absolute correctness into church law, thereby insuring face and imposing his will [hegemony] over all within the catholic domain.

When president Jimmy Carter admitted error in sending the failed hostage rescue team to Iran he "lost face" with the American people and the world. In that time the other leaders in the government as well as many conservative and right wing theologians and politicians of the country reviled him. Through denigration ads in the media the majority of the population came to dislike him and that led the way for the repudiation of the democratic party and the emergence of Ronald Reagan, the republican party, conservatism and the upsurge of the neo-con movement.

In another sense, the superpower myth may be thought of as a cultural credo set forth by the superpower leadership, but additionally it is a dictum that the superpower leadership is bound to also; so their actions too will be constricted by it. In other words, while the superpower myth may be put forth as an expression of freedom, entitlement, superiority, etc. it is as well an expression of self-conditioning, and a form of self-reinforcing delusion that will limit the capacities of the superpower culture. In other words they will be bound to act as superpowers. They will be bard from acting as caring or compassionate or understanding rational human beings. The limits may vary from the inability to relate to other cultures to limits on the patience, and compassion for other cultures as well as limits on change and the capacity to consider new and different options. In effect it is a constricting operation of the superpower mind, i.e. an atrophying of the superpower intellect itself. That is why the superpower mindset operates within a limited range and communicates through simple dogmas, sound bites, slogans and appeals to base emotions or fundamental religiosity.

It is notable that during World War II the United States and Russia worked together as allies against the Germans but after the war the United States emerged with the stronger military industrial complex and the power of the nuclear weapons. The U.S.A. government demonstrated willingness to use nuclear weapons as they unnecessarily dropped two nuclear bombs on Japan even though the United States and Japan were already engaged in talks to end the war. The dropping of the two bombs was an experiment to see the effects of radiation from a plutonium-based bomb and then a uranium based bomb on people in real situations.[27] Later, after the war ended, the United States government experimented in the United States, on its own people, by exploding nuclear bombs and ordering troops to march through the fallout to see the results as they also withheld the information from neighboring towns where the fallout would pass through so there would be no evacuation and the results could be observed.[28] Even as late as 2005 the United States had continued to use a form of nuclear weapons, depleted uranium[29] bomb casings, in the war on Iraq. The willingness to use nuclear weapons on peoples of other countries, especially non-Europeans, as well as the lower classes within the United States population, signals the concept within the *Superpower Syndrome Mandatory Conflict Complex* that there is a difference between the power elite and the lower classes as well as and perhaps even more so, the non-European ethnic groups around the world. Those groups receive the least respect and are considered expendable, used as "cannon fodder" to promote the designs of the Superpower. But according to the Neo-con philosophy, ultimately there can be only one Superpower and even if it means sacrificing or killing other people of European descent, the Superpower will do that if necessary.

During the Iran-Contra affair, the U.S. government consorted with and transacted business with drug dealers to support the Contras that were destabilizing a democratically elected government in Nicaragua. After the end of the scandal, a former CIA agent Richard Brenneke claimed that Swedish prime minister Olof Palme had been assassinated in 1986 because of his refusal to take part in the arms-trade.[30] Just four days before the presidential elections vote (Bush vs. Clinton) that year (1992), Ronald Reagan's defense secretary Caspar Weinberger was implicated during Iran-Contra. Though he claims to have been opposed to the sale on principle, Weinberger participated in the transfer of United States TOW missiles to Iran, and was later indicted on several felony charges of lying to the Iran-

Contra independent counsel during its investigation. The relevance of the situation stopped a late Bush surge in the polls and Republicans howled at the timing. Weinberger received a presidential pardon from president George H. Bush on December 24, 1992, just days before his trial was scheduled to begin.[31] The presidential pardon is important here because if it had not been used the scandal could have implicated not only Ronald Reagan in the Iran-Contra scandal but also George H.W. Bush who was his vice-president.

> Sen. John Kerry's 1988 U.S. Senate Committee on Foreign Relations report on Contra-drug links concluded that "senior U.S. policy makers were not immune to the idea that drug money was a perfect solution to the Contras' funding problems." According to the National Security Archive, Oliver North had been in contact with Manuel Noriega, Panama's drug-baron, whom he personally met.
> In August of 1996, the *San Jose Mercury News* published Gary Webb's "Dark Alliance", a 20,000 word, three-part investigative series which alleged that Nicaraguan drug traffickers had sold and distributed crack cocaine in Los Angeles during the 1980s, and that drug profits were used to fund the CIA-supported Nicaraguan Contras. Webb never asserted that the CIA directly aided drug dealers to raise money for the Contras, but he did imply that the CIA were aware of the transactions (Webb's 1999 book, *Dark Alliance,* substantiated these allegations with copious references). On December 10, 2004, Gary Webb was found dead from gunshots wounds to the head. Coroner Robert Lyons concluded it was suicide.[32]

Reagan projected a noble and perhaps Pollyannaish idea (as in the 1950's) of the United States as an innocent, benevolent, advanced and just country; ideas that most people desired to have of themselves even though racism, sexism, poverty and the rise in the gap between rich and poor were reemerging after a brief relaxation from the 1960's protest period. Reagan epitomized the concept of manufacturing reality, an image of the United States for mass consumption that resulted in manufactured consent by most of the population of the United States; it was what they wanted to see, a presidential president that made people feel good when he spoke and placed the U.S.A. culture in a high pedestal above all other nations. Reagan ushered in a reversal of civil rights gains and renewed the political agenda of destabilizing governments and promoting weakness and dependency in developing countries. Some examples of this are the Iran-Contra Affair scandal and the support of South American dictators.[33] When Reagan issued his famous statement of regret (not apology) for the Iran-Contra scandal, he did so not by admitting culpability but by saying he did what he thought was right and was responsible as head of the government but that he had no knowledge and that the actions were done by his subordinates.

So Reagan represented a conservative ideal but in reality his government was imperialistic and fiscally capitalist as he imposed the idea of "trickle-down" economics, a euphemism for a process wherein the money was given to the rich through tax cuts and other means and they were supposed to invest it and the benefits were supposed to trickle down to the rest of the population. This concept also came to be known as "Reaganomics." The decade of the 1980s became known as the decade of Wall Street excesses wherein "yuppies" [young upwardly mobile professionals] became wealthy on wall street while extreme cuts were made in social programs and the gap between rich and poor widened more.

The neo-conservative movement may be understood as a radical fundamentalist and fanatical expression of the *Superpower syndrome* and the *Superpower Syndrome Mandatory Conflict Complex*. The neo-conservative movement is not to be considered as the same as the traditional conservative movement in the U.S.A. but they both have certain elements in common. The conservative movement has a longstanding history in the United States. However, the conservative movement, unlike the Neo-conservative, has the ideal of establishing and consolidating the United States government and economy but not through fiscal irresponsibility or imperial campaigns. The Neo-con agenda as expressed by president George W. Bush and his advisors revolves around deficit spending to further enrich the rich, and the military industrial complex while setting out to impose the United States model of world economics on the nations of the world, which in practice is opening markets to the United States but not opening United States markets to other nations, especially less developed nations. It also involves keeping less developed nations in a dependent and less developed state, through destabilization of governments and economies through financing opposition groups, covert actions by the CIA or direct military actions to oust government leaders and install puppet governments (neocolonialism). The fiscally conservative ideal was perhaps expressed by George Washington, the first president of the U.S.A., in his farewell address:

> As a very important source of strength and security, cherish public credit. One method of preserving it is to use it as sparingly as possible, avoiding occasions of expense by cultivating peace, but remembering also that timely disbursements to prepare for danger frequently prevent much greater disbursements to repel it; avoiding likewise the accumulation of debt, not only by shunning occasions of expense, but by vigorous exertions in time of peace to discharge the debts which unavoidable wars have occasioned, not ungenerously throwing upon posterity the burden which we ourselves ought to bear.[34]

Washington's views on national finances could be seen as prophetic, reflecting the problems of the present, the country not having followed his advice. While Washington may be considered as a conservative, we must keep in mind that he believed in slavery and the usurpation of lands from the North American Indians or Native Americans as they came to be called later. Yet, at the same time there was also even in the time of Washington a desire for conquest and expansion of the lands adjacent to the growing United States as expressed by Thomas Jefferson, one of its so-called "founding fathers", who was also a slave owner. That desire brought the United States into conflict with the neighboring nations of Canada and Mexico.

> The war (of 1812) was a result of two major causes: a dispute over repeated violations of American sovereignty by Great Britain, and American expansionism, a desire by some Americans to expand their territory and population by conquering Great Britain's Canadian colonies.
> The British Canadian colonies were lightly populated and poorly defended compared to the crowded American states to their south, and many of the settlers were Americans by birth and believed to remain sympathetic to the United States. Some Americans argued that the majority of the population in the British colonies would rise up and greet an American invading

> army as liberators, and that, as Thomas Jefferson suggested in 1812, "the acquisition of Canada this year, as far as the neighborhood of Quebec, will be a mere matter of marching, and will give us the experience for the attack on Halifax, the next and final expulsion of England from the American continent." The belief that the United States was destined to control all of the North American continent would later gain the name Manifest Destiny, but that term was not yet in use at the time of the war.[35]

The term "Manifest Destiny" is a phrase that articulated the conviction that the United States had some form of divinely ordained mission to expand. The term came to be regarded as a synonym for the territorial expansion of the United States across North America towards the Pacific Ocean.[36] But it also was an underlying motivation for expansion to the south (to take over Mexico) and to the north (to take over Canada). Manifest Destiny was also related in United States popular ideology with American exeptionalism as well as a belief in the natural superiority of what was in the nineteenth century referred to as the "Anglo-Saxon race".

"American Exeptionalism", a term said to have been coined by Alexis de Tocqueville in 1831, relates to the perception that the United States is different qualitatively from other developed nations. The difference is supposed to derive from its national credo, unique origins, distinctive political, historical evolution as well as it's religious institutions. This conception ignored the barbarism perpetrated on the women, Native American Indians and on the Africans. Nevertheless, *American exeptionalism* is a form of Romantic nationalism that is supposed to derive from the nobility of the United States and its people who are supposed to hold a special place in the world, because they theoretically offer opportunity and hope for humanity.

It is interesting that in his memoirs, while recalling his participation in the Mexican-American war, president Ulysses S. Grant reprimanded the United States Government for starting the war with Mexico while lying about their placement of troops in Mexican territory to provoke the fight in order to force congress into declaring war against Mexico. This situation was not unlike the

"Gulf of Tonkin incident which was used as an excuse to go to war with North Vietnam or the Weapons of Mass Destruction excuse to go to war with Iraq or the use of the explosion of the American battleship USS *Maine* in Havana harbor as a reason to make war on Spain. All of those "incidents" or "threats" were lies to promote war and expansion of the United States' manifest destiny ideal. The underlying intent was to take possession of Mexico by force to increase the growing "American Empire."

> For myself, I was bitterly opposed to the measure, and to this day regard the war, which resulted, as one of the most unjust ever waged by a stronger against a weaker nation. It was an instance of a republic following the bad example of European monarchies, in not considering justice in their desire to acquire additional territory. Texas was originally a state belonging to the republic of Mexico.[37]

Grant Further explained the United States tactic for starting the Mexican-American War and how it was an opportunist move to capture more lands from a weaker country.

> The presence of United States troops on the edge of the disputed territory furthest from the Mexican settlements, was not sufficient to provoke hostilities. We were sent to provoke a fight, but it was essential that Mexico should commence it. It was very doubtful whether Congress would declare war; but if Mexico should attack our troops, the Executive could announce, "Whereas, war exists by the acts of, etc.," and prosecute the contest with vigor. Once initiated there were but few public men who would have the courage to oppose it.[38]

It is noteworthy that Grant's comment about "following the bad example of European monarchies" would not fit in the present, as the European nations have, in the post World War II era, moved away, to a great extent, from the Machiavellian[39] conceptions of royalty and militaristic imperialism even as the U.S.A moved towards imperialism and world domination. The following excerpt from a program called *The Neocons and Americas Foreign Policy*[40] reveals how incongruous the political culture of the United States seems to confound and at the same time alarm many present day Europeans.

> **John Micklethwait:** I think Europeans on the whole don't understand neo-conservatism very well. They have very little idea of the history of it, they have very little idea that these were originally Democrats who changed to the other side of the political spectrum, and they tend to have somewhat clichéd views of just how powerful the neo-conservatives are within Bush's world, and so they've become a sort of bogeyman for a lot of Europeans, often wrongly I think.
>
> **Ray Suarez:** Clichéd how?
>
> **John Micklethwait:** I think that clichéd version of a neo-conservatism is someone who's obsessively pro-Israel, who is pushed very much towards a preemptive war at virtually all possible opportunities and also the idea that--the very sort of hard right-wingers, and I think in many of those instances there--there are exaggerations there. [41]

The handling of the Israeli-Palestinian situation has never been completely even handed because of the special, though seemingly incongruous relationship between Israel and the U.S.A. Yet it was at least more centrist in prior years as opposed to extremely right winged during the George W. Bush administration. Again, it has been carried out in a way that might impress an onlooker as a deliberate attempt to provoke controversy and conflict. Analysts have stated that a perpetual conflict with the Palestinians has favored the Israelis since they would not need to negotiate and give up any territories they won in their wars of the late 1960s and early 1970s but that does not resolve the situation and forces them to live under the threat of Palestinian suicide bombings and other attacks. So while Israel may be the superpower of the region, its military might has been neutralized by the suicide bomber and eventually they must negotiate a peaceful solution. However, they will not do so as long as they are supported by the U.S.A. and are governed by right winged personalities. Chalmers Johnson said the following about the Israeli-Palestinian situation:

> I do fault the current administration for not continuing the policies of the Clinton administration or all previous administrations to try and produce an equitable and fair reconciliation between the Israelis and the Palestinians. Having abandoned that program, we have no influence at

> all in the Muslim world. But, also, we should be aware of the dangers, long-range dangers, that we are imposing on a society in which we have great emotional interest, namely Israel. It's a tragic situation, in my opinion.[42]

Any conflict in the Middle East that involves Israel legitimizes the need for U.S.A. involvement. Therefore, the longer the conflict lasts the longer and more complex and extensive the U.S.A. involvement in the area can be. However, that involvement has and will lead to greater antipathy by the region's population because of the uneven treatment of the Arab people and the double standard applied to Israel. Such resentments over such protracted periods have provided a fertile ground for anti-western and anti U.S.A. fighters who see their land occupied and their people impoverished for the sake of western imperialism throughout their lives.

Historian Andrew Bacevich has warned that the American foreign interventions are not in the best interest of the U.S.A. Many political observers from politically opposed parties have issued similar statements about this problem. Conservatives such as Pat Buchanan and liberals, such as Tariq Ali, the prominent left-wing writer, have agreed on this issue. Ali makes the case that terrorism acts against the USA, like the September 11, 2001 attacks, are directly connected and are a result of the U.S.A.'s interventions in other countries. Ali states that:

> *"the reasons [for terrorism] are really political. They see the double standards applied by the West: a ten-year bombing campaign against Iraq, sanctions against Iraq which have led to the deaths of hundreds of thousands of children, while doing nothing to restrain Ariel Sharon and the war criminals running Israel from running riot against the Palestinians. Unless the questions of Iraq and Palestine are sorted out, these kids will be attracted to violence regardless of whether Osama bin Laden is gotten dead or alive."*[43]

Symptoms of the Superpower Syndrome.

The *Superpower Syndrome Mandatory Conflict Complex* involves predictable symptoms. A society that adopts the syndrome, due to the delusion of superiority and the false sense of entitlement to rule over all others, will not have the capacity to listen to and or work with others in a cooperative fashion if their desires or demands are not met, which is by definition non-cooperativeness. So, for the superpower, in all dealings there must and will be some degree of hegemony involved and capitulation expected by others. Any other outcome would be seen as anti-Americanism, anti-democracy or humiliation and unacceptable. The syndrome forces the superpower to carry on with deficient communication capacity. That is, the superpower president must remain aloof like the Prince of Machiavellian[44] instruction. However, unlike the Machiavellian Prince, who is supposed to listen and view situations with accurate perception, the superpower prince needs only to believe in expressing his own power and thereby the reality is supposed to adjust itself to the desires of the superpower prince. Another symptom of the superpower syndrome is the incapacity to admit mistakes or error. If there is any admission at all it is usually in the form of apologizing for the mistakes of others under their command but never admitting personal culpability or negligence. One such example is the scandal over the leak of the identity of a CIA agent in order to punish a detractor (Joe Wilson) of the Bush administration.

> ***Bush, Cheney Urged to Apologize for Aides***
> By DOUGLASS K. DANIEL, APWASHINGTON (Oct. 30) - Senate Democratic leader Harry Reid said Sunday that President Bush and Vice President Dick Cheney should apologize for the actions of their aides in the CIA leak case. Reid, D-Nev., also said Bush should pledge not to pardon any aides convicted as a result of the investigation into the disclosure of CIA officer Valerie Plame's identity. "There has not been an apology to the American people for this obvious problem in the White House," Reid said. He said Bush and Cheney "should come clean with the American public." Reid added, "This has gotten way out of hand, and the American people deserve better than this." [45]

Another symptom of the superpower syndrome is the belief in impunity. One primary and representative example is president Nixon, who sought to invoke "executive privilege," essentially that the president is above the law, after it was discovered that he was likely involved in a cover-up to protect operatives of his party who broke into the headquarters of the opposing party to spy on them.[46] That scandal came to be known as "Watergate." What Nixon attempted is similar to what Pope Pius IX achieved through the Papal Infallibility decree. While it may seem that the justice system triumphed in that case it should be borne in mind that Nixon was pardoned by Gerald Ford, the man who assumed the presidency after Nixon stepped down. Therefore, the executive branch of the government protected (shielded itself) and therefore, rose above the law and Nixon escaped legal action. In the year 2005 George W. Bush began to receive intense criticism for the misuse of intelligence to support going to war with Iraq and since the war went badly the recriminations from left wing speakers increased. The reasons for going to war, namely that Saddam Hussein was an imminent threat to the United States because he had weapons of mass destruction had been found to be baseless or perhaps even the result of intentional misleading by the president and his advisors as well as others in the president's party. In the year 2005 criticism was also leveled against the president regarding the actual conduct of the war and the president never admitted wrongdoing but instead intensified rhetoric and sought to redirect the argument for going to war on other grounds such as Saddam Hussein being a tyrant, etc. Throughout the months leading to the invasion of Iraq no government official ever admitted or acknowledged that the United States essentially assisted Saddam Hussein in rising to power and committing the same tyrannical and murderous acts he is being accused of. The U.S.A assisted Hussein in coming to power and assisted Iraq and Iran to make war on each other.

Shaking Hands: Iraqi President Saddam Hussein greets Donald Rumsfeld, then special envoy of President Ronald Reagan, in Baghdad on December 20, 1983

An example in the belief in impunity was the decision of the congress, which is dominated by the president's party, to refuse to investigate illegal wire tapping that the president admitted to authorizing. That decision outraged many liberal and democratic party followers. Yet, it was allowed since most people are not willing to challenge their own government officials and force them to enforce the law on the president.

> ***Civil Liberties Groups Seek Court to Shutdown NSA Spy Program***
> Two civil liberties groups asked the federal courts on Thursday to force the Bush administration to end its warrantless domestic spying program because it violates the privacy and free speech rights of US citizens. The requests from the Center for Constitutional Rights and American Civil Liberties Union came just days after Republicans blocked a Senate investigation into the National Security Agency spy program. ACLU Executive Director Anthony Romero said "In America, no one is above the law, not even the president. The president's allies in Congress are preparing to cover up his illegal program, while others in Congress are standing on the sidelines. When the President breaks the law, Congress should not be giving him a get-out-of-jail free card."[47]

Another salient example of the belief in impunity is the refusal to join and support the *International Criminal Court*[48] in order to protect U.S. nationals, diplomats and troops from prosecutions abroad for violations of international law. There are many U.S.A. government officials either currently in government or retired from serving in government in previous years that would be immediately indicted on charges from murder to war crimes in other countries if the U.S.A were not in a position of superpower. One example is Henry Kissinger, the former secretary of state and national-security advisor. The political critic Christopher Hitchens demonstrates that Kissinger deserves vigorous prosecution,

> "for war crimes, for crimes against humanity, and for offenses against common or customary or international law, including conspiracy to commit murder, kidnap, and torture."
>
> ~ Christopher Hitchens
> *The Trial of Henry Kissinger*

Tactics of the Superpower Syndrome Complex that lead to conflict.

There are several tactics that become manifestations of the superpower syndrome mandatory conflict complex. Among the most important are the following. One tactic is bait and switch [fraud]. As stated earlier, in the year 2005 widespread criticism in the media and from the opposite political party was leveled against the president regarding the reasons for going to war and the incompetent conduct of the war itself. After the war was started and things seemed to go badly in the occupation of Iraq the rhetoric changed from an emphasis on deflecting questions about the reasons for going to war to saying that that is irrelevant and that "what is important now is to figure out what we will do next." This was a tactic to obfuscate the deeper reasons for the war and or the incompetence in handling the war after its initial justification on erroneous or misleading grounds. By creating a problem that the society would have to deal with, the original deception would be rendered inconsequential. In other words the president would be able to get away with the original action by essentially saying that the original reasons don't matter now; now we need to get together to deal with the situation we have in front of us. This tactic would diffuse attempts at recrimination for the original action that was erroneous or even unlawful.

Another tactic is simply to ignore the request to answer for actions done. In other words, the superpower president may ignore or decline to answer any questions. Not until pressure mounts to a fever pitch do superpower presidents answer any questions they do not choose to and even then the final fall back position is to answer by stating their own opinion about a subject and assert that they are correct and all others are wrong. Since follow-up questions or refutations are discouraged from the media as disrespectful or unpatriotic or the fear ensues on the part of reporters that they will be refused access if they press too hard, the leaders expect not to deal with those questions again. Because the system of government has no provision for controlling rogue presidents beyond the "High crimes and misdemeanors" clause of the constitution,[49] the meaning of which is not well defined and little used, most presidents can rest secure in their positions knowing that congress is reluctant to impeach the president because that would mean loss of prestige for the government and the political party and presidents know they can only be voted out or that impeachment could only come through an extraordinary scandal and that only if the opposing party is in power.

Another tactic which is similar to the bait and switch is to publicly endorse or state they seek to promote a particular policy and then call that policy by a name that appears benign or even progressive and then put forth an actual proposal that has the reverse effects of the stated proposed policy but which is in keeping with the general true agenda. This may be thought of as an *opposite speech to intent* tactic. The name or label of a policy appears positive while the intent is the opposite. One example of a foreign policy where the *opposite speech to intent* tactic was used is the issue of torture. The Secretary of State Condoleezza Rice made a statement (December 2005) that the United States does not torture anyone and abides by international laws and the Geneva Convention while at the same time her organization, the Bush administration, was actively seeking to exempt the C.I.A. from prosecution for torturing prisoners. Another example of the *opposite speech to intent* tactic but this time in a social/national policy was the *Clear Skies Act of 2003* and there are many other examples.

The Clear Skies Act of 2003 was a proposed federal law of the United States. The official title as introduced was *"a bill to amend the Clean Air Act to reduce air pollution through expansion of cap-and-trade programs, to provide an alternative regulatory classification for units subject to the cap and trade program, and for other purposes."*

> Criticisms of the Clear Skies Act: The law repeals or reduces air pollution controls, including those environmental protections of the Clean Air Act, including caps on toxins in the air and budget cuts for enforcement. The Act is opposed by conservationist groups such as the Sierra Club with Henry A. Waxman, a Democratic congressman of California, describing its title as "clear propaganda."[50]

Similar charges were leveled against the *Healthy Forests Restoration Act of 2003.* The proposed act promoted more destruction and logging of forests than the previous legislation. The Superpower complex has here led to a confrontation with the truth through lack of ethics. More specifically, there is verbal advocacy for ethical action but practical advocacy for unethical actions and therefore the speech cannot be trusted as there is a disconnect between the speech and the action. The duplicity of United States diplomacy was described by Tecumseh, the famed freedom fighter. Tecumseh realized that the overriding greed of the United States culture would never be satisfied and that the words of the "white man" could not be trusted.

> Brother, I wish you to give me close attention, because I think you do not clearly understand. I want to speak to you about promises that the Americans have made.
> You recall the time when the Jesus Indians of the Delawares lived near the Americans, and had confidence in their promises of friendship, and thought they were secure, yet the Americans murdered all the men, women, and children, even as they prayed to Jesus?[51]

Another tactic is to promote disunity among the factions that are in opposition. This tactic promotes disorganization and weakens the opponents so that the Americans can pick them off individually. Tecumseh explained this tactic.

> It is you, the Americans, by such bad deeds, who push the red men to do mischief. You do not want unity among the tribes, and you destroy it. You try to make differences between them. We, their leaders, wish them to unite and consider their land the common property of all, but you try to keep them from this. You separate the tribes and deal with them that way, one by one, and advise them not to come into this union. Your states have set an example of forming a union among all the Fires, why should you censure the Indians for following that example?[52]

Two years after the invasion of Iraq in 2003, the United States set about to establish a "free" and "democratic" government by the Iraqi people, yet before the commencement of the creation of the new government by the Iraqi people the United States government of occupation instituted new laws which fundamentally changed the Iraqi economy, making it open to foreign investment and plunder. Those same laws in different form were incorporated into the new constitutional process. Also, the ethnic divisions within the country which were previously minor were stirred up and highlighted in the new constitution of Iraq and in the United States national media beyond their true dimensions according to independent journalists. According to them this was a clear attempt to create a weakened state with separate factions that can be manipulated against each other.[53] The Iraqi constitution itself, the creation of which was directed by the United States, is another method of promoting division and weakness in the government because it was devised as a parliamentary system that allows members from the emphasized[54] different groups (Sunni, Shia and Kurd) instead of enforcing on the Iraqis a system like that of the United States which concentrates power in one party and deemphasizes divisions. This is clear evidence that the statements from the United States government about exporting "American style democracy" were merely disreputable rhetoric to obfuscate ulterior opposite outcomes desired. In November 2005 it was revealed that the United States had been paying large sums to Iraqi newspapers [in a covert campaign] to run favorable news reports about the United States military and U.S.A. favored Iraqi politicians.[55] Also, it was becoming clear that the United States has been arming death squads to operate freely in Iraq.[56] Previously, allegations of ballot fixing during the Iraqi elections were widely reported in the United States news media.[57] A government that cares for human rights and if the cause is just would not contemplate these actions which are akin to the system that Saddam Hussein was accused of using previously, election fraud.

> ***Have Some Compassion, Please!***
> ***Could it get any worse for President Bush this fall?*** By GRAYDON CARTER
> Did I mention the war? Forget comparisons to Vietnam. Iraq is increasingly looking like it may go down as one of the worst military blunders in history—up there with Little Bighorn and Balaklava. The vote for Iraq's constitution provided little balm for the president. In some precincts the votes in favor of ratification approached an unlikely 99 percent—talk about exporting American-style democracy to the Middle East![58]

So the question might be asked: Why can't the Iraqis create their own laws without intervention or "help" from the United States? One may even wonder what the need would have been if there had not been an invasion and occupation in the first place. For that matter where would Iraq be now and the Middle East also if the West had not moved to conquest and imperialism in the late 19th and early 20th centuries to carve up the Middle East and Africa into colonies, creating borders between groups that had been related and uniting others that had not been united previously? In reference to the present issue with the new laws in Iraq, on a show provided by N.P.R. an Iraqi poet asked what the need was to include in the new Constitution a reverence for property, calling it sacrosanct.[59] It sounded to him like an attempt to create a free market for western ravaging of the country by western corporations and for the creation of a materialistic society with a nationalistic bent towards capitalism, as one of the first acts of the leader of the C.P.A. (coalition provisional authority) was to open up the country for foreign investment with zero responsibility to reinvest in the country; they could take out all profits. Added to this, we might also wonder why women's rights were being put to the backburner in the new constitution, giving them fewer rights than under the previous regime. Also, the question arose, why the country was being opened up to no bid contracts for President Bush's crony allies and where the lost moneys (8 Billion) of the Iraq reconstruction fund, disappeared to? In other words where is the rule of law for the occupiers, even as they seek to impose it on the occupied, the disenfranchised, and the underdeveloped? The answer is that under the conditions of the *Superpower Syndrome Mandatory Conflict Complex,* the process of hegemony dictates that what the United States says goes. In other words the United States superpower creates its own reality, and that reality is based on the concept of "might makes right." The following article excerpt by Ron Suskind illustrates in stark and blunt terms, the nature of the administration of president Bush and his neo-con advisors' self-concept as seen from their own perspective and their feeling they need not answer to any one and their seeing themselves as above the congress and as creators of the reality of the world, i.e. their own "world order" by virtue of their actions alone in an of themselves. [highlighted text by Ashby]

> In the summer of 2002, after I had written an article in Esquire that the White House didn't like about Bush's former communications director, Karen Hughes, I had a meeting with a senior adviser to Bush. He expressed the White House's displeasure, and then he told me something that at the time I didn't fully comprehend - but which I now believe gets to the very heart of the Bush presidency.
>
> The aide said that guys like me were "in what we call the reality-based community," which he defined as people who "believe that solutions emerge from your judicious study of discernible reality." I nodded and murmured something about enlightenment principles and empiricism. He cut me off. "That's not the way the world really works anymore," he continued. "We're an empire now, and when we act, we create our own reality. And while you're studying that reality - judiciously, as you will - we'll act again, creating other new realities, which you can study too, and that's how things will sort out. We're history's actors . . . and you, all of you, will be left to just study what we do."
>
> Who besides guys like me are part of the reality-based community? Many of the other elected officials in Washington, it would seem. A group of Democratic and Republican members of Congress were called in to discuss Iraq sometime before the October 2002 vote authorizing Bush to move forward. A

> Republican senator recently told Time Magazine that the president walked in and said: "Look, I want your vote. I'm not going to debate it with you." When one of the senators began to ask a question, Bush snapped, "Look, I'm not going to debate it with you."[60]

The frame of mind of the superpower develops hubris due to the deluded idea of self importance and power to "create" its own realities. Just as a mentally ill person would have difficulty in making their way in the real world of external independent realities, the superpower mindset also has difficulties; but unlike the insane individual the superpower leaders can move many resources to try to make the world in the image of their desired reality but that capacity is limited. In other words, the reality that the power elite desires might be insane but for those who agree with the superpower mentality it is not considered insane because it is a superpower and a superpower is supposed to have the power to reshape the world according to its desires and those who want to partake in the spoils of the fruition of the accomplishments of the superpower should accede to the demands of the superpower, defer to them and allow them opportunities that others would not. So the delusion of the superpower is facilitated by deluded followers and ingratiating cronies and other corrupt politicians who want to be rewarded for their support.

The senior CIA officer, Michael Scheuer, author of the book *Imperial Hubris: Why the West is Losing the War on Terrorism,* referred to the same problem of perception and outlook on the world as a source for the incapacity to see beyond the myopic view of American interests and the American way of life:

> "The way we see and interpret people and events outside North America is heavily clouded by arrogance and self-centeredness amounting to what I called 'imperial arrogance' in Through Our Enemies' Eyes. This is not a genetic flaw in Americans that has been present since the Pilgrims splashed ashore at Plymouth Rock, but rather a way of thinking America's elites have acquired since the end of World War II. It is a process of interpreting the

world so it makes sense to us, a process yielding a world in which few events seem alien because we Americanize their components."

Among many examples of the Super Power arrogance is the unwillingness or incapacity to accept criticism or any projection of outcomes other than those that were desired or *decreed* by them as if whatever they desire is supposed to happen as they desire it simply because they want it to be so. Here that delusion manifested as incapacity to accept intelligence estimates of the growing "insurgency" in Iraq after as the president put it "major combat operations" had ceased. Before the war intelligence estimate from the secret intelligence organizations like the CIA and the NSA had cautioned that there likely would be an insurgency and that the invasion and occupation of Iraq would likely require hundreds of thousands of troops because the invasion would likely promote the creation of Islamic extremists but the president and his advisors chose not to heed their warnings.

Former Intel Officials Say White House Ignored Insurgency Warnings

In other news, Knight Ridder is reporting the White House repeatedly ignored early intelligence warnings that the armed insurgency in Iraq was almost entirely local and growing in size. A National Intelligence Estimate as early as October 2003 said the insurgency was fueled mostly by local conditions, such as the presence of US troops in Iraq. It also said outside forces were playing almost no role in the insurgency. Robert Hutchings, the former chair of the National Intelligence Council from 2003 to 2005 said: "Frankly, senior officials simply weren't ready to pay attention to analysis that didn't conform to their own optimistic scenarios." Another former high-ranking intelligence official said: "This was stuff the White House and the Pentagon did not want to hear. They were constantly grumbling that the people who were writing these kind of downbeat assessments `needed to get on the team,' `were not team players' and were `sitting up there (at CIA headquarters) in Langley sucking their thumbs.'"

-Democracynow.org Headlines for March 1, 2006

Among the tactics used to promote its own preeminence the superpower uses the strategy of making war and then paying off the beaten country so it is forced to accept the seizure of their lands and are not so embittered afterwards, feeling at least partly compensated. This tactic was used successfully in the Spanish-American war as well as the Mexican-American war. In the Spanish-American war the United States paid Spain for the Philippines, and Puerto Rico. In the Mexican-American war Texas was paid for. Even though he did not agree with the war Ulysses Grant noted that at least there was compensation. This capacity to pay large sums of money as bribes and payoffs also puts the superpower in a precarious position of believing that in the end moneys can be used to facilitate a political agenda and due to the greed of leaders of other countries or because puppet governments have been set up, the strategy often works.

> It is to the credit of the American nation, however, that after conquering Mexico, and while practically holding the country in our possession, so that we could have retained the whole of it, or made any terms we chose, we paid a round sum for the additional territory taken; more than it was worth, or was likely to be, to Mexico. To us it was an empire and of incalculable value; but it might have been obtained by other means. The Southern rebellion was largely the outgrowth of the Mexican war. Nations, like individuals, are punished for their transgressions. We got our punishment in the most sanguinary and expensive war of modern times.[61]

Another tactic of the superpower is toppling governments and installing dictators. One example of this among others is the installation of the Shah of Iran as an absolute ruler.[62]

> The modern Iranian monarchy was established in 1502 after the Safavid Dynasty came to power under Shah Ismail I, and ended the so-called "fourth era" of political fragmentation. The Shah of Iran was the hereditary ruler of the Iranian monarchy, though the term, when used by Westerners today, generally refers to Mohammad Reza Pahlavi, the last Shah. According to royal order of precedence, the Shah was equal in status to an Emperor. For most of its existence the Iranian monarchy had been an absolute monarchy, although there were attempts to reform it into a constitutional monarchy in the early twentieth century and following World War II. The monarchy was abolished in 1979 when a revolution led by Ayatollah Khomeini forced Shah Mohammad Reza Pahlavi into exile, and established an Islamic Republic in its place. In 1953, Iran's nationalist Prime Minister Mohammed Mossadegh began a period of rapid power

> consolidation, which eventually led to his exiling of Iran's constitutional monarch, the Shah, Mohammad Reza Pahlavi. The United States and Britain, through a now-admitted covert operation of the CIA called Operation Ajax, helped organize protests to overthrow Moussadeq and return the Shah to Iran. After his return, Iran's fledgling attempts at democracy quickly descended into dictatorship as the Shah dismantled the constitutional limitations on his office and began to rule as an absolute monarch.[63]

In speaking about the C.I.A. operation in Iran, the former C.I.A. advisor, professor and author Chalmers Johnson reported that the U.S.A. should have expected "Blowback" [*Backlash*] or a consequence for the actions of the U.S.A. in Iran.

> "This is what blowback means. "Blowback" is a CIA term that means retaliation, or payback. It was first used in the after-action report on our first clandestine overthrow of a foreign government, the overthrow of Mossadegh in Iran in 1953, when, for the sake of the British Petroleum Company, we claimed he was a communist. The Pope would be more likely a communist than Mossadegh.
> In the report, which was finally declassified in 2000, the CIA says, "We should expect some blowback from what we have done here." This was the first model clandestine operation."

Johnson went on to explain why most people in the U.S.A. do not understand the hatred many people feel against the U.S.A. especially when the president disingenuously characterizes the issue as a few malcontents, thugs or criminals that are against democracy or the American way of life. The ignorance of the masses in the U.S.A. makes them easy targets for propaganda that frames the conflict as an "us versus them" issue based on other people's supposed jealousy of American prosperity or other people's supposed religious fundamentalism seeking to destroy American Christianity since there is no historical context being given to people. Since the media in the U.S.A. does not provide that context and the educational system also does not, then most people are rendered ignorant and incapable of acting rationally to promote a proper and equitable solution to the problems in foreign relations that are presented to them.

> By blowback we do not mean just the unintended consequences of events. We mean unintended consequences of events that were kept secret from the American public, so that when the retaliation comes, they have no way to put it into context. Just as after 9/11, you have the president saying, "Why do they hate us?" The people on the receiving end know full well that they hate us because of what was done to them. It's the American public that are in the dark on that subject.

Thus, as fate would determine, the efforts of the United States to control Iran led to the alienation of the Iranian people from the United States that culminated in the removal of the Shah and the establishment of a conservative Islamic government that is in opposition to the United States. That development has led to the current condition in 2006 wherein the United States would like to also invade Iran and cause a "regime change" there as well but the so far failed attempt with Iraq has prevented the United States from any further preemptive, or rather aggressive war of choice to expand its sphere of influence and imperial domain. Failures such as the Hostage situation in the year 1979 led to the loss of prestige of the presidency and Jimmy Carter was blamed for that by the opposing party in order to win the election. Though he partly contributed to the hostage taking from the beginning by allowing the Shah into the U.S. for medical treatment after the mistreatment of Iran by previous administrations and the revolt in Iran that was led by the anti-American religious leader Ayatollah Khomeini, his restraint and humanitarian handling of the situation was overlooked in the feverish rush to excuse the impotence of the United States to do anything about the situation.

Another tactic used by the superpower is to publicly promote freedom and democracy as well as free markets but in actuality the practical action is to promote the dependency of the other country and the open markets of the other country for exploitation by United States corporations without regard to the sustainability of the enterprises or the wellbeing of the people in the other country.

This tactic is also evinced in the United States itself as the masses of people are actually treated as a separate group from the power elite. These are less abused than the populations of the other countries but they are no less subjugated. One example of this is the banning of the use of certain chemicals, such as DDT and adulterated tobacco, within the United States but, yet the permission is given to sell them abroad.

As stated earlier, when president Ronald Reagan issued his famous statement of regret for the Iran-Contra scandal, he did so admitting responsibility but not by admitting culpability, rather by saying he did what he thought was right and others could have a difference of opinion. This idea of opinion implies two sets of legitimate ideas. This is like saying his opinion about breaking the law is the same as his opponent's idea about following the law; in other words, either idea should have equal weight. Therefore, good is equal to evil and there is no objective right or wrong. Such an argument allows criminal behavior as if the offices of government absolve those occupying it from following ethical and or accepted moral standards of behavior; they can make up their own standards. He also said that he was responsible as head of the government but that the actions that were done by his subordinates were without his knowledge. That would mean that in essence, if something wrong happened he is responsible because he is president but in his opinion it was a proper action and others can disagree, but anyway he didn't know anything about what other people [his subordinates] were doing so he cannot be guilty. This kind of tactic for committing immoral and or criminal acts falls under the category of *Plausible Deniability*. So actions could be taken and there could be someone who is responsible but no one who is at fault or guilty. In Reagan's case there was a congress dominated by the opposing party. In a situation of the early 21st century where there was a congress dominated by the same party as the president, the president could rest assured that violations would not be investigated.

> **Plausible deniability** is the term given to the creation of loose and informal chains of command in government which allow controversial instructions given by high-ranking officials to be denied if they become public.
> A Senate committee, the Church Committee in 1974-1975 conducted an investigation of the intelligence agencies. In the course of the investigation, it was revealed that the CIA, going back to the Kennedy administration, had plotted the assassination of a number of foreign rulers, including Cuba's

> Fidel Castro. But the president himself, who clearly was in favor of such actions, was not to be directly involved, so that he could deny knowledge of it. This was given the term **plausible denial**.[64]

In the administration of George W. Bush, even though there were many politicians and private citizens that have cited several possible violations of his constitutional duties under the Crimes and Misdemeanors section of the constitution, there wais no serious expectation of impeachment. Even though the cry for impeachment may be heard from many quarters of the opposing party and from many in the populace at large, most analysts agree that since the congress is controlled by republicans, the same party as the president, and that since they believe or support the religious right and neo-con agenda, there would not be any serious danger of impeachment of George W. Bush. Therefore, it would seem that there is a flaw in the United States constitution, that is, when the same party controls the executive and legislative branches of the government, the actions of the president can suffer less scrutiny and thus he is able to act with greater latitude and impunity (exception from the law). In other words, the same body that is responsible for controlling the president is complicit with him or in support and therefore not willing to exercise its constitutional duties.

Causes of the Superpower Syndrome: The Superpower mentality, racism and the delusion of self-importance

The superpower mentality may be thought of as a massive distortion of self-esteem as well as an overbearing and imperious notion of gender, race and the purpose of life. For the superpower, women are servants of the male agenda and male power, even if given positions that appear to be of elevated power and control of policy. Examples of women serving in high offices of the U.S.A. superpower government who do not make policy but enforce it were Madeline Albright[65] and Condoleezza Rice[66].

The incongruous notion of superiority involves the scheme of cultural and ethnic superiority, which the superpower interprets as racism. Many researchers have speculated as to the source for the problem of racism as it developed in Europe but even more so in the United States. Prior to the advent of the particular form of racism in the Americas and the transatlantic slave[3] trade the concept of white supremacy, as we know it today, was nonexistent. Arabs and Europeans were the first groups to develop technologies and war tactics that allowed them to expand their culture into native areas where they found lesser advanced people who were easily conquered and enslaved. That capacity, along with the development of faith-based religiosity in Europe and Asia Minor that assigned primitive status or barbarian status to anyone not practicing Christianity or Islam and condoned violence against them may have contributed to the development of an ethnic and then racial concept of supremacy that developed into the form of racism that the world is now familiar with. Yet, indentured[4] service did exist on a wide scale that included "white" people as indentured servants. During the time of colonization of the New World a new imperative began, to enslave Africans and use their free labor to create the wealth of the western monarchies and aristocrats. During that time there were whites and Native Americans who were enslaved along with the Africans. Later, in the colonial era of the United States, the Africans came to be the majority of those kept in captivity and slavery came to be relegated to the "black" population exclusively.

Having originated in Europe and following the same beliefs, the people of the United States originally believed in the concept of "White Man's Burden." It represents a self-assigned Eurocentric view of the world. It is a concept that was used to promote the notion that the powerful European nations should adopt an imperial role. This conception specifically promotes a paternalistic view of non-European cultures, to see them as child-like and in need of being civilized [presuming that the Europeans were civilized in objective terms]. This conception alternatively promoted the idea that non-European cultures (including East Europeans who were also seen as lesser beings)[67] were demonic. So in other words, if a

---

[3] [in the form of slavery that developed in the American colonies, one person {black} was owned by another {white} and the owner could do anything to the slave, including kill the slave; the slave has no rights and was considered as an animal and not as a person]

[4] [a form of temporary slavery that ma last for years but which a person can eventually become free of]

culture could not be dominated it was demonized, denigrated and dehumanized so as to make it easier to kill its resisting population.

The idea of the supposed "white" man's superiority and responsibility and therefore permission to conquer "non-white" peoples, is related to the concept of Social Darwinism. It is important to note that Darwin, in his book *The Origin of Species*, called his theory an application of the doctrines of Malthus[68] in an area (evolution) without the "complicating factor of human intelligence."[69] In this context the central task of Social Darwinism became the paradigm that was used as a foundation for the social construct of the superpower mentality. This happens because if the "complicating factor of human intelligence" is removed from people, as Social Darwinism suggests, they can legitimately become, in the minds of the superpower, objects to be manipulated, abused or enslaved since the superpower is "more fit" [survival of the fittest] to do so and therefore has the right to do so, by virtue of its capacity to do so.

> The term "White Man's Burden" is the name of an 1899 poem by Rudyard Kipling, the sentiments of which give insight into this worldview.[70]
>
> The first stanza of the Kipling poem reads:
>
> *Take up the White Man's burden —*
> *Send forth the best ye breed —*
> *Go, bind your sons to exile*
> *To serve your captives' need;*
> *To wait, in heavy harness,*
> *On fluttered folk and wild —*
> *Your new-caught sullen peoples,*
> *Half devil and half child.*

The deluded concept of the "White Man's Burden" has been advanced to explain the current invasions of the Middle East with their Arab [non-white] populations being in need of white help to conduct their governments and other affairs. The statements by some right wing republicans, conservatives and racists, demonstrates the deeper thought processes in those groups that seldom is revealed openly.

Media Matters for America.
Wed, Mar 22, 2006 3:25pm EST

Savage: Iraq war is "white man's burden"[71]

> During the March 20 broadcast of his nationally syndicated radio show, Michael Savage declared that Rudyard Kipling's poem "The White Man's Burden" applied to the situation in Iraq. Kipling's poem, written in 1899, is widely believed to have been written as an endorsement of the U.S. invasion of the Philippines during the Spanish-American War. The poem describes the indigenous, colonized peoples of the world as "half-devil and half-child" and goes on to describe imperialism as a noble, if doomed, venture.
> ... Savage cited Kipling's poem to justify the U.S.-led invasion and occupation of Iraq, claiming that Americans must "choose between American imperialism and Muslim imperialism."

Why was Western Culture Able to Control the Rest of the World?

The researcher Jarrod Diamond[72] postulated that up until recently in human history, the world's populations were about even in terms of their ability to wage war and control the environment. However, the nations of the Eurasian region were able to make use of technologies that allowed them to gain control of the world before other nations could. In Diamond's view, the technological advantage, gained by taking discoveries from far off lands and ingeniously using those to construct war implements, is what spawned longstanding wars amongst European countries and led to the ideal of creating empires by dominating as many nations as possible. Some prime examples of the move to dominate other nations and create modern empires are the colonization of the "New World" (The Americas) and the "Scramble for Africa."[73] History does not present non north Eurasian or Asiatic examples of megalomania.[74] In other words, in the tropical regions of the world there is no record in history of Alexander The Great-like, Caesar-like, Genghis Khan-like, Attila-the-Hun-like, or Napoleon-like personalities, or personalities that have exhibited the desire to extend their power and dominion to encompass the known world.

bar·bar·i·an Pronunciation Key (bär-bâr'ē-ən) *n.*

1. A member of a people considered by those of another nation or group to have a primitive civilization.
2. A fierce, brutal, or cruel person.
3. An insensitive, uncultured person; a boor.

Those people who exhibit disregard for human life, who seek to amass great wealth and power, to rule over their known world, who are brutal and cruel, and may have little regard for other cultures may be considered as barbarians regardless of the amount of technological advancement they may have achieved. Under this definition, the personalities above are included as examples of barbarian leaders throughout history. Furthermore, the people that support those leaders may be considered as barbarians as well. This extended definition includes the Popes who instigated the Crusades and the Arab Islamists who sought to conquer and destroy African and Indian cultures in the way that the present day Sudanese government is doing now and others have done, off and on, since the first conquest of North Africa within 100 years after the death of Muhammad.

There are some evidences that indicate that those peoples who come from the northern hemisphere of the planet earth, especially those above latitude 30°, are more aggressive, militaristic and stressed than those below, especially those between the Tropic of Cancer and the Arctic Circle. For example, the colonization of North America by Europeans was easier in South America because the Native Americans there were not as aggressive as those in North America.[75]

An example of the general peaceful culture that prevailed in Native American culture in the tropical zones is presented by Bartolome De Las Casas, who was an eye witness to the European discovery of the western hemisphere. He speaks here specifically of the peoples that were found there and their existing culture and atrocities committed by the Spaniards on the Island of Hispañola [today Santo Domingo {Dominican Republic} and Haiti. The same occurred in Puerto Rico.

> The Indies were discovered in the year one thousand four hundred and ninety two. In the following year a great many Spaniards went there with the intention of settling the land. Thus, forty-nine years have passed since the first settlers penetrated the land, the first so-claimed being the large and most happy isle called Hispaniola, which is six hundred leagues in circumference.
> ... And of all the infinite universe of humanity, these people are the most guileless, the most devoid of wickedness and duplicity, the most obedient and faithful to their native masters and to the Spanish Christians whom they serve. They are by nature the most humble, patient, and peaceable, holding no grudges, free from embroilments, neither excitable nor quarrelsome. These people are the most devoid of rancors, hatreds, or desire for vengeance of any people in the world. And because they are so weak and complaisant, they are less able to endure heavy labor and soon die of no matter what malady.[76]

Similarly, the peoples of Africa (most of which is located within the tropics), were and continue to be less aggressive in terms of initiating and instituting aggressive and warlike cultures, and social institutions. It is notable that people in the tropics can be made to adopt aggression as a way of life but they did not initiate it or perpetuate it. There are no great historical barbarians in the area of the tropics or in the southern hemisphere of the earth, for that matter. From Genghis Khan and Tamerlane in East Asia to Attila and the Huns in Central Asia, to Alexander, Caesar and the Vandals, Goths, Visigoths, Gauls, Vikings and Crusaders, followed by Napoleon and the British empire in Eurasia, there have been scores of barbarian would be conquerors who pretended to the destiny of world domination [megalomania].[5]

Left: Ghengis Khan. "With Heaven's aid I have conquered for you a huge empire. But my life was too short to achieve the conquest of the world. That task is left for you." -Genghis Khan, to his sons at the end of his life.

[5] A psychopathological condition characterized by delusional fantasies of wealth, power, or omnipotence. a delusion (common in paranoia) that you are much greater and more powerful and influential than you really are. An extremely inflated view of one's own significance and abilities. This may take on a delusional quality in which, for example, the individual may believe himself to be Jesus Christ. In this situation the description of the thoughts is referred to as *delusions of grandeur*.

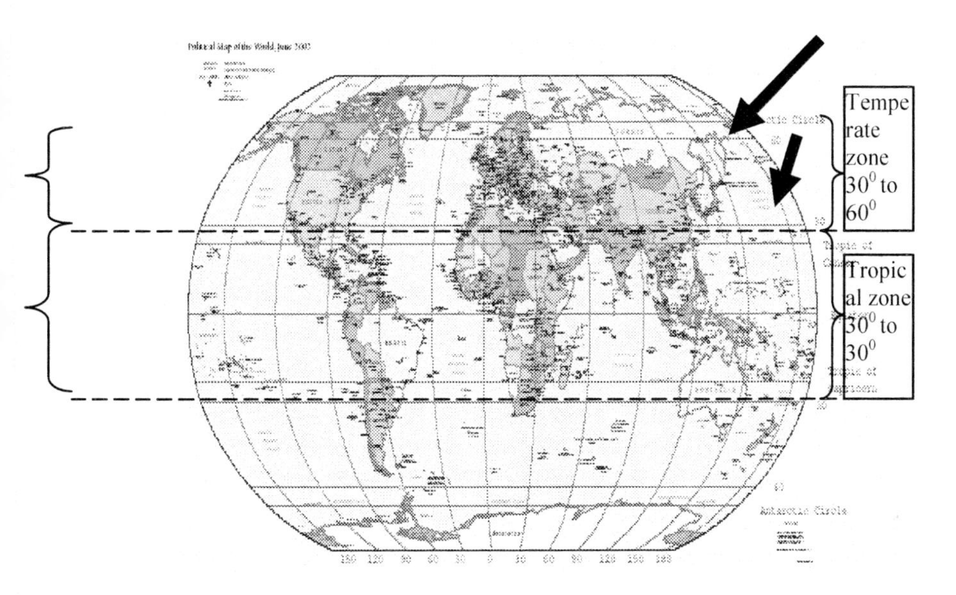

One common factor that generally affected the development of the cultures of the barbarians is the form of climate in the regions of their nations. Scientific studies have documented that changing weather conditions affect moods.[77] Weather changes also affect the immune system and health which is a contributing factor as to why many people contract "colds" at the beginning of the winter "flu season." One of the more prominent well documented ailments based on changing seasons is "***Seasonal affective disorder***," or **S.A.D.**, which is found to affect many people year-round in latitudes of 30°N or South and higher. One important factor which produces less vitality and mental capacity is the nature of sunlight in the affected areas. Only at latitudes between the Tropics is it possible for the sun to be at the zenith. The Tropic of Cancer (cancer (♋) is Latin for *crab*), is the farthest northern latitude at which the sun can appear directly overhead. The reduced amount of sunlight coupled with the constant changes in seasons can lead to changes in the personality. The vegetation as well as the availability of foods is different in the northern hemisphere. People tend to eat more meat products in those geographical areas. Consequently it has also been demonstrated and documented that higher consumption of meat decreases life expectancy,[78] increases diseases such as cancer,[79] diabetes,[80] and produces aggressive behavior.[81]

Another emerging threat to the environment is "Global Dimming" this phenomenon is caused by pollution containing small particles that cause water particles to form on them than thereby produced reflective clouds in the environment. Airplane vapor trails are an example of this occurrence. The sunlight is reflected away and the world has become dimmed. Global Dimming counters the problem of global warming to some degree but if the dimming is reduced, the way it has in the last years, the warming effect will increase more rapidly. Since sunlight affects moods there are some indications that the reason why the seasonal affective disorder syndrome has increased in the past years is related to the Global Dimming problem. Another complication that may be expected is health problems due to vitamin "D" deficiency. Those people who live in colder regions need to cover their bodies more so they do not receive as much sunlight touching their bodies. Direct sunlight stimulates vitamin "D" production in the body. It is necessary for proper nutrition. Its deficiency can cause a myriad of health issues that can add to the stress and anxiety of living in those areas.

All of the stresses related to disease exacerbate the problems due to weather and climate changes. Normal "winter blues" can usually be dampened or extinguished by exercise and increased outdoor activity, particularly on sunny days, resulting in increased solar exposure.[82] The stresses of living in the temperate zones[83] seem to produce rational anxieties [due to the harshness of the environment and the difficulty of making a living there] but also irrational anxieties that are not perceived consciously due to feelings of fear of loss of resources and worry about survival issues. In a sense, the desire to maraud, plunder, pillage, etc., may be thought of as a misguided but cathartic desire to dispel the depression caused by the weather and relieve the anxiety of a precarious existence due to scarce resources. If that activity were directed in positive ways the society could cope with the problem. However, the best solution would be to reproduce the conditions of the lower hemisphere as authentically as possible including the diet, solar exposure, etc. It is sobering to realize that the problem of major conflicts in the world due to aggressive, intolerant, dogmatic philosophies and religions may be in part or mostly due to climate and the indiscriminate migration of human beings out of Africa [where the weather and climate changes are more harmonious -less abrupt and less severe and there is greater availability of fruits and vegetables [year-round] without the need for excessive preparation as is necessary for living in other parts of the world. Thus, the climate syndrome should not be thought of as just an ancient or prehistoric issue that changed people in the northern hemisphere but one that continually affects them even today by stressing the immune system, the mind and personality. As it is impractical for the population of the northern hemisphere to relocate to the south, health strategies including changes in diet, and solar exposure, as well as the practice of meditation, and classes in conflict resolution could mitigate the situation. Therefore, peacefulness and reduced stress can be chosen if the problem is made known in this context and the proper actions are taken; all those in the northern hemisphere can be helped to better cope with the issue of weather in order to lead them towards balance, and peace.

During his reign, an Ancient Egyptian Pharaoh gave instructions to his successor. He did particularly mention the psychological causes for what he termed as the "Miserable Asiatic" mentality. The Sage King from Ancient Egypt who wrote the Wisdom Teaching to Merikara spoke of a reason for the aggressiveness and violent nature of the Asiatics.

Teachings of Meri-ka-ra[84]

Lo, the miserable Asiatic,
He is wretched because of the place he lives in:
Short of water, bare of wood,
Its paths are many and painful because of mountains.
He is nomadic, not dwelling in one place,
The constant need for food propels his legs,
He makes war since the time of Heru,
He is not successful in conquering nor is he conquered,
He is traitorous and does not announce the day of combat,
He is like a thief who darts around a group.
But as I live and shall be what I am,
When the Bowmen were a sealed wall,
I broke through their defenses,
I attack them with the forces from Lower Egypt,
I captured their men and women,
I took their cattle,
Until the Asiatics despised Egypt.
Do not worry about the Asiatic,
The Asiatic is like a crocodile on its shore,
It snatches from a lonely road,
But it cannot capture anything from a populous town.

The Ancient Egyptians referred to the "Asiatics" as the marauding hoards of Middle Easterners, who would later be known as Hyksos, Assyrians, Persians an later the Greeks (Eurasians) who tried for centuries to conquer Egypt. The Asiatic mentality is a state of mind and attitude that is characteristically aggressive, combative and traitorous, and thievish as well as nomadic. Thus, the reason for the Asiatic mentality is the lack of stability, peace and basic needs of life. That upbringing has led to the development of a character [in some members of the population] exemplified by the propensity towards competition, and willingness to use violence for survival wherein cooperation, sharing and laissez-faire (live and let live) capacity is discouraged. That personality is moved to control nature and people, and conquer so as to feed its irrational need for security. The underlying cause for the development of the Asiatic personality is the lack of abundance in terms of food and material wealth in comparison to Africa. This is why the Asiatics were trying to conquer Egypt from the end of the Middle Kingdom Period down to the final conquest of Egypt by Alexander the Great.

Competition, Fear and Greed as Allies of the Superpower Syndrome Mandatory Conflict Complex

George Washington spoke about the dangers of having an overgrown military establishment. He felt that any form of government would be in danger from the inevitable desire that would arise for conquest and the consequent need for war that would divide people and corrupt the government.

> While, then, every part of our country thus feels an immediate and particular interest in union, all the parts combined can not fail to find in the united mass of means and efforts greater strength, greater resource, proportionably greater security from external danger, a less frequent interruption of their peace by foreign nations, and what is of inestimable value, they must derive from union an exemption from those broils and wars between themselves which so frequently afflict neighboring countries not tied together by the same governments, which their own rivalships alone would be sufficient to produce, but which opposite foreign alliances, attachments, and intrigues would stimulate and imbitter. Hence, likewise, they will avoid the necessity of those overgrown military establishments which,

> under any form of government, are inauspicious to liberty, and which are to be regarded as particularly hostile to republican liberty. In this sense it is that your union ought to be considered as a main prop of your liberty, and that the love of the one ought to endear to you the preservation of the other.[85]

The reason why Washington was so interested in the subject of standing armies is that, as an avid student of military history, he knew that the republican form of government could easily turn into a military state since in such a form of government the power is concentrated in the representatives and not in the people directly. There will always be those who would like to use the army to pursue their own agendas. A recent example of this form of thinking came from the U.S.A. ambassador to the U.N., Madeline Albright, who made a revealing statement about U.S.A. military policy when she once told Colin Powel *"what good is your great army if we don't use it?"*[86] James Madison, fourth president and coauthor of the Federalist Papers, also had strong warnings about engaging in wars and what happens to a society when it becomes militarized.

> "Of all the enemies to public liberty war is, perhaps, the most to be dreaded because it comprises and develops the germ of every other. War is the parent of armies; from these proceed debts and taxes...known instruments for bringing the many under the domination of the few. . . No nation could preserve its freedom in the midst of continual warfare."
>
> - James Madison, *Political Observations*, 1795

Washington and Madison had the example of Rome of course but there were other examples in his own day. When wars become the main program of concern of a society the leaders inevitably feel the need to curtail liberties, especially the freedom to dissent. So the media controls and censorships increase and dissenters are labeled as unpatriotic and may even be victims of unusual "accidents." In the U.S.A. new laws such as the "Patriot Act" and the consolidation of the media under wealthy owners and corporations that are closely associated with the government leaders, has produced a situation in which the mainstream media does not press concerning constitutional issues or even factual matters that expose blatant government falsehoods and manipulations. Chalmers Johnson further explores the issue:

> By the end of the first century BC, Rome had seemingly, again, "inadvertently" acquired an empire that surrounded the entire Mediterranean Sea. They then discovered that the inescapable accompaniment, the Siamese twin of imperialism, is militarism. You start needing standing armies. You start having armies that are demobilized, of men who have done nothing but spend all their lives in the military. It's expensive to pay them. You have to now provide them, in the Roman Empire, with farms or things of this sort. They become irritated with the state. And then along comes the military populist, the figure who says, "I understand your problems. I represent your interests against the Roman Senate." And, certainly, Julius Caesar is the model for this. "The only requirement is that I become life dictator for this" -- Napoleon Bonaparte, Juan Peron, this type of figure.[87]

In the speech by president Dwight D. Eisenhower known as the *Military-Industrial Complex Speech,*[88] Eisenhower expressed his concern about what he saw as the development of an out of control military and a social situation of continuous threat, presumably from the Soviet Union or elsewhere that required the need to produce what even he thought of as an unprecedented "armaments industry" and "military organization."

> Our military organization today bears little relation to that known by any of my predecessors in peacetime, or indeed by the fighting men of World War II or Korea. Until the latest of our world conflicts, the United States had no armaments industry.[89]

Eisenhower reluctantly saw the coming of a new society based on this industry and seemed to regret its creation. It was presumably due to the competition between the United States and the Soviet Union that the need arose. Now, fifteen years after the collapse of the Soviet Union, as a superpower the United States maintained its military industrial complex to satisfy the greed of the military industry and now it has fallen under the control of the conservative wing of the conservative (republican) party of the United States which controls the congress of the United States government and the Neo-conservatives who control the executive branch of the government. The choice to go to war with Iraq was an expression of the desire for conquest and expansion of the sphere of influence as dictated by the inevitable desire that arises from having the military capacity to strike out in conquest.

> In the councils of government, we must guard against the acquisition of unwarranted influence, whether sought or unsought, by the military industrial complex. The potential for the disastrous rise of misplaced power exists and will persist. We must never let the weight of this combination endanger our liberties or democratic processes. We should take nothing for granted. Only an alert and knowledgeable citizenry can compel the proper meshing of the huge industrial and military machinery of defense with our peaceful methods and goals, so that security and liberty may prosper together.
> Akin to, and largely responsible for the sweeping changes in our industrial-military posture, has been the technological revolution during recent decades.
> In this revolution, research has become central; it also becomes more formalized, complex, and costly. A steadily increasing share is conducted for, by, or at the direction of, the Federal government.[90]

Eisenhower feared what would happen if the military industrial complex were to gain an overpowering influence on congress. It amounts to *War profiteering*, in particular, active war profiteering, which in addition to directly profiting from a war by selling arms to one or both sides, have a crucial interest not only in starting wars but also prolonging them so as to make or increase profits.[91] Naturally, since the system of government is based on legalized bribery, in the form of contributions by lobbyists, it would not be difficult to imagine such a situation, which was prophetic as the support for Iraq and Iran when they were at war and the attempts by the U.S.A. to prolong that war to weaken the two combatants during the 1980s. In the *Federalist Papers*[92] James Madison spoke about the danger of having a standing army; that the temptation would be to use it. Madison's insights were proven right as later history demonstrated, with the manifest destiny ideas and designs on expanding the United States from coast to coast, into Canada, Texas, and into Spanish territories, etc. Later history books such as the 1899 - *History and Conquest of the Philippines*, clearly state the motivations for material gain and financial interests of the U.S. government to acquire the Philippines. In that book Senator John M. Thurston of Nebraska said:

> "War with Spain would increase the business and earnings of every American railroad, it would increase the output of every American factory, it would stimulate every branch of industry and domestic commerce."

In an interview on the program Democracy Now, [93] hosted by Amy Goodman, guest Antonia Juhasz, visiting scholar at the Institute for Policy Studies, spoke about the blatant statements by Oil company and government contractors about how they would like to see Iraq and the rest of the Middle East invaded by the U.S.A. so that they can control the oil and get government contracts.

> **AMY GOODMAN:** In your chapter "A Mutual Seduction," you have a quote of Ken Derr, the former C.E.O. of Chevron, 1998. I know his tenure well. It was the time in the Niger Delta that Chevron was involved with the killing of two Nigerian villagers, who were protesting yet another oil spill of Chevron and jobs not being given to the local community as they drilled for oil. But your quote here says, "Iraq possesses huge reserves of oil and gas, reserves I would love Chevron to have access to." And then you follow that by a quote of John Gibson, Chief Executive of Halliburton Energy Service Group, who says, "We hope Iraq will be the first domino and that Libya and Iran will follow. We don't like being kept out of markets, because it gives our competitors an unfair advantage."

> **ANTONIA JUHASZ:** I love it when they're honest. It doesn't happen very often. Yeah, these companies have been explicit, for decades, that they want in, particularly to Iraq. The reason is obvious. Iraq certainly has the second largest oil reserves in the world, but some geologists believe it has the largest, at least on par with Saudi Arabia. That's a tremendous pool of wealth. And not just have the companies been clear that they want access to that oil, U.S. leaders -- for example, Dick Cheney, Paul Wolfowitz, Zalmay Khalilzad, Donald Rumsfeld -- have all been explicit for the past 20 years that what the U.S. needs to do is gain increased access to the region's oil, and most explicitly during the '90s, Iraq's oil, that this is something that shouldn't be in the hands of Saddam Hussein.

The statements above clearly show how the economic motivations act to foment wars. Thus, it is possible to see the growing willingness and active search for situations in which to use the military in order to stimulate the economy and expand the economic prospects of the United States throughout its history. It is this factor [war] also that allowed the United States to emerge out of its most profound economic depression and stagnating economy to become the most powerful economy in the world.

So there may be a good motive for speculation as to what kind of culture would have emerged if the conflict with the Soviet Union had been averted after World War II. Yet it was inevitable, due to the desire for preeminence, which the nuclear weapons seemed to provide. Many theorists and political scientists have speculated that the existence of nuclear weapons and their possession by the two "superpowers" prevented war between them. This idea seems to ignore the fact that the conflict was played out through a "Cold War", meaning through surrogates, the developing nations, wherein their economies and governments were destabilized and armed conflicts between them were engendered by both superpowers in which millions of people died. Thus, the two superpowers aided each other, stimulated each other, to reach unprecedented heights of power but also paranoiac-fear, hubris and reckless disregard for human life and the environment.

Eisenhower, having witnessed the horrors of war, seemed to genuinely desire peace, disarmament and justice for all human beings but apparently regretted being unable to promote that goal; he was though, proud of having been able to avert a major war during his tenure as president; Eisenhower's tone and the substance of this message recall to mind the similar statements of Ulysses S. Grant as he reviewed the politics of his own day. Unlike the presidency of George W. Bush's administration, which actively promotes the "us versus them" mentality and egging on the opponents to attack.[94] Never having been in combat themselves, president George W. Bush and his neo-con advisors had not witnessed the horrors of war first hand so it was easier for them and for their supporters (many of whom also had not experienced war first hand) to take a combative posture instead of cooperating and negotiating with others.

> We pray that peoples of all faiths, all races, all nations, may have their great human needs satisfied; that those now denied opportunity shall come to enjoy it to the full; that all who yearn for freedom may experience its spiritual blessings; that those who have freedom will understand, also, its heavy responsibilities; that all who are insensitive to the needs of others will learn charity; that the scourges of poverty, disease and ignorance will be made to disappear from the earth, and that, in the goodness of time, all peoples will come to live together in a peace guaranteed by the binding force of mutual respect and love.[95]

The Asiatic (Superpower syndrome) personality is also evident in United States culture with the treatment of the Native Americans as Tecumseh relates:

> Every year our white intruders become more greedy, exacting, oppressive and overbearing. Every year contentions spring up between them and our people and when blood is shed we have to make atonement whether right or wrong, at the cost of the lives of our greatest chiefs, and the yielding up of large tracts of our lands.[96]

> If there be one here tonight who believes that his rights will not sooner or later be taken from him by the avaricious American pale faces, his ignorance ought to excite pity, for he knows little of our common foe...[97]

Tecumseh noted that no amount of conquest seemed to be enough to satisfy the "white intruders". He noted that the overbearing avarice and greed of the conquerors would eventually lead to the annihilation of the Native American Indians. The point here is that greed seems to be a motivating factor of the Superpower syndrome. Of course not all people of any group are evil or good. Yet in the case of the United States as with other countries, even though the populace may acknowledge the error or unethical nature of a policy, such as graft, killing Indians, slavery, etc. still the population supports the continued existence of the government and its policies, either actively or passively and does not clearly manifest the sense of justice, even to the extent that president Grant manifested in the form of paying reparations to the victims of the manifest destiny policy and the slavery institution. The greed in the masses that operates to cause their support is due to the expectation of someday acquiring wealth and property and of course, security.

So fear, greed and desire are manipulated by the superpower syndrome leaders to promote situations in which people believe they are under attack or that their survival is at stake or that they are justified in some way to engage in the dictates of the superpower dictum. In that way they have become complicit in the superpower culture even though they may as well fall victims to the greater designs of the superpower elite.

This kind of inability to "live and let live" manifests in other areas of social interaction, namely, the religious expressions. While there is a superpower mentality that operates in many religions, out of the major world religions the ones that developed in Asia Minor (Middle East) and Eurasia and in other parts of the geographic temperate zones of the Earth, including Zoroastrianism, Judaism, Christianity and Islam, exhibit an obsessive compulsion to convert all others, that is to say, conquer them, by taking away their religion and forcing them to adopt their own. This is a form of religious fascism. The practice of forcibly converting others and denigrating their culture has been documented in the three main world religions (Judaism, Christianity and Islam) from the time of their inception.[98] That desire to convert others at all cost can manifest as an apocalyptic strategy that includes the destruction of the earth. Robert J. Lifton noted an apocalyptic component to the desire, in some religions, to convert the world by bringing about the destruction of the world presumably so that God would cleanse the world.

> That Japanese cult called Aum Shinrikyo released Sarin gas in the subways in 1995. The important thing about Aum Shinrikyo was the marriage of ultimate zealotry and ultimate weapons. They were a relatively small cult but they really wanted to join in destroying the world in order to create Armageddon. They had a vision of releasing a much larger amount of Sarin gas later on that year so that Americans would think that the Japanese had done it, the Japanese would think that Americans had done it, other world powers would join in what would become World War III, and that would lead to biblical Armageddon. Wild fantasy, of course, but fantasy associated with weapons of mass destruction. They actually manufactured chemical and

> biological weapons and sought unsuccessfully nuclear weapons. They also wanted to be join in what used to be called "forcing the end" by being active in producing Armageddon. Now, when 9-11 occurred, people were struck by the title of my book on Aum Shinrikyo, *Destroying the World to Save It.* That is the ultimate apocalyptic image. And certainly Bin Laden fits into that, has the image of destroying much of the world in service of recreating it in perfect Islamist fashion. But what is little appreciated is that we enter into all of this in our response and ourselves become apocalyptic. That is, with our vision of world control, superpower syndrome, we seek to destroy that which we take to be wrong-headed or evil in the service of a perfect Americanized democratic free enterprise world. So, we want to see ourselves as rational, and non-apocalyptic, but we enter into kind of apocalyptic interplay. What I really have come to believe and say this in my book, there's a kind of a tandem between Al Qaeda on the one hand and ourselves on the other, each reacting to the other, each stimulating the other. Certainly, nobody, I'm sure, was more delighted with our invasion of Iraq than Bin Laden. The two zealots, so to speak, stimulate each other, in a kind of mad dance, which couldn't be more dangerous. [99]

To the above we might add that the neo-conservative political movement may be also considered as an apocalyptic movement or political cult and unlike the previous cults and apocalyptic movements that have come and gone through history, the neo-conservative, racist and sexist leaders have demonstrated the capacity and willingness to use true weapons of mass destruction. The neo-conservative ideal of world domination, megalomania, as an alternative form of zealotry, has as its underlying nature the fear of poverty, fear of being ruled by others, fear of the unknown and greed, for more of everything. So in this context the writers of the science fiction movie *The Day The Earth Stood Still* (1951) were not far off the mark in envisioning the development of humanity in the direction of spreading conquest and nuclear destruction beyond the solar system and attacking other planets just as they attack other countries on earth, for the logic follows that just as governments do to their own people they seek to do to other nations and just as they seek to do to other nations they will seek to do to other planets when they have the capacity to do so.

When president Ronald Reagan proposed creating The Strategic Defense Initiative (S.D.I.), commonly called Star Wars, a space-based system to protect the United States from attack by nuclear missiles many people around the world thought it was an insane move to escalate the Cold War.[100] Indeed, it did infuriate the Soviet Union. But the fact that such a program would be considered to the exclusion of the more obvious, simple and cheap solution, making peace, underscores the factor of psychological impairment that is produced by the superpower syndrome that contributes to creating a mental complex that inevitably leads to conflict. Outspending all other nations the superpower allocate sizeable amounts of money to armaments that could be better spent producing valuable goods or valuable infrastructure, health care needs, education, etc. demonstrating that armaments and combative postures are seen as more valuable than communicating and making peace. Therefore, also it means that to the superpower mentality maintaining power and domination is more important than becoming a member of the family of nations; dying is more important than a peaceful resolution and friendship. Given the policies described above there is little wonder why much of the world sees the United States government as perhaps the greatest threat to world peace. After the passing of the Reagan and Bush Sr. administrations the S.D.I. system lingered in limbo due to its expense and the doubts about its effectiveness until President George W. Bush revived the idea once more.[101]

Most people feel that mass killing is only carried out through the use of weapons of mass destruction. However, many more people have been killed by the superpower countries through carrying out social policies that are injurious to thousands or millions of people. Some researchers, such as Webster G. Tarpley [102] have discovered connections between the writings and philosophy of Rev. Thomas Robert Malthus and the actions of western governments. Malthus wrote about the danger of overpopulation and how that would pose a threat to the ruling class, the oligarchy of the British Empire, as it would lead to a social catastrophe because according to his calculations the human world population supposedly would grow at a faster rate than the food supply. In *An Essay on the Principle of Population*, published in 1798, Malthus predicted population would outrun the food supply, leading to a decrease in food per person.[103]

His writings and economic theories were so influential that much of them were adopted by the leaders of the British Empire and then implemented throughout the countries controlled by the British. In his view, only misery, moral restraint and vice (which for Malthus included contraception) could check excessive population growth. Essentially what this resulted in was the promotion of legislation which degenerated the conditions of the poor in England.[104] As stated earlier, Darwin, in his book *The Origin of Species*, called his theory an application of the doctrines of Malthus in an area without the complicating factor of human intelligence. So in other words, Darwin was, along with a scientific effort to explain evolution, indeed consciously creating a philosophical construct that would justify and promote the objectification and subjugation of the weak elements of the population (the poor, females, and non-Europeans) by the powerful. This concept would later develop into what would be called *Social Darwinism.*[105] Thus, it could be therefore rationalized that it is permissible to enslave others by natural right, simply by having the power and will to do so. In other words, just because one can do a thing gives one the right to do it because one is more fit and therefore has more right to do it. Such positions [Malthusian, social Darwinist, white man's burden, etc.] ignore the moral implications and outcomes of the actions they engender since the complex of fear, greed and superiority clouds the conscience and therefore also the moral capacity of the superpower thinker.

Research and significant empirical evidence have proven Malthus' theories to be wrong.[106] Nevertheless, Malthus continues to have considerable influence up to the present. Recent examples of that influence include the book *The Population Bomb* by Paul R. Ehrlich who predicted that hundreds of millions would die from a coming overpopulation crisis in the 1970s, and that later on by 1980 life expectancy would be only 42 years in the United States, all of which have proven to be in complete error.

However, Malthus's ideas were opposed and perhaps even ridiculed in the middle of the nineteenth century by the writings of Karl Marx and Friedrich Engels who argued that:

> What Malthus saw as the problem of the pressure of population on the means of production was, in fact, that of the pressure of the means of production on population. They thus viewed it in terms of their concept of the labor reserve army. In other words, the seeming excess of population that Malthus attributed to the seemingly innate disposition of the poor to reproduce beyond their means was actually a product of the very dynamic of capitalist economy.

Thus, the draconian measures advocated by Malthus were one of the causes of the *innate disposition of the poor to reproduce*. Studies have found that development in a civilization, especially in the area of elevation of women in a society, as well as education of children and the reduction of poverty, are important factors in reducing the birth rate and promoting sustainable peaceful societies. However, such societies would become economic rivals of the powerful nations, so the powerful nations chose to deal with the issue of population as a reproductive problem instead of as an economic (poverty) problem since approaching it economically would lead to the prospect of their losing dominance. This factor of population increase has concerned some western theorists and avowed racists who see the increasing population in non-western cultures as a threat to the existence of the "white race" and the dominance of western culture especially in view of the reduced birthrate in the west. It is this unconscious fear that is claimed as the source for the perpetuation of the debunked Malthusian concepts of overpopulation in the form of seemingly irrational actions by the United States in its superpower role. Many people find it hard to believe that the United States government would intentionally promote policies nationally or around the world, especially in non-European countries, that lead to disease, famine, and wars; and also have wondered why it seems that the leaders of the United States more often than not pursue policies that seem irrational on their face, that promote large scale death among the national population and populations around the world. In an interview with Robert J. Lifton, Journalist Amy Goodman asked Mr. Lifton about his opinion of a statement by Noam Chomsky and if it related to the superpower syndrome concept.[107]

> **AMY GOODMAN:** Noam Chomsky says that a superpower can exert its power most effectively, not by being rational, but by being irrational, where others in the world cannot predict what this number one superpower in the world, in this case, the United States, will do. What do you think of that?
> **ROBERT JAY LIFTON:** Well, he's certainly right about it being non-rational. In some ways, though, it is almost predictable. I don't think that our behavior has been so unpredictable once we saw its general direction. And part of the argument in my book is that it's part of an ideology which pulls together a kind of military fundamentalism from a more or less secular influence, people like Rumsfeld and Cheney, together with a religious fundamentalism, the influence of the Christian Right to create a doctrine and a policy that has a certain consistency. And it polarizes the world into good and evil. It seeks to dominate militarily and it can employ cynical manipulations because they're in the service of what is perceived as a higher truth. So, in some ways the behavior is certainly consistent. It's certainly non-rational. It's a kind of fantasy of omnipotence, but it is consistent. We're doing this again and again and what we're doing fits into this category.

It seems irrational to promote the despoiling of the environment for profit, creating situations wherein the educational system purposely fails, or preventing the institution of a national healthcare program in the face of abject failure and looming collapse of the inflated private health care model. Other examples include the tacit approval by president George H. Bush of Saddam Hussein's invasion of Kuwait and later the denouncement of it in order to have an excuse to place troops in the Middle East and make the first attempt to attack, control and seize Iraq.[108]

> **The U.S. "Green Light" to Invade Kuwait**
> 12. The Defendants showed absolutely no opposition to Iraq's increasing threats against Iraq. Indeed, when Saddam Hussein requested U.S. Ambassador April Glaspie to explain State Department testimony in Congress about Iraq's threats against Kuwait, she assured him that the United States considered the dispute to be a regional concern, and that it would not intervene militarily. In other words, the United States government gave Saddam Hussein what amounted to a "green light" to invade Kuwait.
> 13. This reprehensible behavior was similar to that of the Carter administration during September of 1980, when United States government officials gave Saddam Hussein the "green light" to invade Iran and thus commence the tragic Iraq-Iran War. A decade later,

> Saddam Hussein simply surmised that he had been given yet another "green light" by the United States government to commit overt aggression against surrounding states. Only this time, the Defendants knowingly intended to lead Iraq into a provocation that could be used to justify intervention and warfare by United States military forces for the real purpose of destroying Iraq as a military power and seizing Arab oil fields in the Persian Gulf.[109]

Later, upon seeing the massive U.S.A. (Gulf War 1991) military buildup, Hussein offered to negotiate a withdrawal if the Israeli-Palestinian issue were resolved. That proposal was rejected by George H. Bush and scarcely appeared in the media. Another example was the withdrawal of arms inspectors from Iraq by George W. Bush in 2003 [before they finished their inspection work after being granted full access to all sites including the ones that the defense secretary and the secretary of state said had weapons for sure] by president George W. Bush, when it was becoming clear they were finding no weapons of mass destruction and that they would not achieve the result of an excuse to pursue the policy of "regime change" and control of Iraq through arms inspections of the U.N., which was the true goal of the invasion. One stark example of seeming irrationality or even amorality during the presidency of Bill Clinton is the killing of tens of thousands of Iraqi children during the intermittent air strikes and embargo/sanctions period between the 1991 Gulf War and the invasion of Iraq by George W. Bush in 2003.

Madeline Albright was appointed ambassador to the U.N., her first diplomatic post, shortly after Clinton was inaugurated. During her tenure at the U.N., she had a rocky relationship with the United Nations Secretary-General, Boutros Boutros-Ghali. After the victory of the U.S.A. in the first gulf war the Iraqi government was controlled through economic sanctions which prevented them from using moneys from oil sales except through a program called "oil for food" in which they received small amounts of money for oil. Yet there developed a large black market of oil tankers carrying oil out of Iraq through Turkey. But most of the money want to bribes and to the Iraqi elite and the poor and the children of Iraq suffered greatly and many died as a result. In fact, it is well known that economic sanctions do not hurt the government and power elite of a country.

The theory is that if people suffer they will overthrow the government that the U.S.A. does not want. The usual outcome is that the country falls economically and the people starve and have less capacity to take any political action except accept their government. In 1996, Madeline Albright made highly controversial remarks in an interview with Leslie Stahl on CBS's Sixty Minutes. Stahl asked her about the effect of sanctions against Iraq: *"We have heard that half a million children have died. I mean, that's more children than died in Hiroshima. And, you know, is the price worth it?"* Albright replied: *"I think this is a very hard choice, but the price -- we think the price is worth it."* When asked about this remark in 2005 she said, *"I never should have made it, it was stupid"*, but she still supported the concept of tailored sanctions. Albright made another statement that displayed the arrogance of U.S.A. military policy when she once told Colin Power *"what good is your great army if we don't use it?"*[110] Such statements show how both political parties have contributed to U.S.A. policies that promote U.S.A. political and economic hegemony along with contempt for human life even to he extent of mass killing. The democrats have tended to use economic subjugation through the I.M.F. and the World Bank and other means while the republican party has tended to use the C.I.A. and military power to achieve the same ends. The I.M.F. and the World Bank are supposed to be institutions by which rich nations channel money into loans to developing countries to raise their standard of living. As of the year 2006 not one single country's standard of living was raised and in fact most had fallen down and that was purposeful since the moneys were given to unrighteous rulers, dictators, and the ruling classes that committed graft and the moneys never benefited the country's infrastructure or went to develop enterprises for the people by developing commerce. Yet after the money was squandered the people were saddled with the debt, insuring they could not raise the standard of living and any income produced would first have to go to pay the debt, which would never be paid, except by refinancing or taking more loans in an endless cycle of debt which might be better described as economic slavery.

Nuclear weapons are perhaps the most apparently irrational area of superpower mentality. Even though it is evident that they cannot be used without engulfing the entire world in a cloud of radiation, there is an almost morbid embrace that recalls the scene in the movie *Beneath the Planet of the Apes* (1970) where astronauts George Taylor (Charlton Heston) and Brent (James Franciscus) encounter humans of the future who are worshipping the ultimate nuclear weapon, a doomsday device, as their god who will protect them from the menacing apes which are essentially evolutions of the aggression, racism and slavery of their earlier human ancestors. That scene seemed irrational to many who could not conceive of a religion based on fear and destruction, yet we see in our own day that the flirtation with nuclear weapons continues unabated with the announcement of the possibility of using new nuclear weapons that are supposed to be less destructive and could destroy distinct city blocks instead of whole cities. If the accuracy of that conception is anything like the accuracy of the so-called smart bombs used in the Iraq war (70% accuracy) the incompetence and strategy of irrationality that Noam Chomsky spoke of could indeed develop into an unintended disaster, thus creating what is not desired due to actions that do not follow the stated policy but which are implemented to promote a general direction towards an outcome of superpower supremacy by making others think there are madmen in control of the superpower. In other words, the superpower leaders will eventually commit a blunder or deceive themselves into becoming what they say they seek to repudiate and deter, by making an error in their calculated irrationality. In that manner they will destroy themselves and the rest of humanity with them, thereby bringing forth their own destruction as inevitably as the lost protagonist of a Greek tragedy who has all of the outs but is unable to take any course that does not lead to his destruction due to ignorance, pride, desire or greed but above all hubris.

> "A secret 1995 study of the Strategic Command, which is responsible for the strategic nuclear arsenal, outlines the basic thinking. Released through the Freedom of Information Act, the study, *Essentials of Post-Cold War Deterrence*, "shows how the United States shifted its deterrent strategy from the defunct Soviet Union to so-called rogue states such as Iraq, Libya, Cuba and North Korea," AP reports. The study advocates that the US exploit its nuclear arsenal to portray itself as "irrational and vindictive if its vital interests are attacked." That "should be a part of the national persona we project to all adversaries," in particular the "rogue states." "It hurts to portray ourselves as too

> fully rational and cool-headed," let alone committed to such silliness as international law and treaty obligations. "The fact that some elements" of the US government "may appear to be potentially 'out of control' can be beneficial to creating and reinforcing fears and doubts within the minds of an adversary's decision makers." The report resurrects Nixon's "madman theory": our enemies should recognize that we are crazed and unpredictable…"[111]

> "We have to have a national persona of irrationality with forces out of control, so we really terrify everybody, and then we can get what we want. And furthermore they're right to be terrified because we're going to have these nuclear weapons right in front of us, which will blow them all up – in fact, blow us all up if they get out of control."[112/113]

The strategy of irrationality perhaps has its most dangerous expression in the "mad man theory" that was developed by Henry Kissinger and Richard Nixon. The theory is that even if you are perfectly sane, sometimes it helps in negotiations if others think you are insane and capable of absolutely anything. The danger comes in when the saber-rattling and threats create over expectations and then the supposedly sane government leader would have to follow through on the action or lose face and appear weak.

The strategy of apparent irrationality is applied to foreign policy but also in national politics as well. Some examples are the irrationality in the approach to *aids* disease prevention and teen pregnancy. In November 2005 it was revealed that president Bush actively supported the abstinence only programs for preventing unwanted pregnancy, venereal disease and abortion so he withdrew funding for programs that included the instruction about the use of condoms.[114] The result was that aids infection rates, especially in Africa, started rising. The governments of the countries affected by this program could not contradict it since they would lose other funding if they did. That is an example of how the superpower country used money to control the lesser developed countries. So the stated goal of preventing aids was a failure and also the other stated goal, to prevent sexual activity, failed. Thus, the outcome that resulted was more deaths through disease and abortions. It seems irrational to support abstinence only programs since those programs have been shown to be ineffective in preventing aids and preventing sexual activity [stated goals of the president].[115] That support by the president was a result of a political ideology and not of science or a practical strategy to confront a real human problem. The issue was politically viable because it is advocated by religious right wing leaders. Since the religious right promotes it, it is an easy way to pander to the religious right votes. In the case of president George W. Bush the support for abstinence programs, that do not work, and the "faith based" grants are a way to ingratiate his administration to the religious conservatives and demagogs, who also advocate policies, not because they are effective but because they are ideologically aligned to the supposed religious dogma and act as instruments to control and mobilize people, either through fear or guilt, as the 2004 presidential election demonstrated.

The net effect of promoting unwanted or poverty inspired pregnancies in the west can be to increase the population at the lower socioeconomic level that can be used as part of the masses of consumers or fodder for the wars of empire; but in the developing world it can be a strain on the economy and a burden on the governments but also a source for more misery and death as well as disaffected youths in developing countries that will grow up to "hate America" and fuel the support for those neoconservatives, war mongers and war profiteers, etc. who call for more militarism in the superpower, to protect it from those disaffected youths that will be labeled as "radicals" or "terrorists." The most important net political effect is that taking a stance against contraception and abortion, even though it does not work as a social policy, does work as a political one since it provides a rallying point to inspire the fundamentalist and extremist elements of the Christian religion. In the 2004 elections, the republican party was able to get more of its constituency to get out and vote by passing out flyers against abortion and insinuating that the democratic opponents were homosexuals or homosexual supporters or supporting supposedly anti-Christian policies like choice for women to have abortions. In this manner the superpower leaders can have a perpetual reason to keep the religious zealots and militarists in power and an indirect method of destabilizing and weakening developing countries and preventing them from becoming opponents. So it is not surprising that this strategy has been seen as a deliberate attempt to cause more deaths among the indigent western and non-western populations and an effort to further burden the governments of the developing countries where the aids rate of infection is the highest in the world (especially sub-Saharan Africa). The strategy of apparent irrationality may be seen as a tactic to intimidate the world; however, the factor that anyone would use such tactics (that can destroy oneself and everything else) may also be seen as a manifestation of actual and not just apparent insanity. In other words, the very possession of nuclear weapons and supporting the research to improve them is a sign of mental illness itself. In this sense the consideration and acceptance of nuclear weapons as a viable deterrent for war is a manifestation of irrationality or mental disease and the strategy of irrationality is merely a manifestation of an actual mental disease of delusion of superiority, greed and fear of weakness and death.

> In the area of education, the government of the United States, during the administration of George W. Bush, repeatedly pushed for higher standards and requirements of both students and teachers mainly through a program called "no child left behind" but also repeatedly reduced the funding for schools and for teachers salaries, making it impossible for schools to alleviate problems [including overcrowded classrooms and lack of educational materials] and provide optimal conditions needed to meet the goals and for the teachers to support themselves. Also, it was common to see effective programs and initiatives be cancelled. Another area of seeming irrationality is the preference for capitalism. While the support for capitalism as a viable socio-economic system for society is touted as the best system by most western economists, corporations and politicians, social researches have repeatedly found that it is not the best system.

Social studies and economics researchers have found that capitalism promotes unemployment, poverty, crime and the disparity between classes; therefore, it is a conflict producing way of social order.

> *Here's the important point.* Among industrial democracies, there are two kinds of political-economic policies emerging in the contemporary world: (1) The Anglo-American model, which creates lots of jobs, many with lousy wages, with huge pools of poverty at the bottom and huge pools of wealth at the top; and (2) the continental European model (for lack of a better term), which creates fewer jobs but better ones and relies on powerful

> states to redistribute sufficient benefits to people and groups to preserve social peace. The disadvantages of the European model are well known: powerful governments, large bureaucracies, higher taxes, and sometimes an inclination for authoritarian "solutions" in hard times. The disadvantages of the Anglo-American model are the very real social costs of vast inequality, such as a large and growing economically and politically marginalized segment of the population characterized by high levels of anxiety and despair; predatory criminality and gang activity in cities; and homegrown terrorists (like the militias of the 1990s).
>
> In the end, vast and increasing levels of inequality have a coercive effect on American social and community life. This happens because high levels of inequality undermine the basis for cooperation in a free society. As many analysts have pointed out, a world with lower inequality is one we would choose without knowing what our eventual place was in it (Galbraith 1998). High levels of inequality make the future certain, undermine the belief that we are all part of a common society, and allow significant segments of the population to opt out of public activities that they would support if their future was unclear and it was possible that (at some future time) they would need those services. In short, rising U.S. inequality is more than just an economic problem. It is a political and cultural one as well.[116]

An important issue in the United States is the growth of the Prison Industrial Complex. The United States has more people incarcerated than any other country in the world even as effective programs for crime prevention are de-funded. This industry is primarily used to control the indigent population that is automatically created in a heavily capitalistic economic system. The capital punishment penalty is used to get rid of the most severely affected persons in such an economy. Since most of the incarcerated are African-American men they suffer the most abuse including state murder. A study demonstrated that the scandalous mistreatment of prisoners and torture techniques used at the Guantanamo Bay (Cuba), Abu Graib (Iraq) and Bagram (Afghanistan) prisons were developed by the C.I.A. and have been used in prisons inside the U.S.A. It reflects a pattern of abuse that stems from European colonialism, to American slavery and killing of Africans and Native Americans. The death penalty and the systematic abuse of the majority of the population through business oriented policies like supporting union-busting tactics by U.S.A. businesses are primary and standard tactics used to control an unwilling population. The acceptance of a system of social order that is designed to produce high numbers of criminals is evidence that the government and the society place a value on a particular way of life and standard of living and they are willing to accept a certain amount of criminality just as they are willing to accept a certain amount of military spending and wars that promote and preserve their superiority and prosperity. The strategy for managing society in this way was called *"Starve-the-beast."*

> **Starve-the-beast** is a strategy of using budget deficits in order to force the government to reduce its social spending; a timely example is the tax cutting policy under U.S. President George W. Bush. The word *beast* in the expression refers to the government and the social programs it funds, such as Social Security, Medicare, Medicaid, and TANF (Temporary Assistance for Needy Families), and implies that these social programs are destructive. A current well-known proponent of starve-the-beast in the U.S. is Grover Norquist. It appears the earliest reference to "starving the beast" as a doctrine was made during the Reagan administration by White House budget director David Stockman, to describe its fiscal philosophy. Some empirical evidence shows that the strategy may actually be counterproductive, with higher taxes actually corresponding to lower spending: "Controlling for the unemployment rate, federal spending [from 1981 to 2000] increased by about one-half percent of GDP for each one percentage point decline in the relative level of federal tax revenues." The article (written by William Niskanen and Peter Van Doren of the Cato Institute) shows that "a tax *increase* may be the most effective policy to reduce the relative level of federal spending," though the authors oppose tax increases for other reasons. Additionally, some economists and politicians see the budget deficits created by this strategy as harmful to the economy.[117]

The idea of "starving" the economy is substantiated and updated by the recent statements of Grover Glenn Norquist.[118] Norquist once said about his and the republican party's strategy for the economy:

> "Shrink the government down to the size that it can be drowned in a bathtub."

About the above quote, the journalist Bill Moyers commented:

> "so much for compassionate conservatism. But at least Norquist says what he means and means what he says; the White House pursues the same homicidal dream without saying so. Instead of shrinking down the government they are filling the bathtub with so much debt that it floods the house, waterlogs the economy and washes away services that have lifted millions of Americans out of destitution for decades. And what happens once the public's property has been flooded, what happens? Privatize it, and sell it at a discounted rate to the corporations. I don't think this is a consequence of ignorance. I think this is deliberate and intentional destruction of the United States Way of Governing."[119]

The actions of the United States government officials and other quotes by Norquist clearly support Moyer's contention as they portray the strategy and mentality of the ruling class that seeks to control society without regard to scientific analysis or sociological study evidences but rather by relying on ideology alone, and powered by privilege, superiority, entitlement, hubris, and promoting rancor in the political process even if it divides the country, erasing the progress in race, sex, gender and other social relations over the past 100 years. Norquist also said:

- "We are trying to change the tones in the state capitals - and turn them toward bitter nastiness and partisanship."
- "Bipartisanship is another name for date rape"
- "We are trying to change the tones in the state capitals -- and turn them toward bitter nastiness and partisanship."[120]
- "And we've had four more years pass where the age cohort that is most Democratic and most pro-statist, are those people who turned 21 years of age between 1932 and 1952--Great Depression, New Deal, World War II--Social Security, the draft--all that stuff. That age cohort is now between the ages of 70 and 90 years old, and every year 2 million of them die. So 8 million people from that age cohort have passed away since the last election; that means, net, maybe 1 million Democrats have disappeared--and even the Republicans in that age group. [...] You know, some Bismarck, German thing, okay? Very un-American. Very *unusual* for America. The reaction to Great Depression, World War II, and so on: Centralization--not as much centralization as the rest of the world got, but much more than is usual in America. We've spent a lot of time dismantling

> some of that and moving away from that level of regimentation: getting rid of the draft."[121]

Noam Chomsky explained that the reason for promoting fiscally unsound expenditures such as swollen deficits, bloated defense budgets and the private health care system which are justified by free markets and fear of enemies, is for the purpose of driving the economy into a state of crisis that will force the drastic action of cutting social programs altogether which will undercut the populace and leave them destitute and at the mercy of the power elite.[122] Therefore, even though the party-line is to praise capitalism and decry socialism and communism, economically, the strategy of the United States government has been to promote capitalism for the middle class and the poor, and socialism or even welfare for the rich through tax cuts, bailouts, subsidies and loopholes. It is interesting to note that the objectives of the policy of *starve-the-beast* are not obtained in the manner suggested by the conservative or neo-conservative economists. Yet, the highest echelon of the upper class profit immensely from this form of economy. In fact, their efforts have the opposite effect but many people suffer and die as a result of those policies. So too, strategies such as that of bringing about peace around the world by means of guns and war will also fail as the strategy is antithetical to the stated goals; and as we have seen the strategies are purposely so. Yet the outcome of fomenting disorganization, uncertainty and strife in the world allows United States corporations to ravage the world economy.

That ravaging, that continues at an expanded rate, is leading to a despoiled world in which social disorder and environmental disaster will destabilize the world economy and the peace between nations. In other words, the political-ideological reasons for the actions taken by the superpower governments will lead to failure of those ideologies because those ideologies are merely dogmas couched in lofty rhetoric to rally the populace and at the same time conceal the ulterior agenda. They are not based in truth nor is their implementation grounded in reality or ethic and they are not meant to be. They are intended to obfuscate the true agenda, which is self-serving, to protect the interests of the plutocratic oligarchic elite.

> "We know that dictators are quick to choose aggression, while free nations strive to resolve differences in peace. We know that oppressive governments support terror, while free governments fight the terrorists in their midst. We know that free peoples embrace progress and life, instead of becoming the recruits for murderous ideologies."[123]

In the statements above president George W. Bush spoke of how dictators choose aggression quickly. Could it not be said that he hastily went to war with Iraq? George W. Bush said that oppressive governments support terror; yet the controversial military doctrine by the U.S.A. military, authorized by Bush, called "shock and awe"[124] and the use of chemical weapons on civilians can and has been characterized as a tactic to cause panic and terror in the enemy nation. The bombing of Baghdad killed many thousands of men, women and children who were non-combatants and that is one of the definitions of a terrorist act, the killing of civilians.[125] George W. Bush said that free peoples do not embrace murderous ideologies; yet the United States adopted the ideology of starving Iraq and allowing thousands of children to die in order to get at Saddam Hussein just as the democratic presidents Kennedy and Johnson instituted illegal economic sanctions against Cuba to punish the Cuban people for having their government. George W. Bush and his father, George H. Bush (Bush Sr.) as well as the neo-cons, adopted the ideologies of capitalism and of enforcing the United States style of freedom on others which has led to torturing and killing innocent as well as suspected subjects. George W. Bush also adopted a belligerent policy, known as the "Bush Doctrine", stating that anyone who is not with the United States is against it and therefore the U.S.A. has the right to conduct preventative [preemptive] wars- attack others before they can attack the U.S.A., which has been seen as a reason for the invasion of Iraq in 2003.[126] preemptive or preventative war is prohibited by international law, so the U.S.A. superpower mentality ignored that as beneath the right of the U.S.A. to do whatever it wants. These kinds of statements and policies can be considered as murderous ideologies since they have led to many deaths in open war, covert operations, torture situations and the killing of civilians in non-combat situations, all without any specific threat to the U.S.A.

> "Our enemies are innovative and resourceful, and so are we. They never stop thinking about new ways to harm our country and our people, and neither do we."
> -George W. Bush, Washington, D.C., Aug. 5, 2004

> "If this were a dictatorship,
> it would be a heck of a lot easier,
> just so long as I'm the dictator."
> -George W. Bush, December 18, 2000

Is there any Effective Opposition to the Hegemony of the Empire?

In an interview on his new book *Failed States*, the renowned intellectual and political critic, Noam Chomsky, spoke about the power of nationalism as a traditional opposition force.

> There have been plenty of barriers. The major barrier is the one that is the usual one throughout the world: independent nationalism. It's called "radical nationalism," which was serious. It was symbolized by Nasser, but also Kassem in Iraq, and others. Well, the U.S. did succeed in overcoming that barrier. How? Israel destroyed Nasser. That was a tremendous service to the United States, to U.S. power, that is, to the energy corporations, to Saudi Arabia, to the main centers of power here, and in fact, it's in – that was 1967, and it was after that victory that the U.S.-Israeli relations really solidified, became what's called a "strategic asset."[127]

Nationalism has been an effective means to mobilize an entire population of a country to oppose internal movements or ideas as well as external ones. The Cuban revolution was in part a nationalistic movement. The movements in South America in the early 21st century to throw off oligarchic leaders and U.S.A. influence are largely nationalistic movements as well. Also it can happen that the growing nationalism may incite the external opposite force to take up arms to force their ideas on the nationalistic population. The U.S.A. government has indeed opposed nationalistic movements and enforced U.S.A. government backed officials even when those countries have selected their governments through internationally certified legitimate elections. One example is Haiti. Haiti held "democratic" elections that met international standards. Nevertheless, president George H. Bush (Bush Sr.) supported the opposition candidate through what was called "democracy promotion measures" which amount to supporting anyone who opposes the established winner. So if a candidate that the U.S.A. supports does not win due to low support, that candidate would receive money to run campaigns and harass the standing government even though they would not have the resources since their policies were not supported by the local population. That would have the effect of destabilizing the legitimately elected government that is not supported by the U.S.A. Insurgency movements have begun in that fashion which has led to civil wars.

In Haiti, after the legitimate elections, the support for the opposition led to a *coup* that was supported by the U.S.A. under the republican party president George H. Bush (Bush Sr.). After the *coup* the U.S.A. under president Clinton, a member of the democratic party, supported the military junta that ruled the country and even authorized the U.S.A. oil companies to deal with them. After the people suffered under the rule of the junta Clinton sent in troops and more people died. The democratically elected president, Aristide, was restored to the government but only if he agreed to include the policies of his opponent who lost the 1990 election, the opponent who was in favor of U.S.A. corporate policies. Haiti's economy failed and people suffered more violence and disruption until on February 29, 2004, the governments of France and the United States exiled president Aristide by forcing him to leave the country and stay in Africa.[128] This move was strongly protested by several governments in the Caribbean. This episode was only the latest display of U.S.A. policy that Noam Chomsky referred to as *"another illustration of the near passionate hatred of democracy, which is consistent and is indeed recognized."*[129]

The traditions of interventions and support of dictators in Haiti has rendered the country used to political unrest and violence. Those policies that promoted destabilization led to generations of civil unrest, dictatorships and social degeneration that are still playing out. What would the culture and government of Haiti, the first country with a majority of African decent to achieve independence from colonial rule, look like if the U.S.A. had not committed the illegal interventions and political regime changes throughout history? What would the U.S.A. look like today if it had been invaded and George Washington, Jefferson, Hamilton, Adams and Franklyn had been murdered or exiled right after they won the war of independence, and the country was invaded and controlled by another power after Britain was pushed out? The point is that when a government foments social policies they have lasting effects whose ramifications and ultimate impact and longevity cannot be fathomed. Thus it is important to promote policies based on ethical ideals so as to reduce the probability of engendering long-lived deleterious social trends that people will come to depend on or become addicted to that will damage culture and civilization and the social order in the longer term.

CONCLUSION

The Super Power syndrome is a psychological and social construct designed to prevent honest and just human interaction and promote dominance by one group over the other. The *Superpower Syndrome Mandatory Conflict Complex* is a mental process that precludes proper interaction among human beings. When communication is strained it is impossible to have good quality understanding among people. It is indeed an expression of perverted animal instinct over the rationality and moral conscience of the human mind that manifests in the form of base instinct as if the world of human activity were a stage for competition and superiority, misusing Darwin's concept of the survival of the fittest. The superpower complex precludes compassion and promotes aggression with impunity.

The Superpower Syndrome is not a modern social problem. It is, rather, an exacerbation of a preexisting social tendency in some populations, predominantly in the northern hemisphere of the world, that has become unrestrained due to the advent of modern technologies, nuclear power and global economies that have allowed previously weak fascist megalomaniac jingoist and sexist personalities to gain control of vast wealth and military power.

The Superpower Syndrome has a quality or life that transcends the individual. It is a philosophy of life by which some people live and lead others but which also has a life of its own that operates in the form of a mythic or legendary mindsets that become themes for vast segments of the culture and drive the population to support the designs of the superpower leadership even if the policies are injurious to the world or even to their population. In effect the society adopts the supremacy ideal of the superpower myth and that facilitates belief in the call, by the superpower leadership, to support the dictum to attack others preventatively or preemptively and to take up arms to face supposed threats. In other words, the policy can be directed but it also has some elements that are unpredictable and uncontrollable. Surely there were many, such as Dwight Eisenhower, who lived in the post World War II era, who regretted what became of the United States but who felt powerless to stop it, even as there were and are others who are pleased to promote conflict, fear and delusion to create more support for arming the country so that they will benefit more in the form of profits, never reflecting upon the cost of the character and quality of life of all peoples affected, either in the present or the future.

In other words, the society may be manipulated through propaganda, contrived situations to facilitate war, or by stimulating rancor in order to make divisions in the population or between the political parties for political gain, but those actions will leave certain impressions in the minds of people and therefore, also certain mental complexes, moods and mindsets that will impact for generations to come and may not be controllable. Yet the superpower mentality is forward thinking to the extent that its plans promote more expansion, and acquisition of wealth and power in the future. It is not primarily concerned with the environment, the degradation of culture or health issues since in the distorted mentality of the superpower those problems can be supposedly overcome through technological advancement or military force or bribes which the superpower would always be able to supply.

The history of the superpower politics, outlined above demonstrates the superpower's willingness to go against stated policy, break laws and social norms, traffic in drugs, avoid the authority of the congress, and engage in criminal activities, including murder, to achieve its ends and its expectation and demand that other nations bow to it. Thus, based on the record of the superpower mindset it might be concluded that in any situation the superpower cannot be seen as acting in or accepting situations without the deference to the superpower.

The superpower mindset is a deep-seated mental complex that has not and will not be eradicated from the superpower psyche for some time to come, except through much development of human culture [considering that humanity survives its own folly] or through a massive social upheaval that renders the superpower elite powerless. However, the powerlessness must be in terms of philosophy and mythic power; if people continue to believe in the superpower myth even if it loses its economic and or military power temporarily, others will revive it sometime in the future. Therefore, what is to be done about the ever-present threat of fascism in the world and the danger of its greatest expression in the form of superpower politics? The Native American leader, Tecumseh, offered some suggestions to confront these issues:

- "But, brother, I mean to bring all the tribes together, in spite of you, and until I have finished, I will not go to visit your president. Maybe I will when I have finished, maybe. The reason I tell you this, you want, by making your distinctions of Indian tribes and allotting to each a particular tract of land, to set them against each other, and thus to weaken us."
- "The only way to stop this evil is for all the red men to unite in claiming an equal right in the land. That is how it was at first, and should be still, for the land never was divided, but was for the use of everyone. Any tribe could go to an empty land and make a home there. And if they left, another tribe could come there and make a home. No groups among us have a right to sell, even to one another, and surely not to outsiders who want all, and will not do with less. Sell a country! Why not sell the air, the clouds, and the Great Sea, as well as the earth? Did not the Great Good Spirit make them all for the use of his children?"[130]

NOTE ON WEAPONS OF MASS DESTRUCTION

The term W.M.D. or weapons of mass destruction, received wide usage in the last few years especially in the U.S.A. particularly with the goal of mobilizing the population to accept attacks against Iraq and other countries. The idea is that the leader of Iraq, Saddam Hussein was amassing WMD and intended to use them against the U.S.A. WMD may be defined as:

> Weapons of mass destruction (WMD) generally include nuclear, biological, chemical and, increasingly, radiological weapons. The term first arose in 1937 in reference to the mass destruction of Guernica, Spain, by aerial bombardment. Following the bombing of Hiroshima and Nagasaki, and progressing through the Cold War, the term came to refer more to non-conventional weapons. The terms ABC, NBC, and CBRN have been used synonymously with WMD, although nuclear weapons have the greatest capacity to cause mass destruction. The phrase entered popular usage in relation to the U.S.-led multinational forces' 2003 invasion of Iraq.

The first record of the term ***Weapon of Mass Destruction*** is from a December 28, 1937 *Times* article on the bombing of Guernica, Spain, by the German Luftwaffe during the Spanish Civil War:

> "*Who can think without horror of what another widespread war would mean, waged as it would be with all the new weapons of mass destruction?*"

This report was in reference to blanket bombing of Guernica, during which 70% of the town was destroyed. Nuclear weapons did not exist at that time, but biological weapons were being researched by Japan (Unit 731), and chemical weapons had seen wide use. Yet the conventional weapons were used as WMD by indiscriminately destroying a city so as to supposedly destroy the will of the people to fight or support their government and thus surrender.

> In 1946, soon after the bombing of Hiroshima and Nagasaki, the United Nations issued its first resolution. It was to create the Atomic Energy Commission (predecessor of the International Atomic Energy Agency (IAEA)), and used the wording:

> "*...atomic weapons and of all other weapons adaptable to mass destruction*".

While much was made of Hussein's use of chemical weapons and bombings of the Iraqi people and the Kurds, even though he was assisted by the U.S.A. to arm himself and create WMD to use against his enemies when it suited the political strategy of the U.S.A.,[6] little is made of the fact that even if Iraq had WMD (which Iraq did not), they had no capacity to deliver any WMD to any target in the U.S.A. and so that was an unfounded pretext to war. That is now well known; What is less well known is that the international arms trade of small arms like rifles and machine guns has led to more killings, coup d'états, more instability and more deaths than all the bombings in the wars.

Small arms weapons like the famous AK-47 rifle have brought more death and devastation than any other source of war. The Russian rifle is so popular because of its simplicity and reliability. The world's biggest arms suppliers are not rogue arms dealers who supply both sides with weapons to kill themselves. The world's biggest arms suppliers are the U.S.A, the U.K., Russia, France and China. It so happens that these same five nations are the five permanent members of the United Nations Security Council. The Security Council of the United Nations is charged with maintaining peace and security between nations. More specifically the Security Council is empowered to make decrees that control other nations while other nations do not have power to control the Security Council nations. So the real power in the U.N. resides in the Security Council. There are about 192 countries in the world so 5 out of 192 total, could control the actions or dictate to the majority. It sounds like a plutocracy but may be better described as an oligarchic-tyrannical-military-corporocratic-plutocracy cabal.

> *While other organs of the United Nations only make recommendations to member governments, the Security Council has the power to make*

---

[6] The US.A. used Iraq as a surrogate to fight against Iran to keep them weak and forestall the present condition of their capacity to achieve nuclear power and the U.S.A. used the Taliban and Mujahideen (including *Osama bin Laden*) against the Soviet Union to prevent them from getting a foothold in Afghanistan; these same fighters that the U.S.A. trained turned against them.

decisions which member governments must carry out under the United Nations Charter. The decisions of the Council are known as UN Security Council Resolutions.[131]

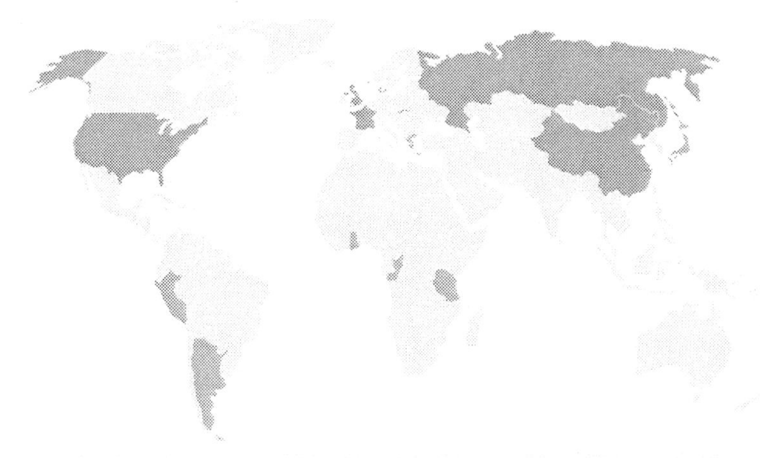

The image above shows the World Map highlighting the UN permanent members of the Security Council of 2006 which are all in the northern hemisphere. The countries highlighted in the tropical zone are only elected members.[132]

It is ironic that the nations that are supposed to control the U.N and promote peace and control conflict around the world are the principle benefactors of war and the biggest purveyors of the means to make war on the rest of the world and assist the world to make war on itself (other nations amongst themselves). The small arms have had a devastating effect on many small countries around the world, especially in Africa, where the coercion of the western and the Arab countries have led to killings of vast numbers of civilians, and making soldiers out of children, sometimes for diamonds, gold or other commodities that are desired by and which dictators and tyrants are used to acquire by proxy or surrogate wars. The recent election of Liberia's new president and first female head of state, Ellen Johnson-Sirleafended ended a period of extreme strife and conflict in the country that was carried out and sustained by small arms. Liberia was recently afflicted by two civil wars (1989–1996 and 1999–2003) that displaced hundreds of thousands of its citizens and destroyed the Liberian economy. Her election, like that of Hugo Chaves and Evo Morales in South America, signals a decided move away from the politics of barbarianism and western hegemony and may also signal a new period of tropical resistance against the temperate zone barbaric temperament that foments war and social conflict. Yet elsewhere in Africa and the world, the philosophy of killing and violence has become so entrenched as to become part of the ideal of the political culture. Mozambique, for example, reveres the AK-47 so much as to include it in its national flag (see below), a symbol which has previously been regarded as the representation of a nation, its aspirations and pride.

Even though blanket bombing is indeed a form of WMD as well as terrorism because it kills combatants and civilians indiscriminately, the U.S.A. used that strategy in World War II[133], Vietnam, among several undeclared wars, and most recently on Iraq to subjugate the Iraqi people in through a program called "Shock and Awe." Wikipedia Encyclopedia describes the Shock and Awe strategy as follows:

> Shock and Awe
> **Shock and Awe** is a military doctrine which advocates attempting to destroy an adversary's will to fight through spectacular displays of power. Its authors label it a subset of **Rapid Dominance**, a concept of defeating an adversary by swift action against all aspects of their ability to resist, rather than strictly military forces. It is a product of the

National Defense University of the United States, and has been notably applied in this country's 2003 invasion of Iraq.

Doctrine of Rapid Dominance
Rapid Dominance is defined by its authors, Harlan K. Ullman and James P. Wade, as attempting "to affect the will, perception, and understanding of the adversary to fit or respond to our strategic policy ends through imposing a regime of Shock and Awe." Further, Rapid Dominance will "impose this overwhelming level of Shock and Awe against an adversary on an immediate or sufficiently timely basis to paralyze its will to carry on . . . to seize control of the environment and paralyze or so overload an adversary's perceptions and understanding of events that the enemy would be incapable of resistance at the tactical and strategic levels."

The military doctrine of shock and awe is perfectly suited for people who have fewer inhibitions about unleashing wonton destruction on other human beings. In much the same way as the Ancient Romans unleashed their own campaign of shock and awe, which included mass killings of segments of any population that resist them, to discourage any one from even thinking about opposing Roman will, here in the 21st century the U.S.A. revived the philosophy of wholesale death and destruction in the name of winning, controlling and subjugating, but using the same excuse that President Harry Truman did when deciding to use atomic weapons on Japan, that it would save American lives by ending the war sooner, never mind that the destruction of the Japanese cities, Hiroshima and Nagasaki killed mostly women and children and never mind that even without the atomic [nuclear] weapons, the conventional bombings in Japan and Europe were devastating those civilian populations in the same way, just not all at once but in the same numbers. Later, in the Vietnam war, there were more bombs dropped on Vietnam and Cambodia than in all the previous wars in history combined, leaving millions of Indochinese people dead while only about 60,000 soldiers from the U.S.A. died. Many critics have objected to the shock and awe strategy and have compared it to terrorism.[134]

Shock and Awe vs. Terrorism
American supporters of Shock and Awe claim that unlike Terrorism, Shock and Awe does not deliberately target civilians although civilians could be killed. Critics however, point to the difficulty in reducing

civilian casualties while bombing locations with high civilian population density.

Criticism
Shock and Awe met significant criticism from both military and civilian sectors. United States theorists had criticized its assumptions of total information awareness, unmatched technology, and assumptions of symmetric warfare.
In coverage by the mass media prior to the United States' invasion of Iraq, "Shock and Awe" was often used to mean an indiscriminate "Doomsday" or terror aerial bombardment. Critics of the war compared the plans of the United States to the bombing of Guernica during the Spanish Civil War, and termed such plans as savagery. The United States armed forces had said that targets, munitions and attack times were chosen to minimize civilian casualties.
Shock and awe style warfare also seems to be less effective against an extended insurgency than it is against an enemy's military.

In April 2004, the United States launched its first assault on Fallujah, Iraq. The city was a stronghold of rebel forces against the occupation of the U.S.A. but there were thousands of civilians, women and children in the city. The U.S. forces nevertheless implemented the mass bombing and sniper killings of combatants and civilians. The conflict was described by a journalist as follows:

AHMED MANSUR: Because time is not sufficient to describe what happened those days, but let me talk about the 9th of April, 2004. It was really like the day of judgment in Fallujah. We were under siege for two days from the U.S. forces and the snipers. We were unable to move, and we decided to take adventure and go to the middle of the city at any price. And we consulted among each other. Some of us said, “No, let's stay.” Then I said, “No, we have to move even if the snipers shoot us.”
When we left the place, we found that Fallujah entirely -- children, women, elderly, all lifting white flags and walking or in their cars leaving the city. It was really a disastrous day for us. When we reached the heart of the city at the hospital, I almost lost my mind from the terror that I saw, people going in each and every direction. Laith was with me and also another colleague, and I felt like we need 1,000 cameras to grab those disastrous pictures: fear, terror, planes bombing, ambulances taking the people dead. And I was shouting and yelling for Laith and my other colleague, and I was shouting, “Camera! Camera!” so that we can take pictures here and there.
At the end, I felt that I have to control myself. The fear was bigger than we could ever handle, and bigger than our journalistic capabilities.

> There's no reporters in the city. We were the only team that was able to enter the city; therefore, we have to transfer what's happening to the whole world. It was an extremely difficult mission. That was the fifth or sixth day we went un-sleeping at all. I didn't know how we were able to stand or move or talk. I used to look at Laith and feel that he is unable to even lift the camera because of the stress on him. Regardless, he was carrying the camera and going and coming. We were trying to move this picture to the whole world, and we felt that we are responsible for all these civilians being bombed from the planes and who are threatened with death, so we have to transfer this picture of suffering to the whole world. It was extremely difficult.
> We wanted to be successful. We wanted to do our humanistic mission to move or transfer that picture to the whole world. And we were under a lot of stress, and Laith -- maybe I was moving by myself with the mic, but Laith was lifting a heavy camera and moving from place to place. It was a very long day. I think this day in my life equals to my entire life, even though I covered Bosnia and Herzegovina war and Afghanistan. But that particular day was the longest in my journalistic view, even for me as a human being.[135]

Despite the U.S.A. army's use of "shock and awe" tactics and the subsequent use of other strange and gruesome chemical weapons like depleted uranium and white phosphorus,[136] the insurgency was not quelled but rather it swelled, to the point that the U.S.A. forces were still not yet in control of the country as of April 2006 and the forces of nationalism and fundamentalism [main factions comprising the Iraqi resistance against the U.S.A.] were gaining more adherents and sympathizers than ever before. This turn of events served to polarize the West and the Arab countries and it allows the western countries, particularly the U.S.A. to create in effect a new cold war but this time between the West and the Arab nations. This kind of cold war promotes animosity that keeps the populations apart and excuses the need to act militarily instead of diplomatically and destabilizes societies so that equitable and just cultures cannot easily develop. This is why many times the populations of countries which have been subjected to this kind of treatment are not suited for non-dictatorship type governments; they seek out "strong dictators" to bring stability and peace at the price of their freedom. That societal condition allows the western economic "hitmen" [agents of the U.S.A. that arrange with the leaders of foreign countries the subjugation of their peoples and the surrender of their national resources to U.S.A. companies] to make deals with the leaders of other countries more easily.

The shock and awe treatment was used on the Native Americans when the Spanish discovered the Americas and soon after their arrival began to enslave and mistreat the indigenous population which they had described as gentle and living in an idyllic society. The Spanish killed thousands of Native Americans through barbaric and cruel tactics using superior armaments. The words of eye-witness Bartolomeo de las Casas reveal that the continuing reliance on a barbaric philosophy of mass destruction with the aim of becoming wealthy, i.e. greed is nothing new in the 21st century but a continuation of a way of living and thinking about the rest of the world that drove the development of Europe, from the days of the Greek empire to the Roman Empire, the Catholic Church Empire, the British, Spanish and now the American Empire. The actions of imperial nations can afflict any other country through neocolonialism and now Globalism, as the cases of so many wars around the world, fomented by the western governments, have demonstrated.

Bartolome De Las Casas - The Devastation of the Indies: A Brief Account (1542)

> The Indies were discovered in the year one thousand four hundred and ninety two. In the following year a great many Spaniards went there with the intention of settling the land. Thus, forty-nine years have passed since the first settlers penetrated the land, the first so-claimed being the large and most happy isle called Hispaniola, which is six hundred leagues in circumference.
>
> ... And of all the infinite universe of humanity, these people are the most guileless, the most devoid of wickedness and duplicity, the most obedient and faithful to their native masters and to the Spanish Christians whom they serve. They are by nature the most humble, patient, and peaceable, holding no grudges, free from embroilments, neither excitable nor quarrelsome. These people are the most devoid of rancors, hatreds, or desire for vengeance of any people in the world. And because they are so weak and

complaisant, they are less able to endure heavy labor and soon die of no matter what malady.

... Yet into this sheepfold, into this land of meek outcasts there came some Spaniards who immediately behaved like ravening wild beasts, wolves, tigers, or lions that had been starved for many days. And Spaniards have behaved in no other way during the past forty years, down to the present time, for they are still acting like ravening beasts, killing, terrorizing, afflicting, torturing, and destroying the native peoples, doing all this with the strangest and most varied new methods of cruelty, never seen or heard of before, and to such a degree that this Island of Hispaniola, once so populous (having a population that I estimated to be more than three millions), has now a population of barely two hundred persons.

The island of Cuba is nearly as long as the distance between Valladolid and Rome; it is now almost completely depopulated. San Juan [Puerto Rico] and Jamaica are two of the largest, most productive and attractive islands; both are now deserted and devastated. On the northern side of Cuba and Hispaniola lie the neighboring Lucayos comprising more than sixty islands including those called Gigantes, beside numerous other islands, some small some large. The least felicitous of them were more fertile and beautiful than the gardens of the King of Seville. They have the healthiest lands in the world, where lived more than five hundred thousand souls; they are now deserted, inhabited by not a single living creature. All the people were slain or died after being taken into captivity and brought to the Island of Hispaniola to be sold as slaves.

... More than thirty other islands in the vicinity of San Juan are for the most p" and for the same reason depopulated, and the land laid waste. On these islands I estimate there are 2,100 leagues of land that have been ruined and depopulated, empty of people.

As for the vast mainland, which is ten times larger than all Spain, even including Aragon and Portugal, containing more land than the distance between Seville and Jerusalem, or more than two thousand leagues, we are sure that our

Spaniards, with their cruel and abominable acts, have devastated the land and exterminated the rational people who fully inhabited it. We can estimate very surely and truthfully that in the forty years that have passed, with the infernal actions of the Christians, there have been unjustly slain more than twelve million men, women, and children. In truth, I believe without trying to deceive myself that the number of the slain is more like fifteen million.

The common ways mainly employed by the Spaniards who call themselves Christian and who have gone there to extirpate those pitiful nations and wipe them off the earth is by unjustly waging cruel and bloody wars. Then, when they have slain all those who fought for their lives or to escape the tortures they would have to endure, that is to say, when they have slain all the native rulers and young men (since the Spaniards usually spare only the women and children, who are subjected to the hardest and bitterest servitude ever suffered by man or beast), they enslave any survivors. With these infernal methods of tyranny they debase and weaken countless numbers of those pitiful Indian nations.

Their reason for killing and destroying such an infinite number of souls is that the Christians have an ultimate aim, which is to acquire gold, and to swell themselves with riches in a very brief time and thus rise to a high estate disproportionate to their merits. It should be kept in mind that their insatiable greed and ambition, the greatest ever seen in the world, is the cause of their villainies. And also, those lands are so rich and felicitous, the native peoples so meek and patient, so easy to subject, that our Spaniards have no more consideration for them than beasts. And I say this from my own knowledge of the acts I witnessed. But I should not say "than beasts" for, thanks be to God, they have treated beasts with some respect; I should say instead like excrement on the public squares.

... And the Christians, with their horses and swords and pikes began to carry out massacres and strange cruelties against them. They attacked the towns and spared neither the children nor the aged nor pregnant women nor women in childbed, not only stabbing them and dismembering them but cutting them to pieces as if dealing with sheep in the slaughter house. They laid bets as to who, with one stroke of the sword, could split a man in two or could cut off his head or spill out his entrails with a single stroke of the pike. They took infants from their mothers' breasts, snatching them by the legs and pitching them headfirst against the crags or snatched them by the arms and threw them into the rivers, roaring with laughter and saying as the babies fell into the water, "Boil there, you offspring of the devil!" Other infants they put to the sword along with their mothers and anyone else who happened to be nearby. They made some low wide gallows on which the hanged victim's feet almost touched the ground, stringing up their victims in lots of thirteen, in memory of Our Redeemer and His twelve Apostles, then set burning wood at their feet and thus burned them alive. To others they attached straw or wrapped their whole bodies in straw and set them afire. With still others, all those they wanted to capture alive, they cut off their hands and hung them round the victim's neck, saying, "Go now, carry the message," meaning, Take the news to the Indians who have fled to the mountain. ... After the wars and the killings had ended, when usually there survived only some boys, some women, and children, these survivors were distributed among the Christians to be slaves. The repartimiento or distribution was made according to the rank and importance of the Christian to whom the Indians were allocated, one of them being given thirty, another forty, still another, one or two hundred, and besides the rank of the Christian there was also to be considered in what favor he stood with the tyrant they called Governor. The pretext was that these allocated Indians were to be instructed in the articles of the Christian Faith. As if those Christians who were as a rule foolish and cruel and greedy and vicious could be caretakers of souls! And the care they took was to send the men to the mines to dig for gold, which is intolerable labor, and to send the women into the fields of the big ranches to hoe and till the land, work suitable for strong men. Nor to either the men or the women did they give any food except herbs and legumes, things of little substance. The milk in the breasts of the women with infants dried up and thus in a short while the infants perished. And since men and women were separated, there could be no marital relations. And the men died in the mines and the women died on the ranches from the same causes, exhaustion and hunger. And thus was depopulated that island which had been densely populated...[137]

War for Profit and Power: Major Military Actions of the United States of America's Imperial Designs under the administration of presidents Franklin D. Roosevelt, Harry Truman, John F. Kennedy, Linden Johnson, Ronald Reagan and George W. Bush and the Neoconservatives

18. All warfare is based on deception.

19. Hence, when able to attack, we must seem unable;
when using our forces, we must seem inactive; when we
are near, we must make the enemy believe we are far away;
when far away, we must make him believe we are near.

20. Hold out baits to entice the enemy. Feign disorder,
and crush him.

--The Art of War, by Sun Tzu

The U.S.A.'s entry into World War II occurred long before the formal declaration of war in 1941. During the 1930s Japan was taken over by a militarist and imperial government and it wanted to secure raw materials and oil for its expansion. The Japanese invaded China in 1931 and during the 1930s was perceived as a competitor in South East Asia by the U.S.A. leaders. In May 1940 president Roosevelt signed an executive order, which was, unpublished (secret) that allowed the U.S. military personnel to resign from the service so that they could participate in a covert operation against Japan in China. That American "Volunteer" group was known as Chennault's Flying Tigers.

The United States and other countries cut fuel oil and other exports to Japan, some via blockade. Taking these actions as acts of war, Japan planned an attack on Sunday, 7 December 1941 on Pearl Harbor, with the purpose of crippling the U.S. Pacific Fleet. The other purpose of starting the war was to capture oil fields in Southeast Asia… oilfields of the Dutch East Indies. The attack on Pearl Harbor achieved military damage to the battleships in the American Fleet, however, the aircraft carriers, which were primary targets, were safe at sea. So the U.S.A. was involved with the war before the formal declaration of war, against its own nonintervention laws. The U.S.A. under Roosevelt wanted to enter the war but was unable to because of anti-war sentiment in the population. Some researchers, such as G. Edward Griffin, have pointed out that one of the reasons why the U.S.A. wanted to join the war was in order to have a hand in the war and its aftermath; to have a legitimate capacity to shape the aftermath of the world. Also, the U.S.A. purposely wanted to hold Japan back because it was becoming a rival in South East Asia for the U.S.A. and for the British colonies that had oil. So it was a competition between two emerging superpowers. In a larger sense World War II was precipitated by an inability of the previous world powers, England, U.S.A. France, etc. to adjust to the emerging powers, Japan and Germany. In like manner many political analysts predict a conflict between the U.S.A. and China if an accommodation is not made to accept China as a world power.

There is compelling evidence that supports the contention that the U.S.A. tried to instigate a war with Japan by provoking the Japanese. There is a quote from Oliver Lyttelton, who was the British Minister of War Production, who is reported to have said, "*... Japan was provoked into attacking the Americans at Pearl Harbor. It is a travesty of history ever to say that America was forced into the war. Everyone knows where American sympathies were. It is incorrect to say that America was truly neutral even before America came into the war on an all-out basis.*" In the book Day of Deceit by Robert Stinnet a memorandum that was prepared by the Office of Naval Intelligence by Lieutenant Commander Arthur McCollum suggests that only a direct attack on U.S.A.'s interests could sway the opinion of the American public to be in favor of direct involvement in the European war, and specifically to be in support of the British. The memo was passed to Captains Walter Anderson and Dudley Knox, who were two of Roosevelt's military advisors on October 7, 1940. Anderson and Knox offered eight specific strategies that were designed to hurt the Japanese Empire and added, *"If by these means Japan could be led to commit an overt act of war, so much the better."* Out of the eight, only one was ever implemented.

The Korean War started as a conflict between South and North Korea. In the U.S.A. the conflict was called a *"police action."* The U.S.A. under president Truman pursued the Korean Conflict, through the United Nations in order to not require a Congressional declaration of war. The Japanese had captured Korea in 1910 and remained there until the end of World War II when the south was captured by the U.S.A. forces and the north by the Soviet forces. The Soviets and the U.S.A. [suppressing democracy] put governments favorable to themselves and against each other in the north and south respectively. In 1949 both Russian and American forces were withdrawn. But in 1950 the north, headed by Kim Il-sung and supported by the Soviets, attacked the south. The intervention by the U.S.A. was an implementation of the *Truman Doctrine,* an ideological policy that promoted the opposition of communism [U.S.S.R. and China] wherever it tried to expand. The idea was that appeasing communism [through diplomacy or negotiation] would only lead to more expansion so it should be confronted militarily. Such ideas later gave birth to a concept called *"domino theory"* which was useful in publicly promoting a fear-based concept for the public to support opposing communism. So the U.S.A forces were brought back to So. Korea and the forces of the north were pushed back above the 38th parallel and in 1953 a cease-fire was agreed but the war never formally ended. Korea was a quagmire because the U.S.A. did not want to enter into full-scale war to defeat the north since the Soviets and Chinese would become more involved which could lead to a more serious conflict involving nuclear weapons. The limited involvement of the Soviets and Chinese was kept secret in order to prevent the need for an expanded war effort.

The conflict arose because of the imperial designs of the U.S.A. and the U.S.S.R. and became the first of such conflicts that led to the deaths of millions and the paranoia in both countries about each other that was played out in the form of a neocolonial cold war that used other countries, especially developing countries, as pawns and in the process turning many of their governments into dictatorships. The Korean War experience led to the idea of a "limited war," a form of conflict in which the two so called superpowers [Soviet Union and U.S.A.] could fight each other without descending to all out war that could then involve nuclear weapons. The concept of "limited war" had its most devastating effect in Vietnam.

The next major military intervention was in Vietnam. The U.S.A. followed the same pattern there and that lead to the deaths of over 59,000 soldiers of the U.S.A. and millions of Vietnamese because the U.S.A. did not want to support the liberation movement there which wanted to free itself from French colonialism. So the U.S.A. replaced the French with the pretext of preventing the communist takeover by Vietnamese communists who had turned to communism due to French imperialism. In time the U.S.A. won every battle but could never establish control of the country and eventually its position in Vietnam militarily and in the U.S.A. politically was unsustainable. For that reason during the invasion and occupation of Iraq and the emergence of an intractable insurgency in Iraq there were many comparisons in the popular media between Iraq and Vietnam. The fighters are different and the religious component is different in Iraq but the common idea of being free of colonialism and occupation is the same. In both cases there is popular support for the rebels, so it is inevitable that the invading force will eventually fail.

The Iran-Contra Affair (also known as "Irangate") is a prime example of the duplicity of U.S.A. foreign policy as well as the capacity of the leadership to escape accountability for its criminal actions; a form of conduct that would be surpassed in the administration of George W. Bush. In the mid-1980s the Iran-Contra Affair became a political scandal in the U.S.A. in which president Ronald Reagan sold arms to Iran [while at the same time selling weapons to Iraq, which was at war with Iran]. Iran was supposed to be an avowed enemy of the U.S.A. because the Iranians supposedly hated the U.S.A. for their political interventions and installing dictators in Iran and taking out the elected government of the Iranian people. The U.S.A. side supposedly hated Iran because they overthrew the Shah [monarch installed by the U.S.A.] and took hostages from the U.S.A. embassy at the end of the Carter administration. At the time, the U.S.A. had troops in Lebanon who were being held hostage there by a group called Hezbollah, which was a militant Shi'a organization that was loyal to the Ayatollah Khomeini [new leader {religious fundamentalist} of Iran]. The government of the U.S.A. claimed that they made the deal because Iran would be influenced by receiving the arms to release the hostages. Iran was at the same time also involved in a war with Iraq and not many countries would sell them weapons. Nevertheless, the investigation into the scandal revealed that the weapons shipments had begun before the first hostage had been taken. Furthermore, the weapons shipments to Iran ended long after the release of the last hostage. The U.S.A. operated the scheme by diverting profits from the sales to Iran to the Contras. The Contras were right wing guerrillas, supported by the U.S.A., who conducted an insurgency [same kind of operation going on in Iraq against the U.S.A. after the U.S.A. invaded Iraq] against the socialist government of Nicaragua which was democratically elected. The Sandinista government of Nicaragua was so named after the original government of Augusto César Sandino (May 18, 1895 - February 21, 1934) who was a Nicaraguan revolutionary and leader who rebelled against the U.S.A. military presence which was in Nicaragua between the years 1927 and 1933; So military intervention [neocolonialism] in Nicaragua stretched back many years.

The sale of weapons as well as the financing of the Contras with the weapons sales violated the stated policy of the Reagan administration as well as legislation that was passed by Congress which at that time was controlled by the Democratic party. Congress had enacted specific legislation to block any further Contra funding, yet Reagan authorized the continued support of the Contras and the sales to Iran clandestinely.

The president Reagan escaped direct accountability because congress did not have hard direct evidence that Reagan approved the deal since Oliver North and others destroyed evidence and accepted responsibility. North accepted the responsibility after having received immunity for his testimony. Since he was free because of the immunity he could say anything and it would not hurt the president since there was no evidence to back up his statements. Since he received immunity he was free no matter what he said. Reagan and his vice-president George H. Bush escaped further scrutiny when the defense secretary, Caspar Weinberger, was pardoned by Bush after Weinberger was implicated in the scandal.

During the military actions started by George W. Bush in Afghanistan, and Iraq prisoners were taken and tortured secretly. Shortly thereafter the scandal of that torture and other related illegal acts such as kidnapping suspects and sending them to secret jails to be tortured broke in the media. The most egregious incidents of torture occurred at the prisons in Guantanamo Bay, [Cuba] Abu Graib [Iraq] and Bagram [Afghanistan] in which the military, under the direction of the Secretary of Defense, Donald Rumsfeld, the Vice-President Richard Bruce Cheney (Dick Cheney) and the President George W. Bush, approved the torture[7] of Iraqi men and women. In the case of the Bush administration, lower ranking military officers and soldiers were blamed and convicted of the atrocities and no further inquiry was allowed by the congress which was controlled by the same political party [republican] as the president.

In the years since the Iran Contra Affair the U.S.A. has invaded other smaller countries with impunity, to change their governments to the liking of the U.S.A. The invasion of Panama and Grenada are most well known. Those military actions were easy victories which emboldened the U.S.A. government after the debacle of Vietnam. In the case of Panama [1989] the invasion was mounted for the stated reason that the Panamanian leader, Gen, Manuel Noriega, was trafficking drugs and because an unarmed U.S. soldier in plain clothes was killed at a roadblock of the Panamanian Defense Forces. Noriega was a former CIA operative and a former head of the secret police of Panama. So his activities were well known and tolerated for many years as investigations revealed. More importantly, the invasion happened days before the administration of the Panama Canal was supposed to be turned over by the U.S.A. to Panamanian

---

[7] See the section of this book entitled: *The True Wounded of Torture and War*

control, in accordance with the timetable that had been set up in the Torrijos-Carter Treaties. The U.S.A. returned the canal-related lands to Panama in 1999, but it reserved the right to apply military intervention in the interest of U.S.A. national security.

During the administration of Ronald Reagan, death squads were authorized and supported in El Salvador. The comparison has been made of Iraq to Vietnam but Journalist Amy Goodman in the alternative news program *Democracy Now* cited the assessment of Peter Moss, from the *New York Times Magazine* that shows how the situation in Iraq may be more aptly compared to the situation of El Salvador.

> **AMY GOODMAN:** On the issue of death squads I wanted to read to you an excerpt from an article that appeared in the *New York Times Magazine* last May by Peter Moss, it was entitled "The Way of the Commandos." We are talking to the man who has just left Iraq as the UN Human Rights Chief, John Pace. We are speaking to him in Sydney, Australia, in his first broadcast interview here in the United States.
> Peter Moss' piece reads, "The template for Iraq today is not Vietnam to which it is often been compared but El Salvador. Where, a right wing government backed by the United States fought a leftist insurgency in a 12-year war beginning in 1980. The cost was high. More than 70,000 people were killed, most of them civilians in a country with a population of just six million. Most of the killing and torturing was done by the army and the right-wing death squads affiliated with it. According to an Amnesty International Report in 2001, violations committed by the army and its associated paramilitaries included extrajudicial killings, other unlawful killings, disappearances and torture while whole villages were targeted by the armed forces and their inhabitants massacred. As part of president Reagan's policy of supporting anti-communist forces, hundreds of millions of dollars in U.S. aid was funneled to the Salvadoran army and a team of 55 special forces advisors led for years by Jim Steele, trained frontline battalions accused of significant human rights abuses."
> Peter Moss' article goes on to say there are far more Americans in Iraq today, some 140,000 troops in all than there were in Salvador. But U.S. soldiers and officers are increasingly moving to a Salvador-style advisory role. In the process, they are backing up local forces that like the military in El Salvador do not shy away from violence. It is no coincidence that this new strategy is most visible in a paramilitary unit that has Steele as its main advisor. Having been a key participant in the

> Salvador conflict, Steele knows how to organize a counter insurgency campaign led by local forces.
> He's not the only American in Iraq with such experience. He was the senior -- the senior U.S. advisor in the ministry of interior which has operational control over the commandos. Steve Castile, a former top official in the drug enforcement operation who spent much of his professional life immersed in the drug wars of Latin America. Castile worked alongside local forces in Peru, Bolivia, and Columbia where he was involved in the hunt for Pablo Escobar, the head of the Medellin cocaine cartel.

The war on Iraq by the U.S.A. was in part an attempt to prevent the huge oil economy of Iraq from being turned over to European currency and insuring the supply of oil to the U.S.A. at favorable prices to the U.S.A. oil companies and U.S.A. economy. In early March 2006 it was revealed that in early 2003 president George W. Bush conspired with the British prime minister Tony Blair to attack Iraq regardless of the outcome of a United Nations vote on a resolution to use force against Iraq. This means that when they were seeking a U.N. resolution to authorize the aggression against Iraq they had already made up their minds to attack and go against international law and their own public statements as well as the public opinion of their countries. This follows the actions of the U.S.A. ordering the withdrawal of the weapons inspectors when it was clear that they were not finding any weapons of mass destruction and that the U.S.A. would not achieve a U.N. vote to attack; so they decided to attack anyway, on their own. However, the British prime minister had pushed for the resolution because of hesitation from his legal council who said the war would be illegal without the U.N. resolution. Yet, in the end the British went along with the U.S.A. desire to invade, as they have sided with the U.S.A. in most instances since the end of World War II, in an effort to ingratiate themselves to the U.S.A. and partake in the wealth of U.S.A. imperial exploits.[138]

Relating to postwar planning, in the run up to the war, even though the Bush administration was warned that the troop levels were too small to mount an effective occupation,[8] the president and his

[8] From the beginning, military experts warned Washington that the task would require, as Army Chief of Staff Eric Shinseki told Congress in February 2003, "hundreds of

advisors decided to press on and go to war anyway, stating that the Iraqi people would meet the U.S.A. soldiers with parades and flowers, etc. The general who suggested they needed more troops was fired because if such a large number was required to hold on to Iraq it would mean that the whole proposition of invading and controlling the country was not as easy as the Bush administration was implying and they would have difficulty convincing the congress and perhaps the public as well, to go along with the invasion. The president and his advisors also ignored a state department plan for postwar reorganization of Iraq, which led to the mishandling of the situation by the Coalition Provisional Authority, a U.S.A. occupation government that was set up to govern Iraq.

> Published on Sunday, October 19, 2003 by the New York Times
> ***State Dept. Study Foresaw Trouble Now Plaguing Iraq* by Eric Schmitt and Joel Brinkley**
>
> WASHINGTON, Oct. 18 — A yearlong State Department study predicted many of the problems that have plagued the American-led occupation of Iraq, according to internal State Department documents and interviews with administration and Congressional officials.
> Beginning in April 2002, the State Department project assembled more than 200 Iraqi lawyers, engineers, business people and other experts into 17 working groups to study topics ranging from creating a new justice system to reorganizing the military to revamping the economy.
> Their findings included a much more dire assessment of Iraq's dilapidated electrical and water systems than many Pentagon officials assumed. They warned of a society so brutalized by Saddam Hussein's rule that many Iraqis might react coolly to Americans' notion of quickly rebuilding civil society.
> Several officials said that many of the findings in the $5 million study were ignored by Pentagon officials until recently, although the Pentagon said they took the findings into account. The work is now being relied on heavily as occupation forces struggle to impose stability in Iraq.
> The working group studying transitional justice was eerily prescient in forecasting the widespread looting in the aftermath of the fall of Mr. Hussein's government, caused in part by thousands of criminals set free from prison, and it recommended force to prevent the chaos.

---

thousands" of troops. **What Went Wrong in Iraq by** Larry Diamond From *Foreign Affairs*, September/October 2004
http://www.foreignaffairs.org/20040901faessay83505/larry-diamond/what-went-wrong-in-iraq.html

By ignoring its own studies, the U.S.A. government was, either due to incompetence or willful intent, actually creating the conditions favorable to "chaos." Going to war with too few soldiers would leave the country, besides the oil fields, unsecured and an armed uprising could more easily develop. If the decision to go to war with less soldiers was done for political reasons, to make it seem as an easy task, or because the secretary of defense, Donald Rumsfeld, thought a leaner army that relied on technology to compensate for larger numbers of personnel was sufficient for the task [a well known policy by Rumsfeld], either reason is evidence of incompetence since the result of the action had catastrophic results. That opposition developed into a formidable force that caused the U.S.A. armed forces leaders to admit the opposition would not be defeated militarily and to urge president Bush to find a political, i.e. negotiated solution. So one way to look at the situation is that the supposedly most powerful military force in the world [U.S.A.] was neutralized by the smaller and less well equipped force.

What resulted from the "chaos" was a protracted conflict in which the U.S.A. would supposedly [according to the same administration that started the war and incompetently carried out the occupation] be required to stay in Iraq for many years instead of having a swift transition from the Hussein regime to complete control of the country by a new Iraqi government which would theoretically require the withdrawal of the U.S.A. troops.

Also, by promoting fear and arguably sadistic and amoral methods of interrogation through psychological and physical torture techniques including sexual debasement as a means of extracting information from people the entire Arab region as well as other countries around the world had confirmed their impressions about the degradation of western culture and particularly the U.S.A.

If it was a miscalculation in the strategy of creating chaos in order to form a pretext for U.S.A. continued presence in Iraq the emergence of a powerful rebellion and the declining popular support in the U.S.A. and Iraq was not foreseen. Also, whatever prestige or moral authority the U.S.A. had in the world previously had seriously eroded. Furthermore, the U.S.A. economy, which was already in a dilapidated condition, sunk even lower due to the wars. Machiavelli had some words to say about such situations.

Machiavelli: ***The Prince*** **CHAPTER V**

CONCERNING THE WAY TO GOVERN CITIES OR PRINCIPALITIES WHICH LIVED UNDER THEIR OWN LAWS BEFORE THEY WERE ANNEXED

Whenever those states which have been acquired as stated have been accustomed to live under their own laws and in freedom, there are three courses for those who wish to hold them: the first is to ruin them, the next is to reside there in person, the third is to permit them to live under their own laws, drawing a tribute, and establishing within it an oligarchy which will keep it friendly to you. Because such a government, being created by the prince, knows that it cannot stand without his friendship and interest, and does it utmost to support him; and therefore he who would keep a city accustomed to freedom will hold it more easily by the means of its own citizens than in any other way.

There are, for example, the Spartans and the Romans. The Spartans held Athens and Thebes, establishing there an oligarchy, nevertheless they lost them. The Romans, in order to hold Capua, Carthage, and Numantia, dismantled them, and did not lose them. They wished to hold Greece as the Spartans held it, making it free and permitting its laws, and did not succeed. So to hold it they were compelled to dismantle many cities in the country, for in truth there is no safe way to retain them otherwise than by ruining them. And he who becomes master of a city accustomed to freedom and does not destroy it, may expect to be destroyed by it, for in rebellion it has always the watchword of liberty and its ancient privileges as a rallying point, which neither time nor benefits will ever cause it to forget. And whatever you may do or provide against, they never forget that name or their privileges unless they are disunited or dispersed, but at every chance they immediately rally to them…

Many progressive critics of the president of the U.S.A. have charged that the president and those in his cabinet are arrogant and incompetent due to their dismal performance in the Iraqi occupation and the emergence of a formidable insurgency in Iraq. Hence, determined fighters with small arms and improvised explosive devices have seemingly neutralized the supposedly mightiest army in human history. Thus, the U.S.A. and Britain were unable to make their technological advances effective there even after centuries of war experience, especially given the wisdom of Machiavelli, referring to the difficulty of occupying another country. The following summary compiled by Stephanie Reich demonstrates how negotiations with Iraq were subverted purposely and how nations were induced, through national bribery, to go along with the U.S.A. plans to invade Iraq.

> Between August 10 and 19, Iraq issued three proposals for resolving the Gulf crisis. The first proposal offered Iraqi withdrawal from Kuwait in exchange for Syrian pullout from Lebanon, and Israeli evacuation of the West Bank and Gaza. The second proposal called for the replacement of US troops assembling in Saudi Arabia by UN forces, and the handling of the Iraq-Kuwait situation within a regional context. The third proposal, delivered to US National Security Adviser Brent Scowcroft, offered Iraq's complete withdrawal from Kuwait in exchange for Iraqi control of the Rumailah oilfield, and for Baghdad's guaranteed access to the Gulf. The US responded to these three Iraqi offerings by continuing its troop buildup in Saudi Arabia.
>
> The US gained its November 29 UN vote authorizing war against Iraq from the other Security Council member states by offering them handsome economic assistance packages. The Soviet Union, for instance, obtained a US pledge of $6 billion in financial aid as payment for its "yes" vote. Colombia, Ethiopia and Zaire were also offered new aid packages, and access to World Bank credits and IMF loans. China's abstention was purchased by ending China's post-Tenanmen Square isolation through a high-level White House meeting with the Chinese ambassador, and by promising to push for the release of China's withheld World Bank credits. Yemen was punished for voting against the resolution with a cutoff of $70 million in US aid.
>
> The Gulf War concluded at the end of February 1991 with the Highway of Death massacre, in which the US Air Force, in violation of international law, strafed and killed tens of thousands of Iraqi troops retreating from Kuwait. The sanctions imposed in August 1990 remained, now tied to Iraqi compliance with Security Council Resolution 687, directing the demolition of its weapons of mass destruction, and compliance inspections at 60-day intervals. It was a moving goalpost that never stopped moving. Lifting the sanctions requires unanimity among the Security Council's permanent members. The US and Britain remain the only holdouts to this day.[139]

Nevertheless, if it is true that the president and those in his cabinet are arrogant and incompetent, the same arrogance and incompetence that has bogged the U.S.A. military in Iraq also prevented any serious contemplation about a full scale invasion of Iran, North Korea or Venezuela, the country headed by Hugo Chaves, a leader of a country with rich oil reserves, that has defied U.S.A. hegemony and who even survived a two day *Coup d'état* that was sponsored and financed by the U.S.A.

> *Decline in Iraqi Troops' Readiness Cited*
> ***Generals Tell Lawmakers They Cannot Predict When U.S. Forces Can Withdraw***
> *By Josh White and Bradley Graham*
> Washington Post Staff Writers
> Friday, September 30, 2005; Page A12
>
> The number of Iraqi army battalions that can fight insurgents without U.S. and coalition help has dropped from three to one, top U.S. generals told Congress yesterday, adding that the security situation in Iraq is too uncertain to predict large-scale American troop withdrawals anytime soon.[140]
>
> ***What the Hell Are We Doing in Iraq?***
>
> U.S. Report on Iraqi Troops Is Mixed
>
> By Robert Burns
> Associated Press
> Saturday, February 25, 2006; Page A13
>
> The number of Iraqi army battalions judged by their American trainers to be capable of fighting insurgents without U.S. help has fallen from one to none since September, Pentagon officials said yesterday.[141]

In an article on the progress in the training of the Iraqi army to take the place of U.S.A. troops, Robert Burns reported that the readiness of the troops had been reduced. Some analysts point out that the U.S.A. could not get men to commit to their side or the side of the Iraqi government set up by the U.S.A because they do not want to be perceived as being against the "insurgents" if the U.S.A. were to pull out. That the condition of the U.S.A. army and U.S.A. government and its Iraqi collaborators did not inspire their confidence speaks volumes about the failed stated policy which was to train a new Iraqi army that could maintain the government left behind, though the U.S.A. never intended to completely pull out of Iraq since they have openly worked on creating four permanent bases and one super embassy, biggest in the world, with its own army, presumably to stay in Iraq no matter what, even if the Iraqi people do not want them there or regardless of what government is there; something like Guantanamo Bay in Cuba. The ideal strategy would be to promote the creation of a friendly government to allow the U.S.A. to stay even if the population disagrees, [neo-colonialism] as the U.S.A. has done elsewhere. But, in any case the strategy would be to remain with a physical presence there and have troops nearby to enforce the U.S.A. agenda.

If the U.S.A. forces were forced to withdraw from Iraq and if the U.S. government was to try to keep the bases around the pipeline it would constitute a new Guantanamo Bay type facility, an illegal establishment of U.S.A. control over land that belongs to another country. However, if such an opposition was to continue and grow, even the most hardened bases would eventually become untenable and they would not easily serve the purpose of protecting oil and gas supplies.

Democracy Now Headlines for March 16, 2006

Top US General in Iraq Says Bases May Be Permanent
In other news, the top US military commander in Iraq has indicated the US may want to hold on to the several military bases it has built in the country. Appearing before a Congressional subcommittee Tuesday, General John Abizaid said the US may want to keep a foothold in Iraq to support regional "moderates" and protect oil supplies.[142]

In early 2006, the political and military situation had deteriorated to such an extent that the rebellion in Iraq had sparked violence between the two main religious factions of the country [Sunni and Shia], which further destabilized the country and further weakened the U.S.A. economy and military. Since the president apparently lied about the reason for war and used manipulation of the intelligence that said Iraq had weapons of mass destruction there were far more people less willing to believe what was said by the U.S.A. in the Fall of the year 2005 statements about the impending threat from Iran. Those statements were intensified since the infamous statement by president George W. Bush using the term **"axis of evil"** in his State of the Union Address on January 29, 2002 describing supposed "regimes that sponsor terror" where he named Iraq, Iran, and North Korea as forming that axis. But this time even the media, which had been accused by critics as being little more than a stenographer for the government, did not echo the call for war with the same enthusiasm as it did previously for the war on Iraq. Nevertheless, the Bush administration kept up intensifying the rhetorical pressure on Iran as if there were an "imminent threat" of nuclear attack from Iran; that pressure was applied even though a report emerged in the Washington Post that stated a contradictory assessment of Iran's nuclear capabilities by the U.S. intelligence review. So, just as was done with Iraq, the military assessments were ignored because they did not fit the geopolitical agenda of attacking and controlling Iran.

Iran Is Judged 10 Years From Nuclear Bomb
U.S. Intelligence Review Contrasts With Administration Statements *By Dafna Linzer*
Washington Post Staff Writer
Tuesday, August 2, 2005; Page A01

A major U.S. intelligence review has projected that Iran is about a decade away from manufacturing the key ingredient for a nuclear weapon, roughly doubling the previous estimate of five years, according to government sources with firsthand knowledge of the new analysis.
The carefully hedged assessments, which represent consensus among U.S. intelligence agencies, contrast with forceful public statements by the White House. Administration officials have asserted, but have not offered proof, that Tehran is moving determinedly toward a nuclear arsenal. The new estimate could provide more time for diplomacy with Iran over its nuclear ambitions. President Bush has said that he wants the crisis resolved diplomatically but that "all options are on the table."

Despite the reports about Iran's nuclear development the president and his advisors continued to make provocative statements and threatening assertions about the supposed danger Iran posed.

Democracy Now **Headlines for March 7, 2006**
Tuesday, March 7th, 2006
US Dismisses Possibility of Compromise on Iran Nuclear Activity

In other news, the United States has dismissed the possibility of reaching a compromise in the international standoff over Iran's nuclear ambitions. Iran has been in talks to move its nuclear enrichment

> activities to Russia. The US announced its stance after U.N. International Atomic Energy Agency head Mohamed ElBaradei said a deal between Moscow and Tehran could prevent Iran's referral to the UN Security Council.

When we examine the political rhetoric that was put out by the U.S.A. government related to Iran we discover a parallel with the kinds of statements that were put out in the time running up to the attack on Iraq. It was a media and public relations effort to sway public opinion to support an attack on Iran. The Republican Party [in power] was not the only source of belligerent statements advocating war on Iran. The following statement came from Democratic Senator Hillary Rodham Clinton of New York, who was speaking at Princeton University in January 2006. Her statement echoes those by other democratic party leaders who support the same imperialist and hegemonic strategies.

> We must move as quickly as feasible for sanctions in the United Nations, and we cannot take any option off the table in sending a clear message to the current leadership of Iran, that they will not be permitted to acquire nuclear weapons.

Vice President Dick Cheney made even more aggressive statements while addressing the American Public Affairs Committee on Tuesday March 7, 2006.

> The Iranian regime needs to know that if it stays on its present course, the international community is prepared to impose meaningful consequences. For our part, the United States is keeping all options on the table in addressing the irresponsible conduct of the regime.

On the same day as Cheney's statements, Donald Rumsfeld, the Defense Secretary, spoke at a Pentagon news conference and said the following, when he was asked about Iran.

> I will say this about Iran. They are currently putting people into Iraq to do things that are harmful to the future of Iraq, and we know it. And it is something that they, I think, will look back on as having been an error in judgment.

After the above and other ominous accusations of Iran, that they were sending fighters into Iraq, the top military officer for all the U.S.A. armed forces was asked about the evidence about that claim. He looked over to his left, at the secretary of defense, Donald Rumsfeld, who had made the aggressive statements earlier, and then he turned to the reporter who asked the question and denied the claim, thereby exposing the disingenuous statements that prompted most progressive commentators to suggest that the purpose of the false statements was to drum up support for attacking Iran.

> **DEMOCRACY NOW, Headlines for March 15, 2006**
>
> ***Top US Military Commander: No Evidence of Iran Links***
> Meanwhile, the top US military commander said Tuesday there is no evidence Iran is aiding the Iraqi insurgency. At a Pentagon briefing, Gen. Peter Pace, chair of the Joint Chiefs of Staff, was asked if he thought Iran was arming militants or sending weapons to Iraq. Pace replied: "I do not sir." Pace's comments appear to contradict recent statements made by both President Bush and Defense Secretary Donald Rumsfeld linking the violence in Iraq to the Iranian government.

Along with the statements described above, journalists such as Seymour Hersh[143] revealed that the administration was considering limited nuclear weapon strikes on Iran's nuclear research sites. Those reports led to controversy since the use of nuclear weapons would seem to be a departure from U.S.A. policy and international relations. The issuance of threats to use nuclear weapons is unfortunately not new. In an interview with journalist Amy Goodman, Daniel Ellsberg, revealed that the late journalist, Jack Anderson, whose files were currently being sought by the F.B.I. in order to confiscate any classified documents he might have uncovered [part of a new program to seize and classify information damaging to the government] revealed the startling history of the use of the threat to use nuclear weapons by presidents Carter and Truman, who were both of the democratic party.

> Jack Anderson, in a little known expose which is in one of his memoirs, also revealed that President Carter was making nuclear threats over a possible intervention by Russia into Iran in 1980. I'll bet even you don't know about that, Amy. It's really very little known, but there's a good deal in print about it now, nobody remarks. Carter was

> threatening to use nuclear weapons in connection with a possible second raid, amounting to an invasion into Iran, which is part of a very long pattern of U.S. making nuclear threats over Iran, as it is doing this week. We're using our nuclear -- we're using our nuclear weapons in Iran right now. We're using them by pointing the nuclear gun at these people, whether we pull the trigger or not.
> Harry Truman claims, in a number of times, that he got the Russians out of northern Iran, Azerbaijan, in 1946, by threatening to use an atomic bomb on it. They didn't. If correct -- and he said it four times -- that would be the first use of our using nuclear weapons since Nagasaki, and that was in Iran, which is on the border of Russia and has oil fields. We don't -- we never wanted to go to Russia, and now we don't want to be under the control of Iranians who are not friendly to us. [144]

If we examine some economic acts by Iran, we may discover some motivating reasons for the U.S.A. government to make such seemingly irrational belligerent and urgent statements about the supposed danger of Iran which sounded like the statements about the supposed danger of Iraq. Saddam Hussein's act of selling oil in Euros instead of dollars in the year 2000 that contributed to the neo-con desire to invade Iraq and control its oil, is to be surpassed by Iran. The following excerpt from an essay by William Clark explains.

> The Iranians are about to commit an "offense" far greater than Saddam Hussein's conversion to the euro of Iraq's oil exports in the fall of 2000. Numerous articles have revealed Pentagon planning for operations against Iran as early as 2005. While the publicly stated reasons will be over Iran's nuclear ambitions, there are unspoken macroeconomic drivers explaining the Real Reasons regarding the 2nd stage of petrodollar warfare - Iran's upcoming euro-based oil Bourse.
> In 2005-2006, The Tehran government has a developed a plan to begin competing with New York's NYMEX and London's IPE with respect to international oil trades - using a euro-denominated international oil-trading mechanism. This means that without some form of US intervention, the euro is going to establish a firm foothold in the international oil trade. Given U.S. debt levels and the stated neoconservative project for U.S. global domination, Tehran's objective constitutes an obvious encroachment on U.S. dollar supremacy in the international oil market[145]

In early 2006 it was revealed through declassified documents that Britain assisted the Israelis to acquire nuclear weapons, in violation of British law and the so called Nuclear Non-proliferation Treaty. This demonstrates what British MP, Tony Benn, called hypocrisy on the part of the British and U.S.A. governments in the treatment of Iran, which only has a nuclear energy facility, and Israel, which threatens its Arab country neighbors with annihilation.

> ***Democracy Now*** *Friday, March 10th, 2006*
> ***Former Labour MP Tony Benn on how Britain Secretly Helped Israel Build Its Nuclear Arsenal***
>
> **REPORT:** BBC News revealed Thursday the British government secretly supplied Israel with hundreds of chemical shipments in the 1960's, despite fears the chemicals could be used to develop nuclear weapons. Analysts say the shipments, which included plutonium, helped speed up Israel's acquisition of an atomic bomb. All told, the BBC reported the British chemicals could have been used to produce bombs 20 times as powerful as those dropped on Hiroshima.
>
> **AMY GOODMAN:** I also heard Mordechai Vanunu interviewed on the BBC, responding to this expose in Britain, and he said, "I continue to call for international inspections" -- or rather, "independent inspections of the Dimona nuclear plant."
>
> **TONY BENN:** Well, you see, the United States and Britain are in total breach of the Non-Proliferation Treaty. The Non-Proliferation Treaty says three things. One, the nuclear powers will agree to disarm collectively. Secondly, that other countries can develop nuclear technology. And thirdly, that nuclear powers will give absolute assurances they will never use nuclear weapons against a non-nuclear state. And both the United States and Britain have now said that if their security was at stake, they would use nuclear weapons. What Bush has done -- I don't think you realize it -- that make the case for the spread of nuclear weapons, because I tell you this, if Iran had nuclear weapons now, he would not dare to attack it. So, actually, Bush is encouraging the spread, and when he went to India the other day, which isn't a signatory to the Non-Proliferation Treaty, he signed an agreement. So, I mean, the thing is total hypocrisy. I think if we could get that clear, then we can consider how we deal with the situation that faces us.

After the defeat of Egypt in 1967 by Israel, the relationship between the U.S.A. and Israel solidified. Since then a special relationship developed in which the Israeli lobby in Washington became powerful and the media became favorable towards Israel. It was also then that Israel began to serve as a friendly base in the Middle East for the U.S.A. and Britain. Noam Chomsky explained further:

> "that was 1967, and it was after that victory that the U.S.-Israeli relations really solidified, became what's called a "strategic asset"... It's also then that the lobby gained its force. It's also then, incidentally, that the educated classes, the intellectual political class entered into an astonishing love affair with Israel, after its demonstration of tremendous power against a third-world enemy, and in fact, that's a very critical component of what's called the lobby."[146]

Returning to the deteriorating situation in Iraq, many calls were heard from retired military officers and even from active ones privately speaking to prominent congress members such as John Mertha[147] who expressed their consternation publicly and stated also that the conflict is un-winnable and that the U.S.A. forces should withdraw from Iraq. Lt. Gen. William Odum (Ret.) echoed his assessment. However, due to the *"Superpower Syndrome Mandatory Conflict Complex"* the U.S.A. could not withdraw from what is widely recognized as a failed policy. It would be an admission of failure. President George W. Bush announced that the fate of U.S. troops in Iraq would be decided by future presidents and future Iraqi governments, meaning it would continue past his administration. If the president could wait until a new president came in he could say that the policy did not fail under his tenure. The incoming president could stop the policy and say it was not his; so both could pass on the situation without losing face but in the mean time hundreds of thousands of people would have to die or be maimed for life in order to allow the superpower presidents to save face. Thus, more lives and money would be sacrificed on the pyre of superpower face saving.

> Once the invasion began in March 2003, all of the ensuing unhappy results became inevitable. The invasion of Iraq may well turn out to be the greatest strategic disaster in American history. In any event, the longer we stay, the worse it will be. Until that is understood, we will make no progress with our allies or in devising a promising alternative strategy.
>
> "Staying the course" may make a good sound bite, but it can be disastrous for strategy. Several of Hitler's generals told him that

> "staying the course" at Stalingrad in 1942 was a strategic mistake, that he should allow the Sixth Army to be withdrawn, saving it to fight defensive actions on reduced frontage against the growing Red Army. He refused, lost the Sixth Army entirely, and left his commanders with fewer forces to defend a wider front. Thus he made the subsequent Soviet offensives westward easier.[148]

This kind of reality is what Daniel Ellsberg, author, of the *Pentagon Papers,* faced when he discovered the document formally known as ***United States-Vietnam Relations, 1945-1967: A Study Prepared by the Department of Defense***, which was a 47 volume, 7,000-page, report on the policy decisions leading to the invasion of Vietnam. Those documents showed that the policy was a failed one because there was no real intent or real expectation to win the war and people were dieing unnecessarily. Parts of the document began to be "leaked" to the *New York Times* in early 1971 and they contributed to the cessation of the U.S.A. involvement in Vietnam which occurred finally in 1975.

In this manner what John Perkins, the Self-Described Economic Hit-Man, called the first true global empire, referring to the global U.S.A. control of the world economy through neocolonialism,[9] Jackals[10] or open military attack [like the Iraq war] was becoming weaker due to the drain on the economy. Lt. Gen. William Odum (Ret.),[149] who has ample combat experience and credibility to assess the conditions in Iraq plainly laid out a detailed review of the reasons to continue the occupation in Iraq and continue fighting the rebels in Iraq, and he also presented reasons why the mission can't be achieved by staying.[150] Odum said: *"If I were a journalist, I would list all the arguments that you hear against pulling U.S. troops out of Iraq, the horrible things that people say would happen, and then ask: Aren't they happening already? Would a pullout really make things worse?"* He found that the conflict cannot be won because the population is aiding the rebel fighters and most ordinary Iraqis when polled said it was OK to kill U.S.A. soldiers.

---

[9] controlling heads of state and preventing democracy in other countries

[10] government assassins to kill those government leaders who do not accept U.S.A. hegemony

Also, most people in the U.S.A., when polled, said they thought the U.S.A. should leave. Odum also said:[151]

> Ask the president: Why should we expect a different outcome in Iraq than in Vietnam?
>
> Ask the president if he intends to leave a pro-American liberal regime in place. Because that's just impossible. Postwar Germany and Japan are *not* models for Iraq. Each had mature (at least a full generation old) constitutional orders by the end of the 19th century. They both endured as constitutional orders until the 1930s. Thus General Clay and General Macarthur were merely reversing a decade and a half totalitarianism -- returning to nearly a century of liberal political change in Japan and a much longer period in Germany.
>
> The civil war we leave behind may well draw in Syria, Turkey and Iran. But already today each of those states is deeply involved in support for or opposition to factions in the ongoing Iraqi civil war. The very act of invading Iraq almost insured that violence would involve the larger region. And so it has and will continue, with, or without, US forces in Iraq.

In one way of looking at it, it is as if the policy pursued by the U.S.A. government under George W. Bush had achieved exactly the opposite of what it stated it intended. By invading Iraq stability had not been produced but rather instability in the entire region. Supposed terrorist groups were not been stamped out but rather emboldened and expanded. Instead of being a threat to Iran, to strike fear into them as to what the U.S.A. may do to them, Iran had become emboldened due to the growing quagmire the U.S.A. found itself in and Iran strategically assisted the Shia in Iraq to arm and has apparently advised them to pursue a political course to political power since they have the majority population. So Iran began to hold significant influence in Iraq which it did not in the past. Also, if the U.S.A. did attack Iraq they could as well cause a mobilization of the Shia in Iraq that would lead to a large scale uprising against the U.S.A. forces there and they could withdraw their oil supplies from the U.S.A. and wreck havoc with the western economies. So a supposed enemy had been strengthened by the U.S.A. actions which were of course illegal under the constitution because the congress never issued a declaration of war against Iraq. Furthermore, the president was warned by the C.I.A. and Arab leaders in the Middle

East that an invasion and occupation of Iraq would lead to the increased following of anti-U.S.A. groups.

In short it would seem as if the strategy in Iraq, from undersupplying troops to disbanding the army instead of retaining them so as to not push them into the hands of the resistance, to the mistreatment of the people as well as the use of torture were designed to promote chaos and conflict; as if the leadership of the U.S.A. wanted to promote a wider war. Another assessment could be that it was all a blunder from a most incompetent executive administration of the president. Yet the resources in human power [for soldiers] to take over and hold territory were not there and would not be there unless a draft was instituted. As of the spring of the year 2006 the recruitment levels of the volunteer army were seriously declining. So unless the U.S.A. government was to propose to institute a draft it could not win any war against a country with at least a neutralizing force like the Iraqi insurgency. Since the draft is politically unpopular and most people who supported the call to war in Iraq came to the opinion that the war was not worth it, the draft would be difficult to establish and probably many young people would flee the country if it were seriously contemplated.

If the U.S.A. were to use even the smallest nuclear weapon it would lose any credibility it may still have around the world and it would instantly turn most of the world [especially the Arab countries] against it not only in opinion polls but many people around the world would feel compelled to actively work against the interests of the U.S.A. using any means at their disposal, including sabotage and indiscriminate murder of U.S.A. nationals (especially the ones abroad) and intelligence estimates have circulated that say such a move would make it highly likely that nuclear weapons, in some form or another, would be used against the U.S.A.

So, as of 2006, the U.S.A. remained in a quagmire and many people had expressed apprehension due to Bush's religious connections and his refusal to accept and admit errors and the unwillingness or inability of the congress to exercise their power to control him, allowing the situation to get worse by continuing the same failed policy in Iraq or getting into new failed policies like an invasion of

Iran. Many people in the government of the U.S.A. and in the Christian religious extremists groups in the U.S.A. had been expressing increased fear about the prospects of Iran's acquisition of nuclear weapons. The claim by the U.S.A. was that creation of nuclear power facilities by the Iranians has been seen as subterfuge for hiding the creation of nuclear weapons.

Ironically it was the imperialist action of the U.S.A., by disrupting the social order and orchestrating *Coup d'état* in Iran that alienated the people and allowed religious fundamentalists to take over control of the country. The reaction to U.S.A. interventions pushed the Iranians [as other countries have] towards fear of the U.S.A., sufficient enough that they want to have weapons to protect themselves. So, the lesson that other countries such as Iran could learn, from the fate of Iraq, is that they indeed should have nuclear weapons so that the big superpower will be afraid to attack them.

The people of the U.S.A., especially those whose families have lived in the U.S.A. for at least two generations and consider themselves "Americans" and believe in the "American Dream" and or the idea of maintaining the "American way of life" and "standard of living" are probably the most fearful because they perhaps second only to the Japanese, know the devastation that can come from a nuclear attack since they launched one on Japan. Since the *"Superpower Syndrome Mandatory Conflict Complex"* precludes humility and friendship with others as equals, the U.S.A. finds it difficult to adjust to a world without U.S.A. supremacy; but in time, if the current period is survived and the ecological crisis and the economic downfall and if the coming rivalry with China are resolved, the U.S.A. will eventually have to accept a position of equal or lesser power and prominence with other nations, as Britain and Russia had to previously.

Speaking of the approach to the problem in Iraq Lt. Gen. William Odum (Ret.), expressed the best course for the U.S.A. involving cooperation with other nations to stabilize the Middle East. However, the price of cooperation would be loss of absolute control, which is apparently something that the U.S.A. policy is not willing to allow even at the cost of national treasure, the lives of soldiers as well as the lives of the people of the invaded countries that have the resources that are desired.

> Thus Brzezinski calls for the United States to lead the states of Europe plus Russia, Japan, and China in a cooperative approach to stabilizing this region so that it cannot spark conflicts among them. As he rightly argues, the task of stabilization is beyond the power of the United States alone. With allies, however, it can manage the challenge.[152]

In the U.S.A. the aristocracy and oligarchy are fearful of losing their grip on control of the population and the economy that produces the means to maintain the current standard of living which is considered extravagant and ostentatious by most other countries. The lesson is that egoistic intentions and actions based on greed or fear, whether in personal life or in geopolitics, lead to cultural and political resentments and conflicts that may take generations to resolve and which in the nuclear age can lead to disastrous consequences in the short term.

At the end of the year 2005 and the beginning of 2006 the administration representatives of President George W. Bush began increasing threats against Iran due to its work on nuclear power plants and the fear they may produce nuclear weapons. Additionally, though less emphasized, were statements about preparations for future confrontations with China; that even though China is the second holder of U.S.A. debt and supposedly one of the most important trading partners for U.S.A. corporations. So the contradictory or perhaps inconsistent foreign policy may lead to the confounding of experts but what is more dubious, according to Chalmers Johnson, is the promotion of Japanese rearmament, which would eventually lead to a confrontation between China and Japan and eventually draw in the U.S.A., which would lose in a conflict against China.

> Such a development promotes hostility between China and Japan, the two superpowers of East Asia, sabotages possible peaceful solutions in those two problem areas, Taiwan and North Korea, left over from the Chinese and Korean civil wars, and lays the foundation for a possible future Sino-American conflict that the United States would almost surely lose. It is unclear whether the ideologues and war lovers of Washington understand what they are unleashing…Let me make clear

> that in East Asia we are not talking about a little regime-change war of the sort that Bush and Cheney advocate. After all, the most salient characteristic of international relations during the last century was the inability of the rich, established powers -- Great Britain and the United States -- to adjust peacefully to the emergence of new centers of power in Germany, Japan, and Russia. The result was two exceedingly bloody world wars, a forty-five-year-long Cold War between Russia and the "West," and innumerable wars of national liberation (such as the quarter-century long one in Vietnam) against the arrogance and racism of European, American, and Japanese imperialism and colonialism. [153]

The profound but succinct statement above precisely describes the main source of war other than religious fundamentalism; that source is greed/power. Greed and power serve the same end, to bolster each other and yield domination. Domination feeds the need for the degraded ego and the debased personality that requires the feeling derived from dominating others in order to raise itself up above others in order to appreciate itself. The dominance of power and the subjugation of the dominated provide the sense of worth and security that the supposedly superior person seeks and cannot find any other way. The need may manifest in purchasing more objects or vacations or seeking more and more pleasurable experiences to drown out the depressive restless heart but these are only symptoms of the true needs which are understanding, peace, and trust. The inability to cede control, to share power and live in friendship is the source of strife between ordinary human beings as well as societies and even countries. The U.S.A. has tended to project military power around the world in the form of bases, in an effort to maintain a grip on power over other nations so as to protect and perpetuate the lifestyle and perceived status of the U.S.A.

How many U.S.A. military bases are there around the world? The former C.I.A. advisor, professor and author Chalmers Johnson reported:

> So there is a lot of misleading information in it, but it's enough to say 700 looks like a pretty good number, whereas it's probably around 1,000. The base world is secret. Americans don't know anything about it. The Congress doesn't do oversight on it. You must remember, 40 percent of the defense budget is black. No congressman can see it. All of the intelligence budgets are black.

> ...In violation of the first Article of the Constitution that says, "The American public shall be given, annually, a report on how their tax money was spent." That has not been true in the United States since the Manhattan Project of World War II, even though it is the clause that gives Congress the power of the purse, the power to supervise.[154]

This means that the strategy of world domination of other countries has taken the form of the establishment of military bases around the world, in strategic places where the U.S.A. power can be projected at will. The effort has created a global network of bases that impacts local economies and causes some nations to want the bases in order to have the revenues from their presence but they also intimidate the local populations of the nations where they are located. In some cases the presence of the bases was accomplished by winning a war [Japan and Germany], in others the local population was coerced into accepting their establishment [like Saudi Arabia] and in some others the local government was forced to accept them [like Iraq]. In this manner foreign policy is dictated by foreign imperious diplomacy and globalized economics and when a country's government refuses to accept that it is branded as communist or tyrannical and the C.I.A. or the military are sent in to overthrow it and then the military creates bases to keep it overthrown. Since the U.S.A. congress has colluded with the executive to secretly fund and create the known and secret bases, in this manner, the military industrial complex has expanded to cover most of the world.

> ... The base world is complex. It has its own airline. It has 234 golf courses around the world. It has something like 70 Lear jet luxury airplanes to fly generals and admirals to the golf courses, to the armed forces ski resort at Garmisch in the Bavarian Alps. Inside the bases, the military does everything in their power to make them look like Little America. I mean, Burger King has just opened at Baghdad International Airport.[155]

The present day U.S.A. military base concept may be considered as an evolution of the model of the military garrison in the way that the base is not just a military installation with military equipment but a self-contained unit of U.S.A. culture that is militarized complete with fast food restaurants and other recreational amenities to help people feel at "home." In this way people are facilitated to be away from their culture by remaining in it as much as possible and insulating themselves as much as possible so as to remain separate and detached from the local population. Considered in a broad sense as a theme in U.S.A. social and political history, the bases are to the world what the suburbs [or gated communities where the wealthy reside] are to U.S.A. national social order, a way to govern the majority from the comforts of an idyllic self-contained world wherein the ruling class does not need to see the rest of the population. In other words it is an evolution of an even earlier model of U.S.A. residential and social arrangements which was prevalent during slavery times. In slavery times in the U.S.A. the European masters lived in the large and comfortable house, far removed from the slave quarters and the degradations perpetrated on them, while the Native American and African American slaves lived separately in uncomfortable and crowded conditions. Just as the national system of social and economic segregation and discrimination in the U.S.A. created and continues to foment class dominance of the wealthy over the poor and race dominance of the ruling white [European] descent peoples over the native, Hispanic and African American peoples [as evinced in the Katrina hurricane situation] the foreign bases also promote discrimination and cultural alienation between the U.S.A. troops [who represent the culture of the U.S.A.] and the local populations. Chalmers Johnson expounds on this issue.

> It's [military base] a foreign antibody stuck into a functioning culture that we don't understand, and that our troops are actually almost cultivated to be systematically contemptuous of. There's no way to avoid the racism and arrogance that goes with the way our people are educated and what they do when they come to countries like this.[156]

In this sense the world becomes tacitly a plantation [in the context of the old European exploitation of the Americas and the Caribbean] and the bases are the houses of the foremen [slave drivers] who enforce the dictates of the slave masters and if the slave country disobeys, the slave driver comes out periodically to apply the whip to exact punishment and reassert the submission of the natives. So the world of nations has been transformed into a world plantation, governed by the power elite and controlled by the world bases. It is a world in which the resources are controlled and the people manipulated from a distance but the foreman position of the old slave plantation has been assumed by the military and the masters are its directors in western governments, and the bankers and the world plantation is serviced by transnational corporations like Kellogg, or Brown & Root, which is a subsidiary of Halliburton Company, the corporation associated with the vice-president Dick Cheney. The term "reservation" may also be applicable in that just as Native Americans were corralled as cattle into particular geographical zones, so too the world population has been many times forced into different borders or hemmed into their own land, preventing the exercise of their movements but always restricting their rights to their own natural resources.

Evolution of Western Imperialism

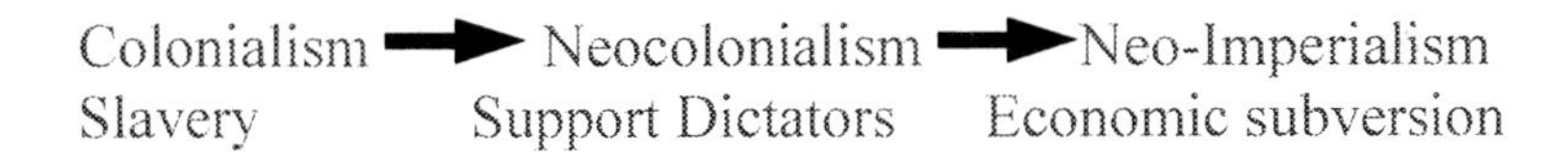

While human beings have remained essentially the same over the last 4,000 years, the old form of empire, such as was developed to a fine tuned machine, by the ancient Romans, 2,000 years ago, but which ultimately failed, gave way to barbarism in the middle ages, colonialism in the European post "Renaissance" and "Age of Enlightenment" periods and neo-imperialism in our times due to technological advances. That renaissance and enlightenment gave rise to countless wars, genocide of indigenous populations and the African slave trade. This demonstrates that while western culture has advanced technologically the people who continue to conduct imperious designs retain their egoism, arrogance, foibles, desires and human flaws.

In our study we have explored the U.S.A. form of empire and the concept of bases but we can perhaps see another way of understanding the usage that goes beyond the original imperial-colonial model. In the model of the earlier empires the colonies served the purpose of extending the colonial powers' culture to other lands but for the modern empire the function of outposts is not to extend the English language and there is no attempt to formally annex territories, etc. Instead, the bases have been made semi-permanent and have been used to effectively control the areas they are located in, essentially to quell protests if the order of things imposed by the U.S.A. government is not accepted, namely the exploitation of those countries by U.S.A. corporations. Thus, the strategy is not to own the world, for owning incurs the difficulty of being a landlord, as in the difficulty posed by the occupation of Iraq. The idea is to control the world. This is an evolution of the economic concept of leverage, not unlike a home mortgage. When a person "purchases" a home by putting say, $20,000 down payment on a $100,000 house, they are using leverage. Leverage is using a small amount to control a larger one and there is no real ownership of the larger amount, just a right to "control" it [that is, as long as the payments are made]. In the case of the U.S.A.'s use of its armed forces, the idea is supposed to be to use the armed forces, which are composed of perhaps a total of 3 million people to control 5.9 billion, the population of the earth.

Where do the people come from who make up the armed forces of the U.S.A.? In any society there are always those people who are fascinated by the military lifestyle and take to it naturally. Others seek to fulfill a genuine desire to serve and protect others. Still others may be in a borderline sociopath or psychotic state or may have preexisting murderous tendencies. It is from this group that individuals may be found who will easily perform tortures, and other atrocities when ordered or will be violent on a regular basis, enjoying making others suffer and feel pain; this kind of personality is not supposed to be allowed to join ordinary police departments because it is prone to acts of police brutality. There are others who may just be seeking a better life and have no other place to turn.

In the year 1973 the U.S.A. armed forces became voluntary instead of conscripted. Since that time many people have joined because they felt their present situation was a dead end so they wanted to seek out better opportunities to see the world and or gain a useful skill or education that could better their lives. So by maintaining a form of economic system that necessarily produces some poor and indigent segments of the population the government can be assured to have a pool of recruits who would "volunteer" for military service, since they have no better options except joining the military or lead a meager or possibly degraded or miserable poor and deprived existence for their whole lives, due to lack of opportunity, discrimination or racism. The case of lack of opportunity was demonstrated in the example of PFC Jessica Lynch. She was wounded at the Iraqi city, Nasiriyah, and when she was asked by a member of the press, *"Why did you join the Army?"* She replied,

> *"I come from Palestine, West Virginia; I couldn't get a job at Wal-Mart"... "I joined the Army to get out of Palestine, West Virginia."*

Her honesty revealed the predicament that many people find themselves in. Having joined the army due to poverty, they are pushed into obediently serving the desires of the government. Thus, by insuring that there will always be an indigent segment of the population, as must occur in the capitalist form of economy, the armed forces personnel will always be replenished.

While it may seem that the invasion of Iraq did not achieve the stated goals of finding weapons of mass destruction which was then changed to "regime change" and or affecting democratic changes in other regional governments, the net effect that is expected geopolitically are least four new bases for the U.S.A. roster. The best expectation of the imperial U.S.A. strategy would be that even if the U.S.A. was forced to withdraw the bulk of U.S.A. troops from Iraq and even if Iraq were to remain in turmoil, that the U.S.A. would retain the bases that are strategically placed along the oil pipelines. In any case the pretexts for going to war such as humanitarian intervention have been revealed as duplicitous because they were given only when it served the strategic goals of the U.S.A. and ignores the U.N. resolutions, which in an ideal world would be the only legitimizing authority for permitting military actions. Humanitarian intervention or the U.S.A. policies of "democracy promotion" programs, as applied by the U.S.A., have therefore been likened to euphemisms for imperialism.

The current foreign policy of securing oil to maintain the U.S.A. ignores the technological reality of oil conservation and alternative forms of propulsion for vehicles. The technology exists today to eliminate the necessity for any oil from the Middle East and yet the strategy of the government remains one of securing oil and perpetuating the oil based economy. In his presidential state of the union address in January 2006 George W. Bush made the statement that *"America is addicted to oil."* What he seemed to be saying was that the political and economic powers that be do not want to move away from an oil based economy because they are addicted to the profits derived from the oil economy. In an interview on the program Democracy Now, journalist Juan Gonzales asked Steve Fretzmaan about the record profits of the oil companies.

> **JUAN GONZALEZ:** Well, your reaction to the report of ExxonMobil's new profit figures?
> **STEVE KRETZMANN:** Well, it's just more of the same from the industry that we've seen over the last few years. I mean, these are record profits that have continued to go up and up. It is shocking, and it's really just sort of the latest evolution in the world's most profitable industry at this point. You have Exxon now becoming the most profitable corporation in the history of the United States. Meanwhile, if you actually are to graph the price of gas for all of us at the pump versus the profits for the oil industry, these are two curves that go up completely parallel. So, what we're seeing is the industry is finding new and ever more inventive ways to pass on costs to the consumers while they are pocketing more and more profits and they are investing, particularly in Exxon's case, less and less in any kind of alternative energy that's actually going to solve the problem of oil dependence in a long run. So, it's a huge problem, and the industry really needs to be taken to task.[157]

The True Wounded of Torture and War

Memo Offered Justification for Use of Torture[158]
Justice Dept. Gave Advice in 2002
By Dana Priest and R. Jeffrey Smith
Washington Post Staff Writers
Tuesday, June 8, 2004; Page A01

In August 2002, the Justice Department advised the White House that torturing al Qaeda terrorists in captivity abroad "may be justified," and that international laws against torture "may be unconstitutional if applied to interrogations" conducted in President Bush's war on terrorism, according to a newly obtained memo.
If a government employee were to torture a suspect in captivity, "he would be doing so in order to prevent further attacks on the United States by the Al Qaeda terrorist network," said the memo, from the Justice Department's office of legal counsel, written in response to a CIA request for legal guidance. It added that arguments centering on "necessity and self-defense could provide justifications that would eliminate any criminal liability" later.

Abu Graib

Many people in the U.S.A. believe that war is a viable alternative to compromising the "National Interests" or "American Interests" which are really a code for "self interests." Compromising the national interests is a code word meaning "way of life." The way of life being discussed here is not anything vital that would endanger the existence of the country. For individuals, the terms "National Interests" or "American Interests" are code words for consumerism and the freedom to pursue pleasure-seeking. These conceptions are extensions of the idea of American entitlement and privilege that the power elite have come to enjoy and expect and to whatever extent the rest of the population has come to enjoy or desire. For corporations the terms mean continued profits and the ability to control markets through American hegemony. However, not all members of the population are free to pursue their desires. Only the power elite are truly free from a financial point of view. However, that freedom is tied to the money and their capacity to maintain or produce it. The power elite of the country has convinced the population either consciously or subconsciously or by coercion, praying on peoples desires, hopes and dreams, that U.S.A. hegemony is a legitimate social policy and that the U.S.A. dominance is to be imposed on any nation that does not comply to U.S.A. standards of civilization. That standard is law and order. But as the great humanitarian, and champion of the poor, dispossessed and downtrodden of society, Dr. Martin Luther King told us, *"Law and order without justice is tyranny."*

So when the U.S.A. acts in contradiction with the basic concepts of its own constitution and topples governments around the world to promote "stability" the peoples of those countries develop resentment and hatred towards their own dictatorship governments or the neocolonial governments set up by the U.S.A. and the U.S.A. itself as well. When the people become unruly and try to rebel against the dictatorial governments put in place by the U.S.A. the government and media pundits in the U.S.A. often apply the strategy of labeling the country as being in danger of being taken over by radicals. The next logical strategy is to advocate the use of U.S.A. troops to go in and reestablish "order." Of course the U.S.A. armed forces do not stay in the country but leave behind a dictatorship with a reconstituted military that is trained by the U.S.A. military[159] and led by personalities beholding to and loyal to the U.S.A. and who are willing to sell the resources of the country to the U.S.A. companies at bargain prices. If a nation were to naturally try to create a government for themselves that was beneficial to the people and that would charge the market prices for the commodities desired by the U.S.A. that would be financially detrimental to the U.S.A. companies so the strategy of destabilization would be used. By financing thugs and murderers a small country could be and has been easily destabilized. An example of this form of tactic was the situation that ensued in Ghana after the Ghana people achieved independence from European colonial rule.

In any such disruptions and impositions of dictatorial rule there are many casualties of the conflict including civilians. Many reports have surfaced of torture techniques used by the dictators and it was discovered that they learned those techniques from the U.S.A. military training. The manuals used by the military to teach torture [even though torture is against the U.S.A. military code and the Geneva conventions] were developed by the C.I.A.[160] The same torture techniques have been used on prisoners from the Iraq and Afghanistan wars, against stated U.S.A. law and international law. Yet the president and his advisors as well as senior military officials who oversee the torture and perpetrate it were not being held accountable for those actions.

Many people think that the perpetration of acts of torture only hurt the person being tortured [victims of torture]. On the contrary, the torturer becomes dehumanized as he or she perpetrates the dehumanizing acts or depraved acts, even if they are not sadists who enjoy hurting others, and even if they do it because they are supposedly following orders or doing it to "serve their country." Torture is like a two edged sword that hurts the victim but also hurts the victimizer as well. This is especially true for supposedly developed societies that send their people to commit heinous acts of brutality and sexual depravity even if it is in the name of protecting their "freedom, "way of life" or "national interests." Often the persons overseeing such acts have sociopath or sadistic tendencies which are aberrations from the norm of psychological balance in human civilized culture. Yet ordinary "normal" people often get caught up as lower level soldiers in situations where they are ordered to participate in dehumanizing acts of aggression or sexual abuse. An unjustified war in itself is a form of torture by one country over another and the remorse from the acts of shooting or bombing or abusing another population also cause mental trauma in the perpetrator, even if the perpetrators are under orders. Even if the war is justified [one country was attacked by another and is defending itself from the other] the act of killing or harming others leaves deep impressions of pain, sorrow and regret in the normal minds of those who partake in the actions.

In all wars, especially those of the 20th century, even on those conflicts wherein the methods of killing have been developed so that a person can be killed from far away and without notice, the stress of war has increased. The Vietnam War produced an unprecedented number of post-traumatic-stress-disorder [PTSD] suffering veterans. The war in Iraq has apparently produced even more stress, given that the soldiers have had to perpetrate acts of abuse and have been subjected to nonstop danger of loss of life, unlike in other wars where they could take extended breaks from the front. That situation led to increasing acts of violence in late 2005 and early 2006 including the indiscriminate killing of non-combatants [including women and children] by the U.S.A. military forces that were similar to the Milai Massacre in the Vietnam war where the soldiers succumbed to the stress of the situation and purposely set out to kill all the people in a Vietnamese village.

> **Study: One in Three Iraq Vets Seek Mental Health Treatment**
> Meanwhile, the Washington Post is reporting an Army study has found that more than one in three US troops who served in Iraq later sought help for mental health problems. According to the report, soldiers and Marines returning from Iraq reported more distress than those returning from Afghanistan and other countries. More than half of all service members returning from Iraq reported that they had "felt in great danger of being killed" there, and over 2,400 reported having suicidal thoughts. Steve Robinson, head of the National Gulf War Resource Center, said: "In Vietnam, there were safe areas where people could go to rest and recuperate. That doesn't happen in Iraq; every place is a war zone."
>
> **-Democracynow.org Headlines for March 1, 2006**

In an interview with journalist Amy Goodman a Veterans Administration nurse who wrote a critical letter about the George W. Bush administration regarding the errors of the Iraq war and the mishandling of the disaster caused by hurricane Katrina explained how the hospitals were seeing increased numbers of World War II veterans who were having relapses of PTSD due to what they were seeing in Iraq war coverage in the news.[161]

> **LAURA BERG:** I wrote this letter. I think, you know, I have -- all of us at the V.A., there's very many compassionate people working there, very many dedicated people. And we've worked with, you know, veterans from Vietnam, veterans from Korea, veterans from World War II. We were seeing more and more World War II veterans, you know, triggered for the first time by Iraq and actually, you know, having memories and nightmares coming out.
> **AMY GOODMAN:** You are saying now that they are triggered?
> **LAURA BERG:** Oh, absolutely. Absolutely.
> **AMY GOODMAN:** So, World War II vets are coming in.
> **LAURA BERG:** Oh, absolutely. Absolutely, so we are seeing --
> **AMY GOODMAN:** What are the complaints?
> **LAURA BERG:** Just nightmares, not able to sleep. More tension, anxiety, irritability, aggressiveness. Some detachment, you know, from reality at the present time. Those kind of things.

So, even veterans of previous wars are affected by current wars and those effects can ripple through a society, as the problems of those veterans become a burden on their families and communities, degrading the mental health of the country as a whole. When laws are broken by one group of people, hurting another, the group perpetrating the injustice suffers culturally because once the human trust has been broken against one people it has been legitimized against all people. That same injustice and violence turns inward as the perpetrating population becomes more violent, criminal and unethical to itself. So when the people of Arabia, Europe, and the American Colonies decided to enslave native populations and Africans and enforce upon them extremely degraded conditions of life, such as mutilations, rape, forced labor, etc. it meant that the perpetrators were also lowering their own humanity and that low psychological state prevents the culture from acquiring mental peace or pursuing deep philosophical or spiritual inquiry. It also means that the perpetrator culture will be unable to develop the wisdom to reverse its self-destructive course. Thus, the humanity of the perpetrator of cruelty or injustice to others is also reduced, and that manifests as a culture that becomes paranoid, and fearful of retribution from those whom they wronged or fearful of punishment from God. Consequently, the perpetrator culture experiences guilt but that guilt is often subconscious or suppressed through entertainments, drugs or lashing out against the victims, or denial and suppression of the memories and guilt or complicity, claiming that the wrongdoings of the past have no bearing on the present, etc.

Due to their debased culture, the perpetrator culture also descends to fundamentalism in religion, nationalism in culture, dictatorship in politics, rampant materialism and consumerism in economics, ambivalence in the sciences (not caring about the ethics of the new creations or inventions), etc. That degraded culture self-destructs through causing disease in humanity and in the ecology because the denial and suppression of the guilt and or pain prevents them from facing the reality of their transgressions of the past or continuing ones, which are justified by the supposed right to crass consumerism and pleasure-seeking that are supported by the superiority complexes and cultural arrogance. Fixing a problem requires facing up to the responsibility of having caused the problem. However if a person does not face their own complicity they cannot assume their capacity and power to fix the problem. Otherwise, a person who wants to continue enjoying some pleasure from ill-gotten gains may not want to face the truth because that would mean that they must face up to loosing the pleasures they desire.

Another negative outcome might be that the culture may sacrifice some of its members so that the rest may survive and prosper. This is in many ways the noble cause that is ascribed to members of the military, that they are nobly sacrificing their lives for the rest of the population. The idea of the nobility of the soldier has been used as a sentimental way of consoling and explaining why (they sacrificed) to the families and survivors for their loss and a means used by survivors to justify their loss, but what does it mean for the dead or those who returned maimed or psychologically damaged for life? Perhaps they sacrificed their lives to pay for some sin of a previous lifetime. Nevertheless, as far as the here and now and future are concerned, since most or all of the wars fought by the U.S.A. since World War II and even previously, have been wars of choice and wars of conquest, that noble cause of the armed forces has, in most cases, been adulterated and made to serve the designs of the profiteers and was not the noble cause of sacrifice in the sense of laying down their lives for the caring of other human beings; therefore what can be expected for wars of the future if the same culture and policies continue to drive the economy and politics of the present?

The very idea of sacrificing for others implies a choice and how can those people, who joined because they had no other better prospects in life, choose freely? How can it be said that they made a noble sacrifice if they joined to gain a skill and make something of their lives but were caught in the military when a war happened to be ordered? How can it be said that a person who is a sadist or a psychopath, who enjoys killing, joined the military and died, sacrificing him/her self for others? How can we say that a person who joined the military because they were shamed by their family or the culture into joining instead of fleeing the country as they wanted to, died sacrificing themselves? These statements are not meant to take away from the nobility of a non-sadist person in the military who dies. The desecration of that death came from the politicians who sent them to die not for protecting the other weaker members of the nation but for some commodity like oil or cheap goods, to insure the perpetuation of a particular lifestyle.

Finally, the members of the perpetrator culture often participate in the same type of degraded behaviors they perpetrated on the others. Ex. forcing others to commit sexual acts is a manifestation of the desire of the perpetrator to commit those acts or the fear of committing those acts. Saying they were ordered to commit certain acts facilitates their relaxing whatever inhibitions they had. Seeing those acts and obsessing over those acts can lead that perpetrator to desire and experience those acts as well. The guilt, shame and fear of retribution over those acts can lead that personality to turn towards fundamentalism in an effort to demarcate the blurred lines of ethics or morality that have been crossed physically or mentally. So the perpetrator society becomes more violent and debauched within itself due to the participation in violence and debauchery, reinforced by leaders of the society. Professor Alfred McCoy spoke about some of the dangers of using psychological and physical torture.

> Now, one of the problems beyond the details of these orders is torture is an extraordinarily dangerous thing. There's an absolute ban on torture for a very good reason. Torture taps into the deepest recesses, unexplored recesses of human consciousness, where creation and destruction coexist, where the infinite human capacity for kindness and infinite human capacity for cruelty coexist, and it has a powerful perverse appeal, and once it starts, both the perpetrators and the powerful who order them, let it spread, and it spreads out of control.
> So, I think when the Bush administration gave those orders for, basically, techniques tantamount to torture at the start of the war on terror, I think it was probably their intention that these be limited to top al-Qaeda suspects, but within months, we were torturing hundreds of Afghanis at Bagram near Kabul, and a few months later in 2003, through these techniques, we were torturing literally thousands of Iraqis.[162]

Since it has been recognized widely by police forces and virtually all other intelligence agencies from the U.S.A. and other countries that psychological and physical torture does not yield useful "actionable" intelligence and that there are better ways to get the information, like gaining the confidence of the individual being questioned, it might be concluded that the purpose of perpetrating the torture and wanton acts of war aggressions is not extracting information to use against other armies but for the purpose of establishing dominance over the other culture through fear and intimidation as in the use of rape, flogging, mutilation, or lynching during the slavery and Jim Crow era of U.S.A. history or like the practice in many species of the animal kingdom where the top male seeks to establish dominance over the younger or weaker males and females. This base and animalistic form of culture leads to hatred and resentment which will lead to acts of "terrorism" [victimized culture strikes back in revenge] but also, just as the Alpha male will one day become tired and weak, so to a degraded culture becomes tired and weak and falls prey to outside forces and self-destruction. When heinous crimes are authorized by society they do not remain confined to the victims but the deep seeded guilt and capacity [capacity is created when inhibitions are reduced due to commission of the acts and creation of a precedent] to perpetrate those acts on anyone else, unleashes the same negative forces on them [those in the perpetrator culture itself]; Hence, the increased incidence of emergence of serial killers in the society.

> A **serial killer** is someone who commits three or more murders over an extended period of time with cooling-off periods in between. A **mass murderer**, on the other hand, is an individual who kills three or more people in a single event and in one location. A **spree killer** commits multiple murders in different locations over a period of time that may vary from a few hours to several days. Unlike serial killers, however, they do not revert to their normal behavior in between slayings. [163]

Given the definitions above, it is possible to see how a seemingly "normal" person, when thrust into a situation of torture, could become a serial, mass murderer or spree killer. Those personalities that are borderline psychotic, sociopath or who were traumatized in their childhood would be more easily coerced into sadistic and cruel behaviors. Again, as we might expect, the incidence of serial killing occurs most often in western countries, which also happen to lie in the temperate geographical zones of the world.

> In terms of reported cases, there appear to be far more serial killers active in developed Western nations than elsewhere. [164]

However, we must realize that an army that makes war for "illegitimate" reasons is perpetrating acts of mass serial-spree killing. In the case of the U.S.A., the internal maladies of crime,[11] sexual depravity and violence against women and children,[12] religious fundamentalism and growing intolerance, continuing and growing racial injustice and discrimination, gender bias, etc. as well as over-consumption, destruction of the environment all lead to the collapse of society.

Sexual depravity and the proliferation of pornography as well as the high number of sex crimes in the U.S.A. are some of the social-cultural aspects of western culture that alarm many in the Arab countries who follow Islam and see the U.S.A. culture as degraded. Since the U.S.A. is regarded primarily as a "Christian country" or at least seems to be controlled by Christians, Christianity is another source of fear especially to those in the Muslim countries or who practice Islam elsewhere around the world. They feel threatened by it and their anxiety causes them to seek to shield themselves from it. Often that is perceived as anti-Americanism, or fundamentalism. Most people in the U.S.A are unaware of how overwhelming the U.S.A. culture can be as it is disseminated through mass media, fueled by corporate interests that want to change foreign cultures in order to make them suitable for selling U.S.A. goods or so that U.S.A. corporations can make money in them selling goods from elsewhere. Domestically, many if not most of the Christian population also feel that the culture's standards of morality have lowered. The religious right has been most agitated by the perceived sexual permissiveness and promiscuity of U.S.A. society and has sought to politically affect the culture. The sexual atrocities and humiliations perpetrated by the U.S.A. domestic prisons and in Iraq,

---

[11] [and having the greatest population imprisoned in the world]

[12] [400,000 children a year are molested and 1 of every 4 women are raped or molested in their lifetime in the U.S.A.]

Afghanistan and other places is actually part of an endemic problem apparently accepted or tolerated by the leadership of the political, legal and military systems of the country. On September 4, 1995, two marines and a sailor from Camp Hansen in central Okinawa abducted, beat, and raped a twelve-year-old girl. The former C.I.A. advisor, professor and author Chalmers Johnson presented researches which demonstrated that sexual attacks by U.S.A. military occur regularly and are widespread.

> The reaction to the rape of 1995 from, for example, General Richard Meyers, who's today chairman of the Joint Chiefs of Staff -- he was then head of U.S. forces in Japan -- was that these were just three bad apples, a tragic incident, unbelievably exceptional. On research, you discover that the rate of sexually violent crimes committed by our troops in Okinawa leading to court martial is two per month! This was not an exceptional incident, expect for the fact that the child was so young and differing from many Okinawa women who would not come forward after being raped, that she was not fully socialized and she wanted to get even.
> … the record of environmental damage, sexual crimes, bar brawls, drunken driving, one thing after another, these all occur in the 725 bases (the Department of Defense -acknowledged number; and the [real] number is actually considerably larger than that) but 725 bases that we have in other people's countries.[165]

Along with sexual attacks, there is widespread usage of prostitution that is also pervasive wherever the U.S.A. bases are located. This denotes a significant preoccupation with sexuality on the part of the U.S.A. military personnel. In some areas of the south east there has developed a special trade of prostitution based on women who have been imported from lesser economically developed areas who were seeking a better life but who were lured there under false pretenses and were forced to turn to prostitution in order to survive. Part of the strategy used by the U.S.A. leadership to cope with the issue of attacks on women around the world is to insulate bases so that the soldiers have all they need on the base and do not need to meet the local population. Since the U.S.A. is developing negative sentiment around the world many U.S.A. citizens are traveling less to many places so the image that people see most of the U.S.A. is the uniformed soldier or sailor; a militarist image of aggressive potential killers or rapists. That isolation leads to further alienation and fear that often degrades to denigration by the U.S.A. soldiers directed at natives and fear by the local population, all of which leads to conflict and misunderstanding and finally mutual hatred.

Religion and the Superpower Culture Part 1: The Henotheism Period, The Counter-Reversion Era the Assurance Age and the Formation of Western Religion

Henotheism Period

During the sixth century B.C.E. there was a special age in human history, which some authors have termed "Axial age" due to its role in history that may be likened to an axis upon which many events turned. However, that period may be better described as a religious "*Counter-Reversion Era.*" The name Counter-Reversion Era was chosen because it describes a time when the religious philosophy of the past [time before that era] was in decline due to the emergence of barbarism and certain religious movements emerged to counter that decline and revert back to the original *perennial philosophy*[166] of religion. During that time, there were several wars of conquest in which several nations in the Middle East developed into conquering forces. Some examples include the Persians and the Assyrians. That period marked a time when the power of Ancient Egypt, which had previously controlled the land areas from present day Sudan to India, at one time in the past, reached its lowest state. Ancient Egypt was under constant siege during that period. However, Egypt did not experience a religious *Counter-Reversion Era*. The Ancient Egyptian religion was a purveyor of the perennial philosophy, the religious tradition of henotheism and panentheism that continued to be practiced openly until the 5th century A.C.E. [1,000 years later] when the Roman Orthodox Christians closed the last Egyptian temples by force.[167] Ancient Egypt had been the beacon of learning and science as well as spiritual wisdom. This is why the ancient pre-Judaic, pre-Christian and pre-Islamic religions had many areas of compatibility with Ancient Egyptian religion and some even included Ancient Egyptian gods and goddesses in their pantheon of divinities. The time prior to the *Counter-Reversion Era* was marked by the practice of henotheism {In philosophy and religion, is a term coined by Max Müller, which means devotion to a single god while accepting the existence of other gods.} and in a more developed format, pantheism {a doctrine identifying the Deity with the universe and its phenomena. Belief in and worship of all gods and goddesses as manifestations of the Supreme Being} and panentheism {the creator is Creation and transcends Creation}.

The Counter-Reversion Era

The *Counter-Reversion Era* covers a period circa the 6th century B.C.E. The philosophies that emerged at that time, such as Pythagoreanism, Buddhism, Jainism, Taoism, and Confucianism had common aspects that hearkened back to and admonished the need to return to a philosophy of mystical spirituality, community service and ethics, such as was taught by the Ancient Egyptians for several thousands of years. Those philosophies, except in Greece, developed in a personalized form, with a personal leader in he form of a realized and or ascended master at its center, as opposed to the priestly format of Ancient Egypt. In other words, the degradation of humanity in the Middle East, due to strife, caused a desire for spirituality that was more personality based instead of mystically based. Ancient Egyptian religion was originally personality based [Ex. God Ra, Osiris or Isis]; however, those personalities did not interfere with the capacity for the practitioners to attain high religious development since the systems introduced by those personalities were based on mystical philosophy with henotheistic components. Therefore, even though the religions that came in during the *Counter-Reversion Era* had specific founding teachers [personalities upon which the religions were based: *Pythagoras, Buddha, Mahavira, Lao-Tzu, Confucius*], whose philosophies pointed to mysticism and the perennial philosophy that has existed before and led people to turn away from violence and towards cooperative peaceful coexistence and a personal quest for enlightenment by discovering the nature of self which transcends the phenomenal and which is essentially a part of the immortal, transcendental Divine, concepts that predated the inception of the new religions and philosophies.

Judaism was practiced in ancient times to the extent that the Torah [the main original Jewish religious texts] is believed by scholars to have been read publicly since the time of Ezra (c. 450 B.C.E. –after the *Counter-Reversion Era*).[168] However, at that time, Judaism did not have the Rabbinical Jewish principles of absolute monotheism as we may understand its practice today which rejects all gods and recognizes only one. At this time Judaism accepted the henotheistic concept which means devotion to a single god while accepting the existence of other gods. However, after the Babylonian conquest of Jerusalem, the Jews (people of Judah, part of the land ruled by the kings Saul, David, Solomon and their descendants)[169] scattered to Egypt and to Babylonia. It seems also contradictory that the Jews who practice the Passover ritual and who commemorate being freed from captivity in Egypt should seek refuge in that same country. Nevertheless, the Egyptian Jews continued to practice the earlier form of Judaism but the Babylonian Jews started to innovate the philosophical tenets of Judaism as a reaction to the debacle caused by the Babylonian destruction of Jerusalem and the Jewish Temple in 586 B.C.E.[170] It is possible that the Babylonian Jews could have come into contact with practitioners of the Zoroastrian tradition at this time. The Babylonian exile period began to set in motion changes in Jewish religion that came to fruition in the next pivotal period of religion in the Middle East that was to have far reaching effects on Christianity and the rest of Western culture in the first and second millenniums A.C.E.

The Coming of the Assurance Age

> "What is now called the Christian religion has existed among the Ancients and was not absent from the beginning of the human race until Christ came in the flesh from which time the true religion which was already in existence began to be called Christian."
>
> St. Augustine (354-430 A.C.E.)

The statement by St. Augustine reveals the admission by early Christian officials that Christianity was nothing new in the sense of its original tenets. Teachings such as the Satan and the apocalyptic notions seem to have come from Zoroastrian influences but the concepts of the resurrection, the Eucharist, the cross symbol, the 14 Stations of the Cross, the concept of the good shepherd, and many others, came directly from Ancient Egyptian religion. This demonstrates the tactic of cooptation through which the Christian officials worked actively to stop the practice of other religions by adopting their traditions and rituals while renaming them as Christian, a process known as co-optation. What did change was the move in Judaism and Christianity towards orthodoxy and faith-based religious practice, supported by literalism, historicity and militarism.

During the early part of the 1st millennium A.C.E., 500 to 700 years after the Counter-Reversion Era, during the period of 70 A.C.E. to 300 A.C.E., a new age emerged that was characterized by the need for certainty or assurance in spiritual practice. This period was marked by wars and national violence and tyranny imposed by the Romans on most other groups at the time, thus forcing upon them harsh conditions and fomenting the creation of religious zealots.[171] The Jewish people lived in Egypt and Palestine and were all under the domination of the Roman Empire, especially after the destruction of the Jewish Temple in c. 70 A.C.E. At that time there were four main sects of Judaism. These comprised what is referred to as the "Jewish People" or followers of the Jewish religion who were, culturally and ethnically speaking, Hebrews. The sects were: *Pharisees, Sadducees, Essenes* and the *Zealots* and were known to have individuals who claimed to be Messiahs who were fighters and preachers that led revolts against the Romans and were revered as liberators —many years before the Jesus, of Christian religion, was supposed to have existed. Each of these groups affected the development of the Jewish scriptures until the time when the Canonization of the Hebrew Bible was essentially complete in c. 90-150 A.C.E.[172]

In this period the search for certainty meant a move away from the uncertainty of mysticism and mystical philosophy to the certainty and simplicity of faith and belief. Religion changed from a discipline dedicated to promoting experience of the divine to a dogma system of believing in or having faith in a particular form of Divine. In essence the religious practice became synonymous with faith in belief itself. This was the beginning of the *Assurance Age* which still continues in those parts of the world affected by the religions that developed in the Middle East that are today known as Zoroastrianism, Judaism, Christianity and Islam.

Zoroastrianism also developed during the same period (6th century B.C.E.) but its tenets were somewhat different than the other religions of the *Counter-Reversion Era* previously mentioned. Zoroastrianism was a departure from henotheism and is often touted as the first monotheistic religion, though it contained within it a dualistic format with divinities of good and evil and the expectation of a great final battle at the end of time, which is a henotheistic format. The concept of the dual opposing forces can be found, for example in the Heru-Set concept of Ancient Egypt and the Yin-Yang of Chinese Taoism. Yet, the preeminence of the Supreme Being, situated as an exclusive and special divinity in Zoroastrianism was a departure from the pantheistic model which would see the Zoroastrian supreme being as a manifestation with equal value as the supreme being in say, Judaism.

The history of religions and cultures besides Ancient Egypt in the period prior to the 6th century B.C.E. is recognized generally by historians as uncertain, though it is known that previously mentioned religions [Judaism, Christianity] had no notions of divinities of evil such that could be equated with or regarded as a "devil". However, religious scholarship has demonstrated that Judaism was not orthodox in the sense of following the particular dogma of monotheism as we know it today. At its inception and up to the rabbinic period, Judaism practiced henotheism. When the earlier Jewish conceptions are examined more closely they reveal a closer affinity to the Ancient Egyptian model that follows the traditional African model of a Supreme Being that is transcendental and with lesser beings that operate effectively in Creation [henotheism]. In fact, the Jews that moved back to Egypt believed that their main god, Jehova [Hebrew: *YHWH*] as *"Yahou who is in Elephantine"*[13]

The early Jewish [non-rabbinic] concept describes the Creation in terms of an act of sexual union. *Elohim* (Ancient Hebrew for gods/goddesses) impregnates the primeval waters with *ruach,* a Hebrew word which means *spirit*, *wind* or the verb *to hover*. The same word means *to brood* in Syriac. Elohim, also called El, was a name used for God in some Hebrew scriptures.[173] Therefore, the original Jewish concept incorporates gods and goddesses within the understanding of a central source divinity in accordance with the previous models of religion and their form of the "theological religious framework" or "God Framework" that was used to determine the religious dogma and relationship between God or Spirit and Human beings.

When the Jewish temple was destroyed in 70 A.C.E. by the Romans, the Jews were scattered and apparently had contact with practitioners of Zoroastrianism and there ensued a new movement in Jewish religion called "Rabbinic Judaism." This period also marked the first Christian writings [Gospels and Letters of Paul 70 A.C.E.-100 A.C.E.] as Christianity developed into a sect of Judaism. Both Judaism and Christianity followed the teachings contained in the Jewish Torah. The term Torah, means "to teach" in Hebrew, and is strictly the first five books of the Old Testament, which are *Genesis, Exodus, Leviticus, Numbers*, and *Deuteronomy* containing laws and customs of Judaism. They are sometimes referred to as the Jewish Bible or the Pentateuch. Moses is generally claimed as the author,

[13] *Jewish Life in Ancient Egypt* by Edward Bleiberg. *Elephantine* is the city in Upper (southern) Egypt today known as "Aswan". The Ancient city was the residence of the ancient Egyptian god *Khnum*, the Creator. *Egyptian Mysteries Vol. 2: The Gods and Goddesses of the Ancient Egyptians* by Muata Ashby

having received inspiration from God on Mt Sinai.[174] There were different sects of Christianity including the Gnostics and the Orthodox.

During the period of Rabbinic Judaism the rabbis were seeking to reinterpret Jewish practices and concepts as the people were in exile and at a time when the Temple was not in existence and there was no anchor for Jewish practice.[175] Prior to the development of the Rabbinic Judaism form of Judaism, Jewish practice included a henotheistic view of Divinity. The same was true in Gnostic Christianity. However, with the development of Rabbinic Judaism there developed the concept of exclusive monotheism that was different from the henotheistic form of monotheism. The Rabbinical movement held that there is only one main God as opposed to the previous view that there was one main god among other lesser gods, which was included in the Ancient Egyptian religions, African religions, Greek religions and Indian religions. Besides the Jewish Torah text the Talmud was developed. The Talmud is a collection of rabbinical writings that were interpretations of the Torah to explain the Torah scriptures and how to apply the Torah teachings. Scholars assign the date of creation of the Talmud as being written between the years of the second and fifth centuries A.C.E. However, Orthodox Jews assign it to an earlier date through oral tradition and thus believe it was revealed to Moses at the same time as the Torah but was preserved orally until the time it was codified by being written down. So the Talmud is regarded as an "Oral Torah," and the Torah or Tanakh is referred to as the "Written Torah."[176]

When Christianity separated from Judaism, now believing in the Old Testament {Jewish Torah} but also the Christian writings, that were later compiled into a “New Testament” and when orthodox Christianity was adopted by the Roman emperors, the form of Christianity that tended towards the universal law or application [catholic] and strict monotheism, as well as male superiority, came into power. Thus, Rabbinic Judaism and Roman Catholic Christianity developed their philosophy by adopting certain Zoroastrian principles which they did not have previously. Rabbinic Judaism also developed a universalistic perspective (that the Torah contained universal truths). Here universalism comes to signify that these truths are universal in the sense that they are real and correct and applicable to all, while other teachings may be speculations but are certainly less than universal and therefore limited and thus not correct. Rabbinic Judaism came into existence after the destruction of the second Jewish Temple in Jerusalem in 70 A.C.E. but had its main development period from the second to sixth centuries A.C.E. By the time of the sixth century Rabbinic Judaism had become established as the normative [dominant- standard] form of Judaism.

Some examples of tenets adopted by Judaism from Zoroastrianism include:

- a tangible, active force for evil (Angra Mainyu, whose attributes were assumed by the later Jewish Satan);
- concept of a final judgment of souls after death;
- and concept of the afterlives in heaven or hell.

Scholars believe that it was possible that the Jews heard those teachings during the period at the end of the Babylonian Exile, under the Persian emperor Cyrus.[177] Prior to the period referred to as the Babylonian captivity (586-538 B.C.E.), Jewish philosophy held that Satan was an agent of God and that he tested man's loyalty to God. Sometime after *Cyrus the Great* permitted the Jews to return to Jerusalem Satan became the personification of evil, a personality wherein evil originated. Therefore, in this new view, evil was not in human beings but outside of them; not inherent or potential, say do to ignorance, error or volition; it was an effect of association with Satan and therefore, anything Satanic must be evil and avoided if not destroyed. Thus, anything in contradiction to the teaching is Satanic and therefore to be repudiated and if possible eradicated. The danger of this kind of philosophy should be noted. Anything that the leaders did not like or that contradicted them could be deemed satanic and therefore evil. Consider the examples of the Spanish inquisition and the Salem Witch trials. This kind of philosophy facilitates closed mindedness and fundamentalist repudiation of anything new or different. Thus, Satan became lord of evil and God's rival.

According to Nesta Ramazani, "Islamic institutions such as *waqf* (religious endowments) and *madreseh* (a theological school attached to a mosque) have their roots in Zoroastrian traditions".[178] However, the concept of Angra Mainyu is not exactly the same as Satan because Angra Mainyu {evil} with Spenta Mainyu {good} were two aspects that came together to complement each other into a whole within Ahura Mazda, the Supreme Being. In Christianity, Satan is a lesser being but may be seen as complementary to Jesus in the philosophical understanding as complementary opposites. However, present Jewish and Christian practice would see Satan as an abomination and completely separate from God and not as an agent of God even though he served a purpose in tempting Jesus [in the Christian gospel accounts] and thus testing his resolve. Yet the attributes from Zoroastrianism were adopted for the Satan character. The dualistic battle of good versus evil in the New Testament was adopted from Zoroastrianism and figures prominently in the Book of Revelation and in Apocalyptic literature.

The henotheistic religions of the pre-Assurance Age were associated with mysticism, pantheism and panentheism. A mystical religion does not require belief in a dogma above practices that promote virtue. Rather, an experience-based religion [mysteries, pantheistic, panentheistic] initially requires faith in the practice of the disciplines that promote purity of body and virtue [purity of heart]. The mystical practitioner should believe in the philosophy of the spiritual practice and develop an understanding of the nature of the divine and when the actual experience of communion and unity with the divine occurs, the belief turns into experience and the faith was fulfilled. Thus, the faith is not perpetual or an end in itself in the mystical religion. It has a purpose that is to be achieved while alive and not just after death. Having experienced the Divine there is no need for faith since the practitioner can rely on memory and experience. The mystical practitioner can believe in him or her self as the source of divinity and can also recognize that same divinity in nature and transcending Creation but in mysticism practice the practitioner learns to transcend the idea of self as ego, to expand beyond the limited concept of self as a finite personality. The mystic would learn that he/she is part of the vast and unfathomable essence of the universe which is *unnamable and un-definable and un-*

circumscribable. The mystic learns that gods and goddesses are metaphors to explain the nature of divinity, so male and female divinities express the duality of existence that is resolved in the unity of human and divine: the individual soul and universal spirit. In mysticism God can be approached as a personality but is not a considered as a particular personality or as confined to a particular form but rather the very essence of all that is perceived and that which transcends what is perceived. In mystical religion God is understood as the essence of all, including the human soul. Therefore, every soul is one with God essentially. Humans have forgotten that essential nature. The discipline of mysticism is to rediscover that essential nature. Therefore, even the notion of a Supreme Being and lesser gods and goddesses is to be transcended in the mystical practice. This concept within the Ancient Egyptian Mysteries {*Shetaut Neter*} was called *Sema* in Ancient Egypt and *Yoga* in post Aryan India. The mystic learns that he/she is not limited except through ignorance of their true nature. In fact they discover that they are one with the universe and with the transcendental self, one with God and transcending even the concept of God.

So due to all those intricate and multifaceted mystical concepts *transcendental divinity, being one with God, indefinable, inexact, etc.* would be perceived by the dogmatic, faith-based-assurance seeking religions of the first and second centuries A.C.E. [Judaism and Christianity], as difficult, indeterminate, or ambiguous and therefore inexact and incorrect and thus wrong.

Mystical philosophy requires some degree of reflective intellectual capacity. The strife of the time left less time for philosophizing about the nature of self and the universe; therefore, a more simplified format of religion was needed. Such a religion would be more easily adopted by the masses and would offer more of a feeling of certainty or assurance to its believers to meet their more immediate needs, like salvation from the Romans. For example, the Gnostic concept of Christ consciousness as found in the Gnostic Gospel of Thomas [not included in the canonical Christian bible] would mean that any individual can attain that state of spiritual elevation. This would also mean that all are potentially daughters and sons of God and not just Jesus. Furthermore, all can be one with God. But that attainment requires philosophical inquiry into the nature of self. In the faith-based religion there is no admittance of a human being to a beatific state of consciousness and that idea would be seen as blasphemy. In the dogmatic Christian religion there is only one Christ and only he has Christ consciousness and salvation after death comes from believing in him. The best that a believer can hope for is being resurrected to live with god in heaven. So in the mysticism-based religious practice there is need for ethical purity as well as philosophy and spiritual research to discover the mysteries of life for oneself; all of that requires time and self-effort spent in working on oneself to transform oneself. In the faith-based religion there is no need for research since all answers are known and recorded in the book [bible] and all that is necessary is to believe in the book. Here there is no time needed beyond attendance at regular worship meetings to reaffirm the faith basis of the religion. That attendance in itself is evidence of keeping faith and therefore the goal of the religion was achieved.

In a religion based on faith, that faith requires and demands belief first and foremost. It cannot tolerate disbelief because without belief there is no religion being practiced. The required belief is conviction in the dogma of the existence of a concrete Creator God who created physical human beings, a concrete universe and who exists as a separate entity somewhere in the universe and is watching constantly the individual human beings who have limited personalities and have no direct connection to God or to nature but who will be taken physically to heaven to exist with God for eternity if they follow his laws and have faith in him.

Since the culture that it emerged from was caught in a struggle for survival, in fear of being put to death, and finding itself readying itself often for war and zealous confrontation against the powers that were in existence at the time, threatening it, the people and the faith-based religion's very survival, the culture became closely associated with fear for survival and therefore, that fear could also be transferred to fear of God. This means that the faith itself was under constant challenge. The Christian response to the Romans or to disbelievers was not through philosophy but through simple dogmas about the faith. The simplest and most important dogma is the dogma of having faith in God or Jesus so as to be resurrected when Jesus comes back. Therefore, the faith was the focus of interest, not the substance of the faith in and of itself.

This kind of religious practice is closely focused on the personality of God and not the essential nature and commonality of the human essence with God's essence. Therefore, the faith-based practice is heavily focused on the actions of God in terms of human understanding of human activities. Thus, just as humans can seek revenge or retribution on other people or punish their children, so too God is seen as ready to punish people if they deviate from a prescribed path that god has supposedly laid out.

How could the Jewish path be the correct path to salvation if there are other religions with different paths and those people are also seeking salvation? The answer would be that the Jewish path must be the only path and all others are false paths. Practitioners of the faith-based religion are concerned more with God's power and capacity for retribution instead of his power for compassion and love. These forms of religion, having adopted the idea of universalism [teaching applies to all] developed the tradition, especially in Christianity, of requiring the conversion of those who are unbelievers in order to sure up the faith [make certain] that is make the religion universal and therefore absolute.

Since there can be only one absolute, that necessarily means that all other religions are false because unlike the faith based religion which is supposedly historical and literal, the other religions are mythic and therefore metaphorical and not literal or historical, which renders them untrue in a phenomenal sense. So the ideal in a faith-based religion is faith in a historical certainty since reality and history must coexist. Therefore, the religion of certainty must also be historical as well as literal since the writings cannot be historical and accurate without being literally true. Conversely, they cannot be literally true without also being historical as well as literal. Thus, all histories that contradict that literal and historical view of religion are false or heretical.

Since those who believe in heresies or who do not come to the "true religion" are going to hell, they may be considered as less than human. This means also that faith or belief without application can be accepted as religious practice. In other words one can say one believes in the Christian faith and be considered "Christian" but that does not require one to act in accordance with any ethical or moral regulation since faith in itself is the religion. This feature of dogmatic [doctrinaire, authoritarian, rigid] religions is evinced in the Christian Church emphasis on expressions of faith but not of virtue and the Jewish Temple's emphasis on ritual and tradition as opposed to virtue. This would mean that even if a person were to act like Jesus or in a manner that is prescribed by the Old Testament or the Koran but the person is not a believer in Judaism, Christianity or Islam that person would be considered as a non-believer by the Jews, Christians or Muslims. For example, Mahatma Gandhi, a follower of Hinduism and a person who upheld the same ethical principles as Jesus would not be considered a Christian and therefore would be going to hell because "he did not believe."

The emphasis of the faith-based religion on faith as a criterion for determining who is a follower of the religion is evinced in the manner in which "sinners" are treated by the religion. A person who claims to be a believer who has attempted and failed in upholding the regulations of the religion is still accepted as a member of the religion. For example, a person who commits adultery has failed in upholding the commandment against adultery but has not been thrown out of the church. Thus, there is a clear implication that faith is more important than virtue. The contradiction in this arises in the case of homosexuality; there are many religious right wing Christian groups that would expel homosexuals, instead of forgive {if it is a sin} and accept them, which is a form of duplicitous treatment, since the adulterer would be accepted and forgiven even though adultery is more prominently mentioned in the bible and should therefore be considered as a greater sin {if it is a sin}. There are many mainstream Christians who may say that they do not support that hard-line on sinners such as homosexuals or adulterers. But support by mainstream Christians of Christianity in general also supports the right wing Christians and since they have more political power the mainstream Christians are supporting their political agenda.

This concept, of emphasis on faith instead of virtue, is perhaps epitomized in the Christian notion of confession wherein a person can be absolved of sins by merely telling a priest about them or by "sincerely" repenting just before death. This concept is rejected in the non-faith-based religions since there is recognition that a person's character is composed of longstanding egoistic desires that must be purified through virtuous deeds over time. Those who treat religion in the way of having faith but also committing unethical acts such as stealing [from mugging to white collar crime], graft, assassination, war, subjugation of other peoples through imperialist tactics, lynching, rape, child molestation, adultery, etc. are often accused of practicing religion in name only, yet that is the logical extension of the faith based religious philosophical idea, to just believe.

Fundamentalists might say that the instructions of the Bible must be practiced literally. Yet, how would *an eye for an eye* {Old Testament} be reconciled with *turn the other cheek* {New Testament}? The contradictions of such concepts coupled with the dogmatic demand to blind faith often has lead to imperfection of practice as evinced in the downfall of Catholic priests who have been convicted of child molestation or other crimes, or of such prominent evangelical preachers as Jimmy Swaggart and Jim Baker whose ministries collapsed due to egregious sins as defined by their religions. Yet those individuals were forgiven and accepted as Christians. Some have manifested patently un-Christian behavior such as the viciousness of promoting the association of foreign leaders or praying for the death of Supreme Court Justices who may not support the right wing religious right political agenda, as Pat Roberson did. This reflects the extreme application of exclusivist and universalistic notions that permeate the faith-based religion that in effect cancels out or invalidates virtue or ethics in the pursuit of what is considered by the religion as greater, i.e. faith. Therefore, sinful behavior can be excused by the religion if the person claims to be Christian; also, crime and unethical behavior can be excused by the religion if the person claims to be Christian and the acts are portrayed as upholding the faith. So killing, making war or crimes in the name of upholding the religion are acceptable; the example of that concept is evinced in the decrees of the Pope advocating the Crusades and in today's Christians making war on other nations and in the corporations of Christians, Jews and Muslims exploiting other peoples around the world. Consequently, if it is acceptable to commit crimes in the support of faith why not commit crimes in support of king and country or family? Is it not necessary to support the family so it can support the church or temple? This line of logic has been presented to demonstrate the subconscious or unconscious or even conscious mental operations that can form the basis for the amorality and cruelty that can manifest from practitioners of faith-based religions and have led to wars as well as oppression on nonbeliever groups.

That confusion in traditional Christianity opens the door for uncertainty, so criticisms are often answered by either calls to believe faithfully and not question the "word of God" since there must be some higher wisdom in those scriptures or the critic may be attacked as an unbeliever or as a hell bound devil worshipper, who was sent to test the faithful believers, or who should be excommunicated and ignored or discredited for being a follower of rationality instead of faith.

That inability or unwillingness to face criticism or apply critical thinking to the scriptural tenets maintains the religion as a faith-based rather than rational practice. Devoid of rationality, the faith-based religion must eventually resort to violent repudiation of that which is criticizing the faith-based dogma as evil and attempting to lure the faithful to ruin. Therefore, the faith based religion must always be alert to reject criticism as well as contradictory ideas. The challenging ideas are not responded to with other rational counterarguments by the faith-based religious practitioners; they are answered with exhortations to have faith. That form of answer closes off debate and negates the need or even discourages critical thinking and spiritual inquiry. When religious zealots or demagogues are able to control the masses of fanatical faith-based religious followers the consequences can be calamitous because the leader can claim to be divinely inspired and since no proof is required beyond the appearance of being touched by the spirit, which can be faked by any skilled con artist, the followers can be manipulated into accepting or partaking in heinous crimes against humanity.

In mystical practice the practitioner is not forced to have faith in a teaching or a teacher or to convert others. All come to that in the fullness of their spiritual development. In experience-based religions the followers are not forced to believe in certain personalities as means to achieve their salvation through those personalities. In mystical religion the aspirant is admonished to trust in the teaching and the teacher until they are able to experience the truth of the teaching for themselves. In mystical religion the aspirant is not pushed to convert others or condemn others who do not follow the same tradition; all follow the paths they are suited to due to their previous desires, feelings and ethical character. A true teacher of the mysteries, a Sage or enlightened being is recognized by mystics as they cleanse their personalities from un-virtuous aspects of character. They essentially discover who is an authentic philosopher by becoming philosophers themselves, by questioning and then practicing the disciplines of the mystery teaching.

Conclusion

What was the cause of the two main religion's, [Judaism and Christianity] turn from henotheism to faith-based religion which concentrates on assurance and certainty, historicity and literalism? These developments [move towards zealotry and dogmatism as well as faith-basis instead of experience-basis in religious practice] may be seen as a reaction to extreme violence and holocaust type experiences at the hands of the Babylonians or Romans. So this means that the extreme violence of the Romans drew a reaction in the form of extreme dogmatism from the Christians. Those religious practitioners were in search of concrete answers to their miseries and immediate salvation from their suffering. So in order to confront the juggernaut of the Roman Empire the counterbalance was the creation of a concretized religious philosophy founded upon the idea of a physical liberator and a physical and final end to the great misery that was being suffered. The apocalyptic vision of Zoroastrianism, which was not originally part of the Judeo-Christian tradition as such, fit into that need.

Additionally, the reliance on historicity and literalism could have the effect of impressing potential followers and luring them away from other religions that were not historically based and therefore not true. In a sense orthodox religion may be seen as a spiritual representation of imperial culture since it, like the political empire, seeks to control and dictate to all the peoples within its domain, what they are to think and believe and do and just as the empire will relate peacefully to its people as long as the people do what they are told, so too the faith-based religions are peaceful towards those followers who believe but hostile to those people who do not. Just as the empire seeks to expand and conquer all, the faith-based orthodox religion must convert all. In another sense the faith-based religions are reactions to the barbarism of their times. Just as the Roman Empire treated them with extreme violence, the faith-based religion must practice religion with and equal measure of zealotry that can leave no unbelievers in peace.

The barbarism of the Romans was matched by the zeal of the zealots who adopted a diametrically opposed ideology in religious terms, to the position of the Roman polytheism. Another factor polarizing religion was the competition between polytheism, as it was understood by the Christians, and their own conception of absolute monotheism. The orthodox Christians regarded the henotheistic religions of their time [ancient Egyptian, Indian, Greek, etc.] as polytheism. In fact henotheism is not the same as polytheism and philosophically speaking is therefore not a diametrically opposed concept to monotheism since in a way henotheism accommodated the monotheistic concept in the framework of a central figure around which peripheral entities are found. It is not unlike the metaphor of the sun and the planets but it is actually even closer to the Christian concept of God and the angels and saints because the concept of angels and saints developed out of the earlier pre-Judeo-Christian traditions. Yet, the dogmatic faith-based followers can accept nothing that is not what they perceive as exactly the same as their concept. That struggle fomented the polarization of that sect of Jews [Christians] that moved them away from their own traditional henotheistic beliefs. This development had a strong effect on the entirety of Jewish religious philosophy and practice.

The intense misery of life can operate to prevent intellectual and mystically oriented thought processes; it creates insensitivity to the subtleties of human experience and promotes hardheartedness and the ideal of concrete [faith] instead of abstract [philosophical] thinking. The predilection towards faith alone as the basis of religious practice discourages deeper religious experiences and hence people come to believe they have the religious experience through expressions of faith instead of expressions of inner spiritual discovery beyond the concrete personality. This same principle applies to the predilection in western countries towards a mechanistic and scientific way of thinking about human development as epitomized in the Cartesian concept of a mechanistic universe [Descartes' reductionistic view was that everything can be dismantled and studied in parts (like a machine) in order to understand the whole] or the mechanistic view of the human body in medical science that persists to this day through allopathic medical practice which repudiates alternative or traditional medical practices that may be just as or more effective. This tendency is also evident in the ideal of western art which revered "realism" instead of the abstract or folkloric forms of art.

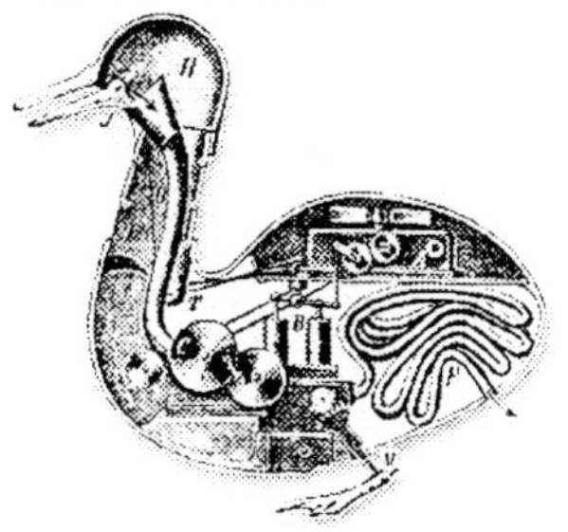

Descartes held that - contrary to humans - animals could be reductively explained as automata - *De homines 1622)*

Certainly not all followers of faith-based religions are insensitive and un-virtuous or uninterested in virtue or a more ecumenical or all-inclusive practice of religion. However, the framework of those religions is designed to promote that form of religious practice that is narrow-minded, fanatical, blind, fearful and intolerant. Therefore, the most fanatical elements of that form of religion actually do reflect the highest perspective enjoined by the traditional form of practice that the religion has developed based on its original tenets.

Under those conditions, those who may consider themselves as moderates or marginal believers could be shamed [coerced] into supporting the more zealous proponents and thereby the zealots would have power to control the actions of the majority.

On May 2, 2006 Madeline Albright made some critical comments about president George W. Bush on "*The Daily Show with John Stewart*". She noted that at a recent meeting between former secretaries of state and defense that president George Bush was not seeking advice and instead issued policy statements. She added, [Highlighted text by Ashby]

> I went back and looked at a lot of America's history and most of our presidents have invoked God in some form or another, what is different about president Bush is that <u>he is so certain about his religion</u>, none of the doubts that president Lincoln raised and I think then what happens is it makes people wonder whose on the other side and anybody who picks a fight with us is picking a fight with God, which is why he has made this so difficult and complicated.

President George W. Bush has made statements about how he prays and is guided by God. In reply to Albrights statement, John Steward said that he thought "that God would be doing a better job in Iraq", referring to the deteriorating war that the president chose to start. In reference to the faled policy related to the war in Iraq, Albright added,

> ...there was no planning for the next part [the occupation of Iraq] and you had Secretary [Colin] Powel on who was explaining that and I think that is the real problem, there was an expectation ther would be dancing in the streets and <u>part of the problem about being so certain</u> that you are getting the message is you never have a plan "B". All the Bush administration wen in was plan "A", everyone would love us, and no idea about plan "B" and the looting and the fact that we would be viewed as occupyers and not as liberators.

The reaction by Madeline Albright is typical of several people who have met with the president. He seems not to listen to advice. At the White House Correspondent's dinner of 2006, comedian Stephen Colbert noted that the president "held on to the same opinion on Wednesday that he had on Monday no matter what happened on

Tuesday." That intractable grasp unto the political or religious dogma denotes a strongly dogmatic personality; A person who holds on to the dogma regardless of any contradictory information. The obstinate grasp on to the projected reality and the certainty of his convictions indicate, again, a personality that is inflexible and whose ideas or deeply held notions are hard to shake. Therefore, such a personality cannot learn from mistakes or improved ways of doing things because they are new and conflict with the accepted absolute beliefs. This is why also such a personality can say one policy for the benefit of others and follow another, closer to the deeply held belief. The president thus presents an extreme example of the religious dogmatic leader that can pose a significant threat to peace as it would find great difficulty in accepting any reality not in accord with its own beliefs. The assessment by Albright confirms the denied statements by George W. Bush which confirm his mindset as a dogmatic personality, relying on religion and projecting his notion of reality, rooted in thc faith-based dogma, onto the world so as to reshape it to his satisfaction, enforcing it on others, regardless of the consequences, because the alternative is worse.

> "I'm driven with a mission from God. God would tell me, George, go and fight those terrorists in Afghanistan. And I did, and then God would tell me, George, go and end the tyranny in Iraq… And I did. And now, again, I feel God's words coming to me, go get the Palestinians their state and get the Israelis their security, and get peace in the Middle East. And by God I'm gonna do it."[179] /[180]

Some political observers and sociologists have examined the presidents actions and some have suggested that the president may not be lying from his perspective in the way that he thinks what he is saying about reality is true from the perspective of how he thinks it should be. Thus, it is indicative of a personality that looks at the world through his own prism, a deluded version of reality, based on an imaginary desired truth founded on the faith-based dogma or ideology. In any case, this vision of reality or the belief that he can reshape reality to fit his idea of reality is either shared or assisted by his advisors. [recall the Ron Suskind article where he quoted one of the Bush advisors as saying: We're history's actors . . . and you, all of you, will be left to just study what we do."][181]

Religion and the Superpower Culture Part 2: How the Religious Far Right, and the Neoconservatives took control of U.S.A. Politics and What is their Agenda?

The rising fundamentalism and extremism {zealotry} of the religious right in the U.S.A. faith-based religions over the last 40 years is partly based on a fundamentalist, literal and fanatical view of the apocalyptic ideas of the Jewish-Christian bible as well as a profound fear of annihilation or being taken over by the forces of evil, the devil or Islam, etc. These pressures have fomented the emergence and expansion of extremist and irrational theological movements in the U.S.A. These movements are bound up with the creation of a Jewish state and what that supposedly means in biblical prophesies and the desire of some to make those prophesies come true.

> If you just had Jews taking up the cudgels for Israel, it wouldn't do it. What you've had from the start is that the country in Europe that was most anxious to have an Israel in the 19th century was Britain, because that's where you have – well, Disraeli was prime minister, but you had a fair Jewish community, and there was this Protestant sense of to have the biblical prophecies come true, Israel had to be restored. And in the United States, the expectations among Christian evangelicals that foreign policy should serve a biblical aspect, in other words, that this should become part of American foreign policy, it's huge...
> ...What you've got is that 45% of American Christians believe in Armageddon, and the more religious ones, the fundamentalists and evangelicals more than anybody else. So, my assumption is that the Bush electorate is probably 50 to 55% people who believe in Armageddon and probably more or less the same numbers who believe that the Antichrist is already on earth.[182]

A Brief History of the Origins of Israel as a Jewish State

Beginning with Abraham (c. 1,500 B.C.E?) and ending with the creation of a Jewish state in 1948 A.C.E., the events surrounding the land today known as Palestine and the creation of the Jewish state of Israel shows the long struggle of the Jewish people to establish a permanent country for themselves and the conflict which ensued when the Jews were successful in taking control of the land which has been considered as the Holy Land for Jews, Christians, and Muslims. The Jewish Bible relates the story of Abraham. The term Abraham, according to the Bible Book of Genesis, means in Hebrew, father of many nations or Abram (ā′ brəm) [Hebrew, exalted father]. In the Jewish Bible, he is progenitor of the Hebrews; in the Islamic Qur'an text he is recognized as ancestor of the Arabs.

> Abraham was the foremost of the Biblical patriarchs. Later in life he went by the name Abraham. There is no contemporary mention of his life, and no source earlier than Genesis mentions him, so it is difficult to know if he was a historical figure. If he was, he probably lived[14] between 2166 BC and 1991 BC.[183]

The idea of the creation of Israel, as a state, had begun in ancient times, as described in the Jewish Old Testament as God purportedly made an agreement with the Hebrews to provide them with a promised land. However, since the time when the early ancient attempts failed, it was not until recent times, the late 1800s A.C.E. that the movement took on strength due to the ability of the Jews to develop political clout and financial backing from their own sources and from the Western countries. The Zionist[15] leaders in Britain always viewed Britain as an important potential supporter in their efforts to create a Jewish state. Britain was at that time the greatest world empire and military power. Jews had been able to settle there in relative peace and security and they had been able to become part of the power elite of the country, producing such political and social leaders as Benjamin Disraeli [who actually became prime minister in 1868 and 1874] and Walter, Lord Rothschild. The Balfour Declaration of 1917, in favor of "the establishment in Palestine of a national home for the Jewish people", was crucial to the plans of the Zionist leaders. In the aftermath of World War II when the Palestinians were weak militarily and the western countries were stronger, Britain took control of the area. This was the opportunity

---

[14] According to the Biblical account.

[15] concept of the creation of a Jewish homeland-promised land

that the Jewish leaders were waiting for since 1896. These factors, coupled with the Western interest in Middle Eastern oil, enabled the Jewish leaders to promote the partitioning of Palestine and obtain the permission and financing to start a settlement in Palestine. The establishment of a Jewish State was not officially part of the original settlement idea as authorized by the previous declarations of the United Nations or the British mandate. Having succeeded in settling the land, the Jews then set out to establish and expand a Jewish State by military force. [184] In order to do that it was necessary to forcibly remove Palestinians (Arab and Muslim inhabitants). The Jews created settlements for the Palestinians, which some observers likened to Bantustans, in which the Palestinians were hemmed in and segregated from the Israeli areas and could only go there with special permits in order to work. Those actions were the first contributing factors of the current rancor between the Arabs and Jews over the Palestinian/Jewish territories. This conflict between the European Jews and others who settled the land by force and the Arab Muslims, led to several wars with no resolution to the issue. Since the late 1960s many Christian groups in the U.S.A. and Britain have supported the state of Israel and that has intensified the problem. This issue promoted anti western sentiment in the Islamic countries [especially in the Middle East] but became a rallying point for right wing politicians who used it as a political issue. The religious right Christian groups and AIPAC, the America Israel Public Affairs Committee gained unprecedented lobbying power in the government that contributed to the general right wing mood of the culture of the U.S.A.

> A dean at Harvard University and a professor at the University of Chicago are coming under intense criticism for publishing an academic critique of the pro-Israel lobby in Washington. The paper charges that the United States has willingly set aside its own security and that of many of its allies, in order to advance the interests of Israel. In addition, the study accuses the pro-Israel lobby, particularly AIPAC, the America Israel Public Affairs Committee, of manipulating the U.S. media, policing academia and silencing critics of Israel by labeling them as anti-Semitic. The study also examines the role played by the pro-Israel neoconservatives in the lead-up to the U.S. invasion of Iraq.[185]

Part of the religious conception of religious right Christian groups is that the Jewish state is to be supported because that is supposedly what the bible demands since that will help to bring about the set of events that will lead to the end times and usher in the return of Jesus and the salvation of the faithful. Therefore, that support and the coincidental agenda of the right wing conservatives, neo-conservatives and European power elites, who want to have a friendly power base in the Middle East, came together for a common goal.

The religious far right in the U.S.A. is composed of those people who believe in literal biblical or traditional fundamentalist teachings of prophecies of the Judeo-Christian bible including the concepts of **Dominionism, Apocalypticism** and **Reconstructionism.**

> **Dominionism** is a term used by some social scientists and critics to describe a trend in Protestant Christian evangelicalism and fundamentalism that encourages political participation in civic society by Christians through appeals to their religious beliefs.
> Politically active conservative Christians rarely use the term dominionism as a self-description; many feel it is a loaded or pejorative term. Use of the term is primarily limited to secular and leftist critics of the Christian Right. The term emerged in relation to the Christian Right in the mid-1990s, but became more widely known due in large part to the U.S. presidential election, 2004 where the media attributed Republican wins to "Evangelical" voters in "Red states" who voted for "moral values". Some poll analysts call this claim over-simplistic. It has been claimed to be a kind of Triumphalism.
> **Apocalypticism** is a worldview based on the idea that important matters are hidden from view and they will soon be revealed in a major confrontation of earth-shaking magnitude that will change the course of history. Apocalypticism is a frequent theme of literature, film and television. It also influences political policy through movements such as Christian Zionism, and in the dualism seen when politicians demonize and scapegoat their enemies as wholly bad, evil, or even Satanic. This process often involves conspiracism in which the apocalyptic enemy is alleged to be engaged in a conspiracy against the good or Godly people. The tendency was especially evident with the approach of the millennial year 2000, but it need not be tied to a particular calendar date.
> **Christian Reconstructionism** is a highly controversial religious and theological movement within Protestant Christianity.
> Reconstructionism relates to the reconstruction of the "literal" meaning

> of the words of he Bible. It calls for Christians to put their faith into action in all areas of life including civil government, and envisions the private and civil enforcement of the general principles of Old Testament and New Testament moral law, including those expounded in the case laws and summarized in the Old Testament Decalogue. In Reconstructionism the idea of *godly* dominion, subject to God, is contrasted with the *autonomous* dominion of mankind in rebellion against God.[186]

Having lost the 1964 elections to the democratic party, the republican party under the direction of Paul Weirich, who was a campaign strategist, developed the idea of expanding the base of the republican party by targeting religious fundamentalists, Pentecostals and members of Charismatic Churches; presumably because those segments of Christianity are most closed minded since they tend to follow religion through blind faith instead of through critical thinking. In the same manner those same sentiments could be manipulated towards blind allegiance to political leaders who seem to be upholding those fundamentalist values.

In the 1960s the Democratic party sought to secularize the population and that drew a backlash from the fundamentalist religious segments of the population. The former republican strategist, Kevin Phillips explained how the religious right embraced the republican party and then a strategy of using the party to acquire control of the government developed.

> Well, the rise of the religious right and the Southernization of the Republican Party has created a role of religion within the Republican Party that is unprecedented in the 20th or 21st century. And this has become a central fact, the extent to which rank-and-file Republicans have a somewhat theocratic view of what government should do and how it should ally with religion, and the extent to which the Republican Party has become the favored party of the most religious conservative segments of Protestantism, Catholicism and Judaism, where you have the Orthodox Jews in the United States turned out in such number -- and they're growing anyway, because of large families[187]

Paul Weirich coined the term Moral Majority in 1979 and that organization claimed to register 9 million new voters. In the year 1981 the Council for National Policy was created to conduct secret meetings for the purpose of formulating strategies to mobilize and control the religious right politically. The council is composed of religious right leaders, gun advocates, anti-tax advocates and financers of the religious right agenda. Its first president was Tim LaHaye, the co-author of the highly successful series of books known as the "left behind series." That series of books, some of which have been made into movies, concerns a fictionalized vision, based on Christian myth and tradition, of the last days of the world in which the true believers in Christianity are taken to heaven and the other people are left behind to suffer for eternity. The following quotation reveals the views of Mr. LaHaye and the message he is putting out through the over 70 million books he has sold.

> "I myself have been a forty-five year student of the centuries-old conspiracy to use government, education, and media to destroy every vestige of Christianity within our society and establish a new world order. Having read at least fifty books on the Illuminati, I am convinced that it exists and can be blamed for many of man's inhumane actions against his fellow man during the past two hundred years." (LaHaye)[188]

It is interesting that LaHaye mentions a conspiracy to use government, education and media since that is exactly what the right wing of the Christian religion has tried to do at least since the mid 1960s. It is also interesting that he demonstrates such concerned about the Illuminati as an enemy of his group and presumably also of Christianity. The concept of denouncing an enemy, even an imaginary one, is a strategy that has been used by many groups to elicit fear in their own members so as to promote more fanaticism or zealous following. It has also been used by some groups to elicit compassion and support from others in an effort to build their ranks or for procuring donations and other considerations. Governments have used this tactic to elicit support for making war on actual or supposed enemies.

The name Illuminati was used by several groups in modern times and historical times. The term Illuminati is a Latin word meaning "enlightened." The term Illuminati as it is most commonly used refers to a specific group known as the Bavarian Illuminati which **was** a society that was founded in Germany just after 1776 A.C.E. by Adam Weishaupt, who was a professor at Ingolstadt. It was popular among the ranks of German rationalists. Rationalism

[Lat.,=belonging to reason], is a philosophy, or theory which holds the concept that one can arrive at basic truth regarding the world through reason alone, without physical experience. The German Illuminati sought knowledge through disciplined thought processes of the mind. The Roman Catholic Church condemned the Illuminati and the government of Bavaria dissolved the organization in 1785 A.C.E.

In Spain and Italy in the 15th and 16th centuries A.C.E., the term *Illuminati,* or *Alumbrado,* referred to persons claiming direct communion with the Holy Spirit, asserting that outward forms of religious life are unnecessary. Their philosophy was akin to Gnosticism, the idea that one can know the Divine through mentally/spiritually experiencing oneness with the Divine. Their claims led to persecution by the Inquisition [by the church]. Other groups using the name have included the Rosicrucians, and certain followers of Jakob Boehme and Emmanuel Swedenborg.[189] So the original purpose of the Illuminati [of Spain and Italy] was to seek self-knowledge, in the tradition of the Ancient Egyptian, and Greek Gnostic spiritual seekers.

It is not too difficult to understand why a Gnostic philosophy would be opposed by the church; it means bypassing interminable years worshipping in a church and paying tithes to the church without achieving higher knowledge of God versus leading life in a way that leads to independence, self-knowledge and inner experience of God without need of the church. Therefore, it is no surprise that the Illuminati in particular and not Freemasons, would be considered as a threat and thus be maligned.

The Freemasons did indeed achieve high positions in governments in Europe and the U.S.A. and they had a philosophy that was more compliant with Christian values, yet their “special” grouping allowed them to conspire together to affect social and economic policies through political institutions. In the present day, the Illuminati are viewed as a cabal that controls governments and economies from behind the scenes. This is of course not the same agenda as the earlier group which followed the Gnostic path. It is well known that some of the United States' founding fathers were Freemasons but there were unfounded suspicions of their being involved with the Illuminati because of the all-seeing pyramid in the Great Seal of the United States [see above]. That symbol was cited as an example of the Illuminati's ever-present watchful eye over Americans; however, Thomas Jefferson, on the other hand, claimed they [the Illuminati] intended to spread information and the principles of true morality. He attributed the secrecy of the Illuminati to what he called "the tyranny of a despot and priests".[190]

Thus, the Illuminati are to be considered separately from Freemasonry. The order [Freemasonry] is thought to have arisen from the English and Scottish fraternities of practicing stonemasons and cathedral builders in the early Middle Ages; traces of the society have been found as early as the 14th cent. Because, however, some documents of the order trace the sciences of masonry and geometry from Egypt, Babylon, and Palestine to England and France, some historians of Masonry claim that the order has roots in antiquity.[191] While the Freemasons may claim to descend from Egypt, Babylon, and Palestine an examination of their philosophy reveals that it does not follow precisely and faithfully the tenets of Ancient Egyptian religion and one would not expect it to since the Christian Bible takes such a dim view of Ancient Egyptian culture[192] and the Freemasonry's oldest extant lodge bylaws,[193] cites religious toleration, loyalty to local government, and political compromise as basic to the Masonic ideal. The principles of Freemasonry supposedly enjoin liberal and democratic politics and the Masons were enjoined to believe in a Supreme Being, and to use a holy book that is appropriate to the religion of the lodge's members. Using the holy book of another religion does not follow the path of Ancient Egypt, which has its own. But the Christian church leaders would not allow any other holy book in their midst besides the Christian bible anyway. So Freemasonry was designed to be compliant to the religion of the practitioners so that they could work in other areas while not being interfered with by the religious groups of the society. In this way it would seem that the Freemasons were the true cabal affecting the social order and that the Illuminati were used as scapegoats to deflect interest in the activities of the Freemasons. The members are admonished to maintain a vow of secrecy concerning the order.

> Many of the leaders of the American Revolution, including John Hancock and Paul Revere, were members of St. Andrew's Lodge in Boston. George Washington became a Mason in 1752. At the time of the Revolution most of the American lodges broke away from their English and Scottish antecedents. Freemasonry has continued to be important in politics; 13 Presidents have been Masons, and at any given time quite a large number of the members of Congress have belonged to Masonic lodges. [194]

Thus, it is clear that from its inception the U.S.A. was founded by people who were in part followers of a secular approach to politics and economics as well as social order even while holding a predilection for Christianity. It is those aspects of culture that upset religious fundamentalists since without a formal theocracy it is difficult to maintain a theocratic order. In other words the country was not founded as a theocracy even though many of its founders were avid believers in Christianity; but even though some predicted the danger of religion in politics none would have predicted the diversity of the culture, the number of different religions that would come to the U.S.A., and the severity of the degradation of culture in relation to crime, debauchery, the scale of white collar crimes and the level of political scheming that developed since their time. Nevertheless, it would seem that a cabal of secular conservatives, the Freemasons, worked to create the social order that became the United States of America and may even be considered as the forerunners of the present day conservatives and neo-conservatives.

Legends of other groups using the name Illuminati, whose purpose is to dominate the world have been circulating for over a century but they are not a shadow conspiracy but rather the very same persons who are trying to gain control of the world economy right now and are the ancestors of those who created slavery, flexible currency, the national banks and transnational corporations in the U.S.A. and Europe under the guise of being religiously tolerant, loyal to government and belief in a Supreme Being. Nevertheless, today those who compose what Jeff Faux calls "The Party of Davos" [power elite-world ruling class] does not need to call itself anything because its money is the universally recognizable code that is accepted by all the power elite all over the world, regardless of language, culture, or religion and, in cases, ethnicity. Yet, some secretive organizational formats still exist but only the power elite within those groups, are part of the ruling class that controls the workings of the economy and of governments.

Many critics of the American Theocratic ideal that is espoused by right wing Christian groups that the U.S.A. was founded as a "Christian country" by Christians and so it should have Christian laws, etc. use The Treaty of Tripoli as an example of the secular political atmosphere that existed right after the creation of the United States government. The Treaty of Tripoli (also known as the Treaty of Peace and Friendship) was a treaty signed on November 4, 1796 as a peace treaty between Tripoli and the United States. The Treaty was approved by President John Adams and Secretary of State Timothy Pickering and ratified by the Senate of the United States on June 10, 1797. It is cited because it contains a statement about the religion of the United States of America in Article 11, which reads:

> "As the Government of the United States of America is not, in any sense, founded on the Christian religion; as it has in itself no character of enmity against the laws, religion, or tranquility, of Mussulmen; and, as the said States never entered into any war, or act of hostility against any Mahometan nation, it is declared by the parties, that no pretext arising from religious opinions, shall ever produce an interruption of the harmony existing between the two countries."

The country was, at least theoretically, supposed to be a refuge for people who were being oppressed due to religious discrimination in Europe. When European settlers started emigrating to the Americas the recent memory of religious oppression and conflict in Europe led many Europeans [ex. The Puritans[16]] to seek freedom in the Americas from the same type of religious demagoguery and intolerance as the religious right wing began to display in the late 20th and early 21st centuries in the United States. So it was designed to have a government that was not controlled by religious interests. Though the "founding fathers" may have envisioned religions other than the European religious sects of Christianity and Judaism in "America" they may not have envisioned the religions from other parts of the world. Nevertheless, varied members of Christian groups have tried, especially in the last 40 years, to characterize the U.S.A. as a Christian country. The tone of the country has indeed become polarized in the sense that the Christian majority has turned more towards religious based ideas in relation to national politics and foreign policies the more internal and external strife is experienced.

In the year 1988 Rev. Pat Robertson[195] founded The Christian Coalition after losing his run for the presidency. The Christian Coalition of America is a U.S.A. Christian political advocacy group, which includes Christian fundamentalists, Evangelicals, Pentecostals, Roman Catholics and members of mainline Protestant churches;[196] the organization claims 2,200,000 members but other

---

[16] A member of a group of English Protestants who in the 16th and 17th centuries advocated strict religious discipline along with simplification of the ceremonies and creeds of the Church of England. Source: *The American Heritage® Dictionary of the English Language, Fourth Edition Copyright © 2000*

sources such as the *People for the American Way* say it has less than 400,000.[197]

The dismantling of the Fairness Doctrine allowed the religious right and conservative organizations to quickly amass and consolidate media ownership and send a singular focused message to many people at once. This consolidation hindered anyone else's capacity to compete or respond to their statements. Oftentimes, as was demonstrated during the 2004 presidential campaign, one baseless accusation after another was launched before the opponent could respond to the first one. By the time a response was put out the damage to public opinion had been accomplished. The strategy of presenting the right wing Christian and neoconservative agendas leaned on the base feelings [fear] and desires [greed] and conceit [hubris] of people. The mood of the country has changed in the past 16 years such that the public readily accepted the installation of George W. Bush as president even though he did not win the popular vote in the year 2000. Other irregularities were also accepted, such as the invasion of Iraq in 2003 and the reelection of Bush in 2004 despite statewide irregularities in the counting of votes and the use of easily hacked electronic voting machines, with no paper trail, supplied by friends of the Bush administration who were known to publicly promise to deliver the state of Ohio to clinch the win of the presidency to Bush.

> *Published on Thursday, August 28, 2003 by the Cleveland Plain Dealer*
>
> ***Voting Machine Controversy***
>
> **by Julie Carr Smyth**
>
> COLUMBUS - The head of a company vying to sell voting machines in Ohio told Republicans in a recent fund-raising letter that he is "committed to helping Ohio deliver its electoral votes to the president next year."
>
> The Aug. 14 letter from Walden O'Dell, chief executive of Diebold Inc. - who has become active in the re-election effort of President Bush - prompted Democrats this week to question the propriety of allowing O'Dell's company to calculate votes in the 2004 presidential election.

While there have been some writers who presented the duplicitous side of the republican party and the neoconservative agenda it was not until the year 2004 that a counterbalancing force on radio emerged that could challenge the relentless message of the conservative organization. That counterbalancing organization was *Air America Radio.*

Theocracy is not an issue in governmental practice if that is the desire of the people who have that form of government. A more literal term for the exact meaning of "theocracy" is "ecclesiocracy," which denotes rule by a religious leader or body, whereas theocracy would literally mean rule by God.[198] What is at issue is the tyranny imposed by such a government, which can be imposed by any government form. So tyranny is the issue, not theology. In other words, a theocratic government is not necessarily tyrannical. The tyranny comes in when the people are forced to accept traditions they do not want or the government imposes dehumanizing or inhuman punishments for disobeying the theocratic rule. Orthodox, religions that promote faith-based practice, absolutism, literalism and historicity are conducive for religious tyranny because they are designed to demand the conversion of all people within their domain. Thus, it is arrogant for a country to dictate the policies of others if that country purports to be a champion of democracy. It is also hypocritical for such a country to promote the ideal of democracy in other countries while curtailing civil rights or discouraging the practice of religion or encouraging certain religions over others in its own social order.

> ***Grants Flow To Bush Allies On Social Issues***
> ***Federal Programs Direct At Least $157 Million*** By Thomas B. Edsall
> Washington Post Staff Writer
> Wednesday, March 22, 2006; Page A01
> For years, conservatives have complained about what they saw as the liberal tilt of federal grant money. Taxpayer funds went to abortion rights groups such as Planned Parenthood to promote birth control, and groups closely aligned with the AFL-CIO got Labor Department grants to run worker-training programs.
> In the Bush administration, conservatives are discovering that turnabout is fair play: Millions of dollars in taxpayer funds have flowed to groups that support President Bush's agenda on abortion and other social issues.[199]

What the article does not discuss is the finding that the grants went to religious right organizations and not to religiously center or left organizations. Also, almost all of the money went to conservative Christian organizations and people who support and can vote for the republican party and not to other religions.[200] Therefore, it is mixing religion with politics and a blatant bribery of spiritual culture, corruption of religion itself to pander for votes by appealing to and supporting religious fundamentalists, Pentecostals and dominionists. If the U.S.A. was supposed to be a place for free practice of religion how would that be possible if the government subsidizes one religion over others? If the constitution of the country prevents the country from being controlled by a religion [which would make it an ecclesiocracy], support or discouragement of one form of religion would be clear violation of that principle.

Establishing such a precedent [government financial support of religion] debases religion because it brings it into the arena of corrupt politics. It has been pointed out by some theologians such as Rev. Forrest Church, that the separation of church and state has actually allowed religion to flourish in the United States of America. A similar contention was presented in the book *A New Religious America* by Diana L. Eck. The radicalization of the religious right has reversed that tradition. Furthermore, whenever an industry or area of culture is subsidized it comes under the control of government because the subsidized group becomes used to the financial support and develops fear of losing it so accedes to the demands of the paying group, the politicians. Thus it would not be unusual to find ministers that promote government policies in order to remain in the good graces of the government. Additionally, conservative preachers have supported political candidates and policies openly or privately, even though that is supposedly against the law.

> On February 22, the day of the Michigan state Republican primaries, Christian Coalition Founder Pat Robertson taped a telephone message for a "shadow" campaign in support of Presidential candidate George W. Bush. The message, which went out on phone banks to thousands of Christian Coalition supporters in Michigan, warned that Bush's rival John McCain was against the First Amendment, that he was pro-labor, and

> that a McCain victory would destroy the Republican Party. Robertson also called McCain's campaign chairman, former New Hampshire Senator Warren Rudman (who is an observant Jew), "a vicious bigot" because Rudman wrote in his 1996 autobiography that the religious right is intolerant. Robertson hoped that his character assassination of Senator McCain would depress voter turnout and swing the closely-contested primary toward Bush, his hand-picked man. But something went wrong. Voter turnout was enormous and McCain carried both Michigan and his home state of Arizona.[201]

On August 22, 2005, Pat Robertson called for the assassination of Venezuelan President Hugo Chavez[202]. However, even though conservative preachers such as Pat Robertson, openly and apparently secretly supported the president and openly spoke out against his opponents, and even advocated assassinating a foreign government leader they were never prosecuted or at least warned by the justice department for inciting a criminal act or contacted by the Internal Revenue Service [I.R.S.] to revoke their status as religious organizations. Yet an anti-war speech [critical of the president] by another pastor did draw that warning. This double standard clearly indicates collusion between the presidential administration and the religious right.

> ***Antiwar Sermon Brings IRS Warning*** [203]
> **All Saints Episcopal Church in Pasadena risks losing its tax-exempt status because of a former rector's remarks in 2004.** By Patricia Ward Biederman and Jason Felch, Times Staff Writers
> November 7, 2005
>
> The Internal Revenue Service has warned one of Southern California's largest and most liberal churches that it is at risk of losing its tax-exempt status because of an antiwar sermon two days before the 2004 presidential election.
> Rector J. Edwin Bacon of All Saints Episcopal Church in Pasadena told many congregants during morning services Sunday that a guest sermon by the church's former rector, the Rev. George F. Regas, on Oct. 31, 2004, had prompted a letter from the IRS.

When religious figures begin to carry on activities that contradict their own religious tenets and even break laws with impunity and or operate in collusion with political leaders and outside the law they have walked into a door that was created by government and religious corruption. The creation of such an alliance in a country that is not supposed to have such alliances signals the condition and direction of the culture, towards corruption and dictatorship.

The issue therefore is not whether theocracy is or is not a proper form of government. There have been theocracies in the past. Ancient Egypt existed for thousands of years as a theocracy ["ecclesiocracy"], based on Maat [divine law], administered by the Pharaoh and the priests and priestesses. The Dalai Lama's rule in Tibet, especially before certain twentieth century changes, has been regarded as theocratic type rule. The issue is that in a country where such a form of government is prohibited, where there are many different theological views, such a development will necessarily lead to conflict and abuse of power, repression of less powerful religions and the imposition of orthodox religious views on the rest of the population, that will engender hatred of the domineering religion as well as animosity between religions and the reverse of the stated spiritual goal, to promote peace and closeness to God.

The steady stream of fundamentalist Pentecostalism in the U.S.A. has led to a religious right wing conservative movement that cannot tolerate other religions, other cultures, or other points of political view or life in a mixed religious and secular society. The following statements by prominent religious right ministers in the U.S.A. illustrate the hostility and supremacist attitude towards religions other than Christianity, coming from typical leaders of the religious right churches. [highlighted text by Ashby]

> ***{Billy} Graham's son not holding back on Islam***[204]
> By Jim Jones -Special to the Star-Telegram
>
> When I heard the Rev. Franklin Graham speak in New Orleans two weeks ago, he focused on proclaiming the saving power of Jesus Christ with only a hint of criticism of Islam.
> "Muhammad didn't die for your sins," he told thousands at the New Orleans Arena. "Buddha didn't die for your sins; Krishna didn't die for your sins. It's Jesus."
> But while in New Orleans, Graham again blasted the Muslim faith under the glare of television lights as he told ABC's Nightline that he hasn't changed his mind about Islam, which he called "a very evil and

wicked religion" Unlike his father, who never uttered a discouraging word against Islam or any other faith, Franklin Graham has joined Christian broadcaster Pat Robertson, the Rev. Jerry Falwell and others as being among the most outspoken against Islam.
After Sept. 11, 2001, he told NBC News: "We're not attacking Islam, but Islam has attacked us. The God of Islam is not the same God. He's not the Son of God of the Christian or Judeo-Christian faith. It's a different God, and I believe it is a very wicked and evil religion."

In another program, Graham also said:

GRAHAM [video clip]: I've been working in Muslim countries now for, oh, 40 years or more. So I know about Islam. If people think Islam is such a wonderful religion, just go to Saudi Arabia and make it your home. Just live there. If you think Islam is such a wonderful religion, I mean, go and live under the Taliban somewhere.

Rev. Pat Robertson said:

ROBERTSON [video clip]: These people are crazed fanatics. And I want to say it now. I believe it's motivated by demonic power. It is satanic. And it's time we recognize what we're dealing with.

On the March 17, 2006 Fox News' program: *The O'Reilly Factor*, the president of the Southern Baptist Theological Seminary, R. Albert Mohler Jr., who also hosts a daily Christian radio show called *The Albert Mohler Program*, agreed with Pat Robertson's [of the *700 Club,*] statements that Muslims are "motivated by demonic power". Mr. Mohler Jr. said:

MOHLER: Well, I would have to say as a Christian that I believe any belief system, any world view, whether it's Zen Buddhism or Hinduism or dialectical materialism for that matter, Marxism, that keeps persons captive and keeps them from coming to faith in the Lord Jesus Christ, yes, is a demonstration of satanic power…

And in the case of the two statements from which you pulled there -- from Dr. Graham and from Pat Robertson, they were speaking a deeply Christian truth there that Christians have believed for 2,000 years. And by the way, not with Muslims, because of course now we have only 14 centuries of dealing with the challenge of Islam, **but any belief system that keeps persons**

> **from coming to Christ we would see as a manifestation of a demonic power.**

It would seem that tragedies such as the Sept. 11, 2001 attack on the U.S.A. were an opportunity for religious extremists to more loudly warn about some impending Armageddon. Even before the tragedy, the religious right had engaged in a campaign of fear about the "end times" being near and the need to repent and accept Jesus for salvation. However, the disaster also allowed them to sound the calls of attack on Islamic followers in general and thus allowing them to present to society a supposedly viable threat to Christianity, which is bound up in the "American way of life" that should be preserved at all costs. This form of demagoguery speaks from an arrogant and hubristic perspective, believing that Christianity is the only true religion and therefore those who follow it are entitled to survive and all others should die if necessary since they are all following false religions and are going to hell anyway [for not believing in and being saved by Jesus]. It is also a fear-based argument that finds many ears and many who agree and support it. The summons to fear and the dilemma of what course of action to take was answered by them not as a call to arms against sin and corruption and to reflection and peacemaking but to hate those who are different as well as against other religions and Islam in particular. It is also a call against secularism and even other forms of Christianity that are not as "zealous". Those people who are unsure of themselves are often caught up in the fervor of the sure sounding words of the religious right preachers or they may acquiesce out of guilt or simple honest faith in their words. In that way, the religious right has gained for itself great power and influence in U.S.A. culture even though it remains a minority, making up perhaps 30% of the population, but with some of the loudest voices among the clergy. Nevertheless, this minority would sacrifice all democratic values in order to force the rest of the country to follow their narrow system of belief.

The ideals of manifest destiny and exeptionalism of the United States, as a superpower, are very much inline with the Judeo-Christian tradition of the special nature and special covenant of the Jews, and therefore the Christians, with God since the culture of the

United States was founded on secular and western Judea-Christian principles.[205] These are ideas that contribute to the notion of superiority over all other religions, and cultures, just as the early Jews assigned to themselves, by means of the dictum from God, the superiority over all other religions. That dictum was and continues to be the entitlement of and mission to conquer the land of Canaan.[206] Only, now, for the United States the land of Canaan, the "promised land," is not just the Middle East but also the entire world.[207] So the roots of the superpower mentality and its causes can be traced to deep-rooted delusions and romanticized ideas, desires and dreams as well as meteorological issues.

The Judeo-Christian religion as it was practiced in Europe has constituted an extreme dogmatic materialistic approach to spirituality and religious practice. It contributes immensely to the Superpower syndrome and its mental complexes that lead to conflict. The Judeo-Christian religion's material culture and reliance on the phenomenology of existence as opposed to the interconnectedness of life and the transcendental nature of human evolution have contributed to the rigidity in the superpower culture with the concomitant disdain for what is not empirical, quantifiable or measurable. Consequently, the religions, values and ideas of other cultures are rejected, in favor of western science and western values and hence western hegemony become the legitimate social imperative and governmental guiding principle.

The religious right [fundamentalists and extremists] supported by acquiescent moderate Christians and the secular populations [by their general support of the government] have attained unprecedented influence in the government upon which they stress the apocalyptic fear of the "end times". That is partly accomplished by citing proposed meanings to Bible prophecies that supposedly speak of Russia leading a coalition of Arabs to destroy Israel[208] and other doomsday scenarios that will trigger events that will lead to Armageddon. Some Christian groups openly advocate using U.S.A. military power to attack all who oppose the U.S.A. to avoid Armageddon. Others advocate such attacks on Arab countries in order to trigger them and bring forth the destruction of civilization to bring about the apocalypse, which is part of a stream of religious thought within Christianity almost from its inception. However, that segment of Christians has been claiming unsuccessfully that the end is near for over 1500 years.

In the late 20th century, the religious right seized upon two issues they could use to incite the ire of ordinary "god fearing" religious people in order to motivate them to get involved with politics and go to cast votes. The two issues were abortion, and homosexual rights. Religious right adherents were motivated against abortion by convincing them it was a sin and against homosexuality because it was also a sin; but these were cataclysmic sins that were dragging the country down and further, that were supported by the democratic party. Therefore, they were motivated out of fear. It is ironic that there are so many other sins mentioned in the bible that are not used to gain such an advantage, like adultery, that if were treated the same way would devastate the leadership of the religious right and republican and democratic parties. The factor of the selective choice of those sins to be concentrated upon and not others and the fact that other sins are mentioned more in the bible but are not mentioned by the religious right leaders reveals a certain double standard and thus also a particular political agenda. Those two issues were used successfully by religious leaders who aligned themselves with the republican party in order to give that party an edge in the electoral process. Those same voters tended to be conservatives and supported the candidates who seemed to be supporting the religious right agenda. However, though the republican party has actually acted in support of the religious right there is overwhelming support for the corporations and the corporate agenda. In a way, the cause of the corporations was merged with that of the religious right, thus making capitalism and republican party affiliation an almost religious duty. Thus, even though the association with the religious right offers a kind of moral veneer to the republican neoconservative and corporate agenda, it remains an unjust and immoral schema for controlling the culture and profiting to the utmost from the labor of ordinary citizens as well as the slave labor of citizens of other countries

Christian Colleges and Universities

One important strategy implemented over 30 years ago was to institute the creation of religious right wing Christian Colleges and Universities for educating professionals who would some day take up leadership positions in the society. Universities such as Liberty University and others, are turning out lawyers, social workers, political science majors, health professionals, etc, who will affect public opinion in the areas ranging from welfare to abortion and foreign policy. Those graduates are indoctrinated with the narrow evangelical, or dominionist or otherwise fanatical view of the religious right that would support ideologically extreme views regardless of rational arguments or scientifically proven contradictory proofs. This strategy may be comparable to but more powerful than the Neo-con strategy of creating “Think Tanks”, that train and put out and support individuals who support the neo-con ideology and agenda, due to the religious fervor of fanatical faith in religious dogma that is involved with the religious following. Those people will have a profound effect on the character of the entire population as they will be diffused throughout the entire population but the important thing is that they will be in leadership positions that offer them the opportunity to shape public opinion. They would not need to act in collusion overtly since their common philosophical religious right wing training would effectively make their actions concerted. Therefore, this is perhaps one of the most important challenges that openness and freedom of religion will face in the future.

Theodore J. Lowi, author of *The End of the Republican Era* (Julian J. Rothbaum Distinguished Lecture Series , Vol. 5), and professor of Government at Cornell University, explained that the republican party has seized the political discourse and debate and have attained the high ground by putting all issues into moralistic terms. In that way they could frame any argument in terms of morality, meaning right or wrong, good or evil. Thus, the other side has no room to argue a different point of view without then being characterized as being against what is good or right or immoral. Therefore, they have been relatively effective at shutting down dissent from the other party or anyone else who disagrees by using the tactic of labeling the other viewpoints as against morality and therefore not to be considered or even given any attention. Even though the republican party does not live up to their own moralistic rhetoric, they nevertheless have appeared as the party of "values"... and who would want to be against values? The scandal that ensued after political lobbyist Jack Abermoff was found to be bribing members of the congress for specific quid pro quo actions[17] raised the potential of implicating enough of the republican politicians as criminals that seriously threatened the republican party characterization of itself as the party of values.

Thus, the merging of the religious right wing agenda with that of the corporate political agenda in the political leadership has allowed the politicians who are in the majority to portray themselves as the moral party even though they have engaged in individual and collective activities that are criminal and or immoral. Nevertheless, there have been several contradictions related to the characterization of the republican party as the party of values and morality. The same group of neoconservative politicians and religious right wing leaders that often spoke about the sanctity of life and were against abortion to protect life seem to be the same group that most foments war, poisoning children, despoiling the environment, expanding poverty, and promoting deadly aids disease transmission [by withdrawing sex education and contraceptives] that has infected millions.

Tim LaHaye, the co-author of the highly successful series of books known as the "left behind series" was the cofounder of the "Federalist Society" in 1982, a right wing think tank that has as its mission to promote conservative judges. The Society has many prominent conservative members, including United States Supreme Court Justices Antonin Scalia and Clarence Thomas, former United States Circuit Court Judge Robert Bork, and former United States Attorney General Edwin Meese. The efforts of the Federalist Society came to fruition in the administration of George W. Bush when two Supreme Court justice vacancies came up. The Federalist society was responsible for the appointment of conservative judges

---

[17] a criminal offence that supposedly goes beyond simple lobbying and political contributions

who are allied to the religious right views, corporate interests, and the elevating of the new Supreme Court justices, John Roberts and Samuel A. Alito, Jr. In an interview with Robert F. Kennedy Jr.[209], Stephanie Hendricks[18] explained that the placement of conservative judges is for the purpose of *"to have anti-environmental judges in every level of the American judicial system."* Robert F. Kennedy Jr. replied, *"well their ultimate goal is to have corporate control of our society; and it would be laughable except for the fact that there are people who believe in this and have actually achieved very high office."*[210]

---

[18] author of ***Divine Destruction: Dominion Theology and American Environmental Policy*** **(Melville Manifestos)** Stephenie Hendricks

IS IT RELATIVE? Lessons from Political Oppression, Media Consolidation and the Manipulation of Public Opinion

In a recent interview of a 32 year old Cuban immigrant to the U.S.A. some interesting perspectives were uncovered that those who consider themselves progressives or anti fascist or anti neo-conservatives, should understand.

This person happens to be an artist. I asked him to explain to me about his experiences in Cuba before coming to the U.S.A. He related that his parents were also artists and that they secretly harbored a desire to leave the oppressive conditions of living in Cuba. He described how in every neighborhood there is an agent of the government to watch for any anti government sentiment and that they can come into the house for any reason at any time. Whenever his parents wanted to speak about any opinions or criticism of the government, they had to whisper in their own house for fear of being overheard by anyone walking by.

One day the authorities came and took him and his parents away because somehow the government heard about their dissident activities. They were all tortured, even he who was only a child at the time. Eventually they were released and they made it to the U.S.A.

I asked him how he felt about what many people [including the recently retired former Supreme Court Justice Sandra Day O'Connor] consider a move in the United States towards dictatorship, like instituting wiretaps in blatant disregard of laws and violating civil liberties.

He replied that people here in the U.S.A. are complaining but they do not know what true repression and loss of rights are. He said that instead of fascism, he feared the left wing move towards communism as he experienced it in Cuba; communism is a form of social order where there is no private ownership but he experienced it along with other features that are not part of the communist or socialist ideal such as no freedom of speech. He felt the situation was bad because there was no incentive to excel because there are no opportunities for advancement because the jobs are government appointed. He further related the idea that governments need to keep certain secrets in order to operate so other countries do not know what they are planning: so we have to trust them [our government] to some degree. In addition, there are many people who come to the U.S.A. from other countries where they were oppressed, like he and his parents, who do not know the system and are just happy to get any job and not say anything. Since they are ignorant and fearful of being sent back they can be easily taken advantage of by unscrupulous business owners. They lived under dire conditions were the government kept them at basic subsistence level income. Many times, they went hungry and he said he witnessed how people's capacity to think was impaired due to malnutrition, so how could they protest or understand how to help themselves?

On hearing his arguments I though about how pre-World War II Germany went down a "slippery slope" of following a fascist dictator [Hitler][211] who wanted to have more room for expansion and protect the German people from the enemies that were supposedly trying to destroy the German culture [artists, philosophers, Jews, democrats, economic competitors, etc.]. I also recalled the current economic statistics of the U.S.A., which show the population of the U.S.A. as working more hours than at any other point in history and more than any other industrialized nation. The working class produces more than in the past but collects less in wages than before. Many people are working to uphold their mortgages, cars, and families and are one or two paychecks away from being in default and possible foreclosure and bankruptcy. In the U.S.A., obesity is now an epidemic and malnutrition is a problem because of over-farming and the use of chemicals in foods. The processing of foods has denatured the foods so that their nutritional value is reduced, so the mind of people of the U.S.A. is also affected. Thus, the difference between oppression in extreme right wing politics [fascism-capitalism] or extreme left wing politics [communism] seems to be one of degrees and not of fundamental difference. Currently, statistics revealed that worker productivity went up in the U.S.A. while worker wages went down. This means that businesses get more products to sell while the cost goes down and workers make less for their labor. In addition, the top 1% of the population received most of the benefits from the expanding economy than the rest of the population. The difference may be that the economic suffering of the Cubans is largely due to the actions of the U.S.A. and not by the Cuban government. That is because the economic situation in Cuba is largely due to the embargo imposed by the U.S.A. just as the economic situation that killed thousands of children in Iraq was due to the embargo on Iraq imposed by the U.S.A. during the 1990s.

In addition, he related that attending government sponsored rallies and protests in Cuba, such as those against the U.S.A., were required under penalty of government sanctions. He did however admit that due to U.S. government policies and cutbacks on education he has noticed that art education has decreased. Furthermore, he informed me that the children that come to his classes are artistically challenged because they have atrophied imaginations. They do not know what to do with simple instruments like a canvas, cooler and a brush. He spoke about the fact that almost all children carry around with them video games and telephones that seem to deprive the mind of creative expression, the right brained activities of the mind. As I listened, I thought of the fact that promoting a generation with less imagination and more left brained thinking would be more pliable for control by propaganda and television. It would be a strategy that coincides with the project of *dumbing down*[212] the population.

He also admitted that it is not so easy to make ends meet in the U.S.A. especially for an artist. For most things in the U.S.A. culture, it is necessary to have money and so if paintings were not selling an artist would be tempted or forced to go into commercial art or degrade the art by making it purposely controversial in order to gain notoriety and drum up sales.

As he spoke, I thought about the similarities between a fascist system and the capitalist system. Both force the people to live on meager rations. Even though the capitalist system allows more people to have more material objects those objects do not bring happiness or a greater sense of wholeness and anyway those material objects are not owned by the people, but by the creditors or ultimately the state, which can confiscate them whenever necessary. But most of all they are a constant source of stress because the objects, like houses, cars, living expenses, child raising expenses [costs], etc. are constantly going up and the wages are constantly going down in relation to inflation. Therefore, in the capitalist system, for most people there is an illusion of freedom to possess objects and perhaps that is why it works better than the fascist system at perpetuating itself, because of the self-sustaining delusion in most people's minds.

He spoke about how much better the U.S.A. system of government is because at least the people in the U.S.A. can "change" their government every few years and not have to deal with the same person for 40 years or more like Castro. As he said that I was thinking about how the "government" changes personnel in the U.S.A. but the policies that promote racism, and sexism, as well as the policies that promote welfare for the rich, allowing them to get richer and capitalism for the middle class and the poor, allowing them to get poorer, remain the same. So here, we find other illusions.

Another illusion is the illusion of trust. In life, it is necessary to trust certain things. One may trust that the bus driver is not drunk or that the pilot is not high on drugs or that a builder did not use substandard materials in a building. One needs to trust one's family members, that the food one eats is not poisoned or that an airplane engine will not fall and hit one on the head, because a bolt was not tightened enough. One should not trust government power to others or to oneself [one's greed, biases, fears and hatreds] but to an equitable and accountable system, controlled by the wise people of a society, the scholars and elders, that promotes sustainability, equality and consensus of the population and not majority rule of factions, like aristocracies or oligarchies that can terrorize the minorities. That is the best way to promote peace, health, prosperity and security for all, through justice and opportunity for all.

After the attacks on the U.S.A. on 9/11/2001 the newscaster Dan Rather said, he was willing to give the government "the benefit of doubt" in handling the response to the attack. That was a pervasive attitude in the media. However, the capitulation of the media was more powerfully compelled through media consolidation and corporate management.

There is another illusion, the illusion of free speech. The media is composed of opinion talk shows and news reports. The talk shows are not news based but rather opinion based. Most of the hosts and speakers on those shows are closely associated with conservatives, right wing groups and the republican party. One of their tactics is to call the media liberal biased. This is a code term apparently meaning that the media is conservative and that it should not become liberal since studies have shown that the media is overwhelmingly conservative if not right winged from the standpoint of opinions and the lack of reporting and follow-up on the wrongdoings of republican and right winged leaders. So by sounding the alarm of fear about too much left wing there is assurance that the left wing will be suppressed because many people will not want to appear liberal [left wing] in their politics ever if there is no such liberal bias. The republican party and the religious right often accuse the "secular humanists" or the "liberal media" for the lowering moral standards of the country and or turning people away from God. The liberal media, including Hollywood (television, movie, game entertainments, etc.) is not the source of degradation in culture. Actually the degradation in the media and entertainments comes from religious and political support of corporations that put out base entertainments to keep ratings up. Both the democratic party and the republican party support the corporations though the republican party and the religious right, have allowed the most deregulation and corporate consolidation under the doctrine of promoting business interests and therefore are most responsible. So the party that says it is for values (republican party) and the religious right wing (Pentecostals, charismatics, fundamentalists, dominionists, etc.) that says it wants to bring Christian values are actually doing the opposite. Politicians from both parties are afraid to control the media for fear of losing political contributions and for that reason are willing to allow businesses to have free reign even if it corrupts politics and society.

In a fascist system, free speech is prohibited but in the capitalist democracy, the speech is permitted and even touted as a virtue. However, in the U.S.A., any person suggesting a move to change the system is labeled as a "liberal elite"[19] or deemed unpatriotic or part of the enemy strategy to turn the U.S.A. into a left wing state like a communist or socialist country. The U.S.A. power elite have succeeded in stigmatizing socialism or social programs and controls on business interests as a negative form of government. There are several socialist governments in Europe that have existed for decades; they do not seem to be failing. What is objected to by the capitalist proponents is the reduced capacity to have extravagantly rich people and economic power to control other governments. Therefore, since the majority of the population has been convinced that socialism and government social programs are a slip towards communism and loss of individual rights to possess property, the so-called "free speech" is inconsequential and that is perhaps worse than the speech in a totalitarian state. At least in the totalitarian state the speech is given weight and validity by the repression of the government that will lead to people taking notice. The dissenting speech in the U.S.A. is cleverly controlled by mass media conglomerates and the virtual national coalition of right wing conservative talk show hosts/neo-con/right wing Christian leaders. The media in the U.S.A. is actually not different from that of a dictatorship since the dictatorship can only survive through popular opinion and the U.S.A. national news media operates as an imperial news service, providing only the news that supports the emperors and demonstrates the virtues of the empire.

The reports below show how the republican/conservative/right wing point of view is aired much more than any dissenting view in the U.S.A. media. That has the effect of neutralizing the dissenting views and drowning the public in right winged ideologies that would be accepted if for no other reason, because there are more people

[19] presumably meaning anti business, for big spending on government social programs, for amorality and permissiveness, etc., i.e. generally "anti-American"

apparently talking about them; and people more often choose positions by going along with a crowd as opposed to practicing critical thinking about an issue.

> ***No room for progressives on cable news inauguration coverage***
> Media Matters for America inventoried all guests who appeared on FOX News, CNN, and MSNBC during the channels' January 20 inauguration coverage. Between 7 a.m. and 5 p.m. ET, Republican and conservative guests and commentators outnumbered Democrats and progressives 19 to 7 on FOX[213], 10 to 1 on CNN (not including a Republican-skewed panel featuring Ohio voters), and 13 to 2 on MSNBC. Moreover, the rare Democrat or progressive guest usually appeared opposite conservatives, whereas most Republican and conservative guests and commentators appeared solo or alongside fellow conservatives.[214]

In the book, *The Media Monopoly* by Ben Bagdikian [1983], the author predicted that the deregulations by president Reagan would lead to the media monopoly and movement toward pro-corporate and right wing controlled media. The book was originally ridiculed when it came out and it was referred to as "alarmist." Now it is praised due to its foresight. In the most recent edition, the author said:

> "I derive no pleasure from having been correct,"[215]

The following study demonstrated how media bias tilted towards conservative think tank [opinion groups funded by corporations] interviews and away from liberal [progressive] think tanks [independent advocacy groups].

> The media watchdog FAIR conducted a Nexus search of major newspapers, radio and TV transcripts for 1995, and came up with the following answer:
>
> Total Number of Think Tank Citations in Major Newspapers, Radio and TV transcripts: (23)
>
> Conservative 7792
> Centrist 6361
> Progressive 1152

> Although there are far more conservative think tanks than liberal ones in the first place, reporters could easily balance the facts if they wanted to simply by consulting academics at universities.[216]

Today, the main media is controlled by five or six parent corporations so the reporting and advisements are controlled in that way. Another way is through advertising revenue. If a newspaper were to run an article contradicting the agenda of a corporation, the corporation may pull their ads. That has happened many times. One example was *Mother Jones* when it ran stories on cigarettes being linked to cancer in 1980. The tabaco companies pulled the ads and the publication lost important income. Today the publications are careful about writing critical articles about any corporation because they do not know which corporation will want to advertise with them in the future.[217]

Returning to the interview with the artist, of course his arguments come from a position of not having studied in detail the history of Cuba and the U.S.A. before Castro. He does not consider that what Cuba turned into is a reaction to and an effect of U.S.A. foreign policy. Like many other Cubans, he does not recall the previous history because he was too young and blames Castro for the life he experienced and always heard other disgruntled people blaming Castro. The voices of those who point out the U.S.A.'s complicity are more often drowned out in the din of Castro bashing through the media.

In a recent interview on his book, *"Overthrow: America's Century of Regime Change from Hawaii to Iraq"*, the author Stephen Kinzer, offered his opinion about the cost of U.S.A. imperial interventions in Cuba since the 1890s.

> It's quite reasonable to say today that had we not intervened in Cuba and prevented Cuba from becoming independent, had we carried out our explicit promise to the Cubans in 1898, we would never have had to face the entire phenomenon of Castro communism all these last 40 years. Now, of course, we would love to have back a moderate democratic regime like the one that was going to come to power in Cuba in 1898, but it's too late for that, and it's an example of how when we frustrate people's legitimate nationalist aspirations, we wind up not

> only casting those countries into instability, but severely undermining our own national security.[218]

After the Spanish-American War, the U.S.A. took over control of Cuba in 1898. The U.S.A. granted Cuba "independence" in 1902. It was not real independence however, because of the limitations due to the Platt Amendment, which was a unilateral policy statement created by the U.S.A. government leaders that granted the U.S.A. a major control in Cuban affairs and forced Cuba to lease Guantánamo Bay to the United States. The Cubans elected a president and had their own government from 1902-1906. In 1906, the U.S.A. sent troops to Cuba under the authority of the Platt Amendment to interfere with the Cuban government for the first time after the Cubans elected their government. The Platt Amendment was supposedly revoked in 1934. However, the U.S.A. extended the Guantanamo Bay lease on their own authority. The Cubans managed to create a liberal government but in the "Revolt of the Sergeants," Fulgencio Batista took over the Cuban government [in a military coup] as military leader on September 4, 1933. The United States concented to the rule of Batista as they concented more recently to the coup that was staged by the military leader Musharaf in Pakistan, against the democratically elected leader, Benazir Bhutto.

> U.S. Ambassador Benjamin Sumner Welles, sent to Cuba in April of 1933 to mediate differences between the government and opposing political groups, found an ally in Batista. "You're the only individual in Cuba today who represents authority," he said to the recently self-appointed Chief of the Military. When Batista asked what the U.S. "wanted done for recognition," Welles replied, "I will lay down no specific terms; the matter of your government is a Cuban matter and it is for you to decide what you will do about it." To Batista, this was an invitation to rule.
>
> On January 14, 1934, Batista forced provisional president Ramón Grau San Martín to resign, and he appointed Carlos Mendieta to the presidency. Within five days, the U.S. recognized Cuba's new government.[219]

Batista remained as the power behind the government and so there were puppet leaders for the next 35 years. During that time, Batista forged alliances with U.S.A. mafia crime bosses like Meyer Lansky and Lucky Luciano. The U.S.A. government concented because they saw that Batista government as more stable [favorable to U.S.A. policies] than the liberal socially oriented movements that were reacting to the dictators and the corruption that had been imposed on Cuba by the U.S.A. hegemony. In 1940, Batista ran for president and was elected over Grau San Martín. Batista increased trade with the U.S.A. and imposed a war tax on the Cuban people. In 1944, Batista lost the election to Grau San Martín who presented an agenda of liberal social and economic change. In 1952, Batista took over the government in a second coup since he knew he could not win the elections. He suspended the constitution, forged stronger alliances with the mafia and the U.S.A. business leaders, and instituted tight controls on the media and repressive controls on the people. Many of his opponents were murdered or "disappeared"; the U.S.A. government sanctioned all of that. Cuba became a major port for trafficking drugs.

> The Havana Post, expressing the attitude of the U.S. business community after a survey of the four years of Batista's second reign, alluded to the disappearance of gangsterism and said, 'All in all, the Batista regime has much to commend it."[220]

Through the 1950's Fidel Castro and other movements in Cuba opposed the Batista Regime and many opposition leaders and fighters died until Batista was forced to resign in 1959. Through that period, the U.S.A. government supported Batista in his dictatorship and government corruption and collusion with the mafia and U.S.A. businesses. The U.S.A. under President Dwight Eisenhower[20] gave Batista planes, ships and tanks, and napalm but even with all the advanced technology Batista lost in the end. He lost because the revolution was popularly supported – by the people who had been oppressed by Batista and the U.S.A. government and the U.S.A. mafia and business leaders who wanted to exploit the island by building casinos and hotels. When Batista left, the mafia and the many well to do Cubans and Cuban collaborators left in panic, many ending up in South Florida.

Due to U.S.A. hostility towards Cuba and Castro, Castro and Che Guevara turned to the U.S.S.R for help and established a one party

[20] same president who warned the American people about the military industrial complex

state. The U.S.A. tried to assassinate Castro through the C.I.A. and also tried to overthrow Castro as they did other governments that had legitimately elected leaders in the Middle East and South America. Having failed to oust Castro the U.S.A. instituted a trade embargo including travel restrictions to Cuba that has caused much hardship on Cubans. When the Soviet Union disintegrated they were no longer able to subsidize the Cuban government which made the economic situation more precarious. Nevertheless, Cubans have survived through other alliances, tourism, rationing resources and preventing U.S.A. subversive activities which necessarily mean repressive policies on the Cuban people.

So, the very thing that is objected to, the Castro government, was a reaction to the U.S.A. policies since the early 1900's and the internal corruption by the Cuban government that was opposed by its own people who supported the revolution, which could not have succeeded without their support. In this way the rise of Castro and the strident anti-U.S.A. stance of the Cuban population are like the anti-U.S.A. stance of the Iranians, as exemplified by the Iranian President Mahmoud Ahmadinejad, a reaction to U.S.A. imperialism and interfereance with their democratic governments. Due to the desire of U.S.A. hegemony, and hostile acts by the U.S.A. government, Cuba has been forced to enact some authoritarian actions to survive and prevent what they see as a return to the Batista days and the U.S.A. lies and deceptions such as occurred with the original agreement to allow Cuba its freedom but then reneging on that in order to extend American Empire to the Island.

It is important to understand that people who come from repressive countries may see the U.S.A. even in the state described by Supreme Court Justice Sandra Day O'Connor as moving towards "dictatorship" as a good or acceptable condition. It is equally important to understand that those who have lived in the U.S.A. and who have accepted the notions of U.S.A. supremacy and hegemony and fear of attack will agree with them. It is also important for those who live in the U.S.A. who consider themselves as progressives or liberal minded, supporters of civil rights and the path of friendship with other countries as opposed to hegemony as a means to promote peace and security with other countries to realize that those people who blindly follow dictators be it due to ignorance of history, having been indoctrinated with propaganda, or out of fear, etc. need to have education, and they need to have an alternative.

If the voices in a country speak out against dictatorship or loss of civil liberties, etc. but yet present no alternative and in the end acquiesce to the propaganda of fear and the illusion of superiority, entitlement or social egoism and illusions about having the best country in the world and having a right to control the world, etc. the problem of imperial policies and unjust economic social policies will never be resolved because the bridge to people's hearts and minds will not be built. They will continue living out of ignorance and fear and supporting the dictates of any government that seems to offer them stability even at the cost of their own liberty and the enslavement of other nations.

Loss of the Fairness Doctrine and the Shaping of Public Opinion

The media plays an important part in shaping public opinion in the U.S.A. So how was the media system in the country allowed to become polarized, presenting mono-views of issues? One reason was the dismantling of the Fairness Doctrine. During the Reagan administration, the religious conservative and neoconservative movements were able to effect a crucial strategic move that allowed them to gain an unprecedented and unnoticed capacity to proselytize the fundamentalist and extremist Christian views as well as train [mentally condition] a large part of the populace to be accepting of conservative religiosity [dogmatism] and the neoconservative agenda by implanting positive messages and ideas favorable to such Agendas as globalization and economic free trade, through treaties such as NAFTA and transnational corporations. They also promoted the idea that trade deficits and the national debt was acceptable for all Americans. The overall tone, especially during the Reagan presidency was that government knows best and should not be challenged. In the George W. Bush presidency a concerted strategy was used to characterize anyone who challenged the government [executive branch] as not a patriot of the U.S.A.

> The Fairness Doctrine is a former policy of the United State's Federal Communications Commission. It required broadcast licensees to present controversial issues of public importance, and to present such issues in an honest, equal and balanced manner.[221]

These messages were presented and reinforced daily and nationally almost without opposition because of the repeal of the Fairness Doctrine by Ronald Reagan in the year 1987, (which had been enacted in 1934), under the guise of deregulating government, when the FCC repealed it in the Syracuse Peace Conference decision. The commission, which was Republican-controlled, claimed the doctrine had grown to a point that it prevented rather than promoted debate. So they suggested the doctrine was probably unconstitutional since there were supposedly many different media voices in the marketplace. Others, noting the subsequent rise of right-wing radio hosts like Rush Limbaugh, suggest the repeal was more likely motivated by a desire to get partisans on the air to help shape public opinion.[222] State Rep. Mark B. Cohen of Philadelphia, a liberal political leader of Pennsylvania said *"The fairness doctrine helped reinforce a politics of moderation and inclusiveness. The collapse of the fairness doctrine and its corollary rules blurred the distinctions between news, political advocacy, and political advertising, and helped lead to the polarizing cacophony of strident talking heads that we have today."* When the matter went to the court it said that since it was a rule established by the FCC and not Congress, it did not need to be enforced. Congress did subsequently pass a bill to transform the fairness doctrine into a congressionally mandated law. Nevertheless, President Reagan vetoed the bill and since there were not sufficient votes to override the veto the legislation was not passed. Since then measures have been put forth in congress but since the takeover of Congress by the republican party in the year 1994 there has been no chance for the legislation to be passed since absence of such rules favors the republican party propaganda efforts. Conservatives, in contrast, see attempts to revive the Doctrine as an attempt to silence conservative voices.[223] It should be noted that the democrats took control of congress and the presidency during the first term of president Clinton and they did not reinstate the fairness doctrine, so they are complicit in the loss of objectivity in the media and the rise of opinion republican pundits and religious right wing preachers on the radio and in television and their unfettered and unchallenged biased portrayal of current events and their support for unregulated corporate interests.

In the Telecommunications Act of 1996 the republican controlled Congress promoted deregulation of the telecommunication industry including cable, local telephone service, long distance telephone service and broadband. Since the Telecommunications Act of 1996, Clear Channel Communications acquired many local radio stations across the United States, and eventually owned more than 1,200 stations which include as many as 7 stations in certain markets. They have created a virtual network so instead of having many local channels that serve local needs the network can put out a national messages. Since there are no restrictions they can put out any message unchallenged under the guise of free speech. This is why pundits like Rush Limbaugh were able to become popular and disseminate editorials [opinions], many of which do not pay close attention to facts, and not worry about competing voices.[224] The Fox News Channel was launched on October 7, 1996 and became a highly popular U.S.A cable and satellite news channel. It is owned by one major shareholder and chief executive officer, Rupert Murdoch. It is known worldwide as a conservative outlet for the republican party and the president. The Fox News Channel did for television what the conservative radio shows did for radio. Other news outlets such as CNN and MSNBC, noting the popularity of Fox News changed their programming to reflect more conservative views. Therefore, progressive or liberal voices became seldom heard in the television media. On June 2, 2003 the Federal Communications Commission [during a republican controlled Congress] voted to relax certain market ownership restrictions. The movement of deregulation allowed unprecedented media consolidation that left 5 corporations in control of the mass media of the entire country. The corporate owners of those companies are the beneficiaries of and contributors to the political parties so those owners have been known to moderate negative stories about the administration and seldom ask hard questions and usually the investigative reporters of those media present only reports of what the administration has told them and do little investigative reporting [such as that which led to the impeachment of president Nixon]. Thus, the U.S.A. media have been accused by critics of being "cheerleaders" of the establishment since if they do not they will be cut out of access to the administration's statements, which has come to be regarded as "news" as opposed to what they may report on independently which is "not news." This format of the media contributed to the public's opinion in reference to the Iraq war.

The months leading up to the War on Iraq demonstrate how the media swayed opinion for the war by manipulating the media. The media monitoring group F.A.I.R. or *Fairness & Accuracy in Reporting* conducted a study of 1,617 on camera sources between the periods of March 20 to April 9th 3003, the critical period just before the start of the war against Iraq when the population was making its mind about the issue. They discovered that 71% of all the sources used in consulting about the issue, like think tanks, were pro-war and only 3% were anti-war. This number is definitively skewed because polls at the time were showing that most people wanted a delay to the war and that the United Nations weapons inspectors should have time to make a full investigation before considering going to war with Iraq.

> ***Poll Shows Most Want War Delay***
> By Patrick E. Tyler and Janet Elder ***New York Times***
> **February 14, 2003**
> Even after the administration's aggressive case for going to war soon in Iraq, a majority of Americans favor giving United Nations weapons inspectors more time to complete their work so that any military operation wins the support of the Security Council, the latest New York Times/CBS News Poll shows.

The report in the New York Times (above) demonstrates that the media was not following public opinion or at least was not even trying to present a balanced viewpoint about the war. Rather, the media continued to interview many more pro-war activists and "authorities". Instead of probing the veracity of the statements by government officials and challenging the opinions of think tank guests and right wing talk show hosts, the media simply reported what they were saying and then recycled what was said by replaying the shows or the statements of government officials or right wing opinion makers. Most of the right wing talk show hosts [especially on Fox News, MSNBC and CNN] and media think tank guests were receiving daily "talking points" memos put out by the Republican party in order to coordinate the message of the day and gain maximum effect on the propaganda efforts nationally. This was an informal way of communicating the desires of the republican party to those who support it in the media so they could coordinate the message of the day. The informality of the system allowed deniability that there was any collusion while still obtaining effective media coverage for the propagandistic messages. The system worked successfully in promoting the pro-war cause as a viable and legitimate point of view even though it violated international law and there was no evidence to support going to war, namely that the U.S.A. was in imminent danger, and threatened by Iraq. However, after the media onslaught a poll from March 11, 2003 revealed increase in those agreeing with war.

New York Times - March 11, 2003
Growing Number in U.S. Back War, Survey Finds
By ADAM NAGOURNEY and JANET ELDER

Americans are growing impatient with the United Nations and say they would support military action against Iraq even if the Security Council refuses to support an invasion, according to the latest New York Times/CBS News Poll.
The poll found that 58 percent of Americans said the United Nations was doing a poor job in managing the Iraqi crisis, a jump of 10 points from a month ago. And 55 percent of respondents in the latest poll would support an American invasion of Iraq, even if it was in defiance of a vote of the Security Council.
But a majority of respondents, 52 percent, say inspectors should be given more time to search for evidence of nuclear, biological or chemical weapons on the ground in Iraq. Still, that number has dropped over the past month, and there has been an increase in the number of Americans who say the United States has done enough to find a diplomatic solution in Iraq. [225]

However, the poll did show a majority that supported more time for the arms inspectors but the media also tended to downplay it.

US Public Opinion and War
By Benjamin I. Page
March 12, 2003

It is FUTURE, retrospective opinion about the actual results of war (casualties among US soldiers and Iraqi civilians; $ costs; duration; turmoil in the region; terrorist attacks, etc) that may bite, as it did with Vietnam. And the ANTICIPATION of such future opinion by decision makers may affect current decisions. Hence I continue to think of Karl Rove, in charge of Bush's reelection, as a possible force for peace if he perceives that his boss is about to jump off a cliff.
The Tuesday 3/11 NYT piece, "Growing Number in U.S. Back War," is misleading on certain fundamental points (see below), but it did document some modest success for the relentless Bush PR campaign. The 10 point rise (to 58%) in judgments that the UN is doing a "poor job" on Iraq reflects Bush's incessant talk. So does the 8 point rise (to 44%) in the "take action...fairly soon" responses as vs. waiting and giving the inspectors more time. The most discouraging finding is that 55% "approve of" (which, however, generally gets 5-6% more people than "favor") "the United States taking military action against Iraq if the U.N. Security Council votes against the [which?] U.S.-sponsored resolution." Though no trend data are given, this suggests substantial

> Bush success at UN bashing and puffing up the existence of imaginary playmates in a "coalition of the willing."
> One misleading aspect of the Times story is the failure to emphasize the continued 52%-44% majority for giving the UN and inspectors more time. A more fundamental weakness is the unaccountable failure to ask questions about ALLIES in an Iraq adventure, which in the past has been seen as even more crucial than UN approval. Various surveys suggest that support for war shrinks to a very low level in the absence of substantial allied backing. Britain, at minimum, seems absolutely crucial. [226]

The repression of anti-war sentiment went further. In the months leading to the attack on Iraq not only were anti-war protestors and activists as well as academics and intellectual left wing think tank guests not invited to talk shows or interviewed for news reports but when activists like Janeane Garofalo, Susan Sarandon and Bishop Melvin Talbert from the United Methodist Church [the church of President George W. Bush] tried to run regular advertisements they were rejected by most networks even though the anti-war protestors wanted to pay for the spots like any other advertisers. Celebrities and artists such as the Dixie Chicks who spoke out against the war and warmongering were ostracized by right wing groups and several commentators the media supported the right wing statements against them, calling for them to be boycotted or that their jobs should be withdrawn. This amounts to unofficial "blacklisting." Criticism of President George W. Bush in 2003, by the Dixie Chicks, led to controversy and a repudiation from the right wing media and from some of their core country audience. On March 10, 2003, as the U.S.A. was planning the invasion of Iraq that was to occur on March 20, Natalie Maines (born in Lubbock, Texas) made some comments between songs during a concert that took place at the Shepherd's Bush Empire theatre in London: *"Just so you know, we're ashamed the President of the United States is from Texas."*[227]

They (especially Maines) received death threats and were ostracized. In 2006 they released a new single called *"Not Ready To Make Nice"*. Some of the lyrics are included below. It would seem that they have regained support from their fans as the actions of the president led him to perhaps the lowest polled approval rating in presidential history, but certainly in his administration, due to the failed policies and the war in Iraq that was entered into by subterfuge and the aftermath of which was poorly handled.

> "I'm not ready to make nice/I'm not ready to back down/I'm still mad as hell and I don't have time to go round and round and round/It's too late to make it right/I probably wouldn't if I could/'Cause I'm mad as hell/Can't bring myself to do what it is you think I should"

Criticizing the death threats, they also said: *" It's a sad sad story when a mother will teach her daughter that she ought to hate a perfect stranger/And how in the world can the words that I said/Send somebody so over the edge that they'd write me a letter sayin' that I better shut up and sing or my life will be over."* In a press release, Robison said, *"The stakes were definitely higher on that song. We knew it was special because it was so autobiographical, and we had to get it right. And once we had that song done, it freed us up to do the rest of the album without that burden."*

Americans Pay Price for Speaking Out

Dissenters Face Job Loss, Arrest, Threats but Activists Not Stopped by Backlash- By Kathleen Kenna

Toronto Star
August 9, 2003

Across the United States, hundreds of Americans have been arrested for protesting the war. The American Civil Liberties Union has documented more than 300 allegations of wrongful arrest and police brutality from demonstrators at anti-war rallies in Washington and New York. Even the silent, peaceful vigils of Women in Black — held regularly in almost every state — have prompted threats of arrest by American police. Actors and spouses Tim Robbins and Susan Sarandon have publicly denounced the backlash against them for their anti-war activism.
Robbins said they were called "traitors" and "supporters of Saddam" and their public appearances at a United Way luncheon in Florida and the Baseball Hall of Fame in Cooperstown, N.Y., this spring were cancelled in reaction to their anti-war stance. Actor/comedian Janeane

> Garofalo was stalked and received death threats for opposing the war in high-profile media appearances.
> MSNBC hosts asked viewers to urge MCI to fire actor and anti-war activist Danny Glover as a spokesperson — the long-distance telephone giant refused to fire him despite the ensuing hate-mail campaign — and one host, former politician Joe Scarborough, urged that anti-war protesters be arrested and charged with sedition.[228]

In the 1991 Gulf War as in the 2003 second War on Iraq the government allowed members of the media to be "embedded" with the troops. It was discovered that the reporters experienced a bond with the soldiers and felt as comrades and took the situation personally, which impaired their ability to report objectively and accurately. One observer likened that to the "Stockholm Syndrome." [The effect of a hostage coming to feel empathy for the captors after a period of time.] Since there was no independent reporting the reports amounted to stenography, repeating the statements of government or armed forces spokespersons. An example of stenography as opposed to investigative reporting in the mainstream media was demonstrated by Robert Fisk during an interview on the alternative news program *Democracy Now*, hosted by Amy Goodman.

> Democracynow.org *Friday, April 7th, 2006*
> ***Robert Fisk on Iraq, Palestine and the Failure of the U.S. Corporate Media to Challenge Authority***[229]
>
> **AMY GOODMAN:** Robert Fisk is our guest, war correspondent for more than 30 years. Your response, once again, to the issue of the planting of stories?
>
> **ROBERT FISK:** Well, I'm surprised the military have to plant stories, because I find that an awful lot of my colleagues are quite happy to go along with stories planted or otherwise. You've only got to see the number of times on the front page of the *New York Times* or the *L.A. Times* or the *Washington Post* when the phrase "American officials say" appears, particularly the *L.A. Times*. I can give an example of that, in which a whole story is repeatedly sourced, after 2003, when we know there weren't any weapons of mass destruction, when we know the press was misled totally in the United States and went along with the war party.
> Still we see everything being sourced and re-sourced back to American officials, as if the U.S. administration is the center of world truth. I'll give you an example. I was actually doing the book tour in Los

> Angeles, picked up my morning *L.A. Times*. Here's a story about Zarqawi, who may or may not exist, of course. "U.S. authorities say," "U.S. officials said," "Said one Justice Department counterterrorism official," "U.S. authorities say," "officials said," "U.S. officials said." It turns to page B-10. It gets worse and worse. Look. "Several U.S. officials said," "those officials said," "U.S. officials confirmed" -- stop me when you want -- "American officials complained," "U.S. officials stressed," "U.S. authorities believe," "Said one U.S. senior intelligence official," "U.S. officials said," "Jordanian officials said" -- Amy, see, there's a slight difference here -- "Several U.S. officials said," "U.S. officials said," "U.S. officials say," "say U.S. officials," "U.S. officials said," "The American officials said," "One U.S. counterterrorism official said." Welcome to American journalism today in Iraq. This is what's wrong.

One way in which misinformation works is to continue repeating it even when it has been proven false. Even when those statements were proven to be inaccuracies or outright lies they continued to be unchallenged.[230] There are other forms of propaganda that governments now use which is especially effective: misinformation by paying newspapers to run planted stories or through "fake news" stories, news reports made to look like reporters are reporting when in reality the corporations or agencies commissioned their filming and content. The use of propaganda on U.S.A. citizens is supposed to be prohibited by the law. Yet there is no law controlling "free speech" that amounts to unchallenged political opinion, which is often skewed in favor of a particular agenda that has the effect of corrupting the political process. In war there is no restriction on propaganda or misinformation. This is why the U.S. government secretly paid Iraqi newspaper reporters to plant favorable stories to the U.S.A. occupation in the Iraqi newspapers (Nov. 2005).[231] However, due to modern technology, the misinformations in other parts of the world do not remain localized; they in fact proliferate and return to their source, the U.S.A., through all media channels reporting on the war in Iraq. Thus, the people in the U.S.A. receive mixed messages such as, "things are going well," but at the same time "the country is in chaos," which lead to confusion and inaction due to a deadlocked population. Nevertheless, the law has historically been violated and U.S.A. citizens have been targets of misinformation directly as well as indirectly. Another recent report in the alternative media examined this issue further.

Democracy Now -Friday, March 24th, 2006
The PsyOps War: A Look at the Lincoln Group and the U.S. Military's Planting of Stories in the Iraqi Press

JUAN GONZALEZ: But there is this other area, not of what, as you say, public relations that they tell us or psychological operations against the enemy, but the public that surrounds, let's say, an insurgent force, and there's been a long history within the United States government of trying to influence public opinion through, quote, "legitimate press." I remember studies written about – in Guatemala, how the C.I.A., in the run-up to the 1954 coup against Arbenz, planted numerous stories in the Guatemalan press to sort of prepare public opinion for it, and most recently the – it was revealed in papers of the COINTELPRO F.B.I. operations in Puerto Rico how the F.B.I. regularly wrote and planted and got editors of legitimate newspapers to plant stories against the independence movement. So, there's been somewhat of a history of our government, unfortunately, resorting to using legitimate press to sort of shape public opinion.
COL. SAM GARDINER: Right, Juan, and you've, you know, you've probably had to mention the C.I.A. in most of those. There is a law which forbids the government to plant false stories in American press. The problem with technology is it's now no longer possible to separate those. So we get false stories that are planted overseas…

Many people think that the planting of propaganda in newspapers is only a foreign occurrence. Actually, it was documented that the U.S.A. government, along with infiltrating protest groups, also colluded with newspapers and other media organizations in the U.S.A. to plant stories in order to control public opinion in the last 40 years. Gary Hart is the author of *The Shield and the Cloak: The Security of the Commons*, and was a Senator and candidate for president of the U.S.A. as well as a member of the Church Commission, a congressional committee set up to investigate conspiracies by the Nixon administrations. He talked with journalist Amy Goodman, on the program *Democracy Now,* about how the C.I.A. worked with major media outlets to deceive the U.S.A. population. The Church investigation led to laws such as the F.I.S.A. act [Foreign Intelligence Surveillance Act] which was supposed to prevent the government and the president in particular, from spying or planting propaganda or misinformation to deceive the U.S.A. population. According to reputable legal sources, that law was violated again between the years 2001-2005 by president George W.

Bush, though he has not been held accountable because his party dominates the congress house and senate.

> **AMY GOODMAN:** And, of course, it's not just -- the C.I.A. can't do it unless they have willing accomplices.
> **GARY HART:** Right.
> **AMY GOODMAN:** And so, you had the *New York Times*, you had the *Louisville Courier-Journal*, you had *Time* magazine, you had CBS, you had *Newsweek*, you had the *Miami Herald*, the *Saturday Evening Post*, you had a lot of publications and news outlets that were willing to work with the C.I.A.
> **GARY HART:** Yes. I think that's fair to say.[232]

Thus, it is the responsibility of responsible persons to avail themselves of alternative media wherein they can obtain credible news and thereby be able to make intelligent decisions about current events, history and the issues that face the culture and humanity in general. It is incumbent upon those who obtain the correct or more objective reports to share those with others so as to prevent the indoctrination of others with inaccuracies that serve the agendas of those who would abuse the people.

The Power Elite and the Neo-Con Agenda

The move towards globalization and the unbridled pursuit of profit has led to the creation of a global market in which multinational corporations can be free to pursue profits without regard to the consequences of national populations. This means that a corporation no longer needs to worry about local workers and their ability to pay their bills or buy their products since they can find cheaper labor abroad and also other markets with people that have money to buy their products. This has caused the loss of manufacturing jobs, which the companies have moved to countries with cheaper labor so the middle class and the poor in the national economy of the U.S.A. have lost income in wages. However, the wealthy investors and company owners have prospered. As the economic situation with the trade deficits and national debt worsen a time will come when the government and the economy will no longer be able to operate with deficit [borrowed] money and there will be a national economic "correction" in which imports will not be sustainable and the standard of living will decrease dramatically for people in the U.S.A. and other nations closely related to the U.S.A. such as Canada due to such agreements as the North American Free Trade Agreement [NAFTA] which entangle Canada, the U.S.A. and Mexico in an economic treaty that benefits multinational companies instead of ordinary people. The proof of that is that one of the stated purposes of the agreement was to bolster the Mexican economy and that never happened. There are as many illegal immigrants seeking to come to the U.S.A. as before. Jorge Castaneda, the Mexican Foreign Minister, said that NAFTA was a deal between the *"rich and powerful"* of Canada, U.S.A. and Mexico that left out the lower classes. That statement corroborates criticism from progressive and liberal groups that charge the Mexican governments for the last several decades as being composed of oligarchs who have purposely maintained low wages in order to draw business and companies from the U.S.A. to do business in and move their factories to Mexico. The oligarchs in Mexico have colluded with the Mexican government to maintain the Mexican masses poor, relative to the U.S.A. economy. That is the reason for the dire economic conditions in Mexico that prompt the people to risk their lives to get into the U.S.A. and find any kind of work. Some of the progressive and liberal speakers also charge that the republican party and the corporations want to turn the U.S.A. population into a new form of mexican low wage center relative to China. The idea would be that as China emerges as a stronger and economically even more dynamic country than the U.S.A. the population of the U.S.A. would assume the position relative to China that Mexico now has to the U.S.A. Multinational corporations would not suffer since they have been released from national restrictions and may even have their headquarters abroad. Unlike ordinary people who live on meager wages and have only one bank account, the corporations can have many assets and accounts around the world, thus minimizing their risks in any economic downturn. In other words, the economic collapse of the U.S.A. would not hurt them as much or at all since in economics losses and gains are in great degree, relative; for example, a rich person in Mexico can be a middle class person in the U.S.A.

The globalized economy has led to what author Jeff Faux calls "The Party of Davos" since the leaders of the governments and corporations controlling the world economy met in Davos to have their annual World Economic Forum.

> That the global economy is developing a global ruling class should come as no shock. All markets generate economic class differences. In stable, self-contained national economies, where capital and labor need each other, political bargaining produces a social contract that allows enough wealth to trickle down from the top to keep the majority loyal. "What's good for General Motors is good for America," Dwight Eisenhower's Defense Secretary famously said in the 1950s. The United Auto Workers agreed, which at the time seemed to toss the notion of class warfare into the dustbin of history.
> But as domestic markets become global, investors increasingly find workers, customers and business partners almost anywhere. Not surprisingly, they have come to share more economic interests with their peers in other countries than with people who simply have the same nationality. They also share a common interest in escaping the restrictions of their domestic social contracts.[233]

The new global class that controls the world economy therefore has allegiances to itself and not to its country of origin. By definition it is global and so its loyalty is to the best way to make money and not the place where it resides. So the relationship between the owners and workers and the lower classes is unhinged and so the responsibility to provide decent wages is diminishing and the rich and powerful are independent from the global middle and lower classes. As Faux explains, Davos has no army but it relies on the U.S. Government to provide the army and keep the economy in operation through the US Treasury, the IMF, and the World Bank. But he also explains that the economic malfeasance and military overreach has weakened the U.S.A. power.

> The crisis on the military side involves blowback from the overreach in Iraq. Bush, Cheney and Rumsfeld--despite their thick transnational corporate connections--have created a disaster for Davos. The war has unleashed an army of enemies of Western modernization that is making global corporations nervous.[234]

In answer to a question about his experiences as a civil rights worker in the 1950s the entertainer and civil rights leader Harry Belafonte expressed the following comments about the F.B.I., espionage on U.S.A. citizens, corruption in government and the new brashness with which politicians openly purvey lies, deceptions to the public, and government operations that are eroding civil rights but also how the complacency and acquiescence of the masses needs to come to an end in order to bring about ethics in government and society.

> Although we suspected that we were being surveilled, we didn't know the extent of it until reports began to be revealed and came out in a number of books that were written. Perhaps the most detailed and one of the best-researched was a writer by the name of Taylor Branch, who did a trilogy called *Parting the Waters* and then *Pillar of Fire*, and the most recent, *Canaan's Edge*. In *Canaan's Edge*, much of his research was drawn from wiretaps, from surveillances, from conversations taped in the White House and the Justice Department and through the F.B.I. These revelations should say to the American people: such a mechanism has been in place for a very, very long time. The essential difference between then and now, in the face of the same horror, is that no previous regime tried to subvert the Constitution. They may have done illegal acts. They may have gone outside the law to do these, but they did them clandestinely. No one stepped to the table as arrogantly as George W. Bush and his friends have done and said, 'We legally want to suspend the rights of citizens, the right to surveil, the right to

> read your mail, the right to arrest you without charge. You do not have the right to counsel if we so decide, and you can stay in prison as long as we want you to, until we're satisfied that we have reached the objectives that we want, despite the Constitution.'
> I think that every person in the United States of America should be up in arms, should be up in rebellion against the reality that we face, that it is that fact that made me say that I think and I feel that we are at the dawnings of a new Gestapo state here in the United States, through the security -- Securities Commission and through the Homeland Security, as well – National Security Agency. All of these different agencies, all of these different bureaucracies have their own special assignments, and then they come – and when you look at the collective, America is playing out a horror theme. The fact that we're a joyous nation, when you see sports and you see so much light, frothy, mindless entertainment bombarding you every day and so much disinformation coming your way, is enough to make any citizen mentally, as well as socially, blurred to truth.[235]

The sentiments of Mr. Belafonte in reference to the unabashed openness of the ruling class in their statements and actions of censorship, breaking social laws such as the constitution, and fascist activities like incarcerating people without due process or spying on them with impunity, are echoed in the words of Arundhati Roy in a speech given at the World Social Forum in Mumbai, January 16, 2004.

> Our project was the World Social Forum. Theirs — to further what many call the "Project for the New American Century". In the great cities of Europe and the US, where a few years ago these things would only have been whispered, now people are openly talking about the good side of imperialism and the need for a strong empire to police an unruly world. The new missionaries want order at the cost of justice. Discipline at the cost of dignity. And ascendancy at any price.

Roy's incisive comment seems to allude to a growing world population in which the masses of people are being mistreated to the extent that they would cry out for a strong dictator, not just of their own country but a dictator for the world, forgetting the ideas of justice or democracy. When people are stressed sufficiently they may desire a dictator just so that the war and violence might end. In this way, the worldwide violence and destabilization of governments can be a strategy to cause most of the people to accept the superpower policing of the world even though it would also mean they would be exploited. One of the most startling and stark examples of the open defiance of law was the admission by president George W. Bush that he authorized secret wire taps of U.S. Citizens without court orders in defiance of the Foreign Intelligence Surveillance Act. A vast majority of constitutional law teachers and congressional watchers agreed that this was an impeachable offence. Yet, the republican party presiding senators refused to open an investigation or seek a court finding which would certainly have forced impeachment hearings.[236]

Propaganda is a key tactic used to influence and condition the minds of the ignorant or the susceptible. Ignorance and intelligence can coexist in the mind of a person. Ignorance is "absence of knowledge of truth." Intelligence is the "ability to acquire and apply knowledge." If the knowledge given to a person is evil it can be used intelligently. Intelligence does not necessarily imply ethics, integrity or reason based on reality or real facts. This is why smart people can commit heinous crimes through inventive and well thought out schemes. Neither the righteous nor the unrighteous person is a true independent human being until they can rationally understand truth AND also live by it through their own volition. Doing what they are told is the child's fate for a reason. The soul must learn to act righteously in the world and must be trained. However, they must understand why righteousness is true and unrighteousness is not. Then they have the capacity to become ethical adult human beings.

> "If you are among the people, gain your supporters by building trust. The trusted are those who do not speak the first thing to come to mind; and they will become leaders. If people of means have a good name, and their face is benign, people will praise them even without their knowledge. Those whose hearts obey their bellies, however, ask for contempt instead of love. Their hearts are naked. Their bodies are unanointed. The greathearted are a gift from God. Those who are ruled by their appetites belong to the enemy."
>
> -Ancient Egyptian Proverb[237]

However, that same capacity and even desire of children to be led, which is a survival instinct, can be turned into a diabolical feature of the personality. Something peculiar happens when a person (males and females, but especially males) is given a uniform and given the authority to discipline others. They take on an altered state of personality and they are then capable of doing previously unimaginable things. If adults can be coerced in this way imagine what children can be made to do, fight wars, commit atrocities and worse. All that is needed is to take away the voices of truth, instill fear of noncompliance, indoctrinate with propaganda and stamp out descent through fear, paranoia and preventing people from thinking for themselves (critical thinking). That is how fascist government support is formed and sustained. Many people thought that the Soviet Union was the ultimate fascist regime but as Noam Chomsky put it, the USA is much more powerful because they do not need guns to keep people in line, they just use narcissistic propaganda about how wonderful and good Americans are and fear propaganda about how bad the world is while dangling the ideal of attaining the "American Dream" just out of reach of most people. Chomsky's term for this process of social control is "Manufacturing Consent." The Nazi regime in Germany used these tactics expertly to control and coerce the population into militarizing and supporting genocide and the quest for world conquest.

> "Why of course the people don't want war. . . . That is understood. But, after all, it is the leaders of the country who determine the policy, and it's always a simple matter to drag the people along whether it's a democracy, a fascist dictatorship, a parliament or a communist dictatorship . . . the people can always be brought to the bidding of the leaders. . . . All you have to do is tell them they are being attacked, and denounce the pacifists for lack of patriotism, and exposing the country to greater danger.
>
> --Hermann Goering, Nazi Reichsmarshal and Luftwaffe chief at Nuremberg trials, 1945

U.S.A. culture has been driven by fear for a long time; fear of European oppression, fear of Native Americans, fear of an African slave revolt, fear of retribution from God for the treatment of Africans and Native Americans, fear of fascism, fear of communists, fear of homosexuals, fear of Islam, fear of the loss of the way of life, etc.; this constitutes an overall fear culture. For many years the actions of the USA have caused much fear of and hatred for the USA in other countries. The events of 9/11/2001 were merely the result of those actions. And as long as the USA government and people refuse to acknowledge the damage to the life and property of others and work to make restitution, the anger and hatred of others will continue to produce the desire for revenge and retribution against the USA. Prior to the Iraq war the Bush administration heightened fears by constantly conjuring up images of "mushroom clouds over American cities," "gathering threats from terrorists and their supporters," (which were baseless) color coded terror alert systems, and linking Saddam Hussein to the September 11, 2001 attack on the united states when there was no evidence. Also, during the 2004 election campaign advertisements were aired that called democrats and other critics of the President's policy on Iraq unpatriotic and the presidential opponent (Kerry) as a disgraced war hero (all false statements). Many people believed the propaganda and the corporate media facilitated the process.

Very small mention was given to any researchers or reporters questioning why the people who attacked on September 11, 2001 felt they had to do so. Also, little mention was given in the press about the stated grievances of those in the Arab countries who felt and continue to feel oppressed by American Imperial Hegemony. The strategy was and continues to be to deflect that line of questioning and label the attackers as terrorists, thugs, mad men or religious fanatics instead of people with legitimate grievances since that would mean that the U.S.A. policy would need to be reviewed and exposed to national and international scrutiny, criticism and would require the possibility of needing to change from the path of domination to a path of peaceful coexistence with other countries.

The president is not the sole architect of the policy of USA hegemony and imperialism, nor is one political party solely responsible. There is a staff of assistants and advisors to the president who devise and implement various propaganda schemes. In the Texas race for governor the political manager Carl Rove, put out the message that the opponents of Bush were gays and gay supporters. That propaganda had the effect of providing a rallying point for fundamentalists Christians who saw an opportunity to create a movement in their congregations to vote against "gays" but in reality supporting the religious right agenda of getting politicians, favorable to their cause, elected. So the republican party mobilized many people in that way who ordinarily did not vote before, bringing them victory in state and national elections. The religious right therefore motivated the simple minded "God fearing" indoctrinated populace who were already caught in the grip of fear due to the decline in the moral standards of the country.

Most people are disillusioned with the government so they do not vote; they are fed up with the mudslinging and insensitivity of politicians as well as their powerlessness over them once elected. That frustration works to the advantage of the power elite politicians because statistics show that the more people that stay away from the electoral process the less progressive votes are cast. So that promotes the power of conservative, fundamentalist and fascist voters. The lack of control over politicians is actually designed into the system of representative government and bolstered by specific constitutional articles such as the Electoral College and the staggered electoral process. Voting for a leader extends no control over what they will do and was never meant to. If we examine the opinions of the "Founding Fathers" of the U.S.A. and their thoughts that went into the creation of the U.S. Constitution that form the basis of the U.S.A. government it becomes evident that actually the USA system of government was designed to take away the power of "the people." Furthermore, it is by design that there is a law of truth in advertising that applies to businesses selling goods but there is no law to require politicians to tell the truth!

James Madison's Virginia Plan idea was to create a republican system of government. In a republic, the people are theoretically the ultimate power. The people then transfer that power to elected or "appointed" representatives. Thus, the republican system reassigns the power of the people to representatives who are supposed to theoretically do the bidding of the people. For Alexander Hamilton, the Virginia Plan of Madison was not enough. Hamilton was of the general opinion that the masses could not be trusted to select the leaders of the United States.[238] So other measures, along with the republican model, were incorporated into the U.S. government to insure control by the American aristocracy instead of the masses.

So there is much dysfunction, psychosis, fear and confusion to go around in the USA social fabric that affects the masses (not the leaders (5%-10% who own 90% or more of the wealth), preside in government and Fortune 500 companies). It is therefore easy to start a panic in such an environment. After the September 11, 2001 incident the president exhorted to all Americans that they should be "patriotic" by going to the shopping mall as often as possible!

In the months leading up to the 2004 presidential elections the color coded "terror alert" system was constantly raised and lowered, having the effect of keeping people constantly in a state of stress over a possible other impending attack. After the election the system hardly received any publicity. At the same time the republican party widely distributed the message that a change in leadership would be dangerous since their party was doing a better job on national security. Judging from the results of the election and the victory of the republican party it would seem that the message, coupled with the stress strategy worked. So in order to maintain control over the population it was important to maintain the constant heightened state of alert along with the urge to be patriotic.

Many people have marveled at the breathtaking number of documented deceptions and outright lies told by the George W. Bush administration but what was most fascinating is the fact that he was still supported by a significant segment of the population [30%-36%] by the middle of his second term, which demonstrated the core of his constituency and his base which was composed of ordinary people who considered themselves as politically conservative and or religiously conservative and did not feel daunted by almost any scandal or impropriety, from warrantless wiretaps on American citizens to lies about weapons of mass destruction in Iraq as a pretext to go to war or outing the name of a C.I.A. operative for political gain.

The ruling class of the world [those rich and powerful people that control the economy and the most powerful military force] may be thought of as elites who see their task as imposing order and amassing power to control the world for all power elites in all countries. The so called neoconservative group that is in control of the U.S.A. government may be thought of as the extreme power elite that are willing and desirous to use military force as well as misinformation to achieve their goals. Several researchers have investigated the source of such a deceptive manner of conducting government and have centered on a little know political philosopher that advanced those ideas as legitimate and necessary strategies for running a government. This philosophy also explains the legitimizing of the plausible deniability concept as a proper and beneficial governing strategy as well.

Leo Strauss (September 20, 1899 – October 18, 1973), was a political philosopher in the U.S.A. of German-Jewish ancestry. He is widely regarded to be one of the principal intellectual creators of neo-conservatism. His ideas have come to be known as "Strausianism". Straus held that "isolated liberal democracies live in constant danger from hostile elements abroad," so policy advisers need to deceive their own people as well as the rulers in order to protect the country. Shadia Drury, author of 1999's *Leo Strauss and the American Right*, explained that "Strauss was neither a liberal nor a democrat," and "perpetual deception of the citizens by those in power is critical (in Strauss's view) because they need to be led, and they need strong rulers to tell them what's good for them… Strauss taught that within societies, "some are fit to lead, and others to be led".[239] Straus once wrote: "Because mankind is intrinsically wicked, he has to be governed."

Drury explained that "Such governance can only be established, however, when men are united--and *they can only be united against other people*." [highlighted text by Ashby] "Strauss thinks that a political order can be stable only if it is united by an external threat,"[240] Drury explained that *"Following Machiavelli, he maintains that if no external threat exists, then one has to be manufactured. Had he lived to see the collapse of the Soviet Union, he would have been deeply troubled because the collapse of the 'evil empire' poses a threat to America's inner stability." "In Strauss' view, you have to fight all the time (to survive)"*[241]

The Straussian concepts of mass deception have been implemented in the form of mass indoctrination in the U.S.A. through media consolidation and the abolition of the Fairness Doctrine, fake news releases and the organized media offensive of the republican party by issuing daily "talking points memos" for all conservative speakers to follow. In other parts of the world such as Iraq, secret stories favorable to the U.S.A. were planted in local newspapers as was discovered in 2005 in order to sway the public opinion in favor of the U.S.A.

The philosophy described above explains the desire to have a visible enemy to rally the people against and cause them to accept the loss of freedoms so as to be controlled more efficiently and that of course was one of the purposes of the U.S.A. Patriot Act that was passed immediately following the attack by Muslim extremists on 9/11/01. The bill was immediately available and ready to be implemented by Congress because it was previously politically impossible to enact it prior to the 9/11 attack, which is why some critics of the act who say it unnecessarily takes too many freedoms away, say it was part of an overall right wing strategy to reduce rights and better control not terrorists but ordinary American citizens.

The work of Straus reaches directly into the neoconservative movement through its main proponents and their influence on the president. Paul Wolfowitz, the Deputy Defense Secretary is probably the most notable proponent of Strausianism since he was an actual student of Strauss during college. Other strongly influential *Straussians* include William Kristol [*Weekly Standard* Chief Editor] and Gary Schmitt, who is the founder, as well as chairman, and director of the Project for the New American Century (PNAC). PNAC is a nine-year-old neoconservative group that includes the current Vice President, Dick Cheney and Secretary of Defense Donald Rumsfeld. The PNAC also includes several other senior foreign policy officials. Interestingly, Wolfowitz himself claimed to be more of a student of Albert Wohlstetter who believed in a special nuclear weapons strategy that amounts to a rethinking of the traditional doctrine known as 'mutual assured destruction' (MAD, in its apt English acronym and the acronym's corresponding synonym), which was the basis for nuclear deterrence during the "Cold War" The Cold War was a political, ideological and geographical struggle between the superpowers U.S.A. and the Soviet Union for world domination, that did not take the form of a direct confrontation but operated through their surrogate or allied countries and a nuclear arms race-between 1947 and 1991].

> In 2003, two French journalists writing for *Le Monde* (Paris) summarized Wohlstetter's ideas on nuclear strategy. Wohlstetter, they said, "was at the origin of the rethinking of the traditional doctrine known as 'mutual assured destruction' (MAD, in its English acronym), which was the basis for nuclear deterrence. According to this theory, two blocs capable of inflicting upon each other irreparable damages would cause leaders to hesitate to unleash the nuclear fire. For Wohlstetter and his pupils, MAD was both immoral -- because of the destruction inflicted on civilian populations -- and ineffective: it led to the mutual neutralization of nuclear arsenals. No statesman endowed with reason, and in any case no American president, would decide on 'reciprocal suicide.' Wohlstetter proposed on the contrary a 'graduated deterrence,' i.e. the acceptance of limited wars, possibly using tactical nuclear arms, together with 'smart' precision-guided weapons capable of hitting the enemy's military apparatus. He criticized the politics of nuclear arms limitations conducted together with Moscow. It amounted, according to him, to constraining the technological creativity of the United States in order to maintain an artificial equilibrium with the USSR." [242]

Thus, Wolfowitz acknowledged he believes in a strategy of using limited or tactical nuclear weapons to achieve military control especially when U.S.A. forces are limited and need to destroy bunkers such as underground command and control centers of so called enemy forces or nuclear installations of countries that have been deemed "enemies" of "American national interests" such as Iran. This explains the continuing reports of secret researches by the U.S.A. and Britain, on suitcase nuclear weapons and small devises that would supposedly not be as destructive as the weapons used on Japan or which have been subsequently developed.[243] Under the conditions of stress and constant rhetoric about how Iran cannot be allowed to acquire nuclear weapons a situation in which such weapons would be justified and the use of which the U.S.A. population would accept, given the climate of fear and the indoctrination to blindly accept the information provided by and decisions of the president, is not unfathomable.

In the usual manner of reporting what U.S. government officials say, a network media report reflected the supposed consensus opinion, which is in reality only an idea supported by the U.S.A., some European countries and a few others that Iran cannot be allowed to acquire nuclear weapons. [Highlighted text by Ashby]

> ***U.S. Critical As Iran Marks Nuke Step*** [244]
> CBS News April 11, 2006
> State Department spokesman Sean McCormack said he could not verify what he called the technical details of Tehran's announcement.
>
> "This is another step by the Iranians in defiance of the international community. Once again they have chosen the pathway of defiance instead of the pathway of cooperation," he said.
>
> The Pentagon is reviewing a variety of contingency plans, **CBS News' Claudia Coffey** reports.
>
> "Everyone agrees that Iran cannot be allowed to possess nuclear weapons. That would be destabilizing for the region as well as the world," McCormack said.

The USA policy of creating an unprecedented war machine and depriving countries it is not allied with and cannot control from obtaining nuclear weapons which they could theoretically use to protect themselves [using the MAD concept discussed above] is in reality hegemony [otherwise known as the Wolfowitz Doctrine]. That strategy is controlling the world's natural resources to make the USA the richest most powerful country and prevent the possibility of any country from emerging as a rival, if necessary by force. The strategy promotes globalization and makes use of institutions like the CIA which destabilize governments and economies so that other countries will then turn to the World Bank, World Trade Organization and the International Monetary Fund or private corporations for help to bail out their economies. The infrastructure for the implementation of the strategy is technology (global communication and weapons) and the glue of the strategy is therefore, greed and power.

Globalization really means "opening up" countries to foreign investors, i.e. western investors and keeping countries in debt to the West. It is a form of slavery that uses contracts, and economic agreements to force governments to devastate their economies by allowing them to be depleted and weakened by the U.S.A. corporations. Those who protest U.S.A. hegemony and "investment" are labeled as undemocratic and corrupt and their regime must be removed so that a "free society" may emerge, i.e. one that is free to do what the U.S.A. wants. Notice that the nations, which disagree with U.S.A. hegemony, are classified as breaking the "rule of law." Never mind that the U.S.A. does not support the world court or victim rights, and emphasizes corporate laws and the profit motive. These features of U.S.A. culture have been cited as resembling the ancient Roman Empire, but which is reaching for new heights of power and worldwide control.

> *It does not matter if they love us, what matters is that they fear us...*
>
> -Ancient Roman statement

The same sentiment expressed in the Roman policy echoed in the writings of Machiavelli and also is evident in the treatment of countries that had rallied to support the U.S.A. after the attack in the U.S.A. on September 11, 2001.

Machiavelli - *The Prince*; Chapter 17

> "The answer is that one would like to be both the one and the other; but because it is difficult to combine them, it is far better to be feared than loved if you cannot be both...Men worry less about doing an injury to one who makes himself loved than to one who makes himself feared. The bond of love is one which men, wretched creatures that they are, break when it is to their advantage to do so; but fear is strengthened by a dread of punishment which is always effective."

A Missed Opportunity

After al Qaeda's attacks in the United States, the European members of NATO invoked Article Five of the North Atlantic Treaty, meaning that they considered the attack on the United States as an attack on them all. Article Five had never been invoked before. Moreover, over 90 countries worldwide joined one or more of five separate coalitions to

> support the U.S. war against al Qaeda. Seldom has the United States had so much international support...
> Over the next year and a half, however, in the run up to the invasion of Iraq, many neoconservatives, both inside and outside the administration, disparaged NATO and other US allies as unnecessary for "transforming the Middle East." Because the United States is a superpower, they insisted, it could handle this task alone. Accordingly, we witnessed Secretary of Defense Donald Rumsfeld's team and some officials in the State Department and the White House (especially in the Vice President's office) gratuitously and repeatedly insult the Europeans, dismissing them as irrelevant. The climax of this sustained campaign to discard our allies came in the UN Security Council struggle for a resolution to legitimize the invasion of Iraq in February-March 2003. From that time on, we have seen most of our allies stand aside and engage in Schadenfreude over our painful bog-down in Iraq. Winston Churchill's glib observation, "the only thing worse than having allies is having none," was once again vindicated. [245]

The Hubris of U.S.A. culture has produced a society that supports a government that is callous and insensible to the needs, desires or rights of other nations. Through a prescribed program of religious proselytizing, corporate investment followed by U.S.A. military investment, the U.S.A. gradually involves itself with a country and eventually ends up turning against its leadership and imposing on that country the U.S.A vision of government and economics. In an interview with journalist Amy Goodman, Stephen Kinzer, the author of the book *"Overthrow: America's Century of Regime Change from Hawaii to Iraq"* explained his researches on the process by which the U.S.A. government has overthrown foreign governments and how those actions of toppling governments has worked to create governments that are worse than the governments they replaced-worse especially for the people of those countries but worse in terms of anti-U.S.A sentiment, which works against U.S.A. interests in the long run.

> There's really a three-stage motivation that I can see when I watch so many of the developments of these coups. The first thing that happens is that the regime in question starts bothering some American company. They start demanding that the company pay taxes or that it observe labor laws or environmental laws...
> Then, the leaders of that company come to the political leadership of the United States to complain about the regime in that country. In the political process, in the White House, the motivation morphs a little bit.

> The U.S. government does not intervene directly to defend the rights of a company, but they transform the motivation from an economic one into a political or geo-strategic one. They make the assumption that any regime that would bother an American company or harass an American company must be anti-American, repressive, dictatorial, and probably the tool of some foreign power or interest that wants to undermine the United States...
> Then, it morphs one more time when the U.S. leaders have to explain the motivation for this operation to the American people. Then they do not use either the economic or the political motivation usually, but they portray these interventions as liberation operations, just a chance to free a poor oppressed nation from the brutality of a regime that we assume is a dictatorship, because what other kind of a regime would be bothering an American company? [246]

The process outline above can be started through missionaries establishing themselves in the "savage" country to proselytize to the heathen natives. That has the effect of changing their culture, destabilizing their traditions, and causing them to look to the western companies for everything from clothing to bibles. Such was the case in several island nations of the south Pacific. Hawaii was a prime example of the takeover of a sovereign country that began first with Christian missionaries from the U.S.A. Then corporations come in to do business with the country and once established begin despoiling the country. Once the local population begins to reject that exploitation and attempts to stop the process of being taken advantage of, the company calls the U.S.A. government officials that they pay bribes [political contributions to] and then the rest of the process, outlined by Mr. Kinzer, ensues.

The philosophy of collectivism has been put forth as an explanation for the movement towards fascism especially in the twentieth century and for the extreme acts of barbarity in torture, toppling sovereign democratically elected governments and supporting belligerent positions such as the U.S.A. has done towards Iraq and not Iran and North Korea. Some psychologists define collectivism as a syndrome of attitudes and behaviors based on the belief that the basic unit of survival lies within a group, not the individual.[247] *Collectivism* is considered to be diametrically opposed to individualism. Individualists believe in private property and capitalism. "Collectivists" believe a free society must abolish private property in favor of collective ownership of property and that the best form of organization for free individuals would be communes. There were the communist states, which often collectivized most of their economic sectors including agriculture. In Israeli there is the example of kibbutzim or the voluntary communes that were set up where people lived and farmed together without private ownership. Another example is the Freetown Christiania community in Denmark which was a small anarchist political experiment which had laws (that abolished private property). In modern political-economic terms, the global power elite may be seen as collectivists in the sense that they want to collectivize the economic, military and political power of the world under their own aegis in order to exercise control over the world but that control need not be through direct ownership of the world but through rights established by means of economic arrangements through world wide economic institutions such as the World Bank and the I.M.F., and by controlling the heads of state, of the countries to be controlled, who wield the military power. The following quote by Benito Mussolini illustrates the ultimate fascist agenda of collectivizing the resources and national sovereignty of the world's nations under the elite rule into a form of fascist collective.

> "For if the nineteenth century was a century of individualism it may be expected that this 20th century will be the century of collectivism and hence the century of the State...."

When examined as a whole and we consider the fact that prior to the Gulf War in 1991 the U.S.A. government [under George H. Bush (Bush Sr.)] refused to accept Iraq's offer to negotiate a solution to the Kuwait issue, and that in the late 1990s relations between Iran and the U.S.A. and North Korea and the U.S.A. were moving towards treaty negotiations and that the George W. Bush administration stopped negotiations and branded those countries as part of an *"axis of evil"* without any provocation from them, so as to provoke a confrontation with them, there begins to emerge a pattern of creating chaos by actions or omission of actions in domestic and foreign policies by the republican party. IF there is sufficient chaos domestically, people will relinquish their rights and allow themselves to be controlled. If there were sufficient chaos abroad and the perception of threats from abroad was sufficiently heightened, then the military options would be more acceptable, with the support of the people and the U.S.A. would move to attain control over the country that the perceived threat is supposed to be coming from. Then those countries could be brought under the control of the U.S.A. power elite.

Pretexts to War

The U.S.A. government officials used several incidents as pretexts to allow them to garner support from the populace to enter into wars with various countries and obtain their territories or natural resources. The Mexican-American war was precipitated by the sending of the U.S. troops into Mexican territory to provoke a counterattack and then tell the congress and the U.S.A. citizens that their country was being invaded and American men were being killed.

The Spanish-American war was precipitated by the mysterious sinking of the American battleship USS *Maine*, in the Cuban harbor. It was later revealed decades later that it was either an internal explosion [accidental or intentional] that produced the sinking of the ship and not by being fired upon by Spanish warships.[248] The news media in the U.S.A. at the time purposely blew up the issue through statements like: *"Our Warship Was Blown Up by an Enemy's Infernal Machine."* [The *New York Journal* headline]

Other apparently contrived events that were later proven to be either suspicious, misinformation or contrived events included the attack on the Lusitania, which facilitated the entry into World War I, the attack on Pearl Harbor, which facilitated the entry into World War II, the Gulf of Tonkin Incident, which facilitated the entry into the Vietnam War, and the September 11, 2001 attack on the world trade center buildings in New York that precipitated the entry into war with Afghanistan and Iraq.

> The **Gulf of Tonkin Incident** was a pair of alleged attacks by North Vietnamese gunboats on two American destroyers, the USS *Maddox* and the USS *C. Turner Joy*, in August of 1964 in the Gulf of Tonkin. Later research, including a report released in 2005 by the National Security Agency, indicates that the second attack did not occur. The Tonkin incident occurred during the first year of the Lyndon B. Johnson administration — less than a year after the Kennedy assassination. While Kennedy had originally supported the policy of sending "military advisors" to Vietnam in an "advisory role", he had begun to change his thinking and shortly before his death in November

1963, he had begun limited recall of American forces. Johnson's views had been likewise complex, but had supported escalation in Vietnam as a means to challenge Soviet-Communist expansion in a policy called "containment".[249]

Declaration of war: On February 15, 1898, the American battleship USS *Maine* in Havana harbor suffered an explosion and quickly sank with a loss of 266 men. Evidence as to the cause of the explosion was inconclusive and contradictory, but the American press, led by the two New York papers, proclaimed that this was certainly a despicable act of sabotage by the Spaniards. The press aroused the public to demand war, with the slogan *"Remember the Maine! To hell with Spain!"*. This chauvinistic belligerent feeling became known as jingoism, a British expression first coined in 1878.[250]

The Attack by the Japanese on the U.S. naval base in Hawaii known as Pearl Harbor precipitated the U.S.A. declaration of war against Japan in 1941 and subsequently also Germany. Historians have noted certain evidences that the U.S.A. had advance intelligence that the Japanese were going to attack Pearl Harbor but took no action to prevent or prepare for it so as to make it appear as a surprise sneak attack by the Japanese. The historians point to this as a means used to enter the U.S.A. into the war. It is also not well known generally that Japan and the U.S.A. were engaged in economic competition. Both were attempting to control countries of the southwest pacific and Japan felt that the U.S.A. was trying to prevent their expansion through political and economic means. So a war was likely anyway. There have been several other incidents that were used by the U.S.A. government as a pretext to engaging in war and some have involved purposely sacrificing human lives in order to goad the population to consent to engaging in war against other nations.

Many observers have pointed to parallels with the attack on the World Trade Center in New York that precipitated the so called "War on Terrorism" due to peculiar facts surrounding the. Critics have pointed to warnings that were received by the U.S.A. government which were ignored that warned of an impending attack and no action was taken to put military forces on high alert. Some of the major warnings received before the attacks are included below. For the entire list see Source: *The Terror Timeline* by Paul Thompson, 2004.[251]

> **June 13, 2001:** Egyptian President Hosni Mubarak claims Bin Laden Wants to Assassinate Bush with an Explosives-Filled Airplane [New York Times, 9/26/01]
> **June 20, 2001:** Time Magazine Mentions al-Qaeda Using Planes as Weapons [Time, 6/20/01]
> **Late summer 2001:** Jordan Warns US That Aircraft Will Be Used in Major Attack Inside the US [International Herald Tribune, 5/21/02; Christian Science Monitor, 5/23/02]
> **July 20-22, 2001:** During G-8 Summit, Italian Military Prepare Against Attack from the Sky [Los Angeles Times, 9/27/01]
> **Late July 2001:** Egypt Warns CIA of 20 al-Qaeda Operatives in US; Four Training to Fly; CIA Is Not Interested [CBS News, 10/9/02]
> **August 2001:** Russian President Vladimir Putin Warns US of Suicide Pilots Training To Attack US Targets [Fox News, 5/17/02]
> **August 2001:** US Learns of Plot to Crash Airplane into US Embassy in Nairobi [9/11 Congressional Inquiry, 9/18/02]
> **August 6, 2001:** Bush Briefing at his Crawford, Texas, ranch is titled Bin Laden Determined to Strike in US [Newsweek, 5/27/02; New York Times, 5/15/02]

In the book *9/11 and American Empire: How should religious people respond?* The author Dr. David Ray Griffin details more evidences of the complicity of U.S.A. business and government officials in the attack. There were unusual purchases for put options on only two airlines [United and American airliners]. Only those airlines were used in the 9/11 attacks and their stock did go down. Those options are used when an investor is betting the stock will go down on a particular company. Dr. Griffin reported that the intelligence services routinely monitor the market for such unusual activities.

> These two examples imply the falsity of the Joint Inquiry's statement that "none of [the intelligence gathered by the US intelligence community] identified the time, place, and specific nature of the attacks." Indeed, one of the FBI agents interviewed by William Grigg reportedly said: "Obviously, people had to know... It's terrible to think this, but this must have been allowed to happen as part of some other agenda."[252]

Conspiracy theorists have pointed to several inconsistencies they consider as evidences of an intentional plan to create what the Project for a New American Century considers a necessity to mobilize people to support the Neo-con agenda, a *"catastrophic and catalyzing event — like a new Pearl Harbor"*[253] or what Dr. Strauss would consider to be an incident that would allow the government to unite the masses, because as Shadia Drury explained, according to his philosophy *"they can only be united against other people"* because *"he maintains that if no external threat exists, then one has to be manufactured."* Dr. Griffin and other researchers have presented evidences they consider as demonstrations of the complicity of the U.S. Government and the military in the 9/11/01 attacks and the cover-up that was presented in the 9/11/01 investigation commission report. Dr. Griffin reported that a "stand-down" order was given on 9/11/01 that canceled the military's standard operating procedures for handling the possibility of hijacked airplanes [flights out of contact or out of their prescribed areas] which happens as much as 100 times per year. The air force may receive a call from the F.A.A.[254] and fighter jets are sent up within 20 minutes to intercept the possible problem plane.[255] On 9/11/01 no planes were sent up. One more peculiar issue stems from a British Broadcasting Corporation [BBC] report that five of the alleged 9/11 hijackers were alive and accounted for after the event. No investigation was made of this report. On March, 7 2006 the INN World Report reported that at least 4 of the men who were supposed to be the dead hijackers according to the FBI are alive and had nothing to do with the attacks.[256]

> Another of the men that were named by the FBI as a hijacker on September 11th has turned up alive and well. The identities of four of the 19 suspects accused of having carried out the attacks are now in doubt. Saudi Arabian pilot Walid Alshiri was one of the 5 men that the FBI said had deliberately crashed American Airlines flight 11 into the World Trade Center. Alshiri is protesting his innocence from Casablanca Morocco and says he was in Morocco when the attacks happened. Abdul Aziz Al-Omari, another of the flight 11 suspects claims to b an engineer with Saudi telecoms and that he lost his passport while studying in Denver. Meanwhile, Asharq Al-Awsat newspaper says it has interviewed Said Al-gamidi who was listed to have been on flight 93.

Soon after the attacks occurred, statements from the Bush administration emerged about using the attacks for embarking on a campaign to change the world. Donald Rumsfeld referred to 9/11/01 as the opportunity "to refashion the world."[257] Congress increased military funding by $40 billion and every additional appropriation asked for by the president was granted. Before the invasion of Afghanistan and Iraq the U.S.A. had hundreds of military bases around the world; the proliferation of bases has continued years after the collapse of the Soviet Union as a superpower adversary. So the purpose was not just to counter the Soviet Union in the Cold War. The other purpose of having those bases is to extend military power easily, to intimidate other countries and protect U.S.A. interests, i.e. preventing other countries from challenging U.S.A. economic hegemony [maintaining the markets of other countries open to U.S.A. transnational corporations, insuring cheap access to oil and other commodities for western corporations and preventing countries from going off the U.S. dollar exchange standard].

The 9/11/01 attack provided the alleged reason for putting more military bases in Central Asia. Zbigniew Brzezinski said having more bases in Central Asia would be imperative for preserving "American primacy" in part due to the large oil reserves that exist in the area of the Caspian Sea.[258] The permanent U.S.A. military bases in Iraq have been strategically placed around the oil pipeline. In his book Brzezinski, explained that the U.S.A. public had previously "supported America's engagement in World War II largely because of the shock effect of the Japanese attack on Pearl Harbor," and he then suggested that the American public of today would also support the necessity of military operations in Central Asia now but only *"in the circumstance of a truly massive and widely perceived direct external threat."*[259]

The question may be asked: in the absence of a rival superpower what would be considered as a sufficient threat to precipitate the peoples consent to war? The September 11 attacks were large but did not rise to the level of a declaration of war such as against an attacking country which has sent its army against the U.S.A. or a worldwide war against all foes. Given the present condition of geopolitics and propaganda, the world accepted the U.S.A. invasion of Afghanistan to get at the perceived perpetrators of the attack but that did not mean that the U.S.A. had permission or the right to call it a war on any government that supposedly supported terrorism or had a despotic regime. If the latter criteria were to be used why did the U.S.A. only brand Iraq, Iran and North Korea as evil and not the dozens of other countries that also supposedly have despotic regimes as perceived by the president? The answer is that that was a red herring to deflect from the true reason to be against those countries. Iraq and Iran have oil and Iran and North Korea could actually resist the U.S.A if they were to acquire nuclear weapons capacity. Given the enmity between those countries with the U.S.A. due to past U.S.A. interference in the governments of those countries, the U.S.A. leaders could arguably feel worry over what they might do to retaliate against the U.S.A.

Even though an attack by a nation-less group cannot logically be extended to additionally mean countries that do not have supposedly acceptable regimes, yet that was the outcome of the statements made and actions that were taken. by fabricating evidence against Iraq [non-existent weapons of mass destruction] and branding certain countries as evil and then proceeding to attack one of them. The continued maintenance by the president of the idea of a war on terrorism implies a perpetual indefinite state of war which would turn out to be a complete fulfillment of Leo Straus's best expectation because it would not be necessary to find new conflicts to rally people and bring them together for a common cause. It would just be necessary to remind them regularly of the state of war and perhaps provide an occasional terror alert or even an actual apparent attack that would confirm the need to remain in a pseudo-state of war that would allow consumerism to continue as usual but would justify the additional military expenditures and foreign policy of intrusiveness and hegemony.

The same effect of providing a pretext for war was achieved through the sinking of the Lusitania; a boat carrying weapons and supplies to England during World War I in contradiction with U.S.A. neutrality laws. The U.S.A. government allowed U.S.A. citizens to board the vessel even though they had received warnings from the German government that it would be in danger by coming to a war zone. The German government tried to place advertisements in over 20 newspapers in the U.S.A. and the U.S.A. government State Department threatened the U.S.A. press, admonishing them against printing the German advertisement. Only the Des Moines Register [newspaper] printed it but the people in New York, where the Lusitania sailed from, never received the warning.[260] When the boat was sunk the U.S.A. government feigned surprise and rallied the U.S.A. populace to war to avenge the U.S.A. citizens and protect the world for democracy in what they referred to as a "war to end all wars."

> The Lusitania was principally a luxury passenger liner built to convey people and property between England and the United States.
>
> It is now known that a secret warning, given to the ship's wealthiest passengers, reported that U-boat activity was to be expected and advised the same not to travel.
>
> There was also a public warning given by the Imperial German Embassy:
>
> > *NOTICE!*
> >
> > *TRAVELERS intending to embark on the Atlantic voyage are reminded that a state of war exists between Germany and her allies and Great Britain and her allies; that the zone of war includes the waters adjacent to the British Isles; that, in accordance with formal notice given by the Imperial German Government, vessels flying the flag of Great Britain, or any of her allies, are liable to destruction in those waters and that travelers sailing in the war zone on the ships of Great Britain or her allies do so at their own risk.*
> >
> > *IMPERIAL GERMAN EMBASSY Washington, D.C.*
> > *April 22, 1915*

Additionally, the Lusitania had 4 boilers and one was ordered to be shut down so that the ship would move more slowly and be a better target and a British warship called the Juno, which was supposed to escort the Lusitania, was called away as the Lusitania entered the dangerous area. The ship was sunk and many people died. The U.S.A. subsequently entered the war.

There is a document from an organization, established in spring 1997, called *The Project for the New American Century*, or PNAC, a Washington, DC based neoconservative think tank that seems to adopt Brzezinski's strategy, discussed earlier. The document, 5 years before, predicted the need for a Pearl Harbor type event to accelerate the agenda of establishing U.S.A. dominance in the world, which follows the philosophy of Machiavelli and Leo Straus, the neoconservative thinker that outlined the neoconservative strategy for political domination of the populace. A line frequently quoted by critics comes from the PNAC document entitled: *Rebuilding America's Defenses,* which famously refers to the possibility of a:

> "catastrophic and catalyzing event — like a new Pearl Harbor" (page 51).

The quote appears in Chapter V; of the document section entitled "Creating Tomorrow's Dominant Force", which discusses the perceived need for the Department of Defense to

> "move more aggressively to experiment with new technologies and operational concepts" (page 50).

The document also contains the following:

> "Further, the process of transformation, even if it brings revolutionary change, is likely to be a long one, absent some catastrophic and catalyzing event – like a new Pearl Harbor."

Some opponents of the Bush administration have used the above quote as evidence for their belief that the US Government was complicit in the 9/11 terrorist attacks. Many critics also claim that the PNAC believed this "new Pearl Harbor" would justify war on Iraq. Critics also point out that throughout the year 2004 there were statements made by former George W. Bush administration officials such as Paul O'Neil,[261] that revealed the Bush/Cheney administration wanted to invade Iraq and had a plan to do so with the intention of removing Saddam Hussein from the beginning of their administration in January 2001 and not just beginning after September 11, 2001.

In April 2006 it was revealed by a CIA head of European operations that the president was informed that Iraq did not have an active nuclear weapons program but they ignored that and went ahead calling for the war even though he knew that Iraq had no weapons of mass destruction.

> ***CIA Official: Bush Ignored Iraq WMD Intelligence***[262]
> The CIA's former top official in Europe has revealed that President Bush ignored intelligence that Iraq did not have weapons of mass destruction. The official, Tyler Drumheller, said former CIA Director George Tenet personally told Bush and Vice President Cheney that Iraq's foreign minister had admitted to U.S. spies that Iraq had no WMD program. Drumheller said the information was ignored. He told 60 Minutes "The policy was set. The war in Iraq was coming and they were looking for intelligence to fit into the policy."

The "Gulf War" between the U.S.A. and Iraq in 1991 also demonstrated a pattern of strategic moves designed to deliberately instigate a pretext for war. The incident occurred as follows. Kuwait was part of Iraq at one time. In 1899 A.C.E., Kuwait became a British protectorate because of the weakness of Iraq as a nation. Kuwait, amassed great wealth through oil revenues, and declared independence in 1961. Iraq challenged this declaration, and claimed that Kuwait was part of Iraqi territory. Iraq did threaten to invade Kuwait, but it was discouraged by the British who had dispatched a military force to the area. At the close of the Iraq-Iran war, Iraq emerged as a strong military force especially with the weaponry it had acquired from the U.S.A., British and other Western firms. Israel felt nervous about that strength and the U.S.A. was concerned about Iraq's capacity to challenge the influence of the U.S.A. in the Middle East. Iraq and Syria moved toward reconciliation, and in March 1990, there was the formation of a joint Iraqi-Jordanian air force squadron containing Mirage fighter aircraft [from France]. Kuwait conspired to lower the price of oil which hurt the Iraqi economy, and refused to forgive the debt that Iraq owed Kuwait for war time sales. In 1989 Kuwait hindered Iraq's access to the Gulf, closed its air space to Iraq and Iraq accused Kuwait of angle drilling for oil into Iraqi territory.

The then secretary of defense Dick Cheney and undersecretary of defense for Policy Paul Wolfowitz, both at that time were working in the presidential administration of George H. Bush (Bush Senior).

Both also worked in the George W. Bush administration. They stated that the U.S.A. would defend Kuwait if it were attacked. The White House later put out a statement that Cheney had spoken with "some liberty", trying to downplay his statements. Later, the State Department spokesperson, Margaret Tutweiler, made a statement that the U.S.A. had no defense treaties or special security agreements with Kuwait. However, she declared that the U.S.A. "remained strongly committed to supporting the individual and collective self-defense of our friends in the Gulf..." Then the US Ambassador to Iraq, April Glaspie, made the statement to Iraq that the U.S. A. had no opinion about inter-Arab conflicts. On that same day, the Assistant Secretary of State, John Kelly, stopped a Voice Of America broadcast that reiterated the warning by Tutweiler.

Once Iraq entered Kuwait, the U.S.A. immediately began to prepare troops to move them to the Gulf and took a posture requiring Iraqi unconditional withdrawal from Kuwait and therefore, dismissed the Iraqi proposals for withdrawal. President Bush Sr. gave Jordanian King Hussein only forty-eight hours to call together a summit in Saudi Arabia for negotiating a settlement. King Hussein negotiated Iraq's agreement to begin troop withdrawals on August 5, which was the first day of the summit; but on August 3, fourteen of the twenty-one Arab foreign ministers voted to condemn the invasion, and so the mini-summit collapsed. On August 6, in exchange for U.S.A. guarantees of military and economic special treatment president Bush persuaded Turkey to shut down the oil pipeline of Iraq.

In an essay on technology and human choice, Rosalind Williams noted how human beings can loose their free will to situations or even technologies.

> The same principle [as with nuclear weapons] can be used with regard to conventional weapons. In the late summer and the autumn of 1989, President George Bush made a series of decisions that had the net effect of putting half a million American troops in an offensive posture against an opponent who had been issued an unacceptable ultimatum. Those circumstances were constructed to ensure that in January 1990 the United States Senate would choose to declare war with Iraq. During the debate, one senator asked "Are we supposed to go to war simply

> because one man-the President-makes a series of unilateral decisions that put us in a box-a box that makes that war, to a greater degree, inevitable?"[21] The onset of Operation Desert Storm four days later provided a clear answer to his question.[263]

After president Bush persuaded Turkey to shut down the oil pipeline of Iraq, Saudi Arabia's "invitation" for the U.S.A. military to come to Saudi Arabia was obtained by the U.S.A. on August 7. That occurred when Secretary of Defense Cheney convinced King Fahad of Saudi Arabia his country was in danger of being invaded by Iraq, even though the C.I.A. and the Defense Intelligence Agency officials had expressed skepticism about the existence of any invasion plans by Iraq and it was confirmed subsequently that there was never any plan nor were there any Iraqi troops on the Saudi Arabian border. General Colin Powell agreed with the assessment and even pointed out that Iraq could have invaded Saudi Arabia without invading Kuwait and that Iraq still could have invaded Saudi Arabia after it invaded Kuwait and never did. Reports later revealed that the British Prime Minister, Margaret Thatcher, had told King Hussein that U.S.A. troops were already on their way to Saudi Arabia even before King Fahad had officially requested them. After the war ended and the Iraqi troops were removed from Kuwait, the U.S.A. troops and U.S.A. contractors never left Saudi Arabia and that presence upset many Muslims in the area, especially those following the sect called Wahhabism. The agitation contributed to and exacerbated the enmity of Osama bin Laden against the west in general and the U.S.A. in particular that apparently led to the attacks on the world trade center towers in New York City in 1993 and their destruction in 2001 and the subsequent invasion and occupation of Afghanistan and Iraq by the U.S.A.

Thus, Iraq was lured into thinking that it could invade Kuwait and that the U.S.A. would not take any action. Later, no Iraqi advances to negotiate a withdrawal were accepted. The goals of the war were to weaken Iraq, to safeguard Israel and to secure access to the Iraqi oil.

---

[21] Senator John Kerry (Democrat, Massachusetts), *Congressional Record 137:* 7 (January 11, 1991).

The fall of the dollar is the reason why it is so expensive to visit Europe and is not the fault of the Europeans. This economic situation of dependency on world markets and the need to sustain the dollar in order to sustain the wealth ["American way of life", "American standard of living"] of the U.S.A. economy was a little known contributing cause for the war on Iraq by the U.S.A. The Iraqi government had been controlled by western governments and again, the dictators were put in place and sustained by the U.S.A. When Saddam Hussein sought to expand his domain and control over the oil fields of Kuwait the Western powers, headed by the U.S.A. moved to stop that control and over the next decade the U.S.A and British governments sought to prevent Iraqi oil from falling under the control of the Chinese, French, German or Russian governments. The message being sent by going to war was two-fold; to other independent nations, do not move away from the dollar, to other potential rival nations, and stay away from the U.S.A. sphere of control.

Innworldreport News Headline 3-22-06

Transcripts from the 1990s show Saddam Hussein
was frustrated that no one believed Iraq had given up banned weapons.
At one meeting with top aides in 1996, transcripts showed that Saddam wondered if U.N. inspectors would "roam Iraq for 50 years." The transcripts are translations recently released by the U.S., and are from audio and videotapes of top-level Iraqi meetings held from 1991 to 1997. Repeatedly, Saddam and his lieutenants reminded each other that Iraq destroyed its chemical and biological weapons in the early 1990s, and shut down the nuclear-bomb program.[264]

Documents Prove Saddam Had No Weapons Of Mass Destruction[265]

March 21, 2006 10:00 p.m. EST
Andrea Moore - All Headline News Staff Reporter
Baghdad, Iraq (AHN) - U.S. government translations of audiotapes shows an exasperated Saddam Hussein and top aides searching for ways in the 1990s to prove to the world that they had given up banned weapons.
In one transcript from 1996, Saddam wondered whether U.N. inspectors would "roam Iraq for 50 years" in a pointless hunt for weapons of mass destruction asking, "When is this going to end?"

> Saddam's goal in the 1990s was to have the Security Council lift the economic sanctions strangling the Iraqi economy but he was thwarted by what he and aides viewed as U.S. hard-liners blocking Security Council action.
> In 2004, after an exhaustive investigation, U.S. experts confirmed Iraq had eliminated its weapons of mass destruction long ago, a finding that discredited the Bush administration's stated rationale for invading Iraq in 2003.

After realizing that the U.S.A. had no intention of lifting trade embargos or stopping no fly zones over Iraq and that the pretext of inspections were a means to perpetually keep Iraq disarmed but also to spy on Iraq and keep Iraq under the pressure of western designs, Hussein expelled the arms inspectors in 1998. But the move that raised the impetus to invade Iraq was not the threat of weapons of mass destruction or links to "terrorist" organizations as was widely disseminated by U.S. government officials and repeated by the media, but rather the move by Iraq to accept payments for oil in Euros instead of dollars in the year 2000.[266] This is one of the reasons why the U.S. Government sought to provoke a war or invade even at the cost of breaking UN resolutions and international laws. This is proven by the decision to invade Iraq even when Iraq agreed to allow arms inspectors back into the country with full access to all sites, including the ones that the U.S.A. officials said they knew had weapons of mass destruction, a supposed condition to prevent war as stated by the U.S. president George W. Bush. When it became clear the inspectors were finding no weapons of mass destruction they were recalled by the U.S. government and the invasion proceeded. The invasion went ahead despite the warnings and predictions by intelligence analysts in the U.S.A. and Arab dictators such as Hasni Mubarak of Egypt that such an invasion would foment animosity and lead to the creation of more opposition and promote more Islamic religious fundamentalism in the Arab world. Proceeding with the idea of making their own reality, the Bush administration became embroiled in a quagmire of dismal military occupation, seemingly playing into the hands of the Arab fundamentalist, Osama bin Laden who invited such a confrontation so as to elevate himself and the cause of resistance against the U.S.A. to mythic proportions as a liberation fighter and Islamic resistance movement against the western "crusaders." Osama bin

Laden's stated belief is that westerners and infidels should not be in Islamic "Holy lands." In this way, the western-Christian fundamentalists, as actually or metaphorically headed by Bush and the Arab-Islamic fundamentalists, headed by bin Laden are once again locked in a continuing struggle for resources but also indirectly as well over which religion is supposedly more correct and worthy to dominate the world.

Conclusion

During the years 2001 and 2005 the presidential administration of George W. Bush had secretly or openly engaged in and had asserted that the president has the right to engage in acts that are outside of the reach of the judicial and legislative authorities including:

The right to engage in preemptive war.
The right to engage in wiretaps without court approval.
The right to indefinitely jail those who are deemed enemies of the state, or enemy combatants without due process of law.
The right to kidnap anyone and send them to countries that torture people.
The right to search people's homes, offices, records, etc. without a court order.

Additionally, John Savage, a reporter at the Boston Globe, reported that president George W. Bush signed over 750 signing statements or letters. Signing letters are statements that the presidents starting with president James Monroe, (April 28, 1758 – July 4, 1831) started to make to accompany the legislation created by the congress. Every time the congress makes a law the presidents have created an accompanying letter stating what they understand about it and how it will be implemented. In common useage, the phrase "signing statement" normaly refers to 'Constitutional' statements that direct how the law is to be applied: Ex. Consitutional, "I'm signing this law, but won't enforce section 2"[267] Critics have charged that George W. Bush has not vetoed any laws passed by congress because he has essentially prepared statements that say what he agrees with or does not and will not follow. Thus, he is directly saying that he will not follow certain laws passed by congress which is in direct contradiction to the intent of the U.S. Constitution. In other words he can disregard whatever laws he wants to ignore. This would mean that the president is above the reach of the law and beyond the constitutional restrictions provided in the constitution to check the powers of the president. Thus, it renders the constitution invalid. This would also mean that the president has powers similar to a dictator or king, including the capacity to invalidate the right to *habeas corpus* or the right of a prisoner to hcallenge the right of his/her captor to keep them in prison (determine of the imprisonment is legal). The realization of what president Bush had done thorugh the signing statements prompted the republican senator Senator Arlen Specter of Pennsylvania to say: "*There may as well soon not be a Congress.*" (5/3/2006)

The activities listed above and the diminishing independence of the legal branch of government due to right wing religious efforts to appoint right wing judges to federal positions and the Supreme Court who are favorable to conservative religious views and the passing of laws such as the U.S.A. Patriot Act [which curtail civil liberties] prompted the retiring Supreme Court Justice Sandra Day O'Connor to publicly speak out on the turn towards dictatorship that the U.S.A had taken. The statement is significant because Sandra Day O'Connor had been perhaps the most respected Supreme Court Justice by both republican party and democratic party leaders and their followers since she balanced the right wing and liberal judges in the Supreme Court. Therefore, her statement, especially using the term, "dictatorship," is especially ominous and should raise the attention, if not alarm, of all interested observers. It is a scathing report on the state of the U.S.A. government and a strong indictment of a government that is slipping away from whatever ethics and democratic-egalitarian values it may have achieved.

DEMOCRACY NOW Headlines for March 14, 2006

Sandra Day O'Connor Warns About U.S. Edging Towards 'Dictatorship'
Former Supreme Court Justice Sandra Day O'Connor warned last week that the United States is in danger of edging towards a dictatorship if right-wingers continued to attack the judiciary. In one of her first public speeches since leaving the bench, O'Connor - who was nominated by Ronald Reagan -- sharply criticized Republicans for strong-arming the judiciary. According to a report on NPR, O'Connor said "It takes a lot of degeneration before a country falls into dictatorship, but we should avoid these ends by avoiding these beginnings."[268]

Many terms have been devised to refer to countries that have governments that are non-responsive to the will of their people; that enact repressive measures; that engage in unrestricted militarism and in which their media do not engage in thoughtful discussion or questioning government policies but merely report what the leaders have said or even cheer them on.

In the 1980's president Reagan devised the term "terrorist states" as a means to refer to countries that were in need of U.S.A. invasion. In the mid 1990's president Clinton devised the term rogue states. In the last 10 years the new term "failed states" was created.

If we were to apply the criteria of a failed state we would have to include the U.S.A. in the list because the U.S.A. government does not follow the wishes of the people, as several polls have demonstrated. For example, most people are for national universal health care, legalized abortion, moving to alternative fuels, and reduced military spending; yet the government leaders continue to promote private healthcare, outlawing abortion, an oil based economy and more military spending and more bases overseas to fight the so called "terrorists."

One example of the rogue nature of the U.S.A. government is that even though president Bush was warned that the policies towards Israel, Saudi Arabia, Iraq and the rest of the Middle East would likely increase terrorism, the Bush administration went ahead anyway and attacked Iraq. According to the findings of the C.I.A., the National Intelligence Council, and other foreign intelligence agencies, as well as independent intelligence specialists the threat of terrorism has increased.[269] It has increased significantly even more because many of the people who have been upset by the attack of the U.S.A. on Iraq were not terrorists previously. However, in the protracted rebellion against the U.S.A. occupation the fighters became skilled soldiers that could pose a significant obstacle to the U.S.A. forces but also could strike at U.S.A. citizens anywhere in the world. Due to the mishandling of the occupation, the killing of so many civilians and the torture of the people, as evinced in the Abu Graib scandal, the U.S.A. has been referred to as an ally of the supposed enemy, Osama Bin Laden. The thesis of the book, *Imperial Hubris: Why the West is Losing the War on Terrorism* by

Michael Scheuer as stated in the book's Introduction is a scathing report on the actions of the administration.

> "As I complete this book, U.S., British, and other coalition forces are trying to govern apparently ungovernable postwar states in Afghanistan and Iraq, while simultaneously fighting growing Islamist insurgencies in each – a state of affairs our leaders call victory. In conducting these activities, and the conventional military campaigns preceding them, U.S. forces and policies are completing the radicalization of the Islamic world, something Osama bin Laden has been trying to do with substantial but incomplete success since the early 1990s. As a result, I think it fair to conclude that the United States of America remains bin Laden's only indispensable ally."

The alternative media and international human rights organizations such as "Human Rights Watch" have cited the U.S.A. as the largest terrorist state as evinced by the killing of over 100,000 people in Iraq alone. The people of the U.S.A. are powerless to influence the current leaders and their efforts are hampered by a media that does not report on dissent with as much vigor as the message of the current rulers and the news reports are hardly critical of the government statements and those are seldom if ever challenged.

> [U.S.] Government policies adopted after the terrorist attacks of September 11, 2001 profoundly altered the human rights landscape in 2002. Although United States citizens continued to enjoy a broad range of civil liberties and government leaders at all levels responded promptly and often effectively to the wave of anti-Arab and anti-Muslim hate crimes that immediately followed the attacks, 2002 was marked by significant steps backward on human rights... Longstanding human rights problems in the United States continued as well, including police abuse, application of the death penalty, overincarceration of low-level offenders, primarily African-Americans and the poor, and the treatment of prisoners.[270]

The reckless and wanton move towards militarism through development of space based weapons and the escalation of nuclear weapons research and construction has led to a new arms race in which countries such as Russia and China have felt the need to increase spending to match the U.S.A. that of course increases the risk of a mistake in nuclear weapons release similar to several that have almost occurred in the past but that if did occur would lead to dire consequences, especially given the state of geopolitics at this time and the right wing dominance over the U.S.A. government. This seemingly incongruous policy of nuclear escalation and preemptive war that scares other governments and makes them want to seek nuclear weapons to protect themselves from the U.S.A. prompted Robert McNamara, the former US Secretary of Defense under president Kennedy to warn of an impending apocalypse.

Apocalypse Soon

"What is shocking is that today, more than a decade after the end of the Cold War, the basic US nuclear policy is unchanged. Of the 8,000 active or operational US warheads, 2,000 are on hair-trigger alert, ready to be launched on 15 minutes' warning. On any given day, as we go about our business, the president is prepared to make a decision within 20 minutes that could launch one of the most devastating weapons in the world. To declare war requires an act of congress, but to launch a nuclear holocaust requires 20 minutes' deliberation by the president and his advisors."

-- Former US Secretary of Defense Robert McNamara, May 2005[271]

While it is true that most previous presidents in the late 20th century including democratic party and republican party presidents and their administrations and the congress, promoted “American hegemony” [president Grover Cleveland was a notable exception] and fiscal irresponsibility, it is also possible that the administration of George W. Bush coupled with the republican dominated congress, exerted the most far reaching and politically eccentric policies in the history of the U.S.A. in regards to domestic and foreign policies.

Part 3: Prospects for the Future

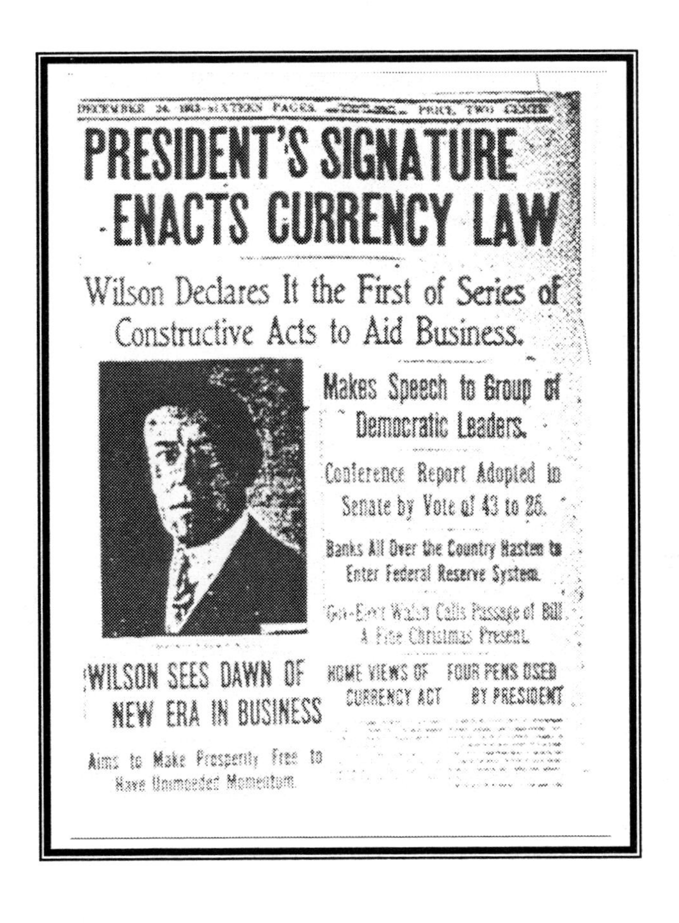
PRICE TWO CENTS

PRESIDENT'S SIGNATURE ENACTS CURRENCY LAW

Wilson Declares It the First of Series of Constructive Acts to Aid Business.

Makes Speech to Group of Democratic Leaders.

Conference Report Adopted in Senate by Vote of 43 to 26.

Banks All Over the Country Hasten to Enter Federal Reserve System.

A Fine Christmas Present.

WILSON SEES DAWN OF NEW ERA IN BUSINESS

Aims to Make Prosperity Free to Have Unimpeded Momentum.

HOME VIEWS OF CURRENCY ACT

FOUR PENS USED BY PRESIDENT

A Dire Scenario of the Future?

Changes in the "economic, political and racial demographics of the United States" and the Possibilities for the Future

> "No one immigrates to the United States anymore. The promise of a better life and opportunity evaporated with the echoes of the optimistic or deluded economists and politicians who said the economy could grow forever. No one comes out into the streets of the great cities anymore. Places like New York, Chicago, Washington D.C. and Los Angeles are now smoldering cauldrons of unrest and violence. In the country that was formerly known as the United States of America, those cities and many others became the sites for the greatest social upheaval that was ever to take place in the modern era. The social unrest was preceded by foreign wars to change foreign regimes and protect the U.S.A. from terrorists that were created by the USA's imperial policies around the world. But domestically, the incessant wars led to public civil disobedience, which led to clashes between protestors, and conservative groups who were supported by the police and national guards. The suspension of the Constitution and perpetual state of martial law and the harshness in which lawbreakers and protestors were treated left no quarter, no compassion, no chance for anyone. There was no freedom of speech or freedom to walk the streets in the wrong neighborhood. Anyone who was not of a particular neighborhood became a legitimate target. The rich now live in exclusive walled compounds which are like self-contained cities and they hardly ever come out. The large corporations have their own paramilitary forces which protect their assets and the neighborhoods of their workers. There were gangs and syndicates controlling most low income neighborhoods. They were so powerful that by the year 2046 it was not possible for the national guard or police or the army to control the lawlessness in the country so the police retreated to their own neighborhoods, like homesteaders circling their wagons to protect themselves from the "savages." This segregation was not only due to race differences, gang wars, or wars for control of territory to promote the drug trade or prostitution but also due to

> animosity between the wealthy and the poor. These territorial disputes between the suburbs of the cities were a battle of control by one neighborhood against others caused by the desire of one group to keep the other one out; the purpose was protection, the desire was survival and the driving force was fear. The U.S. economy collapsed and unemployment went up to 45% so the government could not control the ire of the population left in distress while greedy landlords evicted entire neighborhoods for nonpayment of their home mortgages. By 2050 there were more people of color in the U.S.A. than people of European descent and they resented the fact that there was no non-white president and that promoted the disaffection with the political system that left the minority in control of the government and the economy and left the rest of the population in dire straights. European Americans feared the masses of Latino and African and Asian Americans and resented their desire for political power which promoted rioting and racial conflicts throughout the country."

The description above is the projection, by a futurist, of a possible scenario, a possible outcome of the present course of politics and economic injustices of the United States extended over the next 60 years. By the years 2010- 2015 the "Baby Boomer" generation will constitute the larger segment of those who are retired and those using the healthcare system which is projected to collapse under the weight of the expense and the numbers in need. Also, during those same years, it is projected there will be a decline in the economy due to the exit of the baby boomer generation. The segment of the population that spends the most money and drives the economy is between the ages of 45 to 60. Economic forecasters fear that when that generation passes into the retirement stage the loss of so many people who will not be contributing to the economy will trigger a recession that will lead to loss of confidence in the economy and the U.S. Dollar and will force a depression and other problems in the economy that will last for at least 15 years and possibly over one generation.[272]

In the year 2004 it was announced that the number of Protestants in the U.S.A. had fallen below 50% of the population.[273] Even though the total number of Catholics was 25.9% in 2001 it would seem that, due to their loud voices, the religious conservatives, the fundamentalists and evangelists are the majority. However, the rise in religious fundamentalism could be a factor of the decreasing practice of general Christianity in the United States, down from 88.3% in 1990 to 79.8% in 2001.[274]

Even though Globalism and improvements in technology have progressed, the gap between the rich and the poor has widened even though futurists such as Herman Khan predicted a bright global future in which "worldwide economic affluence and beneficent technology are bright."[275] Rather, the MIT world systems modelers are showing that the economic system of endless growth[276] instead of sustainable development is a looming problem for humanity and the usual answer of "problem solving by growth" [solving economic problems by perpetually expanding the economy] is self-defeating [does not work] and environmentally destructive, i.e., impractical and unsustainable in the long term.

If the current rate of immigration and birthrate are not manipulated, in the year 2050 it is projected that the population demographics of the U.S. will change such that the numbers of those who consider themselves "white" will fall below the numbers of those who consider themselves as "Black," "Hispanic," "Asian," "other," etc. As the recent situation with the devastation of the city of New Orleans and the surrounding areas of the states of Louisiana and Mississippi, due to the impact of hurricanes Katrina and Rita demonstrated, racism and neglect of the poor continue to be stark realities of the United States cultural landscape which will continue into the future [as only small actions are being taken to reverse the problem] just as the construction of new gated communities continues unabated. However, as the city of Santa Monica discovered during the Rodney King riots[277] in Los Angeles, if the general rioting is large enough it can spill over into any community, no matter how separate it may appear to be from the general population. Yet, there is continued perpetuation of the culture of fear, of terrorism, or crime, or remorse about slavery, by rancorous politicians and clergy who stir up strife, etc.[278] which has created a social pattern of alienation between the power elite and the rest of the population of the U.S.A. and the rest of the lower classes of the world, which constitute a majority numerically.

In another scenario, the power elite population would retain political control at least one generation after the ethnic demographic changes. The economic power would be retained for some time longer, perhaps 1-2 more generations or longer after the political change, all of which would engender more animosity against them and promote more fear in them and hence more of a desire to retreat to more secure gated communities that would, as in the imagination of the writer, Neal Stephenson's novel *Snow Crash* exist in a future where gated communities are mass-produced by franchising systems and operate as sovereign city-states. Then there would be a regression to a situation such as was experienced by the Ancient Greeks, who endured many wars for supremacy between the city states. So in other words there would be devolution of civilization that would follow the degraded culture of separatism, segregation, fundamentalism and ignorance.

What actions could be taken to avoid the possible conflict over religion and race, politics and economics? Firstly, more religious, and economic as well as social pluralism needs to be promoted by the leadership so that society may move towards a more social and economic equitable and harmonious condition. That might be considered a manipulation of social order but unlike the positions of fundamentalists, racists and neo-conservatives it is a positive manipulation based on ethics, balance and peace. To the extent that society is able to move in that direction, to that extent it will be able to move towards peace and avoid the great social upheavals that are possible in the future. Of course this is predicated upon the world not experiencing an ecological disaster due to global warming, pollution, over-farming and genetically modifying foods and animals and not experiencing a serious conflict between east (China) and west (United States) or a nuclear disaster due to error or a terrorist attack as retaliation for western economic or religious imperialism. In such a case those factors would complicate the dynamics of the future social conflicts even further. Perhaps the words of John Lennon "***All You Need Is Love***" should be heeded, but in the absence of love perhaps the more important factor is justice which might be more easily attainable; and from there perchance that justice, as the popular saying goes, will lead to peace and conceivably someday in the future, also love among all nations if not all peoples. What would a justice system look like that would produce such a positive outcome? Efforts towards honest sharing of resources and promoting prosperity for all human beings and not just for some countries and the abandonment of the imperialist ideal, as well as the renouncement of religious orthodoxy, absolutism and fundamentalism would lean humanity towards true prosperity and real emancipation from hatred and fear.

Those who deprive any part of life, eventually deprive all life. So any injustice, anywhere in the world, is degradation for everyone and will eventually bring everyone down.

Prospects For the Future: Religion Politics, Economy, Ecology and Health in the 21st Century

Though there are positive signs in people communicating through the internet, many people awakening to the dangers of intolerance, a growing opposition to the imperialism of the U.S. government especially in South America, led by Hugo Chaves and Evo Morales, scientific breakthroughs, etc. that does not seem to be translating into effective actions that influence the course of the dominant culture in the world today. That culture seems to be continuing to lead and accelerate the massive despoiling of the environment, promotion of fundamentalism and animosity between cultures, cruelty to animals and humans and acting politically with impunity to execute its own economic and military designs regardless of the consequences to the environment or to the needs of people or of other countries. Rather, that dominant culture appears to be most interested in protecting the desires of the wealthy and powerful and following a culturally conservative ideological agenda, controlled by an imperial capitalist political imperative and supported by a religiously conservative and fundamentalist ideology. Consequently, four main disasters loom large on the horizon of human existence that will affect all humanity but the people of the U.S.A., as well as those countries closely associated with the U.S.A., most strongly. Those challenges are: a religious-cultural conflict, healthcare crisis, financial collapse, and environmental disaster.

The Religious Crisis

Fueled by dominionist ideals, the religious right Christian groups in the United States of America (U.S.A.) have gained political power and have sought to impose fundamentalist religious principles not only on the rest of the population of the U.S.A. but on the rest of the world which follows the earlier program in U.S.A. history of hegemony through missionary work in other countries preceded or followed by wars of conquest by the government or economic devastation of other countries through colonialism or slavery followed by forced conversions. In the Middle East, Asia and Africa, Islam has gained important ground in gaining adherents and now, almost 1000 years since the first Crusade wars, the Christians and Muslims are again locked in mortal combat for supremacy over the world since Islam also espouses an ideal of converting everyone in the world. So on that account alone (contradictory ideologies) conflict is inevitable, yet, the fundamentalists of either side constitute only a tiny minority; but that minority controls the actions of the masses on both sides, which have been purposely miseducated and radicalized by the ruling classes, the secular capitalists and conservative imperialists who seek to produce enough wealth and military power to rule (control) the world as if it were their "manifest destiny." In this way the desires of religiously right wing Christians and capitalist imperial leaders converge and complement each other.

Religious fundamentalism is an ideological perspective that negates any reality that contradicts its viewpoint. Religious fundamentalism is an assertion of certainty in spiritual knowledge that necessarily requires the believer to declare that the fundamental beliefs are true in the sense of historical facts and since certainties are mutually exclusive [you cannot have two different certainties about the same subject (ex. concepts of God) – only one can be correct to the fundamentalist)] then it follows that the particular fundamentalist religion is the "true" and correct one and all others are false ones. Fundamentalism may also be seen as a fear of uncertainty and grasping on to something that provides peace and assurance through certainty. The fundamentalist mind tends towards literalism and focuses on the power of God instead of the love of God for its guidance. Therefore, God tends to be seen, by a fundamentalist, as a distant, separate but wrathful divinity instead of a close and forgiving divinity.

Thus, fundamentalism and faith-based religion is a form of religious practice required by those who are unsure of their religious convictions and the nature of reality [Creation] or who may have character flaws they cannot come to terms with or forgive itself over; this condition renders the personality weak in terms of not being able to stand on its own without leaning on a power outside of itself for its ability to have a purpose in life or cope and hold on to sanity and peace. The personality is agitated, neurotic, restless and unable to find peace and harmony with itself, the environment or with other human beings, especially those who espouse a different belief system. That insecurity is a source of fear in this personality. The fear acts to cloud the intellect, so the personality focuses on simple teachings [fundamentalism] that can offer assurance. Therefore, the actions of such a personality tent to be fanatical instead of rational and even if rational arguments are presented to them they cannot acknowledge or accept them because they destabilize the fragile peace that is being precariously maintained. It is not secure in itself and therefore tries to find security in the environment by making it reflect a particular ideal of certainty so it can be assured of the truth and thereby be internally secure and assured.

Thus it follows that the need to convert others and eradicate other religions is based on the need for certainty that is confused by the existence of other religions. Thus, it is necessary to block any contradictory information coming from other forms of religion in order to firm up the fundamental beliefs. For that type of personality it is also therefore important to refrain from participating in or fraternizing with practitioners of other religions so as to remain free of information that may contradict the fundamental beliefs or concept of reality based on the dogma(s) they believe in. Finally, if necessary, any information, regardless of its veracity is to be negated if it contradicts the fundamental beliefs because the fundamentalist personality cannot risk breaking the fundamental dogmas since that personality is bound up with them and would be shattered if the belief system were to be proven false. The fundamentalist personality is so due to weakness and is supported through constant activity in asserting and promoting the fundamentalist ideas and avoiding reflecting upon them in the context of other religious ideas for that might lead to critical thinking that could prove error in the tenets, which would shake the confidence in the entire dogma. Following a delusion, be it in politics, religion, economics, etc. in all cases leads to conflict because the fundamentalist search for certainty cannot be complete until it is the sole reality and that can only occur when all others are vanquished.

The study of the crusades is important because it reveals that there was and continues to be deep seeded animosity between western Christians and the Muslims which continues to define relations between the two even today. The desire of the west for oil rekindled the ideal of conquering the oil rich countries of Asia Minor. Today, over 600 years after the last crusade, not much discussion is entertained in the western media or outside of scholarly circles about the legacy of the crusades but in Islamic countries, the mention occurs frequently and without background recapping. This means that when an Arab or Muslim person speaks about the west and references the crusades they do not need to explain the history and background about the crusades to the people they are speaking to.

> *Preaching Islam In America*[279]
> SACRAMENTO, Calif., April 12, 2006
>
> "Almost everyone in the Middle East thinks that America is on a crusade to Christianize the Muslim world, OK. I really hope that is not the case but that's what people believe."
>
> ~Imam Mohammad Azeez

In the same news report by CBS a new poll was presented that demonstrated that fewer than one in five Americans has a favorable view of Islam [19% favorable, 45% unfavorable, 36% no opinion]. Imam Azeez said about the poll, *"it's a stereotype that Muslims themselves must work to change."*

The origins of the crusades in general, and of the First Crusade in particular, as well as the conflict between the Christians and the Muslims reaches further back before the beginning of the first crusade, stemming from events earlier in the Middle Ages of Europe and the first major war between Christians and Muslims.

In the 5th century A.C.E., the Visigoths or western Goths were barbarian-Germanic tribes who had allied with Rome to keep other barbarians away from the Roman border. As payment for their loyalty the Visigoths received the territories of Hispania [Iberian Peninsula-now Spain and Portugal] and Southern Gaul.

In 711 A.C.E. the Muslims attempted to conquer Europe so they crossed the Strait of Gibraltar and attacked the Visigoths, who posed little resistance, and Spain fell under Islamic rule. The Muslims crossed the Pyrenees, and overran the valley of the Rhone. They headed for the Tours, a city in NW central France, on the Loire River, 129mi (208km) SW of Paris. It was the scene of the battle in which Charles Martel defeated the Saracens (Arabs), in A.C.E. 732. The Muslims met the army of the Germans at Tours and were defeated there. Their string of victories in which they overran almost the entire medieval world and North Africa came to an end as they were pushed back into Spain, where they and their descendants remained for over 700 years.

The Crusades were a series of wars undertaken by western European Christians between the 11th and 14th centuries A.C.E. supposedly to recover the Holy Land from the Muslims. In the 7th century, Jerusalem was taken over by the caliph Umar. In the beginning of that period, Christian pilgrimages to Jerusalem were not cut off at first, however early in the 11th century the Fatimid caliph Hakim began to persecute the Christians and despoiled the Holy Sepulcher [church in Jerusalem, officially regarded as the Church of the Resurrection. It is located in the east central part of the Christian quarter, on the supposed site of Jesus' tomb.]. Persecution of the Christians abated after his [caliph Hakim] death in the year 1021 A.C.E., but relations between Christians and Muslims remained strained and became more deteriorated when Jerusalem passed (1071 A.C.E.) from the rule of the Egyptians, who were predominantly Islamic Arabs and were considered to be comparatively tolerant, to the Seljuk Turks, who also in the same year went on to defeat the Byzantine emperor Romanus IV at Manzikert.

In the late part of the 11th century, the Byzantine Emperor Alexius I, leader of the eastern Christian empire, was threatened by the Seljuk Turks. He appealed to the Western Christians for aid. The

First Crusade was started in the year 1095 by Pope Urban II with the stated purpose of regaining control of Jerusalem and the Christian Holy Land from the Muslims. Records of the campaign reveal that the response turned quickly into a wholesale migration and conquest of territories outside of Europe by both peasants and knights from many different nations of Western Europe. They carried out the call to crusade with little central leadership. They traveled by land and by sea to Jerusalem and captured the city in July 1099. This was the only successful crusade. The crusaders established the Kingdom of Jerusalem and some other Crusader states.

In central Western Europe at the end of the first millennium A.C.E. there was relative stability of European borders after the Christianization of the Vikings and Magyars. This development gave rise to a class of warriors who then had very little to do except fight among themselves as well as terrorize the peasant population. Outlets for the violence of those groups were promoted in the form of military campaigns against non-Christians. The Reconquista [re-conquest] in Spain was one such outlet. That conflict in the Iberian Peninsula occupied Spanish knights as well as some mercenaries from around other parts of Europe to fight against the Moors.

The Moors were medieval Muslim inhabitants of North-west Africa and later of al-Andalus (Arabic name for the Iberian Peninsula including the present day Spain and Portugal) and whose culture is often called "Moorish". The Moors were composed of two groups, Arab conqueror leaders, who were originally part of the leading group that had left Asia Minor to conquer North Africa, and Native Africans [Berbers].

The Muslim conquest of Iberia was managed by Arab caliphates. The soldiery of the first wave of invasions was derived predominantly from Berber peoples [indigenous to Northwest Africa i.e. Black Africans,] of North Africa. Upon conquering the Iberian peninsula the Arabs took the best lands and left the inhospitable areas to the Berbers, even though they were all supposedly practicing the same form of Islam. This racism led to protests and conflict that eventually led to disunity and weakening of the Moorish forces. The Visigoth inhabitants, who were now developing the characteristic Christian and Spanish culture, were able to establish themselves in the north and west and from there eventually extend their control over the rest of Spain by engaging in a conflict that lasted from 718 A.C.E. until finally expelling the last of the Moors from Spain in 1492, the same year that Christopher Columbus was sent to find India but arrived in the Americas in error instead. The apparent success of the Visigoths in Spain, who were gradually expelling the Moors from Spain, along with the abundance of fighters in the rest of Europe, emboldened the Christian Pope to advocate for war.

Thus, history shows that while the land of Spain and Portugal was conquered by the Romans and then given over by the Visigoths, who by this time had converted to Christianity. The Visigoths lost Spain to the Moors and then won it back again. The Arabs-Berber-Muslims made the first incursions to conquer the land and at the same time force the inhabitants to convert to Islam by imposing a tax on non-Muslims. History also demonstrates that in Spain as can be seen elsewhere in Arab-Islamic history down to the present situation of the Sudan, the Arab-Muslims tend to force others into conversion and at the same time also practice racial discrimination, segregation and forced miscegenation of conquered populations in order to genetically disperse the conquered population so as to homogenize it and thereby allow the lighter skinned [Arab descent] leaders to dominate it. In the Sudan, as verified by journalists and nongovernmental organizations, the preferred method of conquest by miscegenation is to murder the male population and rape the women. This is a tactic that the Spanish used in conquering the Native Americans.

AMNESTY INTERNATIONAL 19 July 2004

Sudan

Darfur: Rape as a weapon of war: sexual violence and its consequences[280]

"I was sleeping when the attack on Disa started. I was taken away by the attackers, they were all in uniforms. They took dozens of other girls and made us walk for three hours. During the day we were beaten and they were telling us: "You, the black women, we will exterminate you,

you have no god." At night we were raped several times. The Arabs(1) guarded us with arms and we were not given food for three days."

A female refugee from Disa [Masalit village, West Darfur], interviewed by Amnesty International delegates in Goz Amer camp for Sudanese refugees in Chad, May 2004

1. Introduction
In March 2004, Darfur, western Sudan, was described by the then United Nations (UN) Humanitarian Coordinator in Sudan, Mukesh Kapila, as the world's greatest humanitarian crisis". (2) Humanitarian organizations operating in Darfur are warning about malnutrition and famine in the region. (3) Today's "worst humanitarian crisis" has been directly caused by war crimes and crimes against humanity for which the Sudanese government is responsible.

The relative calm of Western Europe, overpopulation, the abundance of armies and the desire for wealth [greed] through conquest and expansion led to a rush to conquer other lands besides the "Holy Lands." So on the way to the Holy Lands the crusaders also sacked the Eastern Roman lands [Byzantium- who were also Christians], as well. Those attacks on Byzantium demonstrate that the motivation was one of greed and not religious. They are not unlike the present day plundering of such countries as the Philippines, Puerto Rico, Venezuela, Panama, Guatemala and others which have a majority Christian population.

The countries of Western Europe did not need to start the crusades. They were wars of choice, not of necessity. Firstly, the west had received calls for help to deal with barbarians, from the Eastern church prior to the late 11th century. Why was there no response to those calls? The west did not have the surplus of manpower or internal security until then but also, the desire for expansion was satiated, up to that time, with internal conquests within Europe. Secondly, if Europeans truly wanted to have the "Holy Lands" why did they not live there to begin with or why did thcy not move there if the land was so special? Why did they not transfer their population and capital to the Middle East? Why did they remain in Europe? Why did the Western Christian crusaders steal from and kill the eastern Christians with the sanction of the western Pope? The answer is that the Holy Land, now Israel and Palestine, was not so important but the excuse it offered to move people out of Europe to capture booty, plunder other lands and gain the spoils of war were the better reasons. In other words, the idealism of a religious war for capturing the Holy Lands was not a good enough reason even though there were some religious zealots who fought for that reason. The profiteering from plundering other countries on the way and capturing new lands was more viable and the Europeans were not ready to do that until the late 11th century A.C.E. So the culture of Europe in the late 11th century was socially and politically driven by religious ideology and economically fueled by secular greed and the mercantile agenda.

In the 21st century there seems to be a similar situation unfolding in the conflict between Arab-Muslim nations and nations in Western Europe and the United States of America. In ancient times the stated desire was to secure the access to the Holy Lands but in reality it was a land grab and looting of various cities by the kings and peasants of Europe. This time the stated desire is to bring peace to the Middle East but in reality the purpose is for the U.S.A. to wrest control over the oil fields from Europe, China and Russia and to stabilize the U.S.A. currency. Supporting president George W. Bush and the conservative republican party agenda was the religious right wing fundamentalist ideologies of Pentecostal, dominionist and Evangelical Protestant Christians and the neo-conservative imperialist agenda of world domination, the corporate agenda of multinational companies seeking to globalize the world economy through privatization of the national wealth assets of other countries and economically subjugating them to the Western economies, to expand profits from worldwide markets.

Pentecostalism is a specific movement within evangelical Christianity that began in the early 20th century. It is typified by enthusiastic religious gatherings and the firm belief that God can empower the Christian for victorious life and service via the Baptism of the Holy Spirit - proof of which is supposedly found in part in the external evidence of tongue speaking. Historic Pentecostalism has its roots in the Holiness Movement and the Revivalism of the "Second Great Awakening" in America during the early 19th century.[281]

> Many secular humanists and fellow Christians criticize some publicly born-again Christians, especially those who became born-again as an overture to entering into politics. They criticize the term, because it allows people to spontaneously become 'Good Christians', and thus receive the uncritical support of a powerful voting bloc, despite the perceived lack of an ethical track record.[282]

As a reaction to the devastation of the Civil War and guilt regarding slavery, rampant corruption, drug abuse, violence and the decline of religious practice in the country many Christians in the second half of the 19th century felt the country needed a religious revival so the fundamentalism that developed in the U.S.A. in the late 19th and early 20th centuries was a reaction to degrading culture that was deteriorating due to low moral values. A similar development occurred in the religion of Islam. In the 18th century a sect of fundamentalist Islam came into being, which is today referred to as Wahhabism.

Wahhabism in Saudi Arabia began with a surge of reformers seeking to reclaim orthodox Islam from innovation by various sects of Sunni Muslims. In the 18th century, it spread with the expansion of the First Saudi State under Muhammad bin Saud and his successors.[283]

As a reaction to western imperialism, many people in the militarily weaker [than the western government] Arab-Islamic state or states where colonialism or neocolonialism had been imposed in the Middle East have sought power and have founded resistance movements through religious fundamentalism. In this sense though religious fundamentalism has had a foundation in Arab culture and in the Islamic tradition itself it has been fomented by western acts perceived by Arabs as imperialist and as unjust. Due to their military inferiority many groups resorted to guerrilla attacks and destabilization of the occupying governments by means of surprise suicide bomb attacks in heavily populated areas which are termed as "terrorism" by western governments. This term is relative since the western governments have bombed entire cities filled with civilian populations and have killed far more people than the Arab-Islamic fundamentalist groups. The suicide attacks have been an effective means to neutralize the military superiority of the western governments [Europe, U.S.A. and Israel], forcing them to negotiate instead of being able to claim outright victory and outright domination of Arab-Islamic populations. The details of how the west helped create and develop Islamic fundamentalism and "terrorism" are detailed in the book *"Devil's Game: How the United States Helped Unleash Fundamentalist Islam"* by Robert Dreyfuss.

Thus, in a sense we are witnessing a modern day form of Crusade via western attempts to colonize the Middle East, supporting favorable dictators and tyrants or outright military occupations that are further inciting Arab animosity, rekindling old grudges and raising hatred between ordinary Muslims and ordinary Christians that will again endure for decades if not centuries. The easy military fall of Arab states to western control has given rise to resistance movements that are more intractable. If any Arab state, with deep resentment and will to oppose the western countries [Europe and the U.S.A.] should achieve or acquire nuclear weapons they would be surely perceived by the west in general and the U.S.A. in particular as a major threat due to longstanding animosities and the dogmatic threats and counter threats by both sides. However, few people reflect upon how countries without nuclear weapons might feel facing the U.S.A. which has used nuclear weapons before and constantly seeks to control other governments by economic or military conquest, causing the weaker nations to seek out the nuclear weapons, perhaps also to protect themselves, by presenting a threat of their own. The case of the conflict between the U.S.A. and Iran is prominent in the present day media. Since the final ouster of the western backed dictator, the Shah, who was put in place by the U.S.A. the relations between the two countries has been strained, especially due to Iran's refusal to accept western cultural and political influences and control of the world economy and the oil of Iran. Consider what would have happened if the U.S.A. had extended true friendship and humanitarian assistance to Iran and sided with the democratically elected government of Iran instead of sponsoring a coup d'é·tat after fomenting social strife and political intrigue? That was not possible due to the U.S.A.'s predilection for control and suppression of other governments in favor of U.S.A. corporations. In this manner, the western countries [especially the

U.S.A in the late 20th century] have promoted, encouraged and supported social and political strife in many parts of the world so as to supposedly prevent them from falling under Soviet influence [during the so called "cold war"] but in reality to produce weakness in other countries and make them fall under the political influence and economic subjugation of the dominant power, all of which has produced much resentment around the world. The proof of this statement is that after the fall of the Soviet Union the U.S.A. continued to act as an imperial power, seeking to control the world through direct military force or preferably through manipulation of financial markets and repeatedly not supporting democratic movements but placing dictators and puppet governments in power.

The Religious Crisis is caused by ignorance and fanaticism. These cloud the intellect and cause one to become callous, cruel and fundamentalist in one's outlook. To avoid the crisis there needs to be openness and the realization that religion does not contradict rationality and anything that is against life and truth is irrational on its face. Anything that promotes hatred and violence is irrational and must be abandoned whether or not it is contained in a holy book or in a tradition, etc. When the negation of hatred, exclusiveness and violence are possible then it will be possible to live by truth, forgiveness and harmony.

As long as nations and governments are influenced by religions that promote exclusivist dogmas and literal interpretations of religious histories that place them as the prominent religion among all other religions or if they consider other religions to be false, there will always develop strife between the religious followers.

As long as there continue to be those religious followers who insist that others be converted to their religion and that they must be saved and can only be saved through their religion and none other, there will be strife between the religious followers.

As long as demagogues are able to control and manipulate populations and as long as there continue to be ignorant peoples who are in search of stability with no prospects for financial justice, social justice or the opportunity to pursue their life in peace and harmony there will be fertile ground for religious fundamentalist followers.

Therefore, in order to prevent the development of fundamentalism it is important to promote social, and economic justice including universal healthcare and compassion for all human beings so that they may not feel the need to resent the rich and powerful who have neglected them or to resent those who have committed crimes against them by taking their land or mistreating their people or economically subjugated them.

First Crusade

Jews, identifiable by their Judenhuts, are being killed by Crusaders, from a 1250 French Bible

The Economic Crisis

The economies of the U.S.A. and the European nations emerged to become the richest in the world because of slave labor. Originally, those nations enslaved their own people through serfdom in the medieval and dark ages and later through indentured service. Later, with the discovery of the "Americas" and the exploration of Africa, those lands were taken by force from their inhabitants and the Native Americans and Africans were enslaved to produce goods at cost that the plantation owners profited from by selling to the merchants who also profited. Those profits were parleyed into private capital used by aristocrats to create businesses and technological developments that led to the industrial revolution. Along the way those aristocrats developed into an oligarchy that controls the government, and they are backed by a plutocracy that controls the world economy via a corpocracy[284] by means of philosophies that include free trade, fiat money [flexible currency] and capitalism. These philosophies have helped the western countries to become wealthy but have not shielded them from wars, and economic depressions and have not provided safety, equality and prosperity for all or most of their populations. This movement has led to economic conditions that are complicated and pose great threats to national as well as international peace and stability.

The capitalist [greed power and wealth] seeking agenda has sought to gain control of the world through economic slavery [subsistence wages, and usurpation of a country's raw materials] and economic undermining of other countries by destabilizing their governments and then saddling them with economically crippling loans from the International Monetary Fund and the World Bank and other proxy institutions. That in itself has caused war, torture, killings either directly by using the U.S.A. armed forces to conquer other countries or by fomenting coup d'états in other countries by supporting dictators who will favor U.S.A. political and economic goals. Overreaching in this way has lead to an unprecedented development of a military industrial complex, which drives the fear, warmongering, profiteering and deficit spending culture of the western countries and in particular the U.S.A.

The modern Western cultures have sought to develop governments and economic systems that will produce opportunities for developing prosperity and wealth through a growth and expansion model of economies. The U.S.A., as a country, has developed with that mentality, from its inception, fueled by people desiring to be rich even beyond the capacity to use the wealth or caring much about the ethical means to achieve it. In a sustainable society the economy is not driven by endless growth because that is unrealistic and it forces periods of growth and recession or depression. In a sustainable culture the relative values of items would stay the same and the society would not be plagued by inflations and depressions but in such a society there can be no fabulously rich people but there would be more even spreading of the wealth and consequently there would be less strife. In order to keep proper fiscal management and budgeting one should not spend more money than one has or will have in the near future. If one does go into debt that will leave one prey to the fluctuations of the economy and the desires of the person holding the mortgage. So economic debt is a form of slavery, and the more debt, the more slavery is strengthened and expanded. Interdependence of economic interaction such as international trade can be positive if it is even trade, but can lead to economic disparity and imbalance and vulnerability of the national economy if left unregulated. The greed of large corporations drove the move towards banking fraud and trade imbalanced that pose serious threats to the U.S.A. economy.

In the year 1971 the U.S.A. abandoned the gold standard. Since abandoning gold backing of the dollar in August of 1971, the country embarked on one of history's greatest experiments in fiat money. Since that day in 1971, debt and credit of every kind expanded at all levels of society. The Federal Reserve Note [U.S. Dollar] has had 96% of its original 1913 value eroded to inflation, according to the CPI. Essentially, the loss of purchasing power in the economy has been caused by the system of economy that has been put in place. It is not natural or absolute, but contrived. Yet most ignorant consumers are content to blame greedy business men for raising prices every year. The United States dollar was once defined as a specific weight of gold or silver, but the years 1913 to 1971 gradually came to be defined by the Federal Reserve Note (FRN) fiat currency principle.

The "U.S. Federal Reserve System" is a banking consortium created by the Federal Reserve Act in 1913. The rich corporation owners of that time, such as Henry Ford, Rockefeller, and bankers such as J. P. Morgan and others pushed for a central bank to provide investment capital to the economy [for their companies to expand] as well as prevent speculative and unstable private banking that produced many bank failures. So the Federal Reserve was supposedly created to provide liquidity [more money] in the economy or contraction in the monetary supply when conditions required that, or otherwise controlling the economy [inflation-deflation] when needed. It is a corporation chartered by the U.S.A. congress and given, by them, the exclusive franchise to create the nations money. The Fed is a hybrid "system" of banks that pool their capital in the Fed. The national board of the Fed is appointed by the president and approved by congress. Essentially it is a collaboration of the government and business. The member banks that are members of the Fed purchase stock certificates in proportion to the capital they put in. In order to get passed the sponsors of the bill, in congress, agreed to put in restrictions. The bill was originally enacted into law with provisions that restricted the capacity to the Fed to create money "out of thin air." Since the Federal Reserve Act was passed it was "amended" over 100 times and the restrictive provisions were gutted and new provisions favorable to government expansion, banking and corporations, were quietly passed in congress that expanded the power of the Federal Reserve System beyond the original enactment.

The central banks in Europe are not hybrids but serve the same function and also create money "out of thin air". Nevertheless, in the time since its creation the economy did not remain stable as it was supposedly intended to be through the Fed. It experienced the crashes of 1921, 1929, great depression of 1931-1939, recessions of 1953, 1957, 1969, 1975, 1981, and the stock market "Black Monday" in 1987. The U.S.A. economy also experienced the highest personal debt than ever before, private and personal bankruptcies at record highs, and interest on national debt that consumes almost half of the tax dollars, banks and savings and loans have failed more than in the past. So the stated objectives of the Fed have not been achieved for the economy but the wealthy power elites holding the reigns of government, banks [the large banks of the east coast [money center banks] that now have branches all over the world-Ex. Chase Manhattan Bank] and transnational corporations have prospered. The Federal Reserve System, instead of democratizing money policy and taking power away from the big banks and large corporations, insured their control over the economy and expanded their economic power and profits. The big banks consolidated their control over the smaller ones by becoming their regulators.

The U.S.A. has managed to get the entire world to base its economy on the U.S. Dollar. After World War II the U.S.A. was the strongest nation and they had a trade surplus. They produced many manufactured goods and brought in more money than was spent. Today there is a monumental trade deficit because the U.S.A. population spends more than it brings in through exports. This problem of trade deficits exploded when deregulations by president Ronald Reagan in the 1980s reduced tariffs on imported goods at the behest of business leaders, saying that that policy was "isolationist". While other countries retained their tariffs the U.S.A. left them low and that benefited businesses like Wal-Mart that import cheap goods. But the trade deficits increased dramatically and that hurt the value of the dollar. So the value of the dollar is dwindling every year, meaning it purchases less and less. China and Japan have been supporting the dollar by purchasing US Treasury Notes, a form of investment in the U.S. Dollar, banking on the "growth" potential of the U.S.A. economy. However, U.S.A. corporations have exported manufacturing jobs for many years [seeking greater profit through lower wages abroad] and now there are more service [low paying] jobs in the U.S.A. than manufacturing [high paying] jobs. So the dollar purchases less and people have less money to purchase things with and save. How degraded is the condition of the U.S.A. economy? In the book *"Empire of Debt: The Rise of an Epic Financial Crisis"* (Nov 11, 2005) the authors, Addison Wiggin and Bill Bonner point out that:

> "It is deeply unpleasant to consider the fact that the U.S. continues to rack up another $80 million of debt every hour, or that our trade deficit has hit an all time high of $725.8 billion."
> "The renowned Levy Institute estimates that the United States will owe foreigners $8 trillion by 2008, a breathtaking 60 percent of our gross domestic product."

If the U.S. dollar should become devalued for any reason to a certain extent the foreign investors could sell and invest in other currencies. If that were to happen the value of the U.S. Dollar would plummet because the dollars would flood the world currency markets and the world economy would go into a depression, and the U.S. economy would go into a major more severe depression than the Great Depression of the 1930s because the more dollars there are, the more the value of the currency needs to be divided into more dollars, therefore making each dollar worth even less. What most people do not talk about is the fact that in 1971 the U.S.A. government made the decision to go off the gold standard and have an economy based on credit. It was a way to artificially expand the economic power of the U.S.A. since if a country were to base the economy on the gold standard and has say 1 trillion in gold reserves it can only print 1 trillion dollars in paper money to represent the gold held in reserves but with a credit economy it can print unlimited dollars backed by nothing of value except the idea that it can have a future value if the economy keeps on growing, expanding, etc. To grow and expand there need to be new markets and more money to develop them.

Now that there is printed paper money [with no real value] all that was needed was new markets, so the move started in earnest in the late 1960s and early 1970's to economically subjugate other countries by destabilizing their governments so a coherent national economic policy could not be developed [so those countries could not develop a manufacturing base to compete with the U.S.A.] and forcing them to accept loans from the I.M.F. or the World Bank and force them to remain indebted and dependent upon the U.S.A. and U.S.A corporations for the products they needed.[285]

Here we may recall the words of Lewis Mumford, who spoke about how the major corporations contrive to maintain mass production. This ties into the imperialist and neocolonial efforts to stifle independent development in developing countries, discussed above.

The techniques used to perpetuate consumerism in reality are unethical devises for sustaining a myth of technological benefit while at the same time promoting more commerce that would not ordinarily occur. In other words, greed has corrupted commerce such that technological advancements, which would have normally led to higher quality and lower production [since fewer products would be needed because the older ones would work longer], are not allowed to be implemented in the economy. In other words, the creation and maintenance of world markets by subjugating other countries is an artificial form of "free market" system, otherwise said, it is actually corruption of the concept of free markets. In fact there is no such thing as a free market where the multinational corporations are involved because they would have too much to lose by allowing the market to be free so it has to be rigged to their advantage. Thus, the propaganda of corporate and technological benefit to society belies the true effect of those institutions, which is to hold back advancement and even to promote devolution by the destruction of resources that occurs through overproduction and over-consumption.

The U.S.A. introduced major credit cards and other credit for consumers to purchase goods in the 1960s. Now in the early 21st century the U.S.A. population has the highest level of debt and lowest savings in history and the desire to spend has not abated.

What would happen if a household spends $4,000 for every $2,000 that comes in through wages income to the home? The home becomes bankrupt very soon. And "the trade deficit only accelerates the speed of decline in the dollar's value."[286] This means that the U.S.A. economy is bankrupt and is only sustained by the confidence in the U.S.A. economy by foreign investors. If confidence should fall, the economy falls and the U.S.A. would no longer be self-sufficient. It depends on oil imports to produce food crops and to sustain the lower levels of manufacturing so the consequences of a financial collapse would affect everyone but more so those who are in debt or without the capacity for self-sufficiency. Many people would go insane or commit suicide due to mounting un-payable debt and the very rich would only suffer physically if there were a social revolution caused by the economic debacle that would cause people at large to violently depose them from their positions of power and remove them from their gated communities. But their income and the value of their assets and savings would be reduced, as it was during the Great Depression of the 1930s. However, if a person has 10 million dollars and their assets are reduced to 3 million they still remain millionaires. But if a person has assets of $300,000 and those assets go down to $50,000 then that person could be in dire straights. Nevertheless, the looming economic collapse would be much more severe than any earlier depression. This is why, in times of financial decline, many wealthy people choose to move their assets into tangible commodities and hard currencies backed by real material goods or in precious metals such as gold or silver during times of financial crisis or devaluations of currency because those assets have real value instead of paper money which in itself has no value.

The conventional wisdom has been that since China has so much invested in the U.S. economy in currency but also in the fact that the same money it invests in the U.S. Treasury Notes is the same money used to purchase Chinese goods. There is also the notion that China would not like to see the U.S. Economy fail because that would depress or cause the Chinese market to fail also, since the U.S.A. population would not be able to buy cheap goods from China anymore, through such outlets as Wal-Mart. Within the past two years China has moved to diversify its investments, moving away from investing in the U.S. dollar and into more stable currencies such as the European Euro, a move that raised tensions in world economic markets. Many other governments have been quietly exchanging the U.S. Dollar for other more stable currencies.

2005 China Revaluation. Yuan Revaluation - Euro's Big Moment?

As China moves towards pegging the CNY to a basket of currencies or floating the Yuan, there could be a notable impact on the Euro. China is the second largest holder of US Treasury debt, approximately $191 billion second only to Japan and Euro Zone. A revaluation of the Yuan will force Chinese policy makers to sell a least part of their US dollar holdings and buy euros and/or yen. Currently there is a growing shift by different countries to diversify their foreign exchange reserves away from dollar and including an increasing amount of Euro's in their mix of currencies. So far we know that Russia will be readjusting their dollar denominated reserve holdings. South Africa and India are also suspected of dumping US treasuries. According to the latest Bank of International Settlements report, oil exporters have reduced their dollar holdings over the past 3 years. Central banks in the Middle East have exchanged some dollar reserves for euros to avoid incurring losses related to the slide in the dollar. Although the euro was only launched in 1999, it has since become the world's second most popular reserve currency. As time passes, we expect more central banks to hold an increasing number of euros as they adjust their reserve holdings to reflect their trade flows. For China, their mix will continue to include the dollar, but by a diminished capacity. However, they are also expected to increase their holdings of Japanese yen and the euro.[287]

***The Attack on the U.S. Dollar and Energy Needs* by Alan Caruba**
March 19, 2006 09:34 AM EST

"As David J. Jonsson, the author of "Clash of Ideologies", pointed out in a recent article, the United States "relies on approximately 70 percent of all foreign-exchange currency to be held in dollars because we sell Treasury debt into that foreign-exchange market." A flight of foreign-exchange reserves away from the dollar would depress its value and, conversely potentially increase the value of the Euro by 20 to 40 percent."[288]

The sensitivity and volatility of the dollar to the Chinese purchases of U.S. Treasury notes was demonstrated in April of 2006:

> The U.S. Dollar fell sharply against the euro and yen in Asia, partly due to a media report suggesting China might reduce its purchases of U.S. treasury holdings.
>
> –International News Network World Report-
> 4/19/06[289]

Up until 1971 the various governments on the world market adhered to the Bretton Woods system of monetary management which used a "managed" Gold Standard. Some economists would like to return to a Bretton Woods–style system, so as to reduce the volatility of currencies. However, the reason it was supposedly dropped is that it's government-ordained exchange ratio is unworkable. This has led followers of Austrian economist's theory such as Ludwig von Mises, Friedrich Hayek and Murray Rothbard to promulgate the idea of a complete freeing up of the gold price in the market from a State-decreed exchange rate as well as the end to the monopoly on the issuance of gold currency by the government.

The Great Depression was a massive global economic depression (or "recession ") that occurred from the year 1929 to 1941. It affected the whole of the industrialized world as well as the trading partners in peripheral nations to the industrialized nations. The most important crash in the 20th century was the 1929 crash in which the Dow Jones Industrial Average dropped 50%; this crash preceded the Great Depression. In succeeding years the Dow Jones dropped a total of over 85%. A stock market crash is a sudden loss of value of shares of stocks of corporations. The stock market system is akin to an auction and sometimes at auctions people overbid for an item that they want. They can recover the price they paid if there are others who want the item for the price they paid or a higher price or if they can hold onto the item until it appreciates to the higher overpriced level. If the price is overvalued eventually other people do not want it so there are no buyers. People may loose confidence in the stock market because the prices are inflated and those holding the stock need to sell at a loss. Emotional selling driven by panic can lead to undermining the market and people want out to get their money out of the stock market before everybody else sells and the prices go lower or dwindle to almost nothing and they lose everything they invested i.e. while they can still get something for the stock. So the stock market is volatile and risky and prone to inflated prices, like a pyramid scheme in which all is ok as long as there is someone at the bottom willing to buy in. If there is no one to buy, the prices go down because demand is low and prices "correct" to their supposedly true levels, i.e. their true market price without the emotional or speculative investing. So crashes often follow speculative stock market bubbles such as the recent dot-com boom and general market downturn in the years 2000-2002.

> In truth Roosevelt had foreseen from early in his Presidency that only a solution to the international trade problem would finally end the depression, and that the New Deal was, to no small extent, a "holding action". He contemplated precipitating a war with Japan early on, in hopes of dealing with the problem early. However, the intensity of the economic crisis convinced him that before the world situation could be dealt with, the United States would have to put its own fiscal house back in order. His original conception was that the New Deal would restore circumstances which would allow for a return to balanced budgets and an international gold standard. It was only gradually that he came to the conclusion that it was essential to remake the U.S. economy in a more extensive fashion, particularly because of the "Roosevelt Recession" of 1937, when he had balanced the budget by restricting fiscal support to the economy.[290]

During the period of the Great Depression president Roosevelt knew that he needed to increase government spending to stimulate the economy out of the depression and that the international trade problems with other countries needed to be resolved as well in order to have a more permanent solution to the problems that led to the depression. He considered engaging the U.S.A. to war with Japan years before the U.S.A. officially entered World War II but there was a strong isolationist sentiment in the country. Prior to the war the U.S.A. economy was transformed and geared towards supplying the European allies of the U.S.A. with munitions and other war supplies and that began to stimulate the U.S.A. economy before the U.S.A. entered the war. So delaying the entry into the war allowed the retooling of industry to produce vast quantities of weapons. This was all accomplished through massive public expenditures and deficit spending. As a consequence of these actions unemployment in the U.S.A. was reduced—from 19% in 1938 (which was already down from a peak of 1933's 24.9%) to 1.2% in 1944—as the labor force grew by ten million.

Along with deficit spending Roosevelt applied socialist economic principles through his "New Deal" program, the reverse of the capitalist principles that had precipitated the Great Depression, in order to stimulate more even distribution of wealth in the economy. For that he was accused of turning America into a *socialist* or even *Stalinist state.*[291] So it is ironic that anti-capitalist measures are needed to reverse the disastrous effects of capitalistic free market corporate driven economics but those measures are only used when there is a financial crisis and not to promote sustainable equitable economics. See below:

> New Deal programs sought to stimulate demand and provide work and relief for the impoverished through increased government spending, by: [292]
>
> - instituting regulations which ended what was called "cut throat competition" (in which large players supposedly used predatory pricing to drive out small players);
> - creating regulations which would raise the wages of ordinary workers, to redistribute wealth so that more people could purchase products.
>
> The original implementation, in the form of the National Recovery Act, brought in direct unemployment relief, and allowed:
>
> - business to set price codes;
> - the NRA board to set labor codes and standards;
> - the Federal government to insure the banking system and provide price supports for agriculture and mining.

World War II was a boon for the U.S.A. economy because the U.S.A. government was able to stimulate the economy through selling supplies to fight the war [profiteering] without domestic danger from damage due to bombings or combat on U.S.A. soil from the war itself. Only people were lost, as people were lost in the previous wars. So it is no surprise that the U.S.A. economy became the most powerful since it was intact and it exported the supplies to reconstruct and sustain other countries after the war. However, just as the British economy plunged after many years of imperialism that had propelled the British pound to become the standard currency for the world economy [reserve currency status] the U.S. dollar is headed for devaluation, due to fiscal mismanagement, but the consequences are much more dire because of the dependency on the dollar by the U.S. Domestic economy and the worldwide markets.

> Reserve currency status, however, is not without its risks. While the United Kingdom enjoyed economic benefits through the 19th Century up until 1914 from the strength of the British Pound and its reserve currency status, the relative weakening of the UK and strengthening of the US economies in the inter-war and post-war periods caused the shift in currency reserves, culminating in a 30% devaluation of the British Pound in 1949 which ended the dominance of the British Pound as a world currency. Weighed down by the debts of fighting World War II, and without the benefits of reserve currency status, the United Kingdom struggled to rebuild its economy, entering a period of economic slowdown and decline that would last over three decades.
> If, as many economists are speculating, current weakness in the dollar were to cause the shift of foreign exchange reserves or oil pricing into another currency such as the Euro, then the reserve currency advantage would also switch to the European Union.[293]

> ***Experts of Standard & Poor's forecast a global economic collapse.***
> The collapse will be caused with the demise of the US dollar rate against the European currency by more than 30 percent. The dollar, specialists say, may lose almost 45 percent of its current value against the euro. The European Central Bank has expressed its concerns with the forecast from Standard & Poor's. The European financial specialists say that the demise of American currency will endanger the global economy on the whole.
> **Pravda Online**, Wednesday, February 01, 2006.[294]

The recent and unprecedented warning from S&P is seen as serious because that organization is one of the most important financial research organizations of the world economy. Despite the efforts to stem the decline of the dollar by controlling Iraq, the U.S. Dollar continued to fall until the S&P[295] issued the warning of the impending collapse of the dollar and the repercussions for the world economy. Meanwhile, the U.S. government has no comment and no advice to offer its people related to any adjustments needed to the economy, but rather the president and his republican party cohorts continued to ask the population to spend money and keep the economy going as a patriotic measure [especially right after the attack on the World Trade Center in New York on 9/11/01] and calling for cutting taxes to the richest segments of the population and to corporations, and continue to raise military spending beyond all previous records; those are moves that independent economists say will surely have the effect of making the economy worse. Unbridled consumer spending and businesses importing goods at a deficit may help corporations in the short term but it does not help the economy in a fundamental and long term way; what are needed are more trade balance and more personal savings. Joan Robinson, a well-known economist in the 1920-1930s close to John Maynard Keynes said:

> "If the capital inflows merely permit an excess of consumption over production, the economy is on the road to ruin. If they permit an excess of investment over home saving, the result depends on the nature of the investment."[296]

The U.S.A. economy has engaged in "excess of consumption over production." That, coupled with other financial mismanagement has promoted a negative economic condition. The continued budget deficit, which is different from the trade deficit, makes the situation worse since the interest on the deficit money must be paid and estimates show that the current spending and tax cuts have already created a situation wherein the current population will not be able to repay the deficit. It will need to be transferred to the taxes from the children of the current population and that is considering that there will not be a financial collapse and that the current levels of income will be maintained and that at some point the deficits must be reversed. Otherwise the population would face perpetual deficit economies that would prevent financing for infrastructure and services that would force the country to become dilapidated in infrastructure and limited in human services that especially the indigent, sick, elderly and the young depend on.

> ***The U.S. Bears A Greater Debt Load Now Than During The Great Depression***
> US debt of consumers, businesses, governments and financial institutions exceeded $40 trillion in 2006, compared with only $11 trillion in output. The nation's debt more than triples its gross domestic product. Compare that to 1933 when debt was only 2 1/2 times the GDP. Also, with the lowest interest rates in four decades applied to this debt, we can only look forward to it growing larger when those rates rise.[297]

As of the date February 11-12, 2006:

> U.S. federal debt was at $8.2 trillion - and growing every second. That leaves each portion of the federal debt to be paid by each individual person in the U.S.A. at over $27,000.
>
> ***US Trade Deficit Continues To Increase***
> The Commerce Department reported Friday that the gap between what America sells abroad and what it imports rose to $725.8 billion last year, up by 17.5 percent from the previous record of $617.6 billion set in 2004.
> It marked the fourth consecutive year that America's trade deficit has set a record as American consumers continued their seemingly insatiable demand for all things foreign from new cars to televisions and electronic goods.
> The increased foreign competition has helped to keep the lid on prices in this country, but critics say the rising trade deficit is a major factor in the loss of nearly 3 million manufacturing jobs since mid-2000 as U.S. companies moved production overseas to lower-waged nations. Many economists believe those manufacturing jobs will never come back.
> "Such a huge trade gap undercuts domestic manufacturing and destroys good U.S. jobs," said Richard Trumka, secretary-treasurer of labor's AFL-CIO. "America's gargantuan trade deficit is a weight around American workers' necks that is pulling them into a cycle of debt, bankruptcy and low-wage service jobs."[298]

The main activity of the Federal Reserve is that it raises and lowers the funds rate to slow down or to speed up economic growth. At least that's the idea. The Federal Reserve operates by the logic that when the economic activity grows too fast (too much lending, prices rising too quickly), you see inflation. To slow inflation down, the

Fed raises the funds rate. This makes it more expensive to borrow money, by increasing the interest rate paid on borrowed money. High interest rates lead to a slowdown in bank lending, because fewer people could afford to pay the cost of borrowing money. Bank lending is what actually creates new money, not the Fed. When the Fed says it's going to "crank up the printing presses," it really means it's going to lower the interest rate on borrowed money. It hopes that by doing so it will encourage banks to make more loans to the public and corporations. It's this lending that creates money "out of thin air."[299] Money that comes "out of thin air" is also referred to by some economists as “flexible currency.”

> “paper money eventually goes down to its intrinsic value – zero.”
>
> ~ Voltaire 1729 A.C.E.

Flexible currency also means the capacity to print money at will. Since the inception of the U.S. Federal Reserve the member banks embarked on a program of using the new capacity to acquire “flexible currency” to entice businesses to borrow money instead of using their own savings. Prior to the creation of the Fed there was a trend of corporations using “sinking funds.” Sinking funds are portions of dividends [profits] paid to stockholders, to buy back stock or reserve until a large enough fund is created in order to build new factories, etc. and thereby expand the company. This is also known as “private capital formation.” Private capital formation is a fiscally responsible way for a company to grow and expand. If companies use their own money they would not need banks and there would be no interest charge to use the borrowed moneys. In those days money was based on real currency like gold and not on thin air. In order to have money they would need to have more gold in their warehouse to back it up. Since there was a set amount of money [gold] there was a set interest rate on real money and there was a set amount of paper money in circulation that was worth the same as the gold. The only way to entice the business men was to provide them money with lower interest rates and the only way to provide them with that was to give them money that had no value because then it would not matter what interest rate was on it since it cost nothing to begin with. This is how the large banks that joined the "cartel" of the Fed, which were based in the east coast of the U.S.A. in the early part of the 20th century became mega banks, controlling not only the U.S.A. economy but much of the world economy as well. The activities of the Fed, enticing corporations and businesses to borrow money, has led to the shaky conditions in which more and more businesses find themselves. If the economy experiences fluctuations they may not be able to service the debt and they would be forced to go into bankruptcy and consequently out of business. Many companies pay more to banks in interest than dividends [profits] to their shareholders. This means that the companies, which did the hard work to produce the money through their enterprises, are paying and sometimes struggling to pay the banks, which did nothing of value except provide the money which costs the banks virtually nothing!

Actually, inflation is caused by adding printed money to the economy faster than the rate of increase of goods and services. If money were added at the same rate as productivity and population increases that purchasing power of money would remain constant. As soon as money has been separated from anything of real value like gold or silver the temptation has always prevailed to print more than the economy needs for the proper economic activity. If a gold or silver standard were used there might even be deflation periods in which the value of the dollar would go up instead of down; with the current system that will not happen. Despite the dire condition of the dollar due to massive deficits and private as well as governmental financial mismanagement, the new head of the Federal Reserve made statements that have been considered by some critics as "wishful thinking."

> CNNMONEY.com
> ***Bernanke: Economy can handle dollar drop***
> ***Fed chairman says a steep decline in greenback wouldn't necessarily disrupt financial markets.***
> March 21, 2006: 6:51 PM EST
> WASHINGTON (Reuters) - The chronic U.S. trade gap need not fuel a "precipitous" decline in the dollar, but the economy could handle it if it did, Federal Reserve Chairman Ben Bernanke said Tuesday.
> "Although U.S. trade deficits cannot continue to widen forever, these deficits need not engender a precipitous decline in the dollar, nor

> should such a decline, were it to occur, necessarily disrupt financial markets, production or employment," Bernanke said in a letter to Rep. Brad Sherman, a California Democrat.[300]

One of the most prominent examples of a deflating economy was the U.S.A. economy in the years 1930-1933 [during the beginning of the Great Depression] when asset prices dropped 10% per year or more. So the value, at the beginning of the year, of a house worth $100,000 would deflate to $90,000 at the end of the year. This is one of the reasons why investors in Japan began investing in gold and in U.S.A. Treasury Notes beginning in the early 1990s and only in 2006 did world economists and the Prime Minister of Japan say in March 2006 that he thought the end was in sight.[301] In that case, if the Japanese economy is coming out of the 15 year deflationary period, after inflating to a comparable state as the current condition of the U.S.A. economy, what will that mean for the U.S.A. economy? Will they now stop investing in the U.S. Treasury Notes? If that were to happen who would take up the slack on supporting the U.S.A. debt? Of course if nobody does that would constitute an untenable situation for the dollar.

What about the question, could a protracted deflationary period occur in the U.S.A. economy? The recently appointed head of the U.S. Federal Reserve Board, Ben S. Bernanke, said the following remarks in the year 2002, at a time when interest rates had gone down to historical lows in the U.S.A. [highlighted portions by Ashby]

> Deflation is defined as a general decline in prices, with emphasis on the word "general." At any given time, especially in a low-inflation economy like that of our recent experience, prices of some goods and services will be falling.
> ...Deflation *per se* occurs only when price declines are so widespread that broad-based indexes of prices, such as the consumer price index, register ongoing declines. The sources of deflation are not a mystery. Deflation is in almost all cases a side effect of a collapse of aggregate demand--a drop in spending so severe that producers must cut prices on an ongoing basis in order to find buyers.
> ... It is true that once the policy rate has been driven down to zero, a central bank can no longer use its *traditional* means of stimulating aggregate demand and thus will be operating in less familiar territory. The central bank's inability to use its traditional methods may

> complicate the policymaking process and introduce uncertainty in the size and timing of the economy's response to policy actions. Hence I agree that the situation is one to be avoided if possible.
> ...Reserve study of the Japanese experience concluded that the deflation there was almost entirely unexpected, by both foreign and Japanese observers alike (Ahearne et al., 2002). So, having said that deflation in the United States is highly unlikely, I would be imprudent to rule out the possibility altogether.

We must remember that the Federal Reserve Note has lost 96% of its original 1913 value. This means that the present dollar purchases only $.04 of the original 1913 dollar [$1.00]. Furthermore, this means that the cumulative interest rate or profit to the banks has been over 1000% on all the money on all the factories, and houses and cars and everything else this money was used on since that time. Additionally, the interest costs more than the item being paid for. For example, if a person were to get an $80,000 home mortgage at 6% and pay it over 30 years the interest on that loan comes to $93,000. The home would cost a total of $173,000. If we multiply this interest figure by the number of homes in the U.S.A. we get a staggering number. We must remember that that interest payment is on money that the bank got for free. Therefore we must conclude that the current banking system is perhaps one of the most usurious and insidious forms of economic commerce that has ever been devised even if we consider loan sharking, or other forms of organized crime because the banking system makes money on all money, the legitimate as well as the illegitimate; and the loan shark worked to get the money he loaned out but the bank did not. This situation can only be compared to a barbarism such as the Vikings pillaging Europe; they would rape and pillage a country and take all the wealth, but at least they had to fight for it, the bank just pays its expenses and manages paper, wherein people have signed their rights away and have concented to pay them the usurious fees. What occurred at the beginning of the 20th century and the beginning of the 21st was foreseen by some of the founders of the U.S.A.

> Thomas Jefferson, third President (1801-1809) of the U.S.A.:
>
> "If the American people ever allow private banks to control the issue of their currency, first by inflation, then by deflation, the banks...will deprive the people of all property until their children wake-up homeless

> on the continent their Fathers conquered.... The issuing power of money should be taken from the banks and restored to the people, to whom it properly belongs."
> ... "A private central bank issuing the public currency is a greater menace to the liberties of the people than a standing army."
>
> James Madison, fourth President (1809-1817) of the U.S.A.:
>
> "History records that the money changers have used every form of abuse, intrigue, deceit, and violent means possible to maintain their control over governments by controlling money and its issuance."

The printing of money "out of thin air" actually constitutes a tax. It is an insidious tax that consumes the entire economy but hurts those who do not have access to the initial buying power of the money. When the treasury prints money and deposits it into the government account, the government gains the first benefit. Once it is borrowed the borrower, or contractors for the government, the corporations, get the next benefit and the banks get their fees but once the money is diffused throughout the economy it has the least value because by that time it has been added to the existing number of dollars already out in the economy. The middle class and poor get the least value and so the dollars they have in the bank and the ones they receive now and in the future are worth less than they were before the new money was printed and circulated. In order to do that the government operates at a deficit. The money is not based on anything real except an I.O.U. that it will be paid sometime in the future. Therefore, the people are losing value over and paying interest on nothing real, nothing of value except the paper produced by the treasury.

People have been conditioned to believe that inflation is a part of life, like death or the sun rising in the morning. They are given meager cost of living increases in the minimum wage but those increases do not keep up with the real state of the economy so no one can live on minimum wage and pay rent, food, utilities, etc. Those increases are always behind the inflation and never given as inflation occurs so that is why people are always behind on their bills and never can catch up, barely trying to keep their heads above water. This is also why two incomes at least are needed to support a home on average wages and why children are often neglected; both parents need to be working and therefore the children are reared by television or open to other pernicious dangers in early life, like predatory adults, negative peer pressure, malnutrition or they may develop depression, anxiety, feelings of abandonment or being unloved, etc. These conditions may lead children to seeking love through sex, drugs or getting pregnant to have somebody be with them or they may develop negative social skills that might lead them to fail in relationships, jobs, etc. So through this strategy, the government and the wealthy can have more money and the population is used to pay for it, but the money is not taken as a legislated tax since that would be unpopular and would precipitate a revolt. This system works as long as the economy is expanding and as long as the economic environment remains the same, so that the masses of people can maintain subsistence level existence with the dream of doing better.

If the population fluctuates [as populations do naturally] the system would collapse or crash regularly, as a pyramid scheme. Thus the government compensates for the shortfall in the population by admitting new immigrants. If immigrants stop coming the economy would contract and the system would collapse under the weight of the massive federal debt that cannot be paid for even with the current amount of people in the population. If other countries want to expand in the same way, and have wealth [like the U.S.A. has done] then the competition will necessarily reduce to the incapacity of having expansion in money [inflation] through trade deficits. If the countries that own treasury notes [subsidizing the national debt and trade deficits] stop buying them the U.S.A. economy would stop and reverse immediately. If the countries that own treasury notes decide they want to liquidate those notes, it would produce a financial crisis of majestic proportions because the money is not there to pay them and the standard of living in the U.S.A. would be lost.

One more thought; the Federal Reserve System is written as a law mandated by the government so that any bank failures that may arise are "guaranteed" by the government. This means that if a bank fails, as many have, the government must step in and pay the depositors. So banks or bank officers do not lose, the government prints new money to cover the losses [bail them out] and the citizens [taxpayers] must pay that back through taxes and inflation.

In order to stem the decline of the dollar the U.S. Federal Reserve,[302] under the chairmanship of Alan Greenspan, slashed [dramatically lowered] interest rates on the money supply after the recession that occurred between the years 2000 and 2003 in which many people lost their life savings in stock investments. This led to a rash of housing refinances and inflation in housing prices and deflation in stock prices. Much of the money gained in home refinances was used for making other purchases such as cars, boats and buying other real estate such as vacation homes. So that money is a loan based on the inflated price of the house due to lower interest rates that allow people to pay less for the same money but the refinances that took money out of the house are like having two loans on the house. So this situation created more debt while artificially raising the value of the economy.

> ...the Fed announced it was worried about deflation even while real inflation of goods we need from food to energy heats up in the economy. The policy statement—which was nothing more than moral suasion—was an attempt by Fed officials to direct the spec community and herd them into playing the yield curve. The result was that money moved into the long-end of the market, driving down interest rates in an explosive bond rally that took 10-year rates down to the 3% level and drove the long bond into the 4% zone. This in turn ushered in lower mortgage rates, which led to another round of mortgage refis putting more debt money into the hands of consumers. The policy objective is to lower the carrying cost of debt in order that more debt can be accumulated (translation: additional consumer spending). Consumer spending now accounts for 90% of U.S. GDP. The U.S. economy has transformed itself from an economy that saved, invested and produced goods into an economy that borrows, consumes and trades off asset bubbles...
>
> In addition to the bond market bubble, which feeds off a continuous supply of cheap credit, a portion of that credit also goes into financial speculation in the stock market. It has become apparent that the Fed is once again trying to re-inflate the stock market bubble along with keeping the real estate bubble inflated in order to avoid a deflationary debt collapse and another depression. Having expanded credit throughout the 90's and now the 2000s, the Fed created a giant asset

> bubble first in stocks, then in real estate. The Fed is now in a fretful state because of the consequences of seeing these bubbles deflate. The result would be the possible collapse of the financial system and a depression. In trying to fight and prevent these two events from occurring, it is expanding credit, monetizing debt, intervening in the financial markets, debasing the currency and using every means of persuasion to direct the markets in an effort to achieve a certain outcome. In this one sense the U.S. economy and financial markets no longer operate freely, but are now centrally planned.[303]

The lowering interest rates created a need for more dollars to be printed and that lowered the value of the dollar more [the more dollars in circulation the less the value per dollar]. So continued devaluation of the dollar occurred while the value of real estate, fueled by investors seeking rapid returns they could no longer get in the stock market, was raised in many parts of the country; some way more than others. This led to the rapid rise of real estate in many parts of the U.S.A., which are far beyond the ordinary capacity of people's incomc to sustain the mortgage payments. Added to these developments, new forms of mortgages were introduced in 2001 that allowed people to purchase bigger more expensive houses and pay the same as they were before or less. The miracle was actually a shell game in which people were lured into adjustable rate mortgages that they could pay only interest on. So, for example, if the payment was supposed to be $2,000 on a $200,000 house that should have been worth only $125,000 [before the artificial inflation] but the person could not afford that $2,000 payment they could now pay only $700 [interest portion] but if the interest rate were to go up and they could only afford to pay $700, the new owner would be forced into an untenable financial crisis very quickly, possibly leading to foreclosure. Even if the interest rate did not go up they would never pay the mortgage down because they are paying interest only, therefore the principal amount would remain the same, and so they would remain in debt perpetually. These manipulations of real estate with inflated values and inflated mortgages in an economy where many people cannot afford the basic expenses of life, is called the "real estate bubble." Many real estate analysts and economists see a looming collapse of the real estate market, a bursting of the "bubble" for many reasons. How does a real estate bubble form and how does it burst?

What has caused U.S. home prices to go up and why it's unsustainable? Houses have become what stocks were in 1999, a can't-miss way of getting rich. Unfortunately, when you buy an asset with credit and credit itself is easy to get, the price of the asset doesn't accurately reflect its true market value. When credit tightens, home values will find their market level.
...this mortgage bubble will not affect all areas of the country in the same way. There is no such thing as a national real estate market. There are hundreds of regional and local markets and thousands of smaller ones. In some places — particularly the Northeast and the West Coast — real estate prices have skyrocketed in the last five years. In these places, home prices are on the brink of the unaffordable for the average household. The numbers will tell you the story. And in these places, homeowners and borrowers have the most to lose in the next few years.
... But bubbles have not. One key ingredient of a bubble is the belief that the asset will keep rising. It's also fueled by a bit of psychological panic: "If I don't get in now, I'll miss it! And everyone else is getting rich!" At some tipping point in the life of a bubble, nearly everyone believes that the asset currently in favor (tulips in Renaissance Holland, Florida real estate, technology stocks, houses) is THE ONLY WAY TO GET RICH. That's when the bubble usually pops — when popular sentiment is nearly unanimous that there's no risk to buying the asset and that it is a nearly guaranteed way to get rich.[304]

'M3 money supply' is about the best measure of the number of U.S. dollars, albeit imperfect. NSA means 'non-seasonally adjusted'. It is the 'hidden' money supply increase, the M3 increase less than the CPI, which is most relevant to bubble formation—because the extra money raises prices of items that are not well represented in the CPI, principally assets such as bonds, stocks, and housing. High M3 growth rates prior to 1990 were matched by similar CPI rates—they did not lead to bubbles because the rising prices were plainly visible in the CPI and monetary authorities were forced to take appropriate actions.)
In the early 1990's the money supply increased at about the CPI, just a few percent per year at most. But from 1995 to September 2003 the number of U.S. dollars increased at about 8% per year, far faster than the combined rates of increase of goods and services and of the CPI. This extra currency flowed into buying assets, thereby, pushing up asset prices. In a bubble, the principle supply-or-demand factor is the oversupply of currency. Similar increases in the amount of currency occurred in most of the world's fiat currencies, and a worldwide bubble in asset prices developed. As of early 2004, the prices of real estate, stocks, and bonds are all well above historical norms.
Starting in September 2003 the rate of increase in the number of US dollars has slowed to about 4% per year. A bubble requires rising asset

> prices to be maintained, because once a belief develops that asset prices are not rising then many people sell assets to repay the borrowed currency they used to buy those assets. Historically, bubbles usually end shortly after the flow of currency into the assets stops or reverses. The data thus suggests that the bubble may end in late 2004 or early 2006.[305]

One of the dangers of the housing bubble is the unprecedented level of "interest only" loans that have been made within the last 4 years. The frenzy to lend out money and the amount that has been lent out without regard to people's ability to pay the loan back has opened much money [1 trillion-dollars] in the economy and many borrowers to extreme risk of default and foreclosure.

> Popular interest-only and adjustable-rate mortgages that have made big houses affordable at low rates to new buyers have a sinister dark side: the repayment. According to a study by Deutsche Bank, some $300 billion in mortgage debt will enter its "adjustable" period next year. Borrowers will have to begin repaying interest AND principal at going market interest rates. By 2007, 12% of U.S. mortgage debt, or $1 trillion, will enter its adjustable period. The chief economist at Freddie Mac, Amy Crews Cutts, even said, "I'm not sure that people are being counseled on really how big of a risk they are taking." I'm sure. They're not being counseled at all. They're buying, and mortgage lenders are eager to lend.[306]

What is even more remarkable is that the risk does not end there. In the last 2 years it has been revealed that the two main lending institutions - government-sponsored enterprises (GSEs) — companies: Freddy Mac & Fannie Mae, have engaged in fraudulent lending practices. Both Fannie Mae and Freddie Mac have admitted to scheming to manipulate their accounting books. The Office of Federal Housing Enterprise Oversight (OFHEO) has also issued an interim report which found irregularities in the GSEs. The Securities and Exchange Commission is already involved with the investigation.

Since these institutions back the real estate market the fraud was compounded as a ripple effect throughout the real estate market as well as the general financial market as a whole. Through a complicated scheme the institutions sold bonds and created a new instrument called "mortgage-backed security." Financial companies such as pension funds, life insurance companies, mutual funds, banks, etc.) have been taking real cash paid to them by shareholders, investors and future retirees and they have been buying either bonds or mortgage-backed securities issued by GSEs. What this has done is to leave the U.S.A. economy dependent upon the financial returns for all the holders of the mortgage-backed securities and bondholders (and therefore by extension, also savers, all the investors and shareholders represented by them); dependent that is, on the ability of millions of homeowners to make their monthly mortgage payments. So now over ***$5 trillion*** in corporate assets are dependent on the ability of U.S.A. homeowners (many of which are now or soon will be overextended ~~when~~ – rather, AS interest rates do go up) to make the monthly mortgage payment. If payments default the GSEs are responsible for paying the bond owners (government pension funds, Corporate America, money market mutual funds, etc.) and that would lead to the collapse of the foundation of all real estate financing. A tangled web; the problem is compounded do to the complex scheme that was set up:

> Even more worrisome, over $7 trillion in household financial assets are invested in private and government pension funds — funds that may or may not own GSE bonds and mortgage-backed securities. In other words, 24% of American household financial assets are tied in with pension funds that are to some degree tied in with the GSEs. To what degree? That is the question. The critical number is 52%. When you combine public and private pension funds with corporate equities and mutual fund shares, you find that 52% of household financial assets are tied up with businesses whose assets are (a) variable and (b) exposed to the risks of the GSEs.[307]

Gretchen Morgenson[308] of The New York Times[309] wrote about why Fannie's accounting fraud problems could be systemic of the entire mortgage lending industry.

> "Fannie Mae 's problems have implications for the entire mortgage market.. .Most of the mortgages under-written in the nation today use automated programs designed by Fannie Mae. 'If allegations that they engineered systems for growth without regard to safety and soundness are correct, other systems, including underwriting, appraisal, and loss

> mitigation systems, should be called into question as well, ' Mr. [Josh] Rosner said."

In a separate article Ms. Morgenson wrote:

> Fannie Mae, the housing-finance giant, for years has fended off critics who contend that the company is too big, too powerful and too risky. But the Securities and Exchange Commission's Wednesday ruling, that Fannie Mae had seriously breached accounting rules, could touch off a chain reaction...[310]

Many people compare the current situation with a similar one that occurred in the 1970s. Then, investors also put money into real estate, however, today the financial conditions are different because:

- in the 1970s the average cost of a house in California was $100,000 and the family income could afford that. As of 2003 the average was $400,000 and the average income could only afford $200,000.
- in the 1970s the average home equity was 70% and homeowners owed banks only 30%. As of 2003 homeowners owe almost half.
- In 1980 a family of four had only $20,000 of debt and As of 2004 the debt is not $100,000

In mid 2003 he said the economic conditions described above and those that follow, related to the U.S. Dollar, prompted one of the most successful worldwide money managers of the past 50 years, John Templeton, to say the following when he was asked about future investment in real estate in the U.S.A.

> *"After home prices go down to one-tenth of the highest price homeowners paid, then buy."*

This would mean a severe decline that would affect the housing industry and all the related industries that produce household materials and products. Even if the U.S. Dollar did not plummet on its own the real estate crash would have a rippling effect on the economy that would lead to the same outcome. Vise versa, a decline in the dollar would affect the real estate market. Either situation would have dire consequences for world financial markets. Thus, the possible economic crises facing the world and the United States are at least three in number: devaluation of the U.S. Dollar [financial "bubble"], the bursting of the real estate "bubble" or the rise in oil consumption which would cause the price of oil to rise and that would have disastrous effects on the economy in itself. The world oil supply is expected to outstrip the demand in the year 2006 so the price of oil will not be going down again.

Unfairness of the U.S. Dollar as the Worldwide Currency Reserve

> "if you postulate a system that depends on one country always following the right policies, you will find that sooner or later no such country exists. The system is eventually going to break down".
>
> — Sam Cross, US Treasury official

This system [the dollar standard] can be criticized because foreign exchange reserves are created as a consequence of balance of payment deficits of the United States without any relationship to world reserve needs. Implicit in this is an unfair advantage to the reserve country, the United States, because it can finance its deficits by paying in its own currency. This makes it too easy to run deficits, and it creates an inflationary element in the monetary system, compared to the classical gold standard...By paying in its own currency, the United States could continue to finance enormous deficits without being forced to introduce adequate deficit reducing measures.

> —Dr. H.J. Witteveen, former director of the International Monetary Fund [I.M.F.], was explaining the dollar reserve phenomenon.

The patent unfairness of the U.S.A.'s imposition of the U.S. dollar on the world as the reserve currency stems from the fact that the U.S. dollar is a fiat currency first of all and second that it is a worthless currency due to the Federal and Trade deficits. As the U.S. prints more money the dollar becomes more worthless while people send goods to the U.S. the U.S. sends them worthless paper money. It is worthless because it is not backed by anything, such as gold or some other tangible asset. So a technically bankrupt country, the U.S.A. has managed to get the world to believe it is the richest country in the world [which it might have been prior to the 1970s] and it sustains the illusion through military force. So in this manner the country as a whole is swindling the economy of the world. Even though foreign countries and investors may seem to own real estate and other assets they, like U.S. citizens, cannot take comfort in those holdings. In a financial crisis those assets would deflate in value and in any case, the U.S. government would seize any assets they could find, including real estate, gold, etc. [as the government did in the past] in order to compensate for any problem; That is exactly what was done by president Roosevelt in the 1930s during the Great Depression. The economic situation of thee devalued dollar is so advanced that the deficits cannot be paid through ordinary income and the U.S. economy can no longer grow to sustain it because manufacturing jobs are dwindling since U.S. corporations want to make more money by moving their manufacturing plants to countries with low wages and many have moved their headquarters overseas so as to evade paying taxes. If the U.S. government were to ask its people to buy less foreign goods, in order to reverse the trade deficit, the myth of the "American way of life", "American standard of living" would become an empty promise; citizens would lose confidence in the economy, become discontented and some would even rebel. The companies that benefit from imports would be upset and that would upset the congress people that they will not give contributions to. The "American standard of living" is actually one of over-consumption and being able to acquire more material goods than are needed and having modern conveniences and being able to eat more meat[22] and hoard more property that is not needed [houses have increased in size over the last 50 years and most of the area is used for storing material objects that are not used]. Many people who came to the U.S.A. (immigrants), lured by the prospect of "making" money and to "lead better lives" or "build better futures" for themselves and their families, who brought skills and expertise needed to support the economy, would go back to their countries of origin and the U.S. population would decline as Europe's is right now. Why do fiat currencies fail?

---

[22] the material wealth of the 20th century allowed people to eat more meat and turn to a meat based diet instead of the plant based diet of the 19th century and prior and that led to the highest increase of cancer and heart disease in human history that have killed more people than *all* of the wars of the 20th century, *all* natural disasters and *all* automobile accidents COMBINED. from *The Rave Diet*

> Fiat currency is created at the whim of politicians and bureaucrats. History's lesson on this point is clear: those in charge of a fiat currency always, eventually, due to some urgent government priority, create too much of the currency and it becomes worth less, and ultimately worthless.
> As a government creates more of its fiat currency then there is an increasing amount of currency to pay for the same amount of goods and services, so the prices of the goods and services rises. The increase in the quantity of currency is called 'inflation', and the consequent rise in prices is measured to some degree by the CPI (consumer price index). The 'value' of a currency (how many goods and services a unit of the currency can buy) depends, in the long run, on how much the country's government inflates its currency.
> Gold, on the other hand, treats everyone equally. Unlike fiat currency, no one can conjure gold up out of thin air to spend for themselves and get others to do their bidding. Gold has to be mined, ounce by hard-won ounce. Because the supply of gold can only ever increase slowly, prices in terms of gold tend to stay roughly constant for centuries—changing mainly due to technological influences that make some goods relatively easier or harder to make.[311]

If the U.S. were to try a fraudulent financial strategy to get out of the predicament of repaying the deficit moneys owed like inflating money so that it is so worthless it is easier to pay off the deficits or institute two currencies, one domestic and one foreign, as some have suggested, that would surpass what is already the greatest swindling of the world economy in human history [reserve currency status] and could precipitate trade embargos from other countries if not direct conflict or even outright war against the U.S. Of course the war need not be with armies but through effective strategies of economic retaliation such as boycotts, embargos or guerilla tactics such as have been employed by so called terrorists: insurgency, guerilla tactics, sabotage, kidnappings, etc. U.S. citizens would not be able to travel abroad without fear of retaliation, etc.; the U.S. would be through as a world power and would become isolated for one or more generations. That is of course if they survive the period without internal implosion and social disarray or escalate conflicts with other countries to the extent of using weapons of mass destruction. The U.S. would be unable to import the material goods it desires and no longer produces domestically and would be forced to go back to a 19th century self-sufficiency based economy. Essentially, the U.S. would revert to a status now assigned to so-called "Third World"[312] countries, as it was when it was beginning to industrialize.

The Failure of the Industrialized Economy combined with Capitalist Ideology

> By encouraging industrial specialization, industrializing countries grew rapidly in population, and therefore needed sources of agricultural goods. The need for cheap agricultural imports, in turn, further pressured states to reduce tariffs and other trade barriers, so as to be able to exchange with the industrial nations for capital goods, such as factory machinery, which were needed to industrialize in turn. Eventually this pressured taxation systems, and pushed nations towards income and sales taxes, and away from tariffs. It also produced a constant downward pressure on wages, which contributed to the "agony of industrialization".[313]

Many people believe in the solvency of the U.S.A. government. Yet at the end of his term the famous chairman of the U.S. Federal Reserve, Alan Greenspan (retired on January 31, 2006, after 18 years as Chairman.) admitted that the economy will not sustain the post World War II generation as they get older. He made the warning that the Congress and White House need to come up with a plan quickly to trim Medicare and Social Security benefits that the 77 million baby boomers are planning to receive as they reach retirement age. Greenspan said,

> "The benefits currently promised cannot be financed by our government and Americans born in the 20 years after World War II[314] needed to be put on notice to start putting away extra retirement savings during their working years. Even under the most optimistic economic assumptions of growth and productivity, government resources will be inadequate to provide the baby boom generation with the level of benefits their parents got".[23]

The issue of the baby boomers getting older also has implications for the gross domestic product. The GDP will degrease because there will be less productive workers and there will be older people [aging population] burdening the economy. Under those conditions

---

[23] government estimates put the shortfalls at 11 trillion however, private studies have put the Medicare and Social Security deficit at over 45 trillion

the 6-7% of GDP that is financed by foreign investment will be definitely unsustainable. Greenspan also said:

> "If we have promised more than our economy has the ability to deliver, ... as I fear we may have, we must recalibrate our public programs so pending retirees have time to adjust through other channels. If we delay, the adjustments could be abrupt and painful."

For these reasons, economists such as the Rodrigo de Rato, the head of the I.M.F., felt the need to say that the U.S.A. rate of savings and deficit spending will be unsustainable within the next 10 years, but he added that a decade can come faster than one expects.[315]

Fiat Currencies as the source of economic failure and Gold as a means to compensate for the downturn in the economy.

> ***Although The Value Of All Currencies Goes Down In Time, Gold Naturally Increases***
> Gold prices remain stable over long-periods of time, while currencies normally lose 90-100 percent of their value every hundred years to inflation. A Dollar today will buy less than ten percent of what it would in 1906, while one ounce of gold would buy the same amount of goods today as it did back then.
> **Gold and silver are the only currencies not created and controlled by governments. All of today's other currencies (dollars, euros, yen, pounds, renminbis, rupees, etc) are 'fiat' currencies, which means they do not represent anything tangible but are only worth something due to government decree (namely legal tender laws).**
> All today's government currencies are 'fiat' currencies. A fiat currency is defined and created by a government. It is given meaning only by legal tender laws, national laws that say that the fiat currency has to be accepted as payment in that country, and thus force people to use the fiat currency.
> The term 'fiat currency' came about because the legal tender laws that give it value are a 'fiat' (or authoritative pronouncement) of government. A fiat currency is a currency brought into existence by government decree (that is, by fiat).
> The value of gold, on the other hand, is independent of any government laws. Unlike fiat currencies, gold is accepted as valuable without needing protection by laws.[316]

Many critics of the U.S. and western form of "faux" economics [fiat currencies], that have been in existence after the rejection of the gold standard; hold that that rejection led to the coming financial debacle. If fiat currency [paper currency by government decree] were to be based on some standard base value that is held by a government such as the gold, or silver standard, etc, then governments could not print more money than the value of the gold they have in reserve; Credit would be limited and development would be slower but inflation and deflation would be manageable. However, it would not be possible to have deficit spending, which allows a country like the U.S. to create vast armies, fabulously rich people and corporations and extend imperialist designs to control the rest of the world through colonial or neo-colonial strategies.

> The gold standard is a monetary system in which the standard economic unit of account is a fixed weight of gold and currency issuers guarantee, under specified rules, to redeem notes in that amount of gold. Nations that employ such a fixed unit of account, and which will redeem their notes to other nations in gold, in principle, share a fixed currency relationship. The intent is to create a system that is resistant to runaway credit and debt expansion, and to enforce a system where money cannot be created through government fiat currency, and will, therefore be safe as an alternative store of value against inflation.[317]

The gold standard is not a perfect system though it is better than the credit based economy founded on fiat money [false or baseless money] used at present which eventually has to fail [as all other fiat currencies have failed in human history!]. Gold is seen as desirable as a backing for currency because it cannot be printed by a government and it exists in limited predictable supplies. The U.S. government went off the gold standard when it had to use deficit spending to get out of the depression and go to war. Previous to the use of the gold standard the U.S. had other systems but the economy fluctuated wildly so a move was made, around the turn of the century, following the rest of the world, to a gold standard and later, as stated earlier the Federal Reserve was created to provide liquidity [more money] or contraction in the monetary supply when conditions required it, to control the economy. The U.S. was the last of the developing nations to accept the gold standard (in 1900) but it did so on a *de jure* status, meaning at their discretion.[318]

An avid student of politics and economics should realize that the two party system as used in the U.S.A. is merely a reflection of two approaches to the conduct of government and economics that differ only in degree and not in substance. Those progressives who want more government regulation to control the economy and social programs are actually promoting the same thing as the conservatives who want more control and stabilization of the economy and less of the social programs but both are controlled by the rich so both want policies that increase their wealth and will not and have never wanted to put in policies that will increase the value of money for the ordinary person. Both want to perpetuate the capitalist system but they differ in how to run it, with more or less controls. In this sense the words of Thomas Jefferson and James Madison and their followers were not heeded. To the contrary, their opponents won the debate; the plan of Alexander Hamilton won. He was a banker and lawyer and the most influential Secretary of the Treasury, who was instrumental in establishing the First Bank of the United States, public credit and the foundations for American capitalism and stock and commodity exchanges.[319] He advocated that the federal government should take over the debt of the states and pay for the war of independence. In that way those who supplied the weapons and supplies to the American rebels would be paid. To produce revenue, Hamilton advocated that there should be a tariff placed on imported manufactures as well as a series of excise taxes. He hoped by these measures to strengthen the national government at the expense of the states and to tie government to men of wealth and prosperity.[320] He also laid the foundation for unprecedented U.S.A. economic and military power. However, Hamilton strongly advocated the abolition of slavery, which George Washington and Thomas Jefferson did not.

In the year 1971 the U.S. government went off the gold standard and embarked on a program of managed currency. Governments of the past, that have created too much fiat currency [money out of thin air], had failed economies within 100 years or less from the time of the fake money introduction. All fiat currencies in the past have ended up being worth very little, collapsing into hyperinflation or threatening to. All of today's fiat currencies have been fiat currencies since 1971 and all government currencies were convertible to gold until 1971. In the 20th century decades prior to 1971 there were no completely fiat currencies, because each currency unit was ultimately defined as a certain weight of gold. For example, in 1971 the United States of America abandoned its commitment to pay $35 U.S. dollars for an ounce of gold. To clarify, this means that in 1971 a U.S. dollar was worth 1/35 of one ounce of gold. As of February 2006 it is worth less than a tenth of that, about 1/550 of an ounce of gold (because gold is about US $550 per ounce –as of 2/2006). So therefore historical evidence demonstrates that the issue is not *if* the U.S. dollar will continue to lose value but only *how quickly* it loses value.

Prior to the use of money as a means of currency in commerce, societies used barter. Barter is a type of trade where goods or services are exchanged for a certain amount of other goods or services, i.e. there is no money involved in the transaction. It can be bilateral or multilateral as trade. Barter trade was common in societies where no monetary system existed or in economies suffering from a very unstable currency (as when hyperinflation hits) or a lack of currency. The disadvantage of using bilateral barter in the past was that it depended on the mutual coincidence of wants. Also, barter becomes more and more difficult when more people become dispossessed of the means of production needed to produce products, including their subsistence needs. For example, if money were totally abolished in the United States, most people would have nothing of value to trade for food (since the farmer can only use so many cars, etc.) Trade and barter were primarily reserved for trade between communities or countries.[321]

Early civilizations did not have so many complexities in their economies. In order to organize production and the distribution of goods and services among the population, many pre-market or pre-capitalist economies counted on tradition, community democracy or top-down command instead of market exchanges. Nations such as Ancient Egypt used these methods. Barbarian nations such as Ancient Greece and Rome attained supremacy by plundering other nations by war and conquest. In modern times market imperialist nations such as Great Britain and the United States attained supremacy by using both the army and financial manipulations of the markets, social and political destabilization of other countries, colonialism, neo-colonialism and globalization. With the market exchange organized system of commerce there inevitably develops a desire by those trading in such a market to manipulate and control it to their advantage and those efforts usually end in failure such as the debacle of the dollar. One example of controlling and devastating the economies of developing countries are the imposed "Structural Adjustment" and privatization (of the country's resources) programs. Those regulations forced those nations to produce crops for export that the country could not use to feed itself, which created food shortages and many other problems in their economies. Another example is the potato famine of Ireland. The famine was not caused by shortage of food but because the price of food, relative to wages, soared; so the food was more profitable as an export as opposed to a means to feed the people-so they were *allowed to die* by the greed of the market and the inherent imperfection of the currency based market exchange organized system. In earlier times reciprocity relations and/or redistribution substituted for market exchange.

Due to the complexity and interrelated economics of the world today it would be difficult to return to a more stable bartering system but some bartering could be reincorporated into the economy. Returning to a "real" gold standard is a more pragmatic solution to the problem. However, its opponents reject that solution because it would slow the economy and restrict governments in their monetary policies. In other words it would tie the hands of government from unlawful actions such as deficits, wars, cronyism, manipulations of the economy to favor the rich, etc.

The case against returning to a gold standard

> Many nations back their currencies in part with gold reserves, using these not to redeem notes, but as a store of value to sell in case their currency is attacked or rapidly devalues. Gold advocates claim that this extra step would no longer be necessary since the currency itself would have its own intrinsic store of value. A Gold Standard then is generally promoted by those who regard a stable store of value as the most important element to business confidence. It is generally opposed by the vast majority of governments and economists, because the gold

standard has frequently been shown to provide insufficient flexibility in the supply of money and in fiscal policy, because the supply of newly mined gold is finite and must be carefully husbanded and accounted for. A single country may also not be able to isolate its economy from depression or inflation in the rest of the world. In addition, the process of adjustment for a country with a payments deficit can be long and painful whenever an increase in unemployment or decline in the rate of economic expansion occurs. One of the foremost opponents of the gold standard was John Maynard Keynes who scorned basing the money supply on "dead metal". Keynesians argue that the gold standard creates deflation which intensifies recessions as people are unwilling to spend money as prices fall, thus creating a downward spiral of economic activity. They also argue that the gold standard also removes the ability of governments to fight recessions by increasing the money supply to boost economic growth.[322]

The Case For Returning to the Gold Standard

Governments and central banks have been suppressing the price of gold since 1995 by lending and selling their gold. They won't be able to keep it up forever. Then the price of gold and silver will soar to its correct level, that it would have been at had there not been any artificial manipulation.[323]

Gold standard proponents point to the era of industrialization and globalization of the 19th century as the proof of the viability and supremacy of the gold standard, and point to the UK's rise to being an imperial power, ruling nearly one quarter of the world's population and forming a trading empire which would eventually become the Commonwealth of Nations as imperial provinces gained independence. Gold standard advocates have a strong following among commodity traders and hedge funds with a bearish orientation. The expectation of a global fiscal meltdown, and the return to a hard gold standard has been central to many hedge financial theories. More moderate goldbugs point to gold as a hedge against commodity inflation, and a representation of resource extraction, in their view gold is a play against monetary policy follies of central banks, and a means of hedging against currency fluctuations, since gold can be sold in any currency, on a highly liquid world market, in nearly any country in the world. For this reason they believe that eventually there will be a return to a gold standard, since this is the only "stable" unit of value. That monetary gold would soar to $5,000 an ounce, about 10 times its current value, may well have something to do with some of the advocacy of a renewed gold standard, holders of gold would stand to make an enormous profit.[324]

Update: the Treasury Secretary of the U.S.A., John Snow, made an important statement. Essentially, he said that the U.S.A. debt ceiling, authorized by congress, will soon be reached and that they need to authorize a higher ceiling and more printed money in order to pay for the government's obligations. He actually said that in accordance with the "law" he has tapped into the *Civil Service Retirement, Pension and Disability Funds* as a means to find more money and apparently he has done all within his power to cope with the deficit. This confirms an unprecedented and unmanageable deficit spending program of the congress and the president that deepens the financial crisis every day.

> **Treasury Secretary John Snow notified Congress on Monday that the administration has now taken "all prudent and legal actions," including tapping certain government retirement funds. This is being done to keep from hitting the $8.2 trillion dollar national debt limit. In a letter to Congress, Snow urged lawmakers to pass a new debt ceiling immediately to avoid the first-ever U.S. default on its obligations. Snow notified lawmakers that the Treasury would begin tapping the Civil Service Retirement and Disability Fund, which Treasury officials said would provide a "few billion" dollars in extra borrowing ability. Treasury has also been taking investments out of a $65.3 billion government pension fund known as the G-fund which is part of the Federal Employees Retirement System.[325]

Welcome to Spend City WashingtonPost.Com By Dana Milbank
Friday, March 17, 2006; A02

> It was the political equivalent of going on a shopping spree the same day you get a credit-line increase on your over-the-limit card. In the morning, the senators increased the federal debt limit by $800 billion, to $9 trillion -- that's with a T. In the afternoon came the Vote-a-Rama, a carnival in which the lawmakers took turns pitching scores of amendments to the 2007 budget measure, most calling for more money for favorite programs.[326]

FREE MARKET GOLD & MONEY REPORT by James Turk

> The $8.2 trillion debt limit -- that has proven inadequate to meet the federal government's borrowing needs -- covers only its direct liabilities. In other words, this $8.2 trillion is the total amount of dollars owed to all the holders of US government debt instruments. Excluded from this total debt are all of the federal government's other liabilities, which total another $38 trillion. In "The 2005 Financial

> Report of the United States Government", US Comptroller General David Walker reported that "the federal government's fiscal exposures now total more than $46 trillion, up from $20 trillion in 2000."[327]

When the well known conservative and former top GOP [republican] strategist Kevin Phillips, the author of *"American Theocracy: The Peril and Politics of Radical Religion, Oil, and Borrowed Money in the 21st Century* was asked if he thought the "American empire" was headed for doom he responded:

> **KEVIN PHILLIPS:** It's certainly headed for some degree of dismantling and loss of international power. Now, to say it's headed for doom -- even when Britain lost its place in the world, it wasn't headed for doom, and it reconstituted itself, and a lot of people are happy and fairly prosperous in the U.K. right now. But we can't go on in the imperial mode, in which we just demand the world's natural resources and that the dollar be the vehicle for everything and that we be able to invade wherever we want. I don't think that will last more than another ten years. I think the crisis builds up sufficiently in the 2010s, that the United States is really going to have to consider what resources it has in terms of energy, what resources it has in terms of the economy, how far it can push its military, a whole set of issues.[328]

The proponents of "free trade" economics could not foresee the pitfalls of economically advanced countries competing with a developing country and the development of trade deficits and their danger to the economy of the more developed country. One prominent economist recently reversed himself after 50 years of teaching economics and spreading his philosophy around the country through his students who have risen to important posts in, finance, government policy-making and business. For more than fifty years professor Paul Samuelson's book *Economics: An Introductory Analysis* was a bestselling textbook used in college economics classes. At the age of 89, the professor announced a very important correction to his philosophy. He explained that free trade might not be a benefit to all parties, after all. That is because:

> In certain circumstances, when a very poor but ambitious nation is trading with a wealthy advanced economy, free trade can turn into a very ugly loser for the wealthy country--inflicting permanent economic loss, stagnant wages, greater inequality and other hurtful consequences. The professor's reasoning is expressed in the abstract language of orthodox economics, but he does name the two countries he has in

> mind--the United States and China. His paper, published in the Summer issue of the *Journal of Economic Perspectives*, bears the lighthearted title, "Where Ricardo and Mill Rebut and Confirm Arguments of Mainstream Economists Supporting Globalization."[329]

The stunning reversal described above demonstrates how modern economics of the western countries in general and the U.S.A. in particular, are based on theory and initial circumstances that favor the more advanced nations in a colonial type environment. But when the economies start to even out, there ensues a desire in the more advanced nation to become "conservative", that is, keep things as they were or reverse the conditions so as to return to and maintain the previous status quo. Attempting to do this is where the strife and belligerence between nations, which lead to wars, have come. The wars are fomented by the desire in the ruling class and middle class of the country with the higher "standard of living" to retain the standard [greed] and power is a means to achieve the end of maintaining economic prominence. It is a choice between sharing and developing equitable sustainable economic policies within a country and with trading partners versus the desire to amass wealth and power to experience inordinate and extravagant pleasures and standards of living.

Another sign of the failing global economy and the power of the "Davos ruling class" is that in Latin America the countries Brazil, Argentina, Venezuela, Uruguay and Bolivia have ousted oligarchs who prospered by means of selling their countries' people and assets to transnational investors.

The Ancient Egyptian Economy: A Model of Ethics in Commerce and Government

The U.S.A. government took the Ancient Egyptian symbols of the Pyramid and the open eye to represent a supposed new world order based on the past order. However, the similarity between the Ancient Egyptian culture and the U.S.A. or Western culture ends there, in a misuse of a religious symbol that has led to misunderstanding of the ancient tradition and misinformation about the present one. A brief overview of Ancient Egyptian economics offers some insights into a workable form of economy that can demonstrate the vast differences between the economic systems and may also present solutions for current problems. Ancient Egyptian religion used the symbol of the spiritual eye[330] to represent the awakening of consciousness. There was a recognition that in order for that awakening to occur there needs to be virtue in a human being.

According to Ancient Egyptian ethics, that necessarily means non-stealing and proper distribution of wealth. In order to have sustained prosperity, peace and security in a country that country must be based on ethical principles. The Ancient Egyptians called that ethical principle "Maat." The Ancient Egyptian government is often referred to as a Theocracy but a more accurate term would be "Ethiocracy" [Ethical-Theocracy]. Theocracy is a form of government based on religious law but in Ancient Egypt the government as all other areas of society, was under the overall rubric of Maat Philosophy, the Ancient Egyptian theological and philosophical framework of spiritual, social, political and economic ethics. This form of government can be corrupted if the values followed are not based on virtue and morality. The Christian Catholic Church suffered this problem of amoral government at various periods throughout its history, which led to dissent and the formation of the protestant movement. Moral theocracy is a kind of shepherding form of government. Morality here means that which is good, i.e. integrity, righteousness, justice, balance, peace, honor and honesty. Morality in the ancient sense cannot be equated with moral relativism or the novel concept of "new morality" or "alternative moral philosophy," which implies sexual freedom, or sexual revolution or situational morality. Maat implies universal moral principles that apply to all, but are not to be forced or imposed on others. In Ancient Egypt the laws had to be based on the philosophy of Maat. Maat is the concept of order, truth and balance in action, similar to Confucianism and Taoism of China and Dharma of Buddhism. The following are injunctions of Maatian order contained in the teachings of the Ancient Egyptian Sage Amenemope.

On Business and Commerce
Sage Amenemope
(48) Do not assess a man who has nothing,
And thus falsify your pen.
If you find a large debt against a poor man, Make it into three parts;
Forgive two, let one stand,
(49) You will find it a path of life.
(66) Haste not to be rich, but be not slothful in thine own interest.
(83) One does not run to reach success,
One does not move to spoil it.
(108) Don't make yourself a ferry on the river, And then strain to seek its fare;

(109) Take the fare from him who is wealthy,
And let pass him who is poor.

The 42 Precepts of Maat are condensed injunctions that form the foundation of Maat Philosophy. They are written in the form of negative statements ["I have not...] reflecting the successful accomplishment of virtuous actions and refraining from actions based on vice. However, in the Ancient Egyptian wisdom texts the Ancient Egyptian sages expounded further on the practical interpretation and application of the precepts in day-to-day life.

> *Do not move the scales, do not change the weights and do not diminish the parts of the bushel... Do not create a bushel that contains two, lest you will near the abyss. The bushel is the eye of Ra. He loathes him who defrauds.*
>
> The teachings of Amenemope

The Ancient Egyptian culture and civilization was the longest-lived and has the record as the longest perpetual civilization [10,000 years][331] in human history. One of the reasons for their success is that the culture was founded and governed by an ethical philosophy that discouraged and prevented government excesses and economic frauds, unlike a market economy or fiat currencies that promote fraud. The country was protected by a legal system that was based on that ethical philosophy that was called "Maat." Maat is a philosophy, a goddess and a universal principle of cosmic order that all human beings need to observe in order to avoid strife and suffering and maintain personal balance, balance with the society and balance with the universe and God. Therefore, any violation of Maat was a serious and egregious act that was dealt with forthwith so as to maintain the order of the society.[332]

The Ancient Egyptians before the "Late Period" did not use coin money like modern society does today. When shopping in an Ancient Egyptian market people would need to bargain on a price. There were few fixed prices and Ancient Egyptians were experienced at calculating the cost of an item. Cost was measured in a unit called *deben*[333] which was a copper weight of .5 ounces. The passage below shows that oil and grain could serve as a kind of currency.

The Middle Kingdom priest Heqanakhte preferred to be paid in grain:

> *Concerning him who will give me payment in oil - he shall give me 1 big jar of oil for 2 sacks of Lower Egyptian barley or for 3 sacks of emmer. Behold, I prefer to be given my property as Lower Egyptian barley.*
>
> 3rd letter of Heqanakhte
> After a German translation on the *Thesaurus Linguae Aegyptiae* website

Gold was not used as a standard per se in Ancient Egypt the way it is conceived in modern times. Gold was seen as a reflection of timeless and immortal qualities of divinity, the sun, so possessing it represented closeness to the spiritual essence of the Divine. The value ratios for the most common commodities would have been known generally. But the wide ranging value combinations brought into existence an abstract value system. Certain amounts were based on a *deben*, *seniu*[334] or, beginning with the New Kingdom, a *kit* of gold, silver and copper were used as units. Generally, no metal appears to have changed hands during the commercial exchanges until the Late Period of Ancient Egyptian history.

The use of metal rings as a standard of a given weight goes back to the Old Kingdom era of Ancient Egyptian history. Among the artifacts found in Queen Hetep-heres I's tomb was a jewel box that had the inscription:

> *Mother of the King of Upper and Lower Egypt, Hetep-heres. Box containing deben rings.*
>
> Reiser, George A. *The Household Furniture of Queen Hetep-heres I*,
> BMFA 27, No. 164, December 1929, pp. 83-90

The introduction of money as we know it today

In the fifth century B.C.E. [early Late Period], foreign coins were being introduced to Kamit [Ancient Egypt]. In the beginning those imported silver and gold pieces were used by the Ancient Egyptians as precious metal of standardized weight rather than true currency money. From the mid 4th century B.C.E. and onwards, as the Greek mercenaries in Egypt began demanding payment *in specie*, and as Mediterranean traders relied more and more on coined metal as means of exchange the Ancient Egyptian mint produced coins[335] [see above] that were similar to Athenian tetradrachms. Under the rule of the Ptolemies coins were later struck that bared the effigies of the Hellenist [Greek] rulers.

IOU's were often written on pot shards [ostraca] or other pieces of matter that were flat enough to be written on.

> *Owed by Apahte, son of Patai: 30 pieces of silver.*
> *Written in the year 28(?), on the 30th of Mesore.*
>
> Demotic ostrakon, Ptolemaic Period,
> Victoria-Museum, Uppsala, inv. no. 982
> My translation from the German[336]

Aside from personal credits the people were able to deposit grain in state warehouses and later write withdrawal orders that served as payment.[337] These grain banks worked by instead of paying interest on the deposit, instead deducted 10% (*demurrage* -Compensation paid for such detention.). Some researchers theorize that due to the demurrage the Ancient Egyptians did not need to hoard their wealth but proceeded to keep on spending it, most often on the maintenance and improvement of the older temples and for the building of new temples. However, since the basic needs of life were provided for through collective work and distribution of goods needed for survival there was no need for saving money for the purpose of developing riches or for inordinate security needs.

During the Hellenistic (Greek) period this banking system became a countrywide and not just a local phenomenon. Accounts were maintained at a central bank in the capital city of Alexandria and the granaries formed a financial system like the British giro[338] network.

Wealth accrues to him who guards it;
Let your hand not scatter it to strangers,
Lest it turn to loss for you.
If wealth is placed where it bears interest,
It comes back lo you redoubled;
Make a storehouse for your own wealth,
Your people will find it on your way.
What is given small returns augmented,
[What is replaced brings abundance.]

The Instruction of Any
M. Lichtheim *Ancient Egyptian Literature* Vol. 2, p.138f

Increasingly, now in the Greek conquest period, the banks began to deal more and more with coin money instead of perishable grain. The example below is of orders for payment crediting and debiting accounts at the royal bank of Greek controlled Ancient Egypt:

[[And there is a notice of payment, as payment for the honourable . . .]] The form of the customary notice of payment is as follows. To be credited to the account of the sacred offices(?). Due to the king from Asklepiades son of Euphris(?), of the Zephyrian deme, as payment for the honourable office of prophet which he purchased in the temple in Menelais of the Menelaite nome, 500 drachmai(?).

P.Mich.:1:9, 257 BCE
APIS record: michigan.apis.1864

The ancient peoples did not have ID cards and social security numbers. However, the Ancient banks were concerned with positive identification of people doing business at the royal bank (which actually served as a central bank). Remember that there were dire consequences for anyone defrauding the bank or committing any crime in ancient Egypt. The bank recorded a person's ancestry, physical characteristics, age, profession and other pertinent information:

> *... through the bank of Sarapion of the Stoa of Athena. Isidoros son of Marion, to Hermas son of Heron, grandson of Hermas, from the second Goose Pen ward, aged forty years with a scar in the middle of his forehead, (acknowledges) that he (Hermas) has received from Isidoros an interest-bearing loan of a principal of one hundred twenty silver drachmas, which he will pay back in the month of Pauni of the current year forthwith.* (second hand) *I, Hermas, have borrowed the one hundred twenty drachmas, which I will pay back in the month of Pauni of the same ninth year, as set forth above.*
>
> ***P.Col.:10:259, 146 CE***
> ***APIS record: columbia.apis.p292***

In the Greek and Roman controlled era of Ancient Egypt the money lenders were concerned about obtaining collateral when lending. The wisdom writings of sage Ankhsheshonq (about 2nd-1st century B.C.E.) gave words of advice to all prospective lenders:

> *"Do not lend money at interest without obtaining a security."* and *"Do not be too trusting lest you become poor."*

Ankhsheshonq also had prudent advice about how borrowed money should be used by a borrower so as to make the most of the money through investment in worthwhile ventures, building its value and progressing in life, instead of squandering it in short term enjoyments:

> *Borrow money at interest and put it in farmland.*
> *Borrow money at interest and take a wife.*
> *Borrow money at interest and celebrate your birthday.*
> *Do not borrow money at interest in order to live well on it.*
>
> M. Lichtheim,
> *Ancient Egyptian Literature*, Vol.3, p.172

A person pledging their property could receive credit. Pawnbrokers did exist in Egypt at least from the time of the Roman conquest period. Some frequent items pawned were jewelry, furniture, utensils and metal implements:

The bronze vessels of Claudius (?) Severus were redeemed when the report of his [property ?] was made ..... and payment was made for the interest on the bond from Epeiph of the 4th year to Tybi [of the 7th year], a period of 31 months, at the rate of 110 drachmas per month, a total 3,410 drachmas, and for the principal 1 talent 5,600 drachmas , and from Theon for the redemption of his Aphrodite 400 drachmas, amounting to 2 talents 3,410 drachmas for principal and interest. The remaining ..... four thousand six hundred drachmas, in total .... talents, 4,600 drachmas [are secured] by the remaining pledges, which are ..... a pair of armlets, a pair of cups, a pair of anklets, a necklace, a spearshaped ornament. Another cupboard was given in addition .....

from P.Mich.inv. 1950, 3rd century CE
APIS record: michigan.apis.1554

Degeneration of the economy

The ancient system of distribution of goods throughout Ancient Egypt operated in a way so that goods were collected by royal decree and the Vizier, governors, and tax collectors and a veritable army of bureaucrats managed the process. So farm crops in the north of Egypt were collected and redistributed so that everyone would get what they needed. Crops of a different sort in the south would in turn be redistributed to the north and so on. Therefore, this was a massive system of economy based on collective sharing of the wealth of the country without leaving some to fend for themselves or creating associations or guilds that segregate people from subsistence level goods. This system of economy may be thought of as a *Barter and Collective Sharing Economy*. One present day similar but small scale system of sharing is called **Community-supported agriculture (CSA).** Typically, CSA farms are small, independent, labor intensive, family farms.[339] In Ancient Egypt the system was country-wide and managed by the central government, the Pharaonic system. By Roman times, however, the Pharaonic state which had controlled the general economy by collecting and redistributing had been mostly dismantled by the Roman conquerors in favor of a colonial administrative system which had the main goal of exploiting Egypt in favor of Rome. Egypt became the "breadbasket" that allowed the Roman empire to grow but Egypt was depleted of its wealth. Trade fell under the control of private persons who often organized themselves in guilds. One such example is the association of the salt merchants of Tebtunis:

The undersigned men, salt merchants of Tebtynis, meeting together have decided by common consent to elect one of their number, a good man, Apynchis, son of Orseus, both supervisor and collector of the public taxes for the coming eighth year of Tiberius

P.Mich.:5:245, 47 CE
APIS record: michigan.apis.2876

After the Romans conquered Egypt a positive interest rate scheme imposed on invested capital was introduced to the economy and the wealth from the profits were taken out of the country, and so the temple sites began to decline. What occurred to Egypt at the hands of the Roman empire recalls what recent colonial powers such as the British empire, the other European colonial powers and most recently the U.S.A. have done to smaller weaker countries as well as the regions of poor people in the U.S.A. itself. The guilds may be likened to today's multinational corporations in some ways. The guilds assigned territories that had special privileges. One example is the territory paid for by one Orseus. Orseus paid 66 drachmas to have a monopoly for selling gypsum in the particular region of Tebtunis.

(they, i.e. the merchants, have decided) that all alike shall sell salt in the aforesaid village of Tebtynis, and that Orseus alone has obtained by lot the sole right to sell gypsum in the aforesaid village of Tebtynis and in the adjacent villages,

P.Mich.:5:245, 47 CE
APIS record: michigan.apis.2876

The guilds also fixed prices. They also set and imposed fines on anyone who would undercut them:

they shall sell the good salt at the rate of two and one-half obols, the light salt at two obols, and the lighter salt at one and one-half obol, by our measure or that of the warehouse. And if anyone shall sell at a lower price than these, let him be fined eight drachmai in silver for the common fund and the same for the public treasury;

P.Mich.:5:245, 47 CE
APIS record: michigan.apis.2876

This very brief overview displays the Ancient Egyptian system of economy and how the Greek and Roman conquerors changed it into an early form of capitalist [imperialist] economy that eventually failed with the downfall of the Greco-Roman cultures. It is interesting to note that the ancient Egyptian culture lasted for thousands of years [ancient Egyptian economic system: 5,000-10,000 years.] while the Greco-Roman cultures only existed for a few hundred years.

The Ecological Crisis

CLIMATE EXPERT SAYS NASA TRIED TO SILENCE HIM
January 29, 2006, Sunday
By ANDREW C. REVKIN (NYT); National Desk
Late Edition - Final, Section 1, Page 1, Column 6, 1615 words

The top climate scientist [**James E. Hansen**] at NASA says the Bush administration has tried to stop him from speaking out since he gave a lecture last month calling for prompt reductions in emissions of greenhouse gases linked to global warming.[340]

In the talk, he [**James E. Hansen**] said that significant emission cuts could be achieved with existing technologies, particularly in the case of motor vehicles, and that without leadership by the United States, climate change would eventually leave the earth "a different planet." The administration's policy is to use voluntary measures to slow, but not reverse, the growth of emissions.[341]

Hansen also said: "We need to stop now, not in a few decades while Exxon/Mobile keeps making record profits."[342]

British Prime Minister Tony Blair lent his name to an official United Kingdom government report warning that the climate impact could be even more serious than previously thought. Blair wrote the forward to the report "Avoiding Dangerous Climate Change," published Jan. 30. The book compiles evidence from a meteorological office conference last February.

"It is clear from the work presented that the risks of climate change may well be greater than we thought," Blair wrote. "It is now plain that the emission of greenhouse gases, associated with industrialization and economic growth from a world population that has increased sixfold in 200 years, is causing global warming at a rate that is unsustainable." With a voice like Blair's behind him, Hansen is no cinch to hush up.[343]

Climate change is *"more serious even than the threat of terrorism"*, according to David King, the government's chief scientific adviser. The Royal Commission on Environmental Pollution says curbing the threat requires a reduction in global greenhouse gas emissions of about 70% by the 22nd century.

– Sir David King,
UK Government Chief Scientific Advisor [2004][344]

Among the reasons climate change is a bigger problem than terrorism, David King tells me, is that the problem is rooted in humanity's burning of oil, coal, and natural gas, "and people don't want to let that go."

– ***While Washington Slept***
BY MARK HERTSGAARD- *the environmental correspondent for* The Nation.

According to King (Sir David King,), even if humanity were to stop emitting carbon dioxide today, "temperatures will keep rising and all the impacts will keep changing for about 25 years."
The upshot is that it has become too late to prevent climate change; we can only adapt to it. This unhappy fact is not well understood by the general public; advocates downplay it, perhaps for fear of fostering a paralyzing despair. But there is no getting around it: because humanity waited so long to take decisive action, we are now stuck with a certain amount of global warming and the climate changes it will bring—rising seas, fiercer heat, deeper droughts, stronger storms. The World Health Organization estimates that climate change is already helping to kill 150,000 people a year, mainly in Africa and Asia. That number is bound to rise as global warming intensifies in the years ahead.

– ***While Washington Slept***
BY MARK HERTSGAARD-

"…we are witnessing a collision between our civilization and the earth, properly understood this is a planetary emergency."

–Al Gore [2005]

Why do so many people ignore the dangers of climate change? Why do corporations seek to ignore climate change when there are technological means to deal with the problem? Why does the government seek to downplay climate change?

The reasons relate to fear, another is greed and still another is religious extremism. As discussed earlier, Dominionism is a driving religious philosophy within Christianity in the U.S.A. The farm industry and the segment of corporations in the U.S.A. that want to pollute freely and despoil the land in order to make more profits have developed an alliance with the dominionist Christians because the industries did not previously have a large constituency to support their efforts. The industry supports those Christian groups and the Christian groups in turn support the corporations and both achieve greater political power within the right wing of the republican party. Conservative right wing Christianity, is not just a religious and political force that leads to hostility towards anyone that is not part of the evangelical, Pentecostal, born again persuasion but this perspective also has devastating effects on the environment as well. Most fundamentalist and main stream Christians believe that the Bible grants the right for Christians to rule over the world and use nature as they desire; so this has translated into despoiling the environment in the pursuit of profit without caring about the consequences. Many fundamentalist Christians even see other Christians who question the despoiling of the environment through pollution and illegal dumping of industrial wastes as un-Christian and traitorous and even blasphemous or otherwise heathenish because the idea is that the destruction of the earth means "Jesus is coming soon", in accordance with supposed bible prophecy. In accordance with this philosophy those extremist politicians [secular neo-conservatives] who support the dominionist views are supported by those groups because they will hasten the end of the world and the coming of Jesus and the supposed ascendancy of true believing Christians into heaven; this perspective ignores the killing of thousands of people and the untold suffering of millions, that might be caused in the process. On one level there is a current of thought in the Christian following that favors business, land development, etc. as well as world domination, war and assassination to subjugate the world for profit. These may be referred to as Theo-Cons or Theo-conservatives. The other current is fundamentalist and hostile to the world, thinking that it is intrinsically evil, and the dwelling place of the devil. They too believe as well in world domination, war and assassination to subjugate the world but for ushering in the end of the world and the coming of Christ.

Global warming has been politically recognized since the problem was highlighted by Jimmy Carter, the former president, in 1980. World temperatures are rising, because greenhouse gases in the environment are rising. The gases are trapping heat from the sun in the atmosphere. The most predominant of the greenhouse gases is Carbon dioxide which is released whenever fossil fuels (oil) are burned or forests are burned or catch fire. However, since the time of Jimmy Carter not much has been done about global warming because powerful forces acting on the government have stifled any strong action to confront the problem. Many corporations and large farms have had a vested interest in denying the reality of Global Warming and the deleterious effects it would have on climate change. In his book *The Heat is On* (1997) Ross Gelbspan exposed an industry strategy memo that revealed the goal of the industry was to "*reposition global warming as theory rather than fact.*"

There are stark examples of how the dominionist philosophy has influenced the political policy and that expose the duplicitous agenda of destruction of life for the purpose of bringing about disease, and death to precipitate chaos and the downfall of society.

EPA Using Data from Human Testing to Evaluate Pesticides[345]

> According to a report released by Senator Barbara Boxer (D-CA) and Representative Henry Waxman (D-CA), the EPA is currently using data from two dozen studies to help evaluate a number of pesticides. The data come from third party sources, most notably pesticide companies seeking to market new pesticides, and the report states that much of the data lack credibility.
> The Congressional report points to a number of studies that deliberately exposed people to toxic doses of pesticides. In one study conducted between 2002 and 2004, scientists exposed young adults to the chemical chloropicrin, a toxic insecticide that was used as a chemical warfare agent in World War I. The participants, mostly college students and minorities, were paid $15 an hour to sit in a chamber and were exposed to insecticide vapor in the air or had the vapor administered to their noses and eyes. This sometimes exposed them to doses 120 times the safe hourly limit as established by the Occupational Safety and Health Administration.

> EPA Administrator Stephen Johnson has been quoted as saying that human pesticide testing is not necessary to protect public health. However, Johnson did support the Children's Health and Environmental Exposure Research Study, or CHEERS, that would have enrolled 60 low-income families who agreed to continue exposing their children to indoor applications of pesticides in exchange for $970, children's clothing, and a camcorder. Johnson was forced to cancel the study due to public outcry and Congressional pressure, but on June 2, he reportedly defended CHEERS, saying that its cancellation was "an unfortunate result of public misunderstanding."

The E.P.A is supposed to be the government agency that promotes the health and well being of the U.S.A. citizens. What business does that agency have in promoting the use of pesticides and chemicals on infants, children and adults? Furthermore, what is the government, headed by George W. Bush, an avowed "born again Christian" accomplishing by appointing Steven Johnson to head the E.P.A.? Steven Johnson is a fundamentalist evangelist, who openly prides himself on his Christianity. The E.P.A. was endorsing studies by corporations specifically to use "abused and neglected children" and "children of limited capacity." This would translate to indigent, low class, children of whom the majority would be composed of African American, and Hispanic children. His proposal of the CHEERS regulations used children as guinea pigs and poisons them; his approval of the Clear Skies act actually allows corporations to put out more pollution than the previous law did; he promoted other laws that allow destruction of forests and natural areas such as north Alaska and others for oil drilling. These actions point to the kind of Christian he is and by appointing him and supporting him, also what kind of Christian George W. Bush was: a Dominionist-corporate advocates who follows statements by dominionists such as because we are in the "end times" and it is "God's will."[346] On a visit to Birmingham Alabama, to comfort the victims of hurricane Katrina the Secretary of State under George W. Bush, Condoleezza Rice, was reported to have told suffering and beleaguered hurricane survivors the following:

> "Don't you see, its OK, this means that Jesus is on his way."[347]

Stephanie Hendricks, author of *Divine Destruction: Dominion Theology and American Environmental Policy*. explained that the messages such as the one above and the experimentation on children coming from the George W. Bush administration from Johnson, Rise or the president himself are meant:

> "to, on a cultural level, reassure the public that the destruction of the earth is Gods will and I would argue that some ministers like pastor Tony Evans in Texas will preach to his congregation that George W. Bush is divinely leading us into God's divinely demanded, dictated destruction. This then justifies lifting of environmental rules, waging wholesale war all over the world the world for resource extraction."

Prior to the landfall of hurricane Katrina on the U.S.A. coast the Louisiana governor formally invoked her authority to declare an emergency and so the president was notified. He had meetings with meteorologists, and the agencies known as "Homeland Security" and F.E.M.A.[348] which were in charge of taking care of disaster preparedness and response to assist and give care to those people affected. In the aftermath of hurricane Katrina's devastation of the Louisiana coast, president George W. Bush publicly stated that he did not think that anyone could have predicted that the hurricane would hit with such force and damage the levies that flooded the city. The Associated Press obtained some confidential video footage of president Bush receiving a final briefing on August 28th, before hurricane Katrina hit the Gulf Coast. On that video he is seen being told of the severe threat and the possibility of the levies breaking and the devastation that would ensue if that were to happen.

> DemocracyNow.org Headlines for March 2, 2006
> ***Video Shows Bush Receiving Dire Warnings Day Before Katrina***
> On the video, President Bush is seen watching the briefing via a videoconference from his Texas ranch. The President does not ask one single question throughout the briefing, yet concludes that the government is: "fully prepared."
> The video shows several federal, state and local officials issuing the warnings. Then-FEMA head Michael Brown tells the President and Homeland Security Director Michael Chertoff: "My gut tells me ... this is a bad one and a big one." At another point in the briefing, , a weather expert says he has "grave concerns" on the levees in New Orleans.
> The video casts further doubt over the White House's claim it wasn't adequately warned about Katrina's possible magnitude. On September

> 1st, President Bush said: "I don't think anybody anticipated the breach of the levees. They did anticipate a serious storm but these levees got breached and as a result much of New Orleans is flooded and now we're having to deal with it and will."
> After viewing the video, New Orleans mayor Ray Nagin said: "I have kind of a sinking feeling in my gut right now… From this tape it looks like everybody was fully aware."

Many political critics of the president have charged him as being incompetent or unfeeling or even racist, since the vast majority of the population that was affected by the hurricane was of African American descent. Yet others, like Noam Chomsky, have pointed out that this kind of act is part of a deliberate strategy to allow and even promote social chaos. Furthermore, the image of a bungling, incompetent administration would be an ideal cover for acts of self-sabotage. Nevertheless, in April 2006 the dissatisfaction with the president fell to an all time low and lower than any other president in modern times. Yet his supporters, which were now the core of his base, composed of the religious right and their supporters along with big business and the wealthy, who receive the tax cuts he supports, still believe in him fervently. Regardless of the revelations of not finding weapons of mass destruction in Iraq and that intelligence was apparently manipulated to get the country to support going to war, the president's supporters continued to make excuses and support him because they believed he was a man of faith and that he would not lie. Having invested him with the status of Christian like themselves, many people may refuse to believe that Bush has committed errors or has ulterior negative agendas because that would mean that the God they think he listens to or follows is also wrong. One of several representative examples of the phenomenon of supporters who make excuses for and continue blind [refusing to consider any ulterior motives or incompetence] support for president George W. Bush even after his statements were exposed as be disingenuous simply because he is perceived as a "man of faith" occurred in a video interview on the program Democracy Now, hosted by Amy Goodman and conducted by Yoruba Richen who was interviewing a Bush supporter by the name of Staci Glick. [highlighted text by Ashby]

> **YORUBA RICHEN:** And they're also asking for answers, and saying that there were lies, that weapons of mass destruction were never found and, you know, what is your response to that?
> **STACI GLICK:** My response is that when the war started, and Saddam Hussein -- this is my understanding, they had given him warning after warning that they were coming in and that they were going to, you know -- he needed to clean up his act. Well, he had plenty of time to move weapons of mass destruction across the border to Syria. And I believe that that's possible. We don't know the intelligence reports that George Bush receives or his advisers receive. So, we have no idea of knowing what actually happened. I believe that they are there or they were there, but I don't -- I have a hard time believing that he lied, that this was all in vain. I have a very difficult time believing it.
> **YORUBA RICHEN:** Why is that? Why do you have a hard time believing that?
> **STACI GLICK:** Well, because, I just -- to me, well, you know, he's a man of faith, and I just don't think that if he is what he says he is, I don't think he would do that. And he's, you know -- there's no reason. There was no reason. I don't think this was something to divert attention away from Afghanistan. I mean, this was -- you know, our -- if we didn't fight today, my son, who is two years old now would have to fight in the future and other people's sons would have to fight in the future for, you know, the Iraqis. They're bringing their children up to hate us and to, you know, make weapons of mass destruction, whatever, and you know, it was going to come to this no matter what. And it had to be taken care of immediately. [349]

As stated earlier, the efforts of the Federalist Society came to fruition in the administration of George W. Bush when two Supreme Court justice vacancies came up. The Federalist society was responsible for the appointment of conservative judges who are allied to the religious right views and corporate interests and the elevating of the new Supreme Court justices, John Roberts and Samuel A. Alito, Jr. In an interview with Robert F. Kennedy Jr., Stephanie Hendricks explained that the placement of conservative judges is for the purpose of: *"to have anti-environmental judges in every level of the American judicial system."* Robert F. Kennedy replied: *"well their ultimate goal is to have corporate control of our society; and it would be laughable except for the fact that there are people who believe in this and have actually achieved very high office."*[350]

Denial of teaching contraception has led to more abortions and more strife and more death. Allowing chemicals in food and the development of the drug industry, is suspected to have led to more deaths from drug interactions [poisonings] than at any time in history and more than from illegal drug abuse; the belief in controlling nature has also led to ignorant faith in the medical sciences as 100,000 people die from medical malpractice and mistakes EACH YEAR! Global warming is and has been a fact and its denial and the attempts to portray the issue as a debate or opinion of scientists is as criminal as lying to protect a murderer. It is a crime to stall or prevent the implementation of technologies that already exist to use renewable sources of energy such as hydrogen or water instead of gasoline. The rise of countries such as China and India into the ranks of industrialized nations, seeking the material riches, that the U.S.A. has gained, presents staggering implications for the global environment. As of now the USA with only 300 million people produces most of the pollution and green house gasses of the world. In the next 25 years China, already with over 1 billion people, will surpass the pollution output of the USA and India will not be far behind. This scenario is not unlike the bleak futures presented in such worlds of science fiction films as *Z.P.G.* [Zero Population Growth] and *Soilent Green.*

The concerning eventuality of the collaboration between dominionists, who believe the bible gives them the right to subdue nature, the corporations who believe they have the right to make profits at all cost without regard for the environment, and government leaders who see their role as facilitators for the dominionists and corporations, in order to get reelected can mean a miscalculation in that their wanton destruction of the environment may lead to irreparable changes or that they may precipitate world war by constantly menacing other countries, pushing confrontations with other nations under the guise of a war on terror when the hidden reason is opposing other nations because they do not want to allow the corporations to steal their natural resources.

The animal based human diet is causing dire consequences to the environment. Half of the fresh water used in the U.S.A. goes to raising cattle for meat consumption and 1 acre of land is cleared [rendering it incapable of producing oxygen and sustaining ecosystems and species of animals and insects that are natural to the environment] every 8 seconds and most of that clearing is for cattle raising. Within 50 years the largest water supply in the U.S.A. will be depleted and arid lands will be produced. Animal waste is so abundant because they are being bred in greater numbers to satisfy the human addiction to meat. The farms producing cattle for meat do not have regulations on animal excrement so cows, which produce 180 times the amount of waste as humans, are saturating the environment with fecal bacteria. In fact, the meats purchased at supermarkets contain ample amounts of cow excrement and therefore also bacteria and so anything that comes into contact with the meat is infected. If the meat is cooked that cooking process kills some bacteria but leaves the meat less digestible and the process of preparing the meat for cooking spreads the bacteria so much so that the toilet is cleaner than the kitchen where meat has been prepared. That is, eating out of a toilet is healthier than eating from the kitchen counter where meat has been prepared!

Meat eating, over fishing, pollution and other despoiling of the environment is leading to a fast approaching ecological disaster that most people used to think would come in the next generation but the accelerated rate of damage to the environment is changing the timeline of adverse effects to the environment.

Faux choice of environmental responsibility or economic growth

Currently, unethical politicians, at the behest of their corporate constituents, are essentially paid [bribed], through political donations, to advocate irrational positions. One of the most effective tactics of unscrupulous politicians or debaters is to frame an idea within a false choice premise. The idea that one is either for environmental responsibility or corporate growth is a false choice, framed within the context of premise that only those two choices exist. Why can there not be corporate growth and environmental responsibility working together? The answer is that the corporation would make less money because for example, if they were mining they would be required to fix the damage they do to the environment after the mining is finished. If they can just walk away they can save the expense. So it is an issue of greed and disregard for the environment which is an irrational position like despoiling one's own home. But the polluters would not see it that way because, according to them, the world is too big to despoil or someone else can worry about it in the future. Well, the changes in the environment regarding ozone depletion, increase in CO^2 and other factors have demonstrated that the world cannot support massive levels of dumping endlessly.

Faux debate of creationism or evolution

There are many Christians who would like to have Creationism taught along side Evolution. The same argument as above applies here as well. Those who would like to promote the idea of Creationism or "Intelligent Design" would like to frame the argument as equivalent options to be chosen. Creationism is Religion and Evolution is science. The argument is nonexistent since to have a debate you would need to have equal elements to compare. In other words, to debate about whether evolution should be taught versus some other discipline, that discipline would need to be a science and not a religion. Likewise, if there were a choice between Christianity and some other philosophy that philosophy would need to be a religion and not a science.

Faux debate of global warming or no global warming

Again, the same argument as above applies here as well. Those who would like to promote the idea that global warming is just a theory without substantiation would like to frame the question as an argument between scientists. The argument is nonexistent because there is no credible dissent on the question of global warming in the scientific community and only scientists should be allowed to debate the question, if there is a question, with other scientists. Writers, political pundits or corporate advocates should not be allowed to enter into a scientific debate on this question. Global warming is a reality because it has been demonstrated by rigorous scientific investigation. Those commentators who say otherwise are often paid advocates or are religious or non-scientist commentators who are not promoting a tenable scientific point of view backed by scientific evidences. All the available scientific evidences point to the ongoing warming of planet earth. It is and will cause climate changes including loss of the ice covering Greenland, which will raise sea levels that in time will, within 25 to 100 years, leave places like certain pacific islands and coastal regions like South Florida [including Miami] and other major coastal cities around the world inundated and uninhabitable. The small island nation of Kiribati is made up of 33 small atolls, none of which is more than 6.5 feet above the South Pacific Ocean, and it is only a matter of time before the entire country is submerged by the rising sea.[351]

> Princeton University geosciences and international affairs professor Michael Oppenheimer, who also advises the advocacy group Environmental Defense, said one of the greatest dangers lies in the disintegration of the Greenland or West Antarctic ice sheets, which together hold about 20 percent of the fresh water on the planet. If either of the two sheets disintegrates, sea level could rise nearly 20 feet in the course of a couple of centuries, swamping the southern third of Florida and Manhattan up to the middle of Greenwich Village..."Once you lost one of these ice sheets, there's really no putting it back for thousands of years, if ever."[352]

There are many other dire consequences to Global Warming, like the formation of new deserts, and new uninhabitable areas on earth, incapacity of farming in certain areas, and a host of other changes to the environment. Certainly there is hope for the future if governments and societies rearranged their priorities to reverse the damage to the environment now. However, the current trend towards greed, and the helplessness of the masses to organize themselves and demand new priorities in their own lives and their governments will continue the move towards the precipice of world ecological disruptions that will have devastating effects for generations to come. The disruptions are not just due to rising sea levels. The thawing of the Arctic will lead to the extinction of polar bears. In Africa, colder mountainous regions are becoming warmer so mosquitoes are moving higher into regions that were previously too cold so there will be more malaria and other diseases in places they were never found before; all due to global warming and the unnatural way of human life based on stressful and poisonous technologies as well as an un-holistic medical care system. Recent reports from a range of news sources have warned that the previous predictions for the effects of Global Warming seem to be wrong because the changes are occurring at a faster rate than was previously estimated.

> **WashingtonPost.Com**
> ***Antarctic Ice Sheet Is Melting Rapidly New Study Warns Of Rising Sea Levels*** By Juliet Eilperin
> Washington Post Staff Writer Friday, March 3, 2006; Page A01
> It is one of a slew of scientific papers in recent weeks that have sought to gauge the impact of climate change on the world's oceans and lakes. Just last month two researchers reported that Greenland's glaciers are melting into the sea twice as fast as previously believed, and a separate paper in Science today predicts that by the end of this century lakes and streams on one-fourth of the African continent could be drying up because of higher temperatures.
> ... The (Antarctic) continent holds 90 percent of the world's ice, and the disappearance of even its smaller West Antarctic ice sheet could raise worldwide sea levels by an estimated 20 feet.
> "The ice sheet is losing mass at a significant rate," said Isabella Velicogna, the study's lead author and a research scientist at Colorado University at Boulder's Cooperative Institute for Research in Environmental Sciences. "It's a good indicator of how the climate is changing. It tells us we have to pay attention."[353]

Ironically, the false debate over whether climate change is happening or not has given way, to some degree, to the debate over the "tipping point" problem. The tipping point is the point at which climate changes become irreversible and unchangeable for many [thousands] years if not permanent. Three special factors are the focus of much concern to most climate scientists.

> There are three specific events that these scientists describe as especially worrisome and potentially imminent, although the time frames are a matter of dispute: widespread coral bleaching that could damage the world's fisheries within three decades; dramatic sea level rise by the end of the century that would take tens of thousands of years to reverse; and, within 200 years, a shutdown of the ocean current that moderates temperatures in northern Europe.[354]

Many people feel that the climate changes going on now are very small and that somehow humanity will adjust and adapt to them.

However, the changes already seen exceed normal fluctuations revealed by core sample studies going back several thousands of years. Some have not been seen by any member of the human race ever.

> Peter B. deMenocal, an associate professor at the Lamont-Doherty Earth Observatory of Columbia University, said that about 8,200 years ago, a very sudden cooling shut down the Atlantic conveyor belt. As a result, the land temperature in Greenland dropped more than 9 degrees Fahrenheit within a decade or two.
> "It's not this abstract notion that happens over millions of years," deMenocal said. "The magnitude of what we're talking about greatly, greatly exceeds anything we've withstood in human history."[355]

<u>What can a person do about this for themselves?</u>

Prepare now;

- Become an advocate for balanced ecological living.
- Choose a lifestyle that is vegetarian and friendly to the environment.
- Become an activist for ethics and environmentally safe government.
- Plan on coping with the conditions that may arise if society continues on its present course.
- The coastal regions of the world will be in danger of disappearing and so those areas are not safe ecologically, economically or socially.
- The environmental disruptions will disturb weather patterns and crops will fail in certain areas and flourish in others but erratically. So it would be wise to become more self-sufficient instead of relying on commercial sources of food items.
- It is also advisable to learn alternative healing methods and adopt a healthy renewable lifestyle that will not be so dependent on the society at large.
- Do not live in large populated areas where social disruptions and disease can take hold easily due to the coming changes.
- If possible try to adopt alternative fuel usage, such as ethanol, bio-diesel or some kind of oil substitute.

The Health Crisis

The overly *technologized* society has become dependent on the allopathic medical system, the economics of which are not sustainable through a private health care system. Unlike other industrialized developed nations the U.S.A. government has refused to implement a universal, government sponsored healthcare system thus, following the desires of drug companies and the medical industry just as it will refuse to pursue peaceful relations with other nations to accede to the demands of corporations and the military industrial complex. Health crises are one of the main reasons why people go bankrupt, yet the legislators in government recently instituted a new bankruptcy law to make it harder for ordinary persons to file for bankruptcy and get out of the weight of their debts. In the year 2008 the so called "baby boom" generation will begin to retire and then eventually within a few years they will make up the majority of the population and the younger minority will not be able to support their healthcare needs.

On the Failure of Modern Medicine:

> "Health care has become too expensive...There are a number of reasons... Some of them are within our control and some of it is beyond our control. For example, medicine made tremendous strides in the early half of the (20th) century in dealing with *acute infectious illness* and as a result of immunization and improved public health and techniques like antibiotics we really rolled back the numbers of people affected by acute infectious illness but what that left doctors dealing with was *chronic degenerative disease* which is by nature much more difficult and not so easy to fix. **So that's a problem that I think was really beyond our control**."
>
> -Andrew Weil M.D.

Due to the preference for processed foods and preference for conveniences, the nutritional content of foods will continue to decrease and the immune systems of more people will fail, leading to more chronic degenerative diseases that the present system of allopathic medicine cannot handle. There will be more disease; more infertility, more suffering and consequently the population will decline in general health as well as in number, due to infertility. The current system of medical theory does not work to cure problems such as cancer and heart disease so more people will die from those problems. Chemotherapy and radiation are poisons, not apt treatments for disease. While there is some interest in Alternative Medicine it is miniscule by comparison to the vast numbers of physicians in practice and in training that receive hardly any instruction in areas outside of drugs and surgery. That will have further dire effects on the economy. The populations of Western Europe are already in decline. The U.S.A. population is rising only due to immigration. When the economic situation of the U.S.A. becomes depressed the immigration will slow or even reverse.

"Cancer is most frequent where carnivorous habits prevail."
Scientific American, 1892 A.C.E.

The "scientific" establishment of the U.S.A., has known since the 19th century, that meat eating causes cancer. Yet no effort is made to control or stop the meat industry while the drug companies and medical establishment continue to search for the "answers" to the problem of cancer and "cures" for cancer. The meat-based diet [which includes cows, chickens, fish, sheep, pigs, dairy products, etc.] is the largest cause of disease in humans and it is the leading source of pain and suffering to animals.

The healthcare system of the western world is designed to promote and support disease by underwriting drug companies and medical procedures to cope with diseases instead of preventing disease. The same is true for the dental establishment. We know that certain kinds of foods (sweets, candies, soft drinks, etc.) deteriorate the teeth and gums. It turns out that those same foods along with cooked foods, meats, pastries, dairy foods etc. debilitate the immune system and upset the pH balance of the body which debilitates the bones and gums. Yet, the dental establishment continues to search for better ways to extract or replace teeth, perform root canals and other disfiguring painful procedures; the reason? It is more financially viable to promote the status quo to stay in business. So ethics in the medical establishment are based on economics and profit instead of responsible medical practice. This all contributes to the decline in health of the entire population.

Neither the medical establishment nor the government leaders want to alter the eating habits of the country because that would hurt profits. The human immune system is the best solution or cure for the body. A vegetarian diet, not medicine, chemotherapy or surgery, is the best way to promote health. However, people must be willing to live by truth instead of the illusion that allows them to eat abnormal poisonous foods. So ordinary people must not be complicit with either the government or the medical establishment or the food industry, which is more interested in profits than health.

It is NOT normal to grow old and have heart disease, cancer, senility, etc. yet this is the notion that the population has accepted. Even today, in countries where there is less or no meat consumption the cancer rate is vastly reduced or non-existent. The conclusion of these surprising findings is that meat is not the best food for human beings. In one medical study, participants who normally ate a vegetarian diet were fed meat for a period of four weeks to assess the effects of eating meat on raising the blood cholesterol level. Participants were also evaluated for changes in mood during the study. Not only did four weeks of eating a meat-inclusive diet increase their cholesterol levels as much as 19% over the control levels (when they ate a vegetarian diet), but the participants also exhibited "significantly higher" scores on the evaluation of five adverse mood factors: anxiety, depression, anger, fatigue and confusion, and a lower score for the positive factor, vigor, during this period[356]. One reason is based on the comparative anatomy, physiology and biochemistry of herbivores (animals that eat only plants), carnivores (animals that primarily eat meat), and omnivores (animals that eat both meat and plants) that clearly shows that humans are more herbivores than anything else. Dr Milton Mills, M.D., compared 19 different features (both anatomical and physiological – i.e., teeth structure, jaw movement, length of intestines, pH of stomach, digestive enzymes, etc.) of carnivores, omnivores and herbivores, and humans fell into the herbivorous category for each parameter[357].

Despite the researches described above, neither government officials nor leaders of the food industry advertise that fact or try to promote more healthy foods. In the U.S.A. the heart diseases and cancer rates are rising, not lowering, despite the fact that the U.S.A. spends more on healthcare than any other country. The healthcare priorities in the culture are skewed towards profits and that leads to disease and the numbers of diseased persons in the country will choke the healthcare system.

The bottom line is: the primary cause of heart disease (the major healthcare issue) is cholesterol buildup- the only dietary source of cholesterol on planet earth is Animal products-cholesterol has killed more people than *all* of the wars of the 20th century, *all* natural disasters and a *all* automobile accidents COMBINED!].[358]

This means that society must restructure its food industry towards a vegetarian based diet and rearrange its political and economic priorities in order to promote health instead of disease and stress. Will this happen before the health and ecological crisis comes to a head?

The Government, prompted by medical industry, drug company and food industry lobbyists is subsidizing meat and other agricultural products which would be much more expensive without the subsidies. For example, a pound of meat without just the water subsidies would cost $35 dollars. So the corrupt government is promoting the ill health of the population in collusion with the corporations, all for a piece of the profits.

See the book *Kemetic Diet: Food For Body, Mind and Spirit* by Dr. Muata Ashby

Part 4: Alternatives to Imperialism and Tyrannical Democracies

One World

Lessons From Botswana: Nationalism, Resistance Movements, Pan-Africanism and Using the deeper Roots of Culture to Achieve the true Goals of Democratic Government

There have always been resistance movements to fight against the tyranny of empires or dictators but not all have been successful. Nationalism is a very strong force for countering negative governmental forces. As stated earlier, Nationalism has been an effective means to mobilize an entire population of a country to oppose internal movements or ideas as well as external ones. The Cuban revolution was in part a nationalistic movement. The movements in South America in the early 21st century to throw off oligarchic leaders and U.S.A. influence are largely nationalistic movements as well. Many peoples around the world have attempted to use their indigenous cultures as a nationalistic ideal to unite around and then use the force from that unity to counteract the forces of dictatorship and imperialism.

> **nationalism**[359]
> n 1: love of country and willingness to sacrifice for it [syn: patriotism] 2: the doctrine that your national culture and interests are superior to any other [ant: multiculturalism, internationalism] 3: the aspiration for national independence felt by people under foreign domination 4: the doctrine that nations should act independently (rather than collectively) to attain their goals [ant: internationalism]

There have been several resistance movements that have developed over the past 100 years in response to western imperialism. Most recently, the movements in South America, led or assisted by Hugo Chaves, have achieved unprecedented power and freedom from American hegemony. The movement headed by Evo Morales [President of Bolivia] is primarily an indigenous movement, strengthened by native culture that overthrew the minority white ruling class. Yet their victory in their struggle is not yet assured. They are still in the process of separating from direct American neocolonialism through local dictators or oligarchies.

The devastation of African countries, due to Arab or European colonialism and or neo-colonialism and now Globalism, led to a situation in which many peoples of African descent were removed from the African continent and their descendants grew up in other lands and sometimes mixed with other cultures. That had the effect of changing the memory of the original land and culture. Nationalism is usually understood as the interest of a people in their own country and national interests. However that definition implies that the people have their own land, their own country. If they have their own country they need to look to their indigenous culture and traditions and reaffirm those and repudiate the imperialistic or hegemonic force that is countering their cultural identity and thereby confusing and weakening their ability to see what has happened to them and how they are being taken advantage of. What happens if those people do not have their own land? Such people would be scattered and weakened by their diffused interests and divergent identities. If we see culture as the foundation of nationalism the people would need to regain their culture and that would answer the question of which land they belong to and what traditions they need to rediscover and reaffirm. That will also lead to a rediscovery of a political agenda and political traditions that can be used effectively to counter the hegemonic force (force of oppression, dictatorship, imperialism, etc.).

The Pan-African movement is another nationalistic movement in a way. It seeks to unite all peoples of African descent as a group with the common goal of overthrowing the oppression imposed by the European nations on the rest of the world. Some peoples of African descent have embraced the idea of Pan-Africanism as a means to reaffirm the forgotten or lost identity and political agenda in order to counter the hegemonic force. However, how would that work if there are various identities that exist simultaneously in the African diaspora? The peoples of African descent in Brazil may have similar needs and similar problems as the peoples of African descent in the U.S.A. but their cultures and religions are different and act to pull them in divergent directions. So the Pan-African ideal has some difficulties to overcome on the way to organizing a viable opposition based on nationality.

The Marcus Garvey movement has sometimes been referred to as a nationalist movement based on an African Legacy. It was largely also based in an economic agenda for elevation of peoples of African descent. That movement occurred in a time when many of the people who joined the movement had recently achieved emancipation from slavery but were still languishing in oppressive conditions due to continued racial discrimination and oppression. Most of the followers were African Americans and most were Christians and most lived in the United States. The Garvey movement achieved great notoriety and a large following but deteriorated due to mismanagement and underhanded financial and legal tactics used by the European establishment. There are even today many who believe in the Garvey movement but they live lives in accordance to the culture where they reside and grew up.

The question arises, what would have been the fate of the Garvey movement if it had its own land, its own religion, its own language, and its own political traditions. Would it have been defeated in the same way? The point is that nationalism, in order to be effective, needs to have its own elements of nationhood in the form of: land, heritage (history), religion, language, and traditions. This would tend to mean that peoples will have more success if they have all those elements as opposed to living in foreign lands and partaking in other economies, etc. However, we have seen some groups do well. For example, there have been groups of Indians (from India), Koreans (from South Korea), Sikhs (from India), etc. who have come to the U.S.A. and have banded together and worked to cooperate and pool their resources and have built great wealth. It was possible because they brought with them their culture [culture = heritage (history), religion, language, and traditions]. However, the succeeding generations after the first tended to disintegrate and adopt the ways of the dominant culture. Therefore, it is not only important to have the culture but for a sustainable culture, land is also important so as to have a separate place to exercise the culture.

So if the land and culture are there, what should be the next step? The next step is to implement the culture and allow that to be the dominant process by which the people live their lives. Here the important aspect will be the political traditions. The political traditions are what allow a people to perpetuate their economics, religion, education, language, etc. In other words, the culture determines the political system and the political system allows the culture to perpetuate itself. The following section of this essay will present an overview of a particular political system that most if not all peoples who follow a general African nationalistic perspective can adopt since it exemplifies perhaps the most advanced application of traditional African principles in existence today which could also perhaps work for any culture that is advanced enough to practice evolved social order and an equitable economic system based on traditional African values of family and community. This value system in social order means taking care of the elderly and the children and seeing all members of the society as human beings to be respected and who deserve opportunity. This value system in social order means all members of the community should have input into the decisions of the country and the leaders cannot exercise independent actions that defy the will of the people. It is possible that this form of government could work for Africans in the diaspora if the other elements of the culture are compatible with the traditional African cultural values.

First of all, if we are going to accept as given that democracy is a good form of government what is democracy and what constitutes a healthy democracy? Four parameters of a healthy democracy have been identified in the book, *Exploring Social Change* by Charles Harper and Kevin Leight.

1. Losing is permissible;
2. Stable sets of parties send clear messages to voters;
3. There is a strong functioning civil society; and
4. Actors focus on processes rather than outcomes.

The criteria above have been demonstrated in other countries around the world, notably, the U.S.A. However, in the U.S.A. there are many discontented people and the government routinely acts in contradiction to the wishes of the people. Is that a model of democracy? Therefore, are the criteria listed above the only criteria that constitute a healthy democracy?

For this essay the country of Botswana in Africa will be examined. Botswana is a landlocked nation in Southern Africa. It was formerly the British protectorate of Bechuanaland. Botswana adopted its new name after becoming independent from British rule on September 30, 1966. Botswana is bordered by Namibia to the west, South Africa to the south, Zimbabwe to the northeast, and Zambia to the north. Botswana has a Constitutional Democracy and parliamentary republic. Botswana has been selected because its system of government is unique on the African continent and the world. It is an example of democratic governance because it more closely operates as a true democratic system. We may begin with the following definition of democracy: *"Government by the people, exercised either directly or through elected representatives. The principles of social equality and respect for the individual within a community"*[360] the central principle of democratic government may be understood as a system wherein the common people are considered as the primary source of political power and in which individual rights are protected from the abuse by the majority if there is one. Right away we can see that this definition of democracy is not the same as what is practiced in countries with a government such as that of the U.S.A. since in that system the majority rules and therefore becomes a tyranny over the losing minority.

Democracy is supposed to be government of, by, and for the people. It is government of a community in which all citizens, rather than favored individuals or groups, have the right and opportunity to participate but the rights of the minorities cannot be violated. This means that just because the majority desires something that does not mean that they can achieve that by voting it in regardless of the hardships caused to others. This is called CONSTITUTIONAL DEMOCRACY. In a democracy, the people are supposed to be sovereign and the ultimate source of authority. However, which people?

In a Pure democracy the law is the reflection of the will of the majority without any legal limit on that power. So it is understandable that many prefer to temper majority power with rule of law by the establishment of a constitution that establishes a stated amount of individual liberty as being inviolable by majority rule. The original framers of the U.S. Constitution saw a danger that majority rule would limit freedom of the individual. For example James Madison, in Federalist No. 10,[361] advocates a republic over "pure democracy" precisely to protect the individual from the will of the majority. However, in creating a republican system for the U.S.A. neither the majority nor the minority of the populace win, rather, the aristocracy won. So, just as "pure capitalism" is an unworkable economic construct to provide for the freedom and prosperity for all people, pure democracy is also an unworkable form of government, except for aristocracies or oligarchies and such. Thus the idea that democracy or capitalism are intrinsically good forms of social order is a misconception, often touted by those who do not truly understand the concepts or who wish to engage in dogmatic rhetorical arguments to oversimplify ideas in order to mislead people or label opponents as "undemocratic." Therefore, since in their true forms democracy and capitalism are not workable there is no such thing as democracy and capitalism, since when modified they cannot be considered as systems that promote the philosophy because they cannot work in their extreme or complete forms. Thus, a democratic form of government that leads to majority rule is actually a "Tyrannical Democracy."

In a constitutional form of government the authority of the majority is limited by legal and institutional means so that the rights of individuals and minorities are respected. This is the form of democracy practiced in Germany, Israel, Japan, the United States, and other countries. However, many governments such as the one used in the United States, do not afford full protection of individual rights. In that country the rights of the majority can take precedent over the rights of individuals or minorities. One example is eminent domain wherein the state may take private property from individuals. Nevertheless, to the extent that the majority of the population remains contented and the individual rights violations are not widespread and that they do not affect the elite or substantial portions of the middle class, democratic-like systems of government that are actually fronts for oligarchies or plutocracies can operate for extended periods without incurring the wrath of the people at a level that would threaten the ruling class.

However, the system of government in Botswana goes further in protecting human rights. In the Botswana government losing is permissible, that is, the losing candidates or parties do not feel the need to foment civil war and the winners do not feel the need to suppress or ban the opposition. The openness of the country's political system has been a significant factor in Botswana's stability and economic growth. General elections are held every 5 years. The next general election will be held in October 2009.[362] One of the reasons why Botswana is a model of higher democracy is because it does not make use of a system of cronyism.

Such systems of government, that include cronyism, allow the party that wins to take all power and place their friends in positions of power regardless of their qualifications. So of course in such a system the losers will be constantly scheming to undermine the victors so that they may become the winners and do to the previous winners what was done to them, and so the cycle goes on because the system is set up to promote that mentality and that form of politics. Or the losers may conspire with the victors so that next time the previous losers may win and keep the status quo so that no one besides the two parties may partake in the government or economic benefits of political power and at the same time the populace would be fooled into believing they are living in a democratic free enterprise system of government when in reality their choices are being limited to the two groups in power which are in reality aspects of one group. Limitation of the people in their participation of government or their choices in electing leaders by definition is not democracy.

In the U.S.A. this system of government was exemplified in 19th century Tammany Hall New York and still survives. It is known as the *spoils system.* The name was derived from the phrase "*to the victor go the spoils*". It was a contentious feature of Andrew Jackson, who introduced it as a democratic measure informed by his understanding of the nature of party politics and democracy. He considered that popular election gave the victorious party a mandate to select officials from its own ranks. The spoils system was closely linked to the new party system which he was instrumental in creating, generally known to scholars as the "second party system" (the first being the system which emerged in the aftermath of the ratification of the American Constitution). The civil service was originally included. Proponents claimed that ordinary Americans were able to discharge the official duties of government offices - not just a special civil service elite. Opponents considered it vulnerable to incompetence and corruption, just like the systems it followed and preceded.[363]

Though the spoils system was formally ended in the U.S.A. in 1883, the government would continue to be formed by the party of the winner of the Presidential election. There are about 3000 government positions that are exempted from the reforms and continue to be part of the spoils system (a more common term used is “cronyism”). The civil service was separated out; appointment to it was based on merit and not tied to any particular government, a state of affairs that continues today. It therefore became difficult if not impossible for voters to have any say in who makes up the civil service.

Botswana has stable sets of parties that send clear messages to voters. Unlike the problem of countries such as the United States, which only has two parties which do not reflect well their differences and in fact, to many voters, seem to have none,[364] which leads to voter apathy, in Botswana there are three main rival parties and a number of smaller parties. In national elections in 2004, the Botswana Democratic Party (BDP) won 44 of 57 contested National Assembly seats, the Botswana National Front (BNF) won 12, and the Botswana Congress Party (BCP) won 1 seat. Individuals elected by the National Assembly hold an additional 4 seats; the ruling BDP currently holds all 4.[365]

In Botswana there is a strong functioning civil society despite the health difficulties that have beset the population due to a high rate of AIDS infections. The openness and fairness of the political system is credited for the flourishing economy. With its proven record of good economic governance, Botswana was ranked as Africa's least corrupt country by Transparency International in 2004, ahead of many European and Asian countries. The World Economic Forum rates Botswana as one of the two most economically competitive nations in Africa. In 2004 Botswana was once again assigned "A" grade credit ratings by Moody's Investors Service and Standard & Poor's. This ranks Botswana as by far the best credit risk in Africa and puts it on par or above many countries in central Europe, East Asia, and Latin America. However, the special feature of Botswana's democratic system which accounts for the fairness and openness of Botswana's government is rooted in Botswana tribal heritage. Unlike many other African nations which have been severely destabilized due to colonialism, neocolonialism, war, disease, etc. and had their tribal traditions damaged, interrupted or dislocated the Botswana leaders created a system of government wherein there is an Executive and a National Assembly but they cannot rule independent of the tribal chiefs who themselves are directly accountable to the people through a village council and a code of fundamental human rights that is part of the constitution.

The advisory House of Chiefs represents the eight principal subgroups of the Botswana tribe, and four other members are elected by the sub chiefs of four of the districts. A draft of any National Assembly bill of tribal concern must be referred to the House of Chiefs for advisory opinion. Chiefs and other leaders preside over customary traditional courts, though all persons have the right to request that their case be considered under the formal British-based legal system. The roots of Botswana's democracy lie in Setswana traditions, exemplified by the Kgotla, or village council, in which the powers of traditional leaders are limited by custom and law. Botswana's High Court has general civil and criminal jurisdiction. Judges are appointed by the president and may be removed only for cause and after a hearing. The constitution has a code of fundamental human rights enforced by the courts, and Botswana has a good human rights record. Local government is administered by nine district councils and five town councils. District commissioners have executive authority and are appointed by the central government and assisted by elected and nominated district councilors and district development committees. However, one area of struggle for improvement in the Botswana political system is that there has been ongoing debate about the political, social, and economic marginalization of the San (indigenous tribal population-also referred to as "Bushmen"). The government's policies for the Basarwa (San) and other remote area dwellers continue to spark controversy.[366]

In Botswana, the Actors in government focus on processes rather than outcomes. In the book *Exploring Social Change* the authors state "Democracy is a way of making decisions. It doesn't guarantee the best decision will be made. If a democracy is only evaluated by the wisdom of the political decisions it produces, then it is in trouble." In Botswana the outcomes are substantially improved because there is less disaffection with the political system since there is more direct control exerted by the people. Yet we may understand then that the constitution or written blueprint or format of the government determines its level of democracy or autocracy, corruption or ethics, as well as its level of capitalism or socialism. So the essence of good democracy lies in its ethical and classless structure. We can recall in history that in ancient Greece, the reputed origin of democratic government, the system was very volatile and people could be easily swayed into voting for war, to conquer other countries, subjugate and enslave their peoples and plunder their wealth; also, only male Greeks could vote, thereby disenfranchising the rest of the population, not to mention the slaves. So just using the term democracy does not automatically imply good government or ethical government or even democratic government. This is why there are many governments which call themselves democratic but which are actually systems of wresting control from other groups or nations and controlling resources. In the Botswana political system it is more possible to have a greater quality in political deliberations and thereby the results of the democratic decision making process are more acceptable and more egalitarian than in other systems such as representative democracies [like the U.S.A.] wherein after candidates are elected they are not directly responsible to the people and so are able to act independently and many times commit crimes with impunity that would, in Botswana, be immediately referred for possible judicial action.

After throwing off the colonial rule, Botswana went back and built its "new" post-colonial society upon its own institutions and social principles. It went back to its roots. Botswana had its own markets and its own form of participatory democracies that operated not just for the country as a whole in a macro sense but in their villages in a micro sense. Unlike the macro system where most of the power lies in the federal or national government, the power in the system used in Botswana is distributed down to the villages.

The system of Botswana government does not work by western democratic standards in that majority is not allowed to rule over the minority. That western format creates disparities and injustices and promotes the formation of interest groups as well as corruption, bribery and promotes dictatorships, oligarchies and plutocracies. For example, In Botswana, in order to handle political affairs, the chief calls a Kgotla or village meeting. The chief then puts the issue before the people of the village. The people then debate the issue until a consensus is agreed upon. In that way all have been heard and all solutions explored and everyone's concerns addressed so as to equitably and justly come up with a solution that is beneficial for all and not just for interest groups such as a business that makes political contributions to get some policy implemented so they alone can make a profit. In Botswana, in order to maintain the social order and promote responsibility of government officials to the needs of the people the cabinet ministers must attend Kgotla meetings weekly.

This format of government and economics makes it more difficult for any despotic ruler to grab power and force national changes not desired by the people locally. Other African countries could use this model of returning to their roots or using the Botswana model to rebuild their government and economic institutions reflecting an indigenous African system that worked prior to the colonial disruptions.

19th Century Wisdom on Dissent and Protest to Promote a More Ethical and Democratic Society

Henry David Thoreau did indeed make more explicit and impassioned arguments for the individual's right to resist both the state and the majority. But it is no less philosophical and yet the power of the arguments derives partially from their simplicity and penetrating incisiveness. They take on a scathing quality that gives no quarter in the pursuit of their goal, freedom from the government which has taken on a life of its own and that directs the lives of people into ruinous affairs such as slavery, war and other problems of society. The question of when is breaking the rules necessary, in order to uphold certain moral or ethical principles, was confronted directly by Thoreau.

Perhaps no other motto more succinctly describes Thoreau's views on government than *"That government is best which governs least."* Many valuable insights can be gained from a careful review of his book *On The Duty Of Civil Disobedience.* Thoreau deeply cared about the injustices perpetrated by the government of the United States of America since that was the land of his birth. However, his sharp and explicit appraisal of politics transcends the U.S.A. since they confront recurring problems in human societies especially in the West. In his time the people who controlled the government of the U.S.A. had designs on the land now known as Texas which was then part of Mexico. Thoreau railed against the policy as illegitimate and an abuse of governmental authority that cost the lives of many men who composed the standing army, not to mention, the Mexicans who also died in the conflict. The current situation with the war on Iraq seems to echo his situation.

> "The standing army is only an arm of the standing government. The government itself, which is only the mode which the people have chosen to execute their will, is equally liable to be abused and perverted before the people can act through it. Witness the present Mexican war, the work of comparatively a few individuals using the standing

> government as their tool; for, in the outset, the people would not have consented to this measure."
>
> ~On The Duty Of Civil Disobedience by Henry David Thoreau

Thoreau noticed a problem of his times that reflects the present day situation. He protests against the fact that the war with Mexico was *the work of comparatively a few individuals.* That situation is the same as the one in the year 2003 when a small group of people who were and continue to be referred to as neo-cons or Neo-conservatives attacked the country, Iraq. They took political power and manipulated the congress into authorizing a war against a country, Iraq, which did not attack the U.S.A. However, just as Mexico had something the imperialists of the U.S.A. government wanted, i.e. land, Iraq had something that the Neo-cons and the plutocrats wanted, oil, which could be used to make money, control economies and have power over other governments and countries. Even though he saw many dire problems with the U.S.A. government Thoreau was not a radical anarchist bent on tearing down the government despite its severe transgressions.

> "But, to speak practically and as a citizen, unlike those who call themselves no-government men, I ask for, not at once no government, but at once a better government. Let every man make known what kind of government would command his respect, and that will be one step toward obtaining it." (On The Duty Of Civil Disobedience.)

Thoreau makes an important point about the misconception of democratic government in that it is touted as a "just" system of government because theoretically everyone gets to have their say in it by means of voting. However, what happens to those who are in the minority in any society? Do their votes really count in a system where majority rules and the winner takes all?

> But a government in which the majority rule in all cases cannot be based on justice, even as far as men understand it. Can there not be a government in which majorities do not virtually decide right and wrong, but conscience? -- in which majorities decide only those questions to which the rule of expediency is applicable? Must the citizen ever for a moment, or in the least degree, resign his conscience to the legislator? Why has every man a conscience, then?
>
> ~On The Duty Of Civil Disobedience by Henry David Thoreau

Most people think of a minority as a small group, such as Jews, African Americans, Asian Americans, etc., within a larger culture. Unless one is a member of the power elite of a country one may consider oneself as part of the minority, even though one may be part of a large ethnic or political group. That is because even though the masses of people can "have their say" by voting, that vote only voices an opinion and has little power in a representative democracy. Since the wealthy minority or powerful control the policies, the masses are part of a minority of power. The concept of majority rule, coupled with the economic system alluded to by John Stuart Mill in his book *On Liberty,* sets up a situation wherein the lower classes, those who are not independently wealthy, are relegated to the duties of soldiering, or supporting the war through burdensome taxes under penalty of law which would be enforced by their fellow underclass compatriots, who are paid by the government to repress their own compatriots. Just as journalists polled people in the year 2003, before the war started, and found that most people disapproved about the war on Iraq and yet the war was perpetrated anyway, Thoreau knew the minds of those who fought for the enforcement of policies that were decided upon without the consent of the people. Thoreau compared the soldiers to machines that had lost their humanity and remarked about the capacity of the government to make human beings into instruments of violence to support its aims.

> "A common and natural result of an undue respect for law is, that you may see a file of soldiers, colonel, captain, corporal, privates, powder-monkeys, and all, marching in admirable order over hill and dale to the wars, against their wills, ay, against their common sense and consciences, which makes it very steep marching indeed, and produces a palpitation of the heart. They have no doubt that it is a damnable business in which they are concerned; they are all peaceably inclined. Now, what are they? Men at all? or small movable forts and magazines, at the service of some unscrupulous man in power? Visit the Navy Yard, and behold a marine, such a man as an American government can make, or such as it can make a man with its black arts -- a mere shadow and reminiscence of humanity, a man laid out alive and standing, and already, as one may say, buried under arms with funeral accompaniments… The mass of men serve the state thus, not as men mainly, but as machines, with their bodies." (ibid.)

The masses are controlled through propaganda, economic subsistence level income and miseducation but those in the armed forces are more intensely indoctrinated, being convinced that they cannot protest being used as cannon fodder by a code of following a chain of command under penalty of death or other punishments. Miseducation is like a darkness that leads people to live blindly for the benefit of others and to die doing the bidding of others even while they may be convinced they are doing a service to God, country or community. The following excerpt from Thoreau reminds one of a world, as described in the Indian *Bhagavad Gita* that has its priorities upturned.

> Gita--Chapter 2:69. *That which is night to all beings, in that a man of controlled (intuitive) mind keeps awake, but that in which all beings of the world keep awake (ignorance), is night for the Sage who sees the Self.*

In other words, what people should revere they disparage and what they should disparage they revere as virtue or view it as laudable and proper.

> He who gives himself entirely to his fellow-men appears to them useless and selfish; but he who gives himself partially to them is pronounced a benefactor and philanthropist.
>
> ~On The Duty Of Civil Disobedience by Henry David Thoreau

There are many people who, as Mill stated, defer to the Princes (government leaders). There are also people who may disagree with the policies but who have been convinced that they must do the bidding of the government and that feeling in them to comply with that command is supported by the incapacity of their ability to apply critical thinking ("Judgment") but also they are as Mill explained, susceptible to the crowd or mob group mentality: *People more happily situated, who sometimes hear their opinions disputed, and are not wholly unused to be set right when they are wrong, place the same unbounded reliance only on such of their opinions as are shared by all who surround them, or to whom they habitually defer.* (John Stuart Mill. *On Liberty* Chapter 2) There are also those who support the government with their taxes and remain quiet for fear of losing their property or source of income. Unlike Mill, however, Thoreau proposed that the better and more powerful way to promote the dissenting point of view is to disassociate from the government and not lend it any support.

> How does it become a man to behave toward this American government to-day? I answer, that he cannot without disgrace be associated with it. I cannot for an instant recognize that political organization as my government which is the slave's government also. (ibid)

Thoreau saw that just complaining about government wrongdoing but still paying taxes or otherwise aiding and abetting the government as it carries out its illegitimate (not consented to by the populace) policies is not much different than those who openly and actively support the government. The people who acquiesce are actually prolonging the injustices that they themselves suffer since they themselves are the ones who bear the brunt of deaths in war and the burden of taxation at all times (during war & peace). People were, in the time of Thoreau and are still in the present, convinced that they must support the government to maintain order and or because the government officials and especially the commander in chief, must be obeyed without question; as Thoreau puts it: *Thus, under the name of Order and Civil Government, we are all made at last to pay homage to and support our own meanness.* (ibid)

One of the important aspects of Thoreau was his abolitionism. This aspect of the U.S.A. experience, he found to be particularly abhorrent. So he resolved to disengage from the government on this point as well. There are many people in a society who believe the adage, promulgated in society, that the U.S.A. is not perfect but its better than all other systems and that even though bad things happen that we must still go on and support the government and somehow things will work out better in the future. That thought process sustains the government even as those same people continue to be mistreated by the government. Thoreau's solution would be to allow the government to fall if necessary in order to repair the problems and then go on if possible but in any case, the injustice should be stopped even though it might disrupt the peace or continued operation of the government, commerce, etc. *But Paley appears never to have contemplated those cases to which the rule of expediency does not apply, in which a people, as well as an individual, must do justice, cost what it may.*. (ibid)

In the following statement Thoreau pointed out the ineffectiveness and feebleness of those who acquiesce to the desires of the government's imperialism and slavery.

> There are thousands who are in opinion opposed to slavery and to the war, who yet in effect do nothing to put an end to them; who, esteeming themselves children of Washington and Franklin, sit down with their hands in their pockets, and say that they know not what to do, and do nothing; who even postpone the question of freedom to the question of free-trade, and quietly read the prices-current along with the latest advices from Mexico, after dinner, and, it may be, fall asleep over them both. What is the price-current of an honest man and patriot to-day? They hesitate, and they regret, and sometimes they petition; but they do nothing in earnest and with effect. They will wait, well disposed, for others to remedy the evil, that they may no longer have it to regret. At most, they give only a cheap vote, and a feeble countenance and Godspeed, to the right, as it goes by them. (ibid)

The history of slavery and racism that has racked the U.S.A. from the colonial period and continues to wreck havoc with U.S.A. society could be considered as an example of the acquiescent approach's results. Slavery might have ended even before it started if certain groups, Africans, Europeans, Catholic Church, or others, had taken a firm stand against it instead of deciding to profit by it while at the same time justifying the atrocious human sufferings that were going on. Some simply blinded themselves to the immorality of the institution of slavery even though they did not take direct part in it. But in any case the entire western culture benefited by the usurpation of native lands and slave labor. Certainly these important issues (war, slavery) are cause for the ethical modern professional to protest in the strongest possible terms. Thoreau pointed out that many thousands opposed slavery but did nothing actively to oppose it by making their desire to stop it felt in the halls of government leaders; so their votes fell on deaf ears as part of a silent minority that might have become a majority if they had been more boisterous and organized in their efforts to promote change.

> Even voting for the right is doing nothing for it. It is only expressing to men feebly your desire that it should prevail. (ibid)

This point highlights a major flaw in the U.S.A. government system at least from the perspective of the minority or dissenting opinions. It is set up as a winner takes all scheme which acts to concentrate power in fewer individuals. In order to make the system more balanced there would need to be an adjustment such that even the minority could have some power at least to control their own destiny if not to restrict the power of the majority in society over them. That could be a system of government that is more democratic than the current U.S.A. system of government. And indeed other governments have moved in that direction so it is not correct to say that the U.S.A. system of government is the best form of government or democracy that has ever been devised by human beings. Thoreau refuted an interesting thesis by a person who was considered as a moral authority which proposed that as long as the government exists and cannot be changed it has been granted a kind of divine dispensation to be and so people must comply to its demands until it cannot compel them anymore.

> Paley, a common authority with many on moral questions, in his chapter on the "Duty of Submission to Civil Government," resolves all civil obligation into expediency; and he proceeds to say that "so long as the interest of the whole society requires it, that is, so long as the established government cannot be resisted or changed without public inconveniency, it is the will of God... that the established government be obeyed, and no longer.... (ibid)

This is like saying that it is right for a thief to steal a person's belongings until that person can stop the thief but as long as they cannot stop the thief the thief is in the right! Herein lays the difficulty in assigning what is moral or ethical when there is no objective standard to use as a guideline for all moral questions. For example, if the objective standard is that all human beings have inalienable rights then all should be free, but if the morality is bigoted, which can only occur through disregarding objective reality, then the morality becomes arbitrary and partisan and thus, it ceases to be morality but more dogma and propaganda in support of one group's views as superior over another.

Thoreau made another important point about the voting system.

> But no: I find that the respectable man, so called, has immediately drifted from his position, and despairs of his country, when his country has more reason to despair of him. He forthwith adopts one of the candidates thus selected as the only available one, thus proving that he is himself available for any purposes of the demagogue. His vote is of no more worth than that of any unprincipled foreigner or hireling native, who may have been bought. Oh for a man who is a man, and, as my neighbor says, has a bone in his back which you cannot pass your hand through! (ibid)

A more democratic system would allow for the possibility of any qualified person the opportunity to run for elections without needing to have large amounts of money that require donors who will then want something in return for their donations. Yet the system of the U.S.A. as well as that of other countries is set up specifically so that there can only be two candidates [in the presidential elections for example] and those are selected by party officials, corporate supporters and political cronies. So they are then presented to the people so that they may make their choice, yet, the choice has already been made for them, even before the candidates were selected, since much of the populace have already been indoctrinated by the propaganda of the culture, to accept the system and the values of the candidates and in any case either one of the two would be acceptable to the established power elite who control the economy and the government. Thoreau's argument is therefore that voting in such a system is a waste and that it shows that those who vote are submitting to the bidding of the one they are electing.

Thus, dissenting by putting forth differing views is necessary to promote the soundness of the ideas upon which a society conducts its affairs and the work should not stop at just protesting. There should be a plan to promote those ideals so that they gain the widest possible audience and then they should be juxtaposed with the prevailing notions. If protest is not effective it can become part of the established order that facilitates despotism. If dissenters are too timid to take actions that actually change the system and not just express their feelings, they risk the danger of becoming ineffectual instruments to release cultural stress; merely a facilitator, a safety valve for the wrong that has been perpetrated. Such kinds of protests actually facilitate the dominance of the power elite and their government by supposedly proving to everyone that there is freedom of speech and thus there is an implication that freedom and exchange of ideas has occurred and the best ones won in the end and were accepted; so the people would appear to have gotten what they wanted… thus, people would think that the system works after all. Author and activist Arundhati Roy gave a very pertinent statement on what needs to happen in order to have effective protest and dissent.

> "What we need to discuss urgently is strategies of resistance. We need to aim at real targets, wage real battles and inflict real damage. Gandhi's Salt March was not just political theatre. When, in a simple act of defiance, thousands of Indians marched to the sea and made their own salt, they broke the salt tax laws. It was a direct strike at the economic underpinning of the British Empire. It was real. While our movement has won some important victories, we must not allow non-violent resistance to atrophy into ineffectual, feel-good, political theatre. It is a very precious weapon that needs to be constantly honed and re-imagined. It cannot be allowed to become a mere spectacle, a photo opportunity for the media."[367]

But even those suggestions may fail if those who hold the reigns of power and the erroneous ideas or who promote unjust laws are uncaring or even apathetic? What form of dissent is appropriate when gross injustices are being perpetrated or atrocities are being committed or people are dieing due to the policies or actions of the government? Thoreau presents similar questions and then his solutions:

> Unjust laws exist; shall we be content to obey them, or shall we endeavor to amend them, and obey them until we have succeeded, or shall we transgress them at once? Men generally, under such a government as this, think that they ought to wait until they have persuaded the majority to alter them. They think that, if they should resist, the remedy would be worse than the evil. But it is the fault of the

> government itself that the remedy is worse than the evil. It makes it worse.
> What I have to do is to see, at any rate, that I do not lend myself to the wrong which I condemn.
> It is not my business to be petitioning the Governor or the Legislature any more than it is theirs to petition me; and if they should not hear my petition, what should I do then? But in this case the State has provided no way; its very Constitution is the evil. This may seem to be harsh and stubborn and unconciliatory; but it is to treat with the utmost kindness and consideration the only spirit that can appreciate or deserves it. So is an change for the better, like birth and death which convulse the body. (ibid)

Thoreau made what would be considered by indoctrinated patriots as a form of sacrilege when he points out that the problem is with the constitution itself. Thoreau was denouncing the Constitution of the United States of America because it is the document that contains the framework for the system of government that was implemented that provides for slavery, subjugation of women, and the "one party take all the power" format. It also establishes that people will only vote for their top rulers indirectly, through the "electoral college" and Senators. Therefore, the power to select and elect the leaders does not reside with the people ultimately. Thus, Thoreau's logic about resisting by nonparticipation in the apparently counterfeit electoral process seems more supported. Thoreau went on to propose a form of "peaceful revolution" by refusing to pay the taxes that support the government. However, that rout would only work, it would seem, if a large segment of the population were to participate in such an insurrection, because they would be hard to marginalize or imprison.

> A minority is powerless while it conforms to the majority; it is not even a minority then; but it is irresistible when it clogs by its whole weight. If the alternative is to keep all just men in prison, or give up war and slavery, the State will not hesitate which to choose. If a thousand men were not to pay their tax-bills this year, that would not be a violent and bloody measure, as it would be to pay them, and enable the State to commit violence and shed innocent blood. This is, in fact, the definition of a peaceable revolution, if any such is possible. If the tax-gatherer, or any other public officer, asks me, as one has done, "But what shall I do?" my answer is, "If you really wish to do anything, resign your office." When the subject has refused allegiance, and the officer has resigned his office, then the revolution is accomplished. But even

> suppose blood should flow. Is there not a sort of blood shed when the conscience is wounded? Through this wound a man's real manhood and immortality flow out, and he bleeds to an everlasting death. I see this blood flowing now. (ibid)

Many people who have become involved with the U.S.A. politics adopted the idea of "changing the system from the inside." According to Thoreau that idea would be based on a false premise that the system is capable of changing and or that the system is willing to change; neither of which would seem to be the case since the constitution, is set up to produce a certain kind of social order and economic structure for the government that according to Thoreau and other critics is one of the important causes for the possibility of injustices to exist with impunity. Further, the constitution had and still has many ardent supporters in the powerful classes of professionals and bureaucrats as well as the indoctrinated masses.

> Statesmen and legislators, standing so completely within the institution, never distinctly and nakedly behold it. They speak of moving society, but have no resting-place without it...
> The lawyer's truth is not truth, but consistency or a consistent expediency. Truth is always in harmony with herself, and is not concerned chiefly to reveal the justice that may consist with wrong-doing. He well deserves to be called, as he has been called, the Defender of the Constitution. There are really no blows to be given by him but defensive ones. He is not a leader, but a follower. His leaders are the men of '87. "I have never made an effort," he says, "and never propose to make an effort; I have never countenanced an effort, and never mean to countenance an effort, to disturb the arrangement as originally made, by which the various States came into the Union." Still thinking of the sanction which the Constitution gives to slavery, he says, "Because it was a part of the original compact -- let it stand." (ibid)

The idea of a minority withholding their participation appears to contain the more profound notion that the act of withdrawal will cause those who withdraw to remove not only their financial support but also their mental support, i.e. they will become free, having disassociated, to turn their energies towards their own capacity to resist injustices instead of placing their faith in false electoral processes that do not work for them.

Perhaps no other argument for dissent and for disassociation from what one deems as untoward is the factor of the degradation of one's own humanity.

> I can afford to refuse allegiance to Massachusetts, and her right to my property and life. It costs me less in every sense to incur the penalty of disobedience to the State than it would to obey. I should feel as if I were worth less in that case. (ibid)

Thoreau made the point that for a self-respecting and principled individual, participation in such a system that serves its own corrupt and mercenary ends, is not only the surrender of the finances or property or the body, but that which is more valuable, the conscience and the soul, for without integrity and virtue the finer transcendental aspects of life cannot be experienced. So even the highest class as well as the lowest and also the middle, who support such a government cannot attain the heights of those who refuse to sacrifice their honor and prudence to the state that professes to uphold inalienable rights but which in reality protects itself and the rights and privilege of the power elite, before anything else. Thus, breaking the rules [set up by the government to stifle dissent and legitimate opposition] is sometimes necessary whenever virtue is in danger of being supplanted by the designs of the adulterated and demeaning authorities controlling the government; for it is from virtue that true humanity and civil government is born and without which moral government and any goodness that can come of it are impossible. Thoreau focused on the injunction by Confucius who said, *"If a state is governed by the principles of reason, poverty and misery are subjects of shame; if a state is not governed by the principles of reason, riches and honors are the subjects of shame."* (ibid)

We could add that any form of government is only as good as the virtuous qualities of its leaders and especially its prince. In the case of the U.S.A. the traditional position of the Prince [political ruler] is occupied by the President but in reality the presidency was supposed to be more of a figurehead to provide the impression of a person in charge and the appearance of change through transference of power from one administration to another. True power resides potentially in the congress and out of the two houses of congress more power resides perhaps in the Senate since the true power rests with the body in government that are the representatives of the aristocracy, who represent the interests of the heads of corporations as well as the wealthy and can control the power of the purse.

Just as a family and its integrity as well as its values are determined by the parents, so too a government's honor and integrity are determined by its executive or the level of virtue of its aristocracy. This is because governments are composed of human beings and most are imperfect individuals, with desires and defects which can be corrupted into a form of group consciousness that promotes a certain objective, of which primarily is the desire to survive and next to experience pleasure and not pain. In the absence of an environment of virtue those desires and faults are transformed into feelings of entitlement, exclusivity and indifference or even cruelty towards those who are less fortunate. However, those directives and policies that make such class separations within the society possible arise from the structure of the government (the constitution) and in the leadership of the executive, which is the most powerful force that shapes the feeling and tone of a society by guiding its feelings and aspirations towards what is virtuous or towards what is base. In this way the Prince is the parent of the country and with those persons rests the power to mold the society and the capacity to shape the future. So in this line Confucius said, *"There is government, when the prince is prince, and the minister is minister; when the father is father, and the son is son."*

In comparing the present condition of government in the U.S.A. in the early 21st century with that which Thoreau describes that existed in his times, it would seem that technology has changed but corrupt government has only changed in that it has become bigger, more powerful, and more adept at deception and manipulation of human beings. The demagoguery and fear mongering of many politicians and fundamentalist or evangelical religious leaders has not changed but has become more dangerous because it reaches more people through mass media. The politicians and weapons producers have more profoundly mastered and improved on propaganda, killing in war, sophistic statements and polemical arguments, and adding to these, timorous speech, phobic fear-mongering and an overblown superpower mentality so much so that the U.S.A. has become isolated, in great measure, from the community of world nations. There are consequences to the demagoguery and warmongering and fear mongering that leads to what the C.I.A. calls "blowback" or in other words, "chickens coming home to roost."

> **Democracy Now – March 10, 2006**
> ***Dubai Firm Pulls Out of U.S. Port Deal***
> The Dubai-based firm DP World has announced it will not take control of operations at six U.S. ports following a firestorm of criticism. Instead the company said it would transfer the management of the ports to an unnamed U.S. entity. It remains unclear whether DP World plans to sell off its U.S. assets or set up a U.S.-based subsidiary to run the ports. Congress had threatened to derail the handover of port operations to DP World claiming national security would be endangered if a company run by the United Arab Emirates operated the ports. But President Bush vowed to veto any legislation put forward by Congress to block DP World from taking over port operations.[368]

One example of the consequences of actions and how actions lead to certain unintended consequences was the George W. Bush administration's bid to contract a company from the United Arab Emirates. When the public, the democrats and others found out about the deal to allow the Arab based company to operate six or more ports in the continental U.S.A. a major opposition was mounted by congress and people in the democrat ranks as well as the republican ranks arose ultimately killing the deal; however, the deal did not die before extremists on both sides used the issue for election year posturing and denigrating the country as an Arab country, whipping up the fears about Arab nations as spawning grounds for terrorists, an idea implanted in most people's minds by the president and his advisors who had promoted that very fear in an effort to drum up support for the invasion of Iraq. So, what was started as political rhetoric using fear of Arabs has led to widespread belief among many people that all Arabs and the Islamic religion are dangerous and so the president's plans to enter into the deal have been thwarted by conditions of his own making. The danger in negative and politically motivated rhetoric is not just in losing business deals but in entire nations fearing other nations and thereby becoming easily manipulated by unscrupulous leaders into aggressive actions against those that are feared even if the fear is irrational or based on illusions.

> ***Poll: Half of Americans Negative About Islam***
> More Americans are expressing a negative attitude toward Islam, according to a new poll released this week. The survey by THE WASHINGTON POST and ABC News found that nearly half of those responding said they had an unfavorable opinion of Islam. More than a third said they thought Islam encourages violence. The percentages show a significant increase from a similar survey taken in 2001 shortly after the September 11 terrorist attacks.[369]

Under such conditions dissent by citizens is branded as unpatriotic and though thousands or millions around the world may die because of the policies whose disingenuousness has been proven but yet still garner support for the leaders from the general populace and their core constituents, who follow them as automatons, repeating the party line or conservative agenda as they hear it and then proceed to follow it in lockstep. The citizens of the country that the U.S.A. or the European nations deem as vital to their "national interests" might have its economy manipulated, as Japan's was before W.W. II and if the country were to descend into chaos it would be branded as a "failed state" in need of intervention. Protestors in that country would be identified as malcontents, communists or now, terrorists, in order to legitimize invading and occupying the country and putting down its people's objections. Arundhati Roy touched on this subject succinctly in a speech given at the World Social Forum in Mumbai, January 16, 2004.

> "New imperialism" is already upon us. It's a remodeled, streamlined version of what we once knew. For the first time in history, a single empire with an arsenal of weapons that could obliterate the world in an afternoon has complete, unipolar, economic and military hegemony. It uses different weapons to break open different markets. There isn't a country that is not caught in the cross hairs of the US cruise missile and the International Monetary Fund (IMF) chequebook.
> Poor countries that are geo-politically of strategic value to empire, or have a "market" of any size, or infrastructure that can be privatised, or natural resources of value — oil, gold, diamonds, cobalt, coal — must do as they're told, or become military targets.
> … Those who have been fired upon are immediately called militants.

> In the era of the "war on terror", poverty is being slyly conflated with terrorism. In the era of corporate globalization, poverty is a crime. Protesting against further impoverishment is terrorism.
> Like old imperialism, new imperialism relies for its success on a network of agents — corrupt, local elites who service Empire.

It is an unfortunate aspect of human culture to see how many lives are wasted in the pursuit of ignominious efforts. As Thoreau put it *The mass of men lead lives of quiet desperation. What is called resignation is confirmed desperation.* (Henry David Thoreau, *Walden*) It is amazing to clearly see that the struggles of humanity that have existed for ages and which manifested in the days of Thoreau are still with us today. Perhaps it is heartening to know that there are those human beings who are not willing to live lives of quiet desperation but who are willing to pursue and live for the betterment of all humanity and to make their skills and faculties available to that task as opposed to acquiescing to the powers that be and in effect becoming part of the cogs of industry which disintegrate the bodies and minds of people in the pursuit of wealth and power. Like Thoreau, there are many who live with the desire to know life and to live life and his work contributes a powerful instrument for moving forward in power and dignity to discover and experience the meaning of life.

> *"I went to the woods because I wished to live deliberately, to front only the essential facts of life, and not discover when I came to die that I had not lived."*
>
> ~Henry David Thoreau, *Walden*

Afterword: What Could Happen in the Near Future?

What could happen to the U.S.A. and world economy if the current course of affairs continues? What are the consequences to the U.S.A. economy due to the financial mismanagement, deficits, consumerism and the profit motive of the multinational corporations?

> Thanks to George W. Bush's reckless fiscal deficits, the government will have less ability to overcome an economic crisis through borrow-and-spend, as it did in the last economic downturn. With the appetite for America's IOUs diminishing, US politicians will have their hands full dealing with rising energy costs and the tottering finances of healthcare, education and pensions.
> The basics of a harder-times scenario are not much in dispute. The debate is between those who foresee a hard landing and those who believe that the world's central bankers will somehow figure out a way to avoid a global financial meltdown. But hard landing or soft, even the staunchest supporters of globalization admit that lower living standards are already in the cards.[370]

Here is what some prominent political and economic leaders in the U.S.A. had to say in relation to the upcoming future economic conditions of the U.S.A.:

- N. Gregory Mankiw, the George W. Bush administration's economist said that the U.S.A.'s reliance on foreign investors to support its high level of consumption will mean a *"less prosperous future."*
- In the year 2005 Paul Volker,[371] a member of the power elite of the U.S.A. and former chairman of the U.S.A, Federal Reserve said that there was a *75% chance of an economic catastrophe within 5 years.*

- Financier Warren Buffett concluded in 2004 that the U.S.A. is moving towards *"significant political unrest."*
- Democratic Senator Max Baucus, [January 2006] who is a supporter of globalization, told Chinese business executives recently that China should cut their country's trade deficit with the U.S.A. by withholding exports or else *"US politics will become unmanageable."*

Any of several possible scenarios could cause the economy of the U.S.A. to collapse and if it does its collapse will reverberate through the world financial markets and adversely affect other economies. Some recent examples of financial collapse were the devaluation of the Mexican and Argentinean currencies and before that the British also experienced a collapse. The same could likely happen to the U.S.A. but there is a possibility that the downturn could be more severe.

> Anyplace one or more of the four factors you're about to discover could have an impact on America's petroleum supply I call an "oil chokepoint." A combination of any of these (although each of them could do it single-handedly) has the potential to not just make the U.S. oil outlook grim, but to spell the *end of our world as we know it* - a world where we can't afford to consume to our heart's content, and where America's oil interests aren't sovereign...
> In other words: A world where you may not have a steady job, where many of your investments (even blue chips) have tanked, where everything from groceries to heating oil costs a fortune, where the United States isn't the top dog economically or militarily anymore and where you'll no longer be able to just fly or drive anywhere you want. A world where your freedom and livelihood are *put in mortal jeopardy.*[372]

Possible scenarios for the near future based on financial disturbance to the economy:

Scenario 1: Recession- the economy becomes depressed as in the 1970s and early 1980s and there would be difficult times but people get by.

Scenario 2: Depression- severe economic distress but country goes on with severe economic downturn. [Hard Times] The current generation would define their lives as the older Great Depression generation did, by the deprivation and destitute nature of life. Nevertheless, as with the Great Depression, the rich will continue to be rich and control the population with coercion or police and army.

Scenario 3: Financial Collapse of the world Economy:

- U.S. dollar falls 30% or more relative to the euro and loses its status as world reserve currency and the U.S.A. can no longer finance the deficits of the past and must stop any deficit spending.
- The Euro takes over as the world reserve currency and the European Union becomes the economic world power while the U.S.A. remains as the world military power due only to its nuclear arsenal.
- pump price for gasoline *skyrockets to $5.32 per gallon* or more
- Crude oil prices *explode to more than $150* per barrel
- Over *2 million American jobs or more vanish* across varied sectors and the unemployment figures can rise to 20% or more, even higher than the Great Depression of the 1930's
- The Standard & Poor 500 blue chip stock index *drops by 28%*
- An *instant recession* all but cripples the U.S. economy, followed by full scale depression.

The consequences of the conditions outlined above would include:

- Due to high costs people can't travel because airlines are grounded because people can't pay the higher costs- or they (airlines and people) may be even forced into bankruptcy.
- Some people who are fortunate enough to hold onto their jobs will not be able to get to work since bus schedules would be cut.

- Grocery store shelves get increasingly bare because it is too costly to ship anything or because the costs to produce things or import them gets to high.
- New car sales plunge as the "Big Three" auto makers of Detroit [Chrysler, GM and Ford] struggle for solvency.
- There would be no money left for entertainment, travel, retail buying or entrepreneurship. People would be forced into subsistence level living as it was before the present "standard of living" was achieved through imperialism, underhanded economics. People would be forced to live in a way they are not used to but out of the illusory way that has led to hubris and social pretentiousness, etc. i.e. the country would be humbled-but would find it hard to accept.
- There would be shortages of food since the economy was based on imports, so food prices will go up and some people will not have money to pay so they will starve and there will be large famines since the government will be slow to respond if at all.
- Minorities in the country [especially illegal immigrants and African-Americans] would be used as scapegoats and persecuted for the country's ills.
- The whole U.S. economy would *stall on the way to full collapse*.

One possible positive effect of the financial collapse would be the inability of the U.S.A to conduct wars. So the move into attacking and occupying Iraq and the continued drain on the economy due to the continuing resistance to U.S.A. occupation is hastening the demise of the U.S. Dollar and the U.S.A. economy.

In the event of a major financial collapse in the U.S.A. everyone would want to survive and perpetuate the culture and eventually there would be a sorting out and reorganization of the economy but not before some traumatic social events. The country may experience conditions like those of the Great Depression coupled with social strife like the 1960s. Surely there would emerge religious animosity and conflict as some fundamentalist Christian groups would claim that God has forsaken the U.S.A. for its sins of allowing "Jews", "gays" and "fornicators" or "immigrants" and other "undesirables" from entering and running the country down. Also, racism, which still exists, would experience a resurgence as many of the majority population, which is still of mostly European descent ["white" people] even though they may have some non European (including African) ancestry], enter into active efforts to expel non-whites [African-Americans, Asian-Americans, Hispanic-Americans, Native-Americans, etc.] but not before demonizing them and or blaming them for the dire conditions of the country. Unscrupulous politicians, demagogs, would fan the flames of hatred and discontent so as to get the masses, seeking stability, to grant them power to "make things better." There would be many people incarcerated and the social strife would lead to many deaths. There will be many of European descent who would object to the treatment of minorities but just as they objected to other social ills, like the war on Iraq, without much effect, their efforts will be inconsequential, without real conviction or political organization and consequently would be of no consequence, and their calls would go unheeded. One reason is because they would not have the fortitude to cope with the struggle of life and at the same time challenge the power of the power elite, being backed by those who follow them blindly or through a deluded sense of patriotism.

Strategies to cope with the challenges of the future:

- Reduce debts.
    - Do not get a larger house when a smaller one will do. Avoid large mortgage payments.
    - Do not get a new car if the older one is in good running order. Avoid car payments.
- If possible, move from an overprized real estate location to a less overprized location. If possible, use the profit [before the real estate bubble and dollar bubble] deflate the cost of real estate to purchase a home to live in that requires no mortgage expense or does not require as much mortgage expense.
- Stop eating meat and processed foods.

- Learn to have your own garden and water supply in case of any emergencies.
- Place some assets in tangible commodities such as gold and silver and real estate in other countries to spread the risk from having assets in the U.S.A. Keep in mind that real estate is not as liquid as currency or other assets and is susceptible to deflation.
- Live in an area where you would not be susceptible to social violence;
    - where there is a community of ethical people who will not turn to violence and degradation, looting and hatred as an outlet for their despair and fear in times of strife.
    - Prepare to leave the country if necessary by having other real estate assets and income producing capacities in other countries.
- In other words gain a skill that would be necessary in any society such as a trade or other form of self-sufficient endeavor.
- Look into ways to simplify life, reduce debts and become self-sufficient.
- If possible move to an area where the climate is milder, such as the tropical zone, and will not require as much energy to heat up in the winter or cool down in the summer.
- Live with or close to others of like mind who you can cooperate with and who can support you if the society deteriorates.
- Simplify your life, divest from high mortgages, and places were it is expensive to live.
    - Learn to live a simple life without extravagant needs.
    - Turn your attention towards the deeper meaning of life and realize that the strife of society, not just the troubles ahead, but all troubles, are designed to lead you to understand that there is no perfect situation in the world even though some may seem to last longer than others.

Q & A

Question

I hope this mail reaches you in the best of health. I have a couple of questions that I would like the esteemed elder to enlighten me on. Given the subject of this book I wanted to know if there is any correlation between its subject and the prophesies of Native Americans. Is December 21, 2012 a date that we should be preparing for since I am hearing a lot of talk about this date? Is this the end of the world? If yes, what's the story behind this and how do we prepare?

Thank you

Answer

The date "December 21, 2012" has been the object of much speculation in some circles because the Mayan calendar ends on that date (give or take a year). In that year also there will be some astronomical conjunctions of heavenly bodies. Some people have speculated that the world will end. Mind you, the Christians have been saying that the world would end for the last 1900 years, most recently in 1970 and we see what happened with that! Some New Age spiritualists have said that the world would end on the date 5/5/2000 and we see what happened with that! Some others have made wild speculations such as:

- Hyperspatial Breakthrough
- Planetesimal Impact
- Alien Contact
- Historical Metamorphosis
- Metamorphosis of Natural Law
- Solar Explosion
- Quasar Ignition at the Galactic Core
- Resurrection of Osiris

Surviving Maya elders are upset because ignorant people have been prophesying and speculating in their name. They say the world will not end but will be transformed. It is more likely that the world will end or rather that human civilization will end due to nuclear war or the destruction of the environment, economic crisis or health disasters rather than the conjunction of astronomical objects or the end of calendars, which are only descriptions of segments of time as we experience it, a piece of eternity. The world is always transformed every day; things always change.

The world will go through changes. In order to be prepared, for the best or the worst, all should follow the advice given here, to become self-sufficient, reduce expenses, turn to a healthier lifestyle and gain the skills necessary to survive in the troubled economy of the future. This would be a good time also for philosophical research. What is the meaning of life and why is humanity going through this stage? Those kinds of questions will help you find personal meaning and also your place in the world. Working to answer these kinds of questions will bring peace in the time ahead and will allow you to be secure that you will make it to the other side.

Conclusion: What happens next?

As a summary I would like to include a statement by Dr. David Ray Griffin, a professor emeritus of philosophy of religion and theology, at the Claremont School of Theology in Claremont, California, from his essay *9/11 and American Empire: How should religious people respond?*

> I suggested earlier that seeing the true connections between 9/11 and the global domination project helps us understand how fully this project reflects "fanaticism based on a deeply perverted value system." This is a value system that is diametrically opposed to the value systems on which all the great religious and moral traditions of the world have been based. These traditional value systems say that we should not covet, steal, and murder, and that we should make sure that everyone has the necessary means for a decent life. But our government's project for global domination is carried out in the name of the greed of the "haves" of the world to have still more, even if it means killing hundreds of thousands of people and letting millions more die every year of starvation and poverty-related diseases. We can now see, furthermore, that some political and military leaders are so fanatically infected with these perverted values that they are willing to kill thousands of their own citizens, then endlessly use a deceptive account of these terrorist attacks to justify "a war on terror," in the name of which they claim the right to do virtually anything they wish, ignoring all principles of morality and international law.

What is the purpose for amassing great quantities of wealth; more than one can possibly use? Power can be a form of compensation for insecurity but power can also be a high for a person who "has everything" and is bored with life. The economic maelstrom created by the world plutocracy is no longer just for pleasure seeking in the ordinary sense, buying big houses and fancy cars and land, etc. it is evident that the purpose is power. It has been done before, by the empires of the past, and was described in detail by Machiavelli. However, the current level of power-seeking is unprecedented in that the goal is not just to acquire and control territories or commodities but to control whole governments and whole countries along with the people in them. Thus, there is great investment in mass media, genetic manipulation of food and more effective means to control people physically [riot control methods].

As Noam Chomsky[373] explained, the reason for the power elite promoting fiscally unsound expenditures such as swollen deficits, bloated defense budgets and the private health care system which are justified by fear of enemies, is for the purpose of driving the economy into a state of crisis that will force the drastic action of cutting social programs altogether which will undercut the populace and leave them destitute and at the mercy of the power elite with their vast military power. This means that the population within the developed country would become conditioned through terror alerts, and fear of dire economic conditions to accept becoming relatively as destitute as those people in the developing countries and would become more pliable to the control of the power elite.

So what Alexander and Caesar and Napoleon and Genghis Khan and Attila or the British Empire and others could not do is now being attempted by the world power elite through such strategies as fiat currency, and institutions such as the I.M.F. and the World Bank, as well as conditioning of the minds of people through propaganda, mindless entertainments and barbaric sporting events, meat eating and chemicals in foods, and fear instead of cooperation.

Many of the problems faced by the U.S.A. society in particular and the world in general [political-social-economic] occurred in ancient civilizations such as ancient Rome. Ancient Rome faced the barbarians at the gates. With the disengagement of the dollar from the gold standard, the present devaluation of the dollar, the real estate bubble, the rise of global warming and the coming healthcare crisis it appears to be Rome all over again. Who are the barbarians now? –the political and religious fundamentalists and corporations who have blinded themselves to rationality and espouse ideas that are destructive to society. This should remind us of movies such as Robocop, and others where the corporations take over the insolvent government and the tyrants are in the board room! So the source of social degradation is the society itself due to not acting in ways that are in harmony with truth. Living in a way that promotes pleasure-seeking and disregard for truth, promotes pain and suffering to other humans and to animals as well as nature itself. This is the source of ill health as well as a contributing source of distress, anger and hatred in the world. It is more than ironic that that pain and suffering meted out by humanity is being returned to humanity in the form of degenerative and infectious diseases and inhabitable environments.

There are voices of reason in today's society, though they are drowned out by the din of fear mongering and warmongering and apocalyptic fanaticism or the corporate blind championing of capitalism.

Gary Hart is the author of *The Shield and the Cloak: The Security of the Commons*, and was a Senator and candidate for president of the U.S.A. In his book and in an interview on news program *Democracy Now* he talked about military security, government corruption and the needed political reforms for the U.S.A. government in order to turn away from the current course.

> "Basically, what the country is going through now is a rerun of what happened during periods of the Vietnam War, in which largely the Nixon administration undertook illegal activities to place American citizens under surveillance and accuse them of unpatriotic conduct, and justifying support for the war -- using support for the war as a justification for violation of constitutional rights and liberties. So, what's happening now is a rerun of history, in effect…"
> "…I think we have to broaden our understanding of what it means to be secure in the 21st century. The 20th century clearly was a century of ideology. We defeated imperialism, we defeated fascism. We stood off communism. And that ended in 1991. And now, we're not clear on -- I mean, war on terrorism replaced containment of communism as our central organizing principle. But if you've lost your job, you're not secure. If your children are contaminated by pollutants, you're not secure. If your son or daughter loses their lives -- their life in Gulf War III, IV or V, so your neighbor can drive his Humvee, you're not secure. So we have to broaden our understanding of what security means to include the environment, to include energy, to include economic livelihood. And I don't know anyone else that's making this argument. And second, the idea of national security is simply eroding, because America can't be secure if the rest of the world is insecure. So rather than go it alone, as we are right now, we desperately need international alliances and friends and partners, both to deal with terrorism, but also to address issues like global warming. The challenges of the 21st century include mass migration south to north -- the Europeans and we are suffering -- I mean, are experiencing this; climate change and global warming; weapons of mass destruction; and the list goes on.

> Those do not lend themselves to military solutions, nor can any single nation solve any of those problems."[374]

The community of humanity must work to reduce and ultimately abandon the idea of nationalistic exclusiveness in which nations seek to selfishly promote their own agendas, excluding the needs of other nations. Just as a family cannot operate well if some members of the family are selfish, so too, the human community will not function well. It will be continuously beset with conflicts and strife.

You as an individual must stand up for your own financial and physical health. Those who want to rely on the government or on authorities or on anyone else to provide for their security are deluded. Seek to understand the meaning of life, simplify your life and create conditions that are conducive to peace in your life, community, nation and world.

That U.S.A. culture is headed for hard times is now accepted by economists and environmental scientists as well as social scientists. Financially, the reason is that will be the only way to balance the trade deficit and start to pay for the government debt. Environmentally, the reason is that the raising of the global temperature is and will cause severe problems for humanity. In health the reason is that most people continue to accept the notion of eating animal products which are poisonous to the body and the production of which is degenerative to the environment.

There are many people in society who choose not to face these issues and when the result of those social policies reaches a certain level that will be undeniable and uncontrollable those people will be surprised. When we look around us we see people driving, buying cars, houses, boats and using their credit cards, going to movies, watching TV and carrying on as if everything is OK and thinking that the government will perpetuate the current situation indefinitely we might tend to fall into that delusion along with them. Yet it cannot continue indefinitely because the government does not exist in a vacuum or in a world that it can control indefinitely. Other people will inevitably develop their economies to the extent that they will not want to support U.S.A. consumerism at the expense of their own economies and that has already started to happen in several parts of the world. As was demonstrated with the situation in Iraq, the U.S.A military power is limited. So if sufficient numbers of people arise and throw off the U.S.A. economic hegemony from their countries the U.S.A. economy will fall- and that process has already begun.

Most people in the U.S.A. who are finding out about these issues and who have ethical consciousness or who are fearful of the future, are overwhelmed and do not know what to do. They have been inculcated with sentimental ideals of the American Dream or are too lost in the day-to-day struggle to pay their bills and cannot pay attention and reorient their lives to control their government and the people running it.

So the same type of belt tightening measures that the I.M.F. imposes on other countries will be felt in the U.S.A. The question is how harsh will the coming austerity period be and how long it will last? Looking at the cases of the United Kingdom, Mexico, and Argentina it will be a situation that the current generation has never seen and factoring the extreme and unprecedented depth of the negative financial condition it will be more severe. This is why there will be civil unrest and social strife. The so-called "American way of life" and the "American standard of living" will be lost to the middle and lower classes of the society. But in order to maintain order, the police forces will be well paid and police brutality and abuses will increase, until the society may approach the level of martial law. Yet, life will go on, though people know intrinsically that they have been living in a bubble reality. Nevertheless, they will not want to accept the new condition and so there will be strife, anger and widespread disgust and lawlessness.

Perhaps the most amazing phenomenon of this research is that while western culture has given perhaps the most freedom of speech than other government systems in modern times, most of its people generally seem to be intoxicated with the luxuries of consumerism and are smitten with their government leaders in such a way that the leaders can do what they please as long as the economy allows the consumerism to continue. It is as if the culture is disconnected from its humanity and does not understand the interconnectedness of life which demands retribution for unethical behavior, complacency and acquiescence.

The biosphere of the earth is one connected system, so if a part of it is distressed it will affect other parts, so the nineteenth century mechanistic idea of the world as a machine with separate parts, does not work. The human race is also not a machine. The injustices perpetrated on one group are visited on the other in the fullness of time just as pollution in one country affects all other countries around the world. So it is indeed the responsibility of every human being to promote equity and justice for all populations and for the earth and to resist the temptation to become lost in the sea of greed and self-centered vanity.

It is incumbent upon every human being to discover the means to understand the plight of the world today and not get caught up in the rhetoric and propaganda of war and pleasure-seeking that cloud the intellect to the true meaning of life and the possibilities for making the world a better place while at the same time discovering one's purpose and true happiness in life. While the hard times ahead may not be avoided the lessons from the past must be faced and the truth must be upheld through direct pursuit of justice for all peoples in all countries. Until that happens there will be no end to empires, no end to tyrants and dictators because if injustice is allowed abroad and not at home the injustice in the heart will manifest at home unconsciously and silently until it destroys the fabric of culture and its very foundation, which is the justice system. Complacency and apathy are not lost all at once but year in and year out, in degrees, after many struggles in paying bills and mortgages and listening to propaganda day in and day out. As with any cycle we are coming to the end of the U.S.A. empire as we have known it for the last 60 years but there is always some other emperor waiting in the wings, to pull the wool over the eyes of the ignorant, the tired, the hungry or the fanatical. So knowledge is a key, self-sufficiency is a key, organization is a key and ethics is a key to establishing the next society if it is to be governed by balance, justice, equitable economics, natural health and compassion for all human beings.

> "When opulence and extravagance are a necessity instead of righteousness and truth, society will be governed by greed and injustice."
>
> -Ancient Egyptian Proverb[375]

On February 15th and 16th 2003, some 10 million or more people around the world expressed their overwhelming opposition to the war in Iraq through marches and demonstrations. This was an unprecedented move by the world's people who are cognizant of the danger of militarism and many of whom have experienced the devastation of an unjust world market economy. Citing the failure of Brazil's leader, and South Africa's leader Nelson Mandela to truly transform a political victory, ousting the corporocracy and establishing a government and economy that serves the common people, Arundhati Roy made some astute observations.

> I'm thinking here of President Luiz Inacio "Lula" da Silva of Brazil. Lula was the hero of the World Social Forum last year. This year he's busy implementing IMF guidelines, reducing pension benefits and purging radicals from the Workers' Party. I'm thinking also of ex-president of South Africa, Nelson Mandela. Within two years of taking office in 1994, his government genuflected with hardly a caveat to the market god. It instituted a massive program of privatization and structural adjustment, which has left millions of people homeless, jobless and without water and electricity.
> Why does this happen? There's little point in beating our breasts and feeling betrayed. Lula and Mandela are, by any reckoning, magnificent men. But the moment they cross the floor from the opposition into government they become hostage to a spectrum of threats — most malevolent among them the threat of capital flight, which can destroy any government overnight.
> ...Radical change will not be negotiated by governments; it can only be enforced by people.
> ... While our movement has won some important victories, we must not allow non-violent resistance to atrophy into ineffectual, feel-good, political theatre. It is a very precious weapon that needs to be constantly honed and re-imagined. It cannot be allowed to become a mere spectacle, a photo opportunity for the media.[376]

If there is a solution to the problem of the world power elite and their military industrial complex, it likely is the uprising of millions of individuals who refuse to go along with plans that enrich the rich and slowly drain the life out of the poor and which call for the constant conflict and warmongering that cause people to succumb to their fears and render them weak, malleable subjects, ripe for manipulation and self-destruction. That will be the death of empire by popular demand. But that will hold as long as people remember and are vigilant, for the seeds of imperialism remain in the egoistic psyche and the desire filled personality that wants to rule and become rich.

A Window of Opportunity?

The title of this book, *The Death of American Empire,* contains the word and concept of death, but death should not be thought of in the ordinary way, as a final and absolute end. Affording to some spiritual traditions there is an afterlife and to others there is reincarnation. The imperial idea will not die for ever but it will die as we know it and the culture that gave birth to it will continue but in an unknown different form. In time people will forget the past just as they have forgotten about the "Great Depression" of the 1930s. Then there will be a time of seeming prosperity and another crash and people will say then why didn't we do the right thing? Why didn't we learn from the last crash? Before that happens there may be an opportunity to change things, to change the way that society is arranged and to institute sustainable and renewable economies. There are many groups that would like to see the U.S.A. fall; some because they are scared of U.S.A. hegemony and others because they are rivals of U.S.A. imperialist power and would like to take its place. Still others would like to see the downfall because of grievances due to past U.S.A wrongdoings to other countries and dissidents. In Ancient Egyptian Philosophy and Indian Hindu Buddhist Philosophies, there is a concept called *ariu* in Ancient Egypt and *karma* in India. This concept holds that the past actions lead to present conditions. Thus, the present negative conditions being faced would be due to past unrighteousness. Thus, the result is a kind of punishment for the past actions. Others might call this "chickens coming home to roost." Nevertheless, the results lead to suffering that is supposed to teach lessons. If the sufferers do not learn the lessons and become virtuous, they are bound to commit the same actions again that will lead to more suffering in this life or the next. Nations have *ariu* or *karma* just as individual do. One example of that is the trouble encountered by the U.S.A. with Iran and various South American countries due to a backlash from the U.S.A. sponsored toppling of their legitimate governments and supporting dictators, etc. Since under these concepts [*ariu* or *karma*], there is no death in the western sense, people reincarnate and suffer for their past actions and do not escape their wrongdoings.

Yet, the downfall will cause worldwide problems for all nations but eventually others may try to take the place of the U.S.A., perhaps Russia or China, and that will lead to strife. So provisions should be made to promote a family of nations that promote the common good instead of individual agendas; that was the original goal of the United Nations.

The empire that is the United States, as the Roman, Ottoman, British and other empires that came before, will come to an end as we know it today. There will be a necessity to scale back all areas of society. It will not be possible to have unrestricted consumerism and deficit spending. The government will not be able to sustain armies all over the world. All of this will cause innumerable problems in the economy as the consumerism comes to an end. There will be massive social disruption of the previous way of life. Government officials will have difficulty governing so there will be repressive measures imposed.

During this period of reorganization of society, which may last about one generation, there will be much strife, scapegoating and political demagoguery as well as religious fundamentalism and fanaticism. But amidst the chaos there will be an opportunity that is not now possible. The lifestyle of consumerism and world dominance that has been perpetuated since the end of World War II that has become accepted and expected by most people will be shattered and so too the unwillingness of most people to listen to the voices of reason, to face the reality of the error of consumerism, capitalism and selfishness will be reduced. But even so, the capacity for the population to make use of this opportunity will depend on how much the people want to hold on to the bogus notions of "American Supremacy" or "the American Dream" and the illusory value of the U.S. Dollar.

If the society turns away from hegemony to cooperation and real promotion of democracy and freedom around the world instead of promoting dictators that favor U.S.A. political and economic designs the world may indeed move in a new direction that could lead to a positive outcome for all humanity. How are those who want to promote a better society in the future to know the true direction of government policies? And how are they to control government and make sure that the policies of sustainable, ethical government are enacted and enforced?

The true agenda of any government is not determined by the rhetoric of its leaders but by the items contained in the government's budget. For instance, while the president spoke about supporting veterans, he was at the same time cutting veteran's benefits. There will be an opportunity to expose this kind of duplicity in government and to implant ethical values in government that will manifest in fiscal responsibility in government; which will also mean an end to fiat money and budget deficits.

In order to make a new society the government and economic systems must be changed. The current constitutional system of the U.S.A. allowed the country to become what it has and so those errors must be confronted, if possible by amendments but if not by changing to a new system of government that takes power from government officials and makes them accountable to the masses. The power of corporations and their mandate to make profits at all cost must be abolished. The oil based economy must be changed to renewable fuels, with all due haste as an emergency.

It is important to end the corporate scheme of society and to institute regulations that protect workers and human rights both nationally and internationally. U.S.A. corporations should not be allowed to collude with foreign governments to enslave their populations with meager wages in order to produce cheap goods to sell to the U.S.A. population and elsewhere. This can be done by ending the legalized government bribery system that is lobbying and the legal status of corporations as "persons."

It is important to join the world community that is overwhelmingly in favor of facing the global warming issue instead of forestalling efforts by obfuscating the truth so as to prolong corporate irresponsibility and profits. The U.S.A. government should also join the International World Court and humble itself to international law.

There are many people who speak of the lofty ideals of the U.S.A. constitution and the Bill of Rights. They often tout it as a beacon of light for the world. If that is true the upcoming period may offer the opportunity for those who believe in those ideals to create a movement in society that might cause a retreat from militarism, racism and sexism and the rule of the government and the economy by a minority of men of European descent.

Nevertheless, it would seem that if the U.S. constitution has such lofty ideals there is some flaw in it that allowed the culture to be degraded to the degree that it has, with government officials that collude to take bribes and break laws with impunity. So it is apparent that greater effort should be made in raising an ethical society and correcting the flaws in the constitution in order to better prevent these kinds of situations.

So what will you do to work towards that high ideal? How will you prepare yourself to meet the upcoming challenges to survival? What organizations will you join in order to promote those high ideals? How will you position yourself and your family in order to protect and preserve health? This is the time to reflect on these questions. But the reflection time should not be too long since it is necessary to take action soon to begin preparations.

Concluding Thoughts

The inability to cede control, to share power and live in friendship is the source of strife between ordinary human beings as well as societies and even countries. Sometimes excuses may be given, such as cultural differences but underlying the surface pretext lurks the restless soul. It is that soul that great teachers and philosophers have sought to understand and heal and not until that soul of humanity is healed and allowed to rest will there be lasting peace between neighbors, communities or nations. This is perhaps one of the major questions for humanity [true needs of human beings] in the 21st century since it guides other actions.

> The major question for the twenty-first century is whether this fateful inability to adjust to changes in the global power-structure can be overcome. Thus far the signs are negative. Can the United States and Japan, today's versions of rich, established powers, adjust to the reemergence of China -- the world's oldest, continuously extant civilization -- this time as a modern superpower? Or is China's ascendancy to be marked by yet another world war, when the pretensions of European civilization in its U.S. and Japanese projections are finally put to rest? That is what is at stake.[377]

Just as a desperate person may rob, cheat or steal to save themselves or their family, so too nations can feel fear and anxiety and take actions that are self-serving and yet at the same time self-destructive even while knowing the damage that is being done. In this manner the west has forged ahead towards development regardless of the consequences to the environment, the economy or to health of the body. But just as the body can take only so much stress before the organs fail, so too the economy, the environment and the mind of the people have limits because those stresses are unnatural.[378] If a lion was chasing a person it is natural for them to feel stress and run but once they get away the stress level should go down. On the contrary, western culture has lived in stress for centuries, trying to get rich and remain rich, trying to become dominant and stay in a position of dominance, etc. by hook or by crook. Those stresses must be resolved if the human race is to survive. Life places all human beings into situations that will force them to change and societies, as well as nations, also must change. When they have difficulty changing they have wars and if they do not learn from history they must receive the lesson again. So it is incumbent upon the wise elders and scholars of society to teach the leaders the wisdom of understanding and peace. The masses need to be taught the ethical life and an ecumenical basis of spirituality so they will not be duped by charlatan politicians and religious demagogues. Then humanity will be well served and on the path to discover its higher capacity, to explore the meaning of life, provide for the welfare of nature and humankind and promote advanced culture and civilization for all.

Bringing people together to constitute a viable opposing force to counteract the actions that are despoiling the environment is extremely difficult in the age of mass media and in a society that has been coerced into consent with the superpower mentality and which has been subjugated economically through mortgages, inflationary capitalism, subsistence (paycheck-to-paycheck) lifestyles and media propaganda. Yet the effort does keep the alternative ideal alive and does benefit those who pursue it in allowing them to have a higher outlook for what humanity can be. Gore Vidal, the historian, essayist, playwright and novelist, speculated that the downfall of the United States superpower elite would not come from the opposing party but from powerful traditional conservatives that will reign in the power of the radical neo-conservatives; their power was demonstrated in the removal of Harriet Myers from consideration for the position of Supreme Court Justice when she was nominated by president George W. Bush in the year 2005. In an interview with Robert J. Lifton, Journalist Amy Goodman asked Mr. Lifton, "So, how do you break the cycle?" (of the superpower syndrome). Lifton replied:

> "You can break that cycle. You can change things in this country. There still are democratic expressions, maybe this program is one of them, in which we have our voices, don't use them as much as we should. We have to act both within the electoral system and outside of it. One thing that's very important and my book tries to address is that I don't think that Americans realize how extreme our government has been. And if you put it within this superpower and apocalyptic structure,

> you can begin to see its extremity. However, Americans are beginning to doubt what we are doing. It's as if reality is catching up with us. Because so much of this projection is a kind of fantasy that isn't borne out by actual events, as we're seeing in Iraq, and as we're seeing with our unsuccessful diatribes against nuclear proliferation rather than taking more constructive universal and international approaches."[379]

It is interesting to note that throughout history there have been many societies that have lived peacefully for hundreds of years in terms of not engendering a superpower culture; examples include Native American cultures and African cultures. Yet when a certain level of disruption in the culture occurs [death of leadership, loss of language, traditions, and spiritual values, etc.] the culture tends to disintegrate and loose its values and ethics, leaving it susceptible to fascist ideologies and alien agendas from conquering forces. In a sense, the problem that Tecumseh spoke of, relating to the Native Americans selling their lands to the white man or the actions of some African chiefs, selling Africans into slavery to the white European slave traders are examples of the degradation of culture. Nations that have previously observed the rule of law and humanitarian ethics, can suddenly turn to fascism; pre and post Nazi Germany may be an example of that. The point here is that while this rule does not apply to all individuals, as there are always some who possess an innate ethical nature, there is no genetic predisposition for rationality or ethics for any given nation. In general, ethics are learned and passed on from one generation to the next just as power, privilege and the superpower mentality are also passed down. The tendency towards ethics or vice comes from spiritual maturity and the capacity to realize the oneness of humanity and the interconnectedness of the ecology with humanity. When a society's culture of self-identity and connection with nature is disrupted, the progeny of that culture can be misguided. Cicero, the famous Roman Philosopher (106-43 BC) once said:

> "There is no more important knowledge to a people than their history and culture. If they do not know this they are lost in the world."

Therefore, it is important to use the wisdom that has been gained throughout the history of a society to uphold righteous humanitarian culture once it has been attained and establish regulations on culture while at the same time remaining vigilant and ensuring their proper application in succeeding generations. The problem arises in that human beings have short memories, that is, the wisdom of one generation can be lost to another even if the previous generation made an attempt to pass it on simply because the new generation did not experience it through struggle and the learning process and did not do the necessary work to arrive at it and so they develop arrogance and that arrogance leads to complacency and the sense of entitlement and hubris. This would mean that after the coming ecological disaster, if any survive, people will learn and will do better but their progeny may forget at some point in the future and the same thing may happen again if they do not learn the lesson well.

So societies develop in cyclical fashion, experiencing highs and lows of culture and civilization. However, just as positive societal developments can be eradicated from a society by eliminating the purveyors of it and the symbols and legacy of it, so too the negative aspects can as well be eradicated. Societies have indeed attempted this method of radical change, by killing of the elite of a society, such as the monarchy, as in the case of the Bolshevik revolution in Russia, or the killing of the educated members of society, educated that is, in the manners, beliefs and customs of the previous culture as in the case of the cultural revolution in Cambodia which was influenced by the Chinese cultural revolution. It was an attempt to erase the memory of the past culture. The Khmer Rouge regime of Cambodia arrested and eventually executed nearly anyone[380] suspected of connections with the former government or with foreign governments, as well as professionals and intellectuals who were the class targets of the Khmer Rouge.

Nevertheless, it must be realized that either magnanimous developments or misanthropic developments in a society are due to previous and many times longstanding courses of action and thinking in a society that may run their course in time or may be abruptly altered due to historical events such as wars or revolutions. However, once the fascism has run its course by disintegrating or being defeated by outside forces, the pendulum may swing to the other movement, progressiveness and reform; then wise personalities once again can lead society, that is, if extreme left wing demagogs [those who promote extreme liberalism or communism] do not take over. A complicating new factor in modern history is the technology to create, maintain and monitor systems that perpetuate and promote propaganda to support certain ideals and those systems would artificially maintain the manufactured consent longer than it normally would exist were it allowed to run its course in a pre-information society culture. So here independent media and information sources as well as education not just for promoting careers but also in the arts and in civics as well as ethics, becomes more critically important if there is a viable system of government for them to have an effect. Otherwise their efforts will be futile and simply window-dressing for a society that claims it has freedom of speech but wherein free speech has no efficacy or is of no consequence.

However, if the culture is degraded to a certain extent, it will not reemerge, but it will rather be subsumed in a new culture, that is, provided there is a world for it to emerge into [ex. Roman Empire, Greek culture, etc.]. Given the level and rate of damage to the environment and the food supply of the world, there is much work needed to ensure the continued existence of the human race on planet earth.

While it may be argued that the United States in principle stands for high ideals in culture and civilization, because of the ideals stated in its constitution, it is also impossible to find any time when those ideals have been implemented for all its citizens or promoted and implemented for humanity worldwide. Thus, no one should pay homage and offer blind allegiance to a "beast"[381] that offers neither comfort nor nurturing, neither security nor justice. Many people have died in service to the ideals of the United States Constitution, never having experienced the fruits of its promise. That too is part of the myth of the "American dream", that someday in the future there will be a Utopia Americana, but in the mean time the populace should be satisfied with football, pornography, beer and pay-per-view on one hand or religious fundamentalism [that promotes blind faith] and gated communities [that promote a false sense of security and elitism] on the other; all of that is to occur while the environment is despoiled and the treasury is plundered by corporations and the rest of the world is enslaved so that every greedy household may have cheap appliances that need to be replaced every other year.

From its inception the United States has systematically deprived whole segments of its population and the populations of the world from full integration, full rights and equal opportunity. From a practical perspective, the United States could repair the damage caused by the superpower mentality as well as its other flaws (racism, sexism, cronyism, militarism, etc.) by outlawing those policies and renouncing the superpower myths while accepting a position as one in a family of nations. But the leadership would have to give up the superpower myth as well as the contrived advantages supplied by clandestine schemes of social institutions such as conservative "think tanks" and manipulations of the world economies, governments, etc. Unless these adjustments are possible the efforts to curb the superpower's mandamus to conflict will be futile.

Peace

NOTES

[1] Wikipedia Encyclopedia
[2] Kellner, Douglas. American Exceptionalism; http://www.gseis.ucla.edu/courses/ed253a/american-exceptionalism.htm
[3] Lens (2003), op. cit. Book jacket
[4] Lens, Sidney (2003). *The Forging of the American Empire*, Haymarket Books and Pluto Press. ISBN 0745321003. Book jacket.
[5] Buchanan, Patrick (1999). *A Republic, Not and Empire*, Regnery Publishing. ISBN 089526272X. p. 165.
[6] Chomsky, Noam (1988). *Manufacturing Consent*, Pantheon Books. ISBN 0375714499 url=http://www.thirdworldtraveler.com/Herman%20/Manufac_Consent_Prop_Model.html.
[7] Miller (1982), op. cit. p. 136.
[8] Wikipedia Encyclopedia
[9] **Chalmers Johnson** is a professor emeritus of the University of California, San Diego. He is also president and co-founder of the Japan Policy Research Institute, an organization promoting public education about Japan and the rest of Asia.
[10] Miller, Stuart Creighton (1982). *"Benevolent Assimilation" The American Conquest of the Philippines, 1899-1903*, Yale University Press. ISBN 0300026978. p. 3.
[11] Foster, John Bellamy (July-August 2003). "The New Age of Imperialism". *Monthly Review*.
[12] Foster, John Bellamy (July-August 2003). "The New Age of Imperialism". *Monthly Review*.
[13] JOHN PERKINS interview on Democracynow, Democracynow.org, Democracy now Self-Described Economic Hit Man John Perkins- We Have Created the Worlds First Truly Global Empire *Wednesday, February 15th, 2006*
[14] http://www.deliberatedumbingdown.com/pages/book.htm
[15] is a neologism originally used by Jacob Talmon is his book *Origins of Totalitarian Democracy* (1951) to describe the "democracy by force" doctrines of Jean-Jacques Rousseau and its philosophical decedents, as an effective tyranny that demotes democratic principle to rhetorical use only. Variants include *totalitarian democracy* and *Jacobin democracy*.
[16] The Nation Magazine ARTICLE | *posted December 4, 2003 (December 22, 2003 issue)* American Apocalypse by Robert Jay Lifton (http://www.thenation.com/doc/20031222/lifton)
[17] *Democracy Now* with Amy Goodman, Newsmaker interview with Robert J. Lifton [Broadcast 01/05/04]
[18] Source: *The American Heritage® Stedman's Medical Dictionary*
[19] *The Deliberate Dumbing Down of America* by Charlotte Thomson Iserbyt, former Senior Policy Advisor in the U.S. Department of Education
[20] *Faith, Certainty and the Presidency of George W. Bush* by Ron Suskind OCTOBER 17, 2004
[21] Backarak, who is known for his musical compositions and much successful collaboration, felt the need to create a new album with a Rap artist to protest the current political order.
[22] *The Prince* by Machiavelli
[23] Face refers to two separate but related concepts in Chinese social relations. One is **mianzi**. The other is **lianzi**.

Lian is the confidence of society in a person's moral character, while *mianzi* represents social perceptions of a person's prestige. (Prestige means good reputation or high esteem, although it originally meant a delusion or magician's trick (Latin *præstigum*).)
[24] Of, relating to, or manifesting behavior that is habitual, maladaptive, and compulsive – from Dictionary.com
[25] Example: opposition of Iran. Documentary- Playing Brinkmanship with Iran or Will this be Americas Next War, Link TV Length: 00:30 Type of program: Current Affairs
[26] In Roman Catholic theology, papal infallibility is the dogma that the Pope, when he solemnly defines a matter of faith or morals *ex cathedra* (that is, officially and as pastor of the universal Church), is correct, and thus does not have the possibility of error. This doctrine has a long history, but was not defined dogmatically until the First Vatican Council of 1870. [Wikipedia] Convened by Pope Pius IX to deal with certain contemporary problems, such as rising liberalism and rationalism, the Council is perhaps best remembered for its declaration of papal infallibility, causing widespread protest and minor secessions from the Church. It was cut short by the interference of Italian troops. [Random House Encyclopedia]
[27] Documentary: *Deadly Arrogance: Nuclear Nightmare*
[28] Documentary: *Deadly Arrogance: Nuclear Nightmare*
[29] Iraqi cities 'hot' with depleted uranium • By Sara Flounders editor and a contributing author of the book "Metal of Dishonor: Depleted Uranium," and helped produce a video by the same - http://www.iacenter.org/images/du-703.pdf
[30] From Wikipedia, the free encyclopedia.
[31] ibid
[32] ibid
[33] Example: The U.S. diverted proceeds from the sale to the Contras, anti-Communist guerrillas engaged in an insurgency against the elected socialist Sandinista government of Nicaragua. [From Wikipedia, the free encyclopedia.]
[34] George Washington Farewell Address Philadelphia, September 17, 1796
[35] Wikipedia Encyclopedia
[36] From Wikipedia, the free encyclopedia
[37] LETTERS & PERSONAL MEMOIRS OF U. S. GRANT, CHAPTER III. ARMY LIFE--CAUSES OF THE MEXICAN WAR--CAMP SALUBRITY [the war with Mexico began in April, 1846. Grant was promoted to a first-lieutenancy September, 1847. The Mexican War closed in 1848. Both this war and the Civil War he characterizes in his _Memoirs_ as "unholy."]
[38] ibid
[39] *The Prince* by Machiavelli
[40]http://www.americaabroadmedia.org/radio-details.php?id=126&PHPSESSID=e363a1d68c2536bfff8e11e7d41cc471
[41] John Micklethwait is US Editor of *The Economist* and author of *The Right Nation.*
[42] Chalmers Johnson Interview: Conversations with History; Institute of International Studies, with Harry Kreisler UC Berkeley
[43] Ali, Tariq (October 2001). "Tariq Ali on 9/11". *Left Business Observer* (98).
[44] *The Prince* by Machiavelli
[45] *Copyright 2005 The Associated Press*
[46] *Watergate* scandal
[47] Democracy Now, *Friday,* **Civil Liberties Groups Seek Court to Shutdown NSA Spy Program** *March 10th, 2006*
[48] The International Criminal Court (ICC) was established in 2002 as a permanent tribunal to prosecute individuals for genocide, crimes against humanity, and war crimes, as defined

by several international agreements, most prominently the Rome Statute of the International Criminal Court.
[49] United States Constitution, Article II, Section 4:
[50]From Wikipedia, the free encyclopedia.
[51] *Quotations from a statement reported to have been spoken to William Henry Harrison, Governor of the Indiana Territory* (11 August 1810)
[52] ibid
[53] Hot Talk with Saul Landau. Dahr Jamil, The journalist recounts his experiences in Iraq between 2003-05. [http://video.csupomona.edu/streaming/inc/ht_index.html]
[54] This format exemplifies ethnic divisions instead of unify under a single national concept.
[55] INN World Report –Dish TV DeC. 1 2005 [INNWorldReport.net]
[56] ibid
[57] The New York Times, Vanityfair.com
[58] ibid
[59] National Public Radio NPR.org-Iraq: Vivid Language from Iraq's Constitution Oct-22-2005, All Things Considered
[60] *Without a Doubt* By Ron Suskind The New York Times, Saturday 17 October 2004 [*Ron Suskind was the senior national-affairs reporter for The Wall Street Journal from 1993 to 2000. He is the author most recently of "The Price of Loyalty: George W. Bush, the White House and the Education of Paul O'Neill."]*
[61] LETTERS & PERSONAL MEMOIRS OF U. S. GRANT, CHAPTER III. ARMY LIFE--CAUSES OF THE MEXICAN WAR--CAMP SALUBRITY
[62] CIA Operation Ajax to overthrow democratically chosen Prime Minister Mohammed Mossadegh and restore the exiled Shah. (From Wikipedia, the free encyclopedia.)
[63] From Wikipedia, the free encyclopedia.
[64] Zinn, Howard (1991). *Declarations of Independence: Cross Examining American Ideology*, Perennial. ISBN 0060921080., pg 16
[65] ambassador to the United Nations for president Bill Clinton
[66] National Security Advisor for president George W. Bush
[67] At various times Northern-Western Europeans have viewed southern Europeans as lesser beings because of their association with North Africans, specifically Rome with Carthage in ancient times and Spain with Morocco and the Arab conquest of Spain. The hue of skin, hair and eyes of the southern Europeans generally tending towards swarthiness, and darker color relegates them to a lower status of European elite.
[68] (February, 1766 – December 23, 1834), who is usually known as Thomas Malthus, although he preferred to be known as "Robert Malthus," was Parson, an English demographer and political economist best known for his pessimistic but highly influential views.
[69] ibid
70 From Wikipedia, the free encyclopedia
71 Media Matters for America. Wed, Mar 22, 2006 3:25pm EST - http://mediamatters.org/items/200603220010
72 Guns, Germs, and Steel by Jared Diamond
73 From Wikipedia, the free encyclopedia. Retrieved from http://en.wikipedia.org/wiki/Scramble_for_Africa
74 1. a delusional mental disorder that is marked by infantile feelings of personal omnipotence and grandeur Source: *Merriam-Webster's Medical Dictionary, © 2002 Merriam-Webster, Inc.* 2. A psychopathological condition characterized by delusional fantasies of wealth, power, or omnipotence. *The American Heritage® Dictionary of the English Language, Fourth Edition Copyright © 2000 by Houghton Mifflin Company.*
[75] The Western Tradition by Ugen Webber, Professor of History, UCLA

[76] Bartolome De Las Casas - The Devastation of the Indies: A Brief Account (1542)
[77] Seasonal affective disorder, or SAD, is an affective, or mood disorder. Most SAD sufferers experience normal mental health throughout most of the year, but experience depressive symptoms in the winter. SAD is rare, if existent at all, in the tropics, but is measurably present at latitudes of 30°N (or S) and higher.
[78] Singh PN. Does low meat consumption contribute to greater longevity? In: Sabaté J, ed. Vegetarian nutrition. Boca Raton, FL: CRC Press, 2001:135–70.
[79] Gottlieb S. Evidence grows that eating red meat increases cancer risk.
BMJ. 2005 Jan 15;330(7483):111. No abstract available. PMID: 15649914 [PubMed - as supplied by publisher]
[80] Fung TT, Schulze M, Manson JE, Willett WC, Hu FB. Dietary patterns, meat intake, and the risk of type 2 diabetes in women. Arch Intern Med. 2004 Nov 8;164(20):2235-40. PMID: 15534160 [PubMed - indexed for MEDLINE]
[81] *The Kemetic Diet*- by Muata Ashby
[82] From Wikipedia, the free encyclopedia
[83] In geography, temperate latitudes of the globe lie between the tropics and the polar circles. From Wikipedia, the free encyclopedia
[84] Ancient Egyptian Wisdom Texts
[85] George Washington Farewell Address Philadelphia, September 17, 1796
[86] statement in the 1990's during the Clinton [Democratic administration]
[87] Chalmers Johnson Interview: Conversations with History; Institute of International Studies, with Harry Kreisler UC Berkeley
[88] Dwight D. Eisenhower, 1961 Public Papers of the Presidents, Dwight D. Eisenhower, 1960, p. 1035- 1040
[89] ibid
[90] ibid
[91] Example: Basil Zaharoff's Vickers Company sold weapons to all the parties involved in the Chaco War. Basil Zaharoff's Vickers Company sold weapons to all the parties involved in the Chaco War. Example 2: William Randolph Hearst was believed by many to have drummed-up the Spanish-American War of 1898 to encourage sales of his newspaper. From Wikipedia, the free encyclopedia
[92] The Federalist Papers are a series of 85 articles about the United States Constitution, first published serially in New York City newspapers (the *Independent Journal*, the *New-York Packet* and the *Daily Advertiser*) between October 27, 1787 and May 28, 1788. A compilation, called *The Federalist*, was published in 1788. The Federalist Papers were intended to explain the new Constitution to the residents of New York state and persuade them to ratify it. The articles were written by James Madison, Alexander Hamilton, and John Jay, under the pseudonym "Publius" in honor of Publius Valerius Publicola.
[93] Democracy now transcript **Antonia Juhasz on The Bush Agenda- Invading the World, One Economy at a Time** Tuesday, April 25th, 2006
[94] USA Today, WASHINGTON (AP) — President Bush said Wednesday that American troops under fire in Iraq aren't about to pull out, and he challenged those tempted to attack U.S. forces, "Bring them on."
[95] ibid
[96] Speech before a joint council of the Choctaw and Chickasaw nations (1811)
[97] ibid
[98] book *African Origins of Civilization* by Muata Ashby
[99] Robert J. Lifton- Interview with Amy Goodman *Democracy Now*
[100] PBS http://www.pbs.org/wgbh/pages/frontline/shows/missile/view/

[101] FRONTLINE: *Bush's Missile Doctrine* George W. Bush names Donald Rumsfeld his secretary of defense, and the administration vows to make missile defense a reality by 2004.
[102] Historian, Investigative Journalist –books: *911 Synthetic Terrorism. Bush: Unauthorized Bio. Against Oligarchy* www.tarpley.net.
[103] Case & Fair, 1999: 790
[104] From Wikipedia, the free encyclopedia
[105] Social Darwinism is a social theory which holds that Darwin's theory of evolution by natural selection is not only a model for the development of biological traits in a population, but can also be applied to human social institutions. Social Darwinisim was popular in the late 19th century to the end of World War II, although some have claimed that contemporary sociobiology could be classified as a form of Social Darwinism. Proponents of Social Darwinism often used the theory to justify social inequality. Others used it to justify racism and imperialism. At its most extreme, some Social Darwinism appears to anticipate eugenics and the race doctrines of the Nazis. From Wikipedia, the free encyclopedia.
[106] ibid
[107] *Democracy Now* with Amy Goodman, Newsmaker interview with Robert J. Lifton [Broadcast 01/05/04]
[108] The U.S. "Green Light" to Invade Kuwait -*American War Crimes During the Gulf War* by Francis A. Boyle (The author served as Legal Advisor: to the Palestine Liberation Organization on Creation of the State of Palestine (1987-1989), to the Palestinian Delegation to the Middle East Peace Negotiations (1991-1993) and sometime to the Provisional Government of the State of Palestine.
http://www.mediamonitors.net/francis19.html
[109] *ibid*
[110] statement in the 1990's during the Clinton [Democratic administration]
[111] *Rogue States* by Noam Chomsky
[112] *Nuclear Terror at Home* By Noam Chomsky
[113] In 1995 the Russian president Boris Yeltsin came within 12 seconds of releasing nuclear weapons on the United States due to an error. [Documentary: *Deadly Arrogance: Nuclear Nightmare*]
[114] *Democracy Now*
[115] A study by researchers at Texas A&M University (when George W. Bush was governor) found "Teen sex increased after abstinence program." More from Reuters: Despite taking courses emphasizing abstinence-only themes, teenagers in 29 high schools became increasingly sexually active, mirroring the overall state trends, according to the study conducted by researchers at Texas A&M University. "We didn't see any strong indications that these programs were having an impact in the direction desired," said Dr. Buzz Pruitt, who directed the study. Bush's record in Texas on teen pregnancies, via Advocates for Youth: Texas ranks dead last in the decline in teen birth rates among 15-to 17-year-olds, ranking 50th out of 50. Between 1991 and 1998, the teen birth rate in this age group dropped by more than 21 percent in the United States as a whole; Texas' rate declined by only 10 percent.
[116] *Exploring Social Change* by Harper and Leicht pp 63-64
[117] From Wikipedia, the free encyclopedia. [2005]
[118] Grover Glenn Norquist (born October 19, 1956), the president of the noted anti-tax lobbying group Americans for Tax Reform, is a well-connected conservative activist with close ties to business and the media. His close business and political ties to recently-indicted lobbyist Jack Abramoff are the subject of a current federal investigation. From

Wikipedia, the free encyclopedia. Grover Norquist has been a partner of Karl Christian Rove (born December 25, 1950) is an American political consultant, and (as of 2005) U.S. President George W. Bush's senior advisor, chief political strategist, and Deputy White House Chief of Staff in charge of policy. From Wikipedia, the free encyclopedia. Both have conspired together(even though Norquist does not have a formal government elected or appointed position) to determine the agenda of the executive branch and who gets to communicate with the president. (NPR: *Fresh Air from WHYY*, December 1, 2005 · Political scientists Jacob Hacker and Paul Pierson are the authors of the new book *Off Center: The Republican Revolution and the Erosion of American Democracy*.) Note: This book is a must read for anyone who wants to know what strategies the Republican party, aided by neo-conservatives and the religious right, used to take control of the United States government beginning in the late 19960s.

[119] Speech at *Take Back America* conference.

[120] Grover Norquist -quoted in John Aloysius Farrell, "Rancor becomes top D.C. export: GOP leads charge in ideological war," Denver Post, May 26, 2003

[121] Grover Norquist -interview with Pablo Pardo from the Spanish periodical *El Mundo* as transcribed from the recording by *The Weekly Standard*

[122] Documentary: *Deadly Arrogance: Nuclear Nightmare*

[123] George W. Bush (president)-Speech to United Nations General Assembly (September 21, 2004)

[124] Shock and Awe is a controversial military doctrine which advocates attempting to destroy an adversary's will to fight through spectacular displays of power. Its authors label it a subset of Rapid Dominance, a concept of defeating an adversary by swift action against all aspects of their ability to resist, rather than strictly military forces. It is a product of the National Defense University of the United States, and has been notably applied in the 2003 U.S. invasion of Iraq. From Wikipedia, the free encyclopedia.

[125] More than 100,000 deaths according to Johns Hopkins University study, October 2004, published in *The Lancet*

[126] Bacevich, Andrew J. *The New American Militarism: How Americans Are Seduced By War*, New York & London, Oxford University Press, 2005. ISBN 0195173384, Dolan, Chris J. and Betty Glad (eds.) *Striking First: The Preventive War Doctrine and the Reshaping of U.S. Foreign Policy*, New York & London, Palgrave Macmillan, 2004. ISBN 140396548X, Donnelly, Thomas *The Military We Need: The Defense Requirements of the Bush Doctrine*, Washington, D.C., American Enterprise Institute Press, 2005. ISBN 0844742295, Woodward, Bob *Plan of Attack*, New York, Simon & Schuster, 2004. ISBN 074325547X

[127] Democracy Now *Friday, March 31st, 2006* EXCLUSIVE...Noam Chomsky on Failed States: The Abuse of Power and the Assault on Democracy

[128] http://en.wikipedia.org/wiki/Aristide

[129] ibid

[130] *Quotations from a statement reported to have been spokenby Tecumseh to William Henry Harrison, Governor of the Indiana Territory* (11 August 1810)

[131] Wikipedia encyclopedia

[132] Image based on Image:BlankMap-World.png by Vardion.

[133] Description by Howard Zinn

[134] From Wikipedia, the free encyclopedia

[135] Democracy Now.org with Amy Goodman interviewing AHMED MANSUR

[136] Italian broadcasting agency RAI has released a documentary "The Hidden Massacre" that clearly indicates that the U.S. military used the chemical weapon white phosphorus

during their attack on Fallujah in November, 2004.
http://www.rainews24.rai.it/ran24/inchiesta/default_02112005.asp
[137] Voices of a People's History of the United States by Howard Zinn and Anthony Arnove Seven Stories Press, 2004, paper p87
[138] **American Ally: Tony Blair and the War on Terror by Con Coughlin**
[139] *Slow Motion Holocaust US designs on Iraq* by Stephanie Reich CovertAction Quarterly, Spring 2002
[140]http://www.washingtonpost.com/wp-dyn/content/article/2005/09/29/AR2005092902085.html
[141] http://polardonkey.blogspot.com/2006_02_01_polardonkey_archive.html
[142] Democracynow.org
[143] Hersh: Nukes Unlikely Vs. Iran WASHINGTON, April 10, 2006 (CBS) Pulitzer Prize-winning reporter Seymour Hersh writes in the latest issue of The New Yorker magazine that the use of tactical nuclear weapons is one option being considered by the administration if Tehran doesn't abandon what Washington and other nations suspect are efforts by Iran to develop nuclear weapons.
http://www.cbsnews.com/stories/2006/04/10/earlyshow/main1483568.shtml
[144] Democracy now transcript Pentagon Papers Whistleblower Daniel Ellsberg to Government Insiders: Risk Prison to Leak Information Exposing Illegal Government Actions *Wednesday, April 26th, 2006*
145 The Real Reasons Why Iran is the Next Target: The Emerging Euro-denominated International Oil Marker by William Clark www.globalresearch.ca 27 October 2004 The URL of this article is: http://globalresearch.ca/articles/CLA410A.html
[146] Democracynow.org *Friday, March 31st, 2006* EXCLUSIVE...Noam Chomsky on Failed States: The Abuse of Power and the Assault on Democracy
[147] John Mertha (D-PA), ranking member of the House Appropriations Defense Subcommittee
[148] Want stability in the Middle East? Get out of Iraq! By William E. Odom | November 11, 2005
[149] Senior Fellow with Hudson Institute and a professor at Yale University. He was Director of the National Security Agency from 1985 to 1988. From 1981 to 1985, he served as Assistant Chief of Staff for Intelligence, the Army's senior intelligence officer. From 1977 to 1981, he was Military Assistant to the President's Assistant for National Security Affairs, Zbigniew Brzezinski.
[150] In two articles published by the Nieman Foundation for Journalism at Harvard University. http://www.randomduck.com/2005/11/
[151] **What's wrong with cutting and running?** By Lt. Gen. William Odum (Ret.) August 03, 2005
[152] Lt. Gen. William Odum (Ret.) speaking about the suggestion by Former national security adviser Zbigniew Brzezinski
[153] No Longer the 'Lone' Superpower Coming to Terms with China by Chalmers Johnson March 15, 2005 http://www.zmag.org/content/showarticle.cfm?ItemID=7446
[154] Chalmers Johnson Interview: Conversations with History; Institute of International Studies, with Harry Kreisler UC Berkeley
[155] ibid
[156] ibid
[157] **Steve Kretzmann**, Executive Director of Oil Change International. The group recently released a report called "Crude Designs: The Rip-Off of Iraq's Oil Wealth." The report argues that Iraqi oil policy has guaranteed massive profits to foreign companies through awarding them with secret contracts. http://www.crudedesigns.org/ **With Exxon Making a**

Record $5 Million Per Hour, a Look at Bush's Energy Policies Ahead of His State of the Union Democracynow.org *Tuesday, January 31st, 2006*

[158] http://www.washingtonpost.com/wp-dyn/articles/A23373-2004Jun7.html

[159] The **Western Hemisphere Institute for Security Cooperation (WHISC)**, formerly **School of the Americas (SOA)**, is a US Army facility at Fort Benning in Columbus, Georgia, USA. It is a training facility operated in the Spanish language, especially for Latin American military personnel. In 1946, the SOA was established in Panama as the Latin American Training Center - Ground Division. It was renamed the US Army School of the Americas in 1963. It relocated to Fort Benning in 1984 following the signing of the Panama Canal Treaty. Repeated efforts in Congress to curtail training at WHISC have failed. In 1999, after disclosures about torture manuals being used in the training, the U.S. House of Representatives adopted a bill to abolish the school, but its passage was stymied in a House-Senate conference committee. In 2000, mounting pressure upon the United States Congress to stop funding the SOA reached a point where the Pentagon decided to rename the school the Western Hemisphere Institute for Security Cooperation, abbreviated as WHISC or WHINSEC. [from Wikipedia encyclopedia]

[160] **Professor McCoy Exposes the History of CIA Interrogation, From the Cold War to the War on Terror** Democracynow.org *Friday, February 17th, 2006*

Alfred McCoy, professor of history at the University of Wisconsin-Madison. Author of "A Question of Torture: CIA Interrogation, From the Cold War to the War on Terror" and also "The Politics of Heroin: CIA Complicity in the Global Drug Trade."

[161] **V.A. Nurse Accused of Sedition After Publishing Letter Critical of Bush on Katrina, Iraq** Democracynow.org *Thursday, March 2nd, 2006*

[162] **Professor McCoy Exposes the History of CIA Interrogation, From the Cold War to the War on Terror** Democracynow.org *Friday, February 17th, 2006*

[163] From Wikipedia encyclopedia

[164] ibid

[165] Chalmers Johnson Interview: Conversations with History; Institute of International Studies, with Harry Kreisler UC Berkeley

166 The Perennial Philosophy (Latin philosophia perennis) is the idea that a universal set of truths common to all people and cultures exists. The term was first used by the German mathematician and philosopher Gottfried Leibniz to designate the common, eternal philosophy that underlies all religious movements, in particular the mystical streams within them. The term was later popularized by Aldous Huxley in his 1945 book The Perennial Philosophy. The term "perennial philosophy" has also been used to translate the concept of the "eternal or perennial truth" in the Sanskrit Sanatana Dharma.

The concept of perennial philosophy is the fundamental tenet of the Traditionalist School, formalized in the writings of 20th century metaphysicians René Guénon and Frithjof Schuon. The Indian scholar and writer Ananda Coomaraswamy, associated with the Traditionalists, also wrote extensively about the perennial philosophy.

http://en.wikipedia.org/wiki/Perennial_philosophy

[167] *African Origins of Civilization*, by Muata Ashby, *Mystical Journey From Jesus to Christ*, by Muata Ashby

168 Essential Judiasm: A Complete Guide to Beliefs, Customs and Rituals by George Robinson (Pocket Books, 2000). "Torah, Torah, Torah: The Unfolding of a Tradition." Judaism for Dummies (Hungry Minds, 2001). Tracey R. Rich, "Torah." Judaism 101 (1995-99).

169 While the term Jewish is used largely as a religious or and ethnic designation it is actually a religious designation or name.

170 Jewish Life in Ancient Egypt by Edward Bleiberg for the Brooklyn Museum 2002

[171] **Zealot** A member of a Jewish movement of the first century A.D. that fought against Roman rule in Palestine as incompatible with strict monotheism. Source: *The American Heritage® Dictionary of the English Language, Fourth Edition Copyright © 2000 by Houghton Mifflin Company*

[172] 1. George Robinson, *Essential Judaism* (Pocket Books, 2000), 541-50. 2. John Bowker, ed., *Cambridge Illustrated History of Religions*. 3. "Judaism." *Encyclopædia Britannica* (Encyclopædia Britannica Premium Service, 2004).
[173] *Mystical journey From Jesus to Christ* by Muata Ashby, 1998, p. 55
174 Random House Encyclopedia Copyright (C) 1983,1990 by Random House Inc.

175 Essential Judiasm: A Complete Guide to Beliefs, Customs and Rituals by George Robinson (Pocket Books, 2000). "Torah, Torah, Torah: The Unfolding of a Tradition." Judaism for Dummies (Hungry Minds, 2001). Tracey R. Rich, "Torah." Judaism 101 (1995-99).

176 "Talmud and Midrash." Encyclopædia Britannica. Encyclopædia Britannica Premium Service (2004). Essential Judiasm: A Complete Guide to Beliefs, Customs and Rituals by George Robinson (Pocket Books, 2000). "Torah, Torah, Torah: The Unfolding of a Tradition." Judaism for Dummies (Hungry Minds, 2001). Tracey R. Rich, "Torah." Judaism 101 (1995-99).

177 Contemporary Zoroastrians: An Unstructured Nation. Lanham, MD: University Press of America.
Zaehner, R.C. 1961. (Zaehner, 20-21)
178 Zoroastrianism: an Ethnic Perspective. Bombay: Good Impressions. (Ramazani, 21)
Ramazani, Nesta. 1997.

[179] [http://news.bbc.co.uk/2/hi/americas/4317498.stm, White House denies Bush God claim The White House has dismissed as "absurd" allegations made in a BBC TV series that President Bush claimed God told him to invade Iraq.]
[180] According to Palestinian negotiator Nabil Shaath, said by Bush to him, apparently in the same June 2003 meeting, as reported by BBC News. Shaath later disclaimed the quote. [http://news.bbc.co.uk/2/hi/americas/4320586.stm, Bush God comments 'not literal' A Palestinian official who said the US president had claimed God told him to invade Iraq and Afghanistan says he did not take George Bush's words literally.], Denied by White House spokesperson Scott McClellan, October 6, 2005, and by Mahmoud Abbas who attended the meeting in question. [http://www.smh.com.au/news/world/abbas-denies-bushs-mission-from-god-remark/2005/10/08/1128563027485.html, **Abbas denies Bush's 'mission from God' remark,** October 8, 2005 - 12:23PM
[181] *Without a Doubt* By Ron Suskind The New York Times, Saturday 17 October 2004 [*Ron Suskind was the senior national-affairs reporter for The Wall Street Journal from 1993 to 2000. He is the author most recently of "The Price of Loyalty: George W. Bush, the White House and the Education of Paul O'Neill."]*
[182] Democracy Now.org ***Fmr. GOP Strategist Kevin Phillips on American Theocracy: The Peril and Politics of Radical Religion, Oil, and Borrowed Money in the 21st Century*** **3-21-06**
[183] From Wikipedia Encyclopedia, http://en.wikipedia.org/wiki/Abraham
[184] see the full history in the book *Mystical Journey From Jesus to Christ* by Muata Ashby
[185] Democracy Now.org *Friday, March 31st, 2006* **EXCLUSIVE...Noam Chomsky on Failed States: The Abuse of Power and the Assault on Democracy**
[186] ibid
[187] Democracy Now.org ***Fmr. GOP Strategist Kevin Phillips on American Theocracy: The Peril and Politics of Radical Religion, Oil, and Borrowed Money in the 21st Century*** **3-21-06**
[188] Quoted from the book : Tim LaHaye (September 1998). *Rapture: Under Attack*, Multnomah Publishers.
[189] From Wikipedia encyclopedia
[190] ibid
[191] The Columbia Electronic Encyclopedia Copyright © 2004, Columbia University Press.
[192] *The Mystical Journey from Jesus to Christ* by Muata Ashby
[193] *Anderson's Constitutions* (1723) the bylaws of the Grand Lodge of England,
[194] The Columbia Electronic Encyclopedia Copyright © 2004, Columbia University Press.

---

[195] who in the year 2005 publicly advocated the assassination of Hugo Chaves, the president of Venezuela
[196] From Wikipedia encyclopedia
[197] http://www.pfaw.org/pfaw/general/default.aspx?oid=4307 *People for the American Way* **Founded in:** 1989 **Membership:** Claims nearly 2 million members, but other data suggests 300,000-400,000 members.
[198] http://en.wikipedia.org/wiki/Theocracy
[199] http://www.washingtonpost.com/wp-dyn/content/article/2006/03/21/AR2006032101723.html
[200] PBS *NOW*, with David Brincoccio
[201] http://www.sullivan-county.com/news/pat_quotes/big_lie.htm
[202] http://mediamatters.org/items/200508220006
[203] http://www.latimes.com/news/local/la-me-allsaints7nov07,0,6769876.story?coll=la-home-headlines
[204] http://www.dfw.com/mld/dfw/living/religion/14176450.htm
[205] *African Origins of Civilization* by Muata Ashby
[206] present day Palestine
[207] *African Origins of Western Civilization, Religion and Philosophy*- by Dr. Muata Ashby,
[208] One example among many is *Jerusalem Countdown: A Warning to the World* by Pastor John Hagee
[209] Mr. Kennedy serves as Chief Prosecuting Attorney for the Hudson Riverkeeper and President of Waterkeeper Alliance. He is also a Clinical Professor and Supervising Attorney at Pace University School of Law's Environmental Litigation Clinic and is co-host of Ring of Fire on Air America Radio. Earlier in his career he served as Assistant District Attorney in New York City. He has worked on several political campaigns including the presidential campaigns of Edward M. Kennedy in 1980, Al Gore in 2000 and John Kerry in 2004. http://www.robertfkennedyjr.com/about.html
[210] Ring of Fire- *Air America Radio* interview Stephenie Hendricks March 4, 2006
[211] Hitler also claimed to be a follower of the Catholic Religion
[212] *The Deliberate Dumbing Down of America* by Charlotte Thomson Iserbyt, former Senior Policy Advisor in the U.S. Department of Education
[213] The original version of this item mistakenly omitted Lott and Chambliss from "Republicans and conservatives" on FOX and Pelosi from "Democrats and progressives" on FOX. These additions changed the FOX tally from 17 to 6 in the original version to 19 to 7 in the corrected version. —Media Matters staff
[214] MEDIAMATTERS.org http://mediamatters.org/items/200501210001
[215] Ben Bagdikian, *The Media Monopoly* (Boston: Beacon Press, 1984 [1992]) p. ix.
[216] **Part of the Liberalism Resurgent web site © Copyright by Steve Kangas, editor** http://www.huppi.com/kangaroo/L-liberalmedia.htm
[217] ibid
[218] Democracy Now **Overthrow: America's Century of Regime Change from Hawaii to Iraq,** *Friday, April 21st, 2006,* DemocracyNow .org
[219] Fulgenico Batista by Jerry A. Sierra http://thescreamonline.com/essays/essays4-1/batista.html
[220] ibid
[221] From Wikipedia encyclopedia
[222] From Wikipedia encyclopedia
[223] From Wikipedia encyclopedia
[224] http://mediamatters.org/

---

[225] **New York Times** - March 11, 2003
http://www.nytimes.com/2003/03/11/politics/11POLL.html?ex=1143608400&en=218e0fabdb4df771&ei=5070
[226] US Public Opinion and War, By Benjamin I. Page **March 12, 2003**
http://www.globalpolicy.org/ngos/advocacy/protest/iraq/2003/0312uspublic.htm
[227] Clarke, Betty (2003). "The Dixie Chicks" *Guardian Unlimited* (accessed April 13, 2006)
http://arts.guardian.co.uk/reviews/story/0,,912236,00.html
[228] Americans Pay Price for Speaking Out, ***Dissenters Face Job Loss, Arrest, Threats but Activists Not Stopped*** by Backlash- By Kathleen Kenna, ***Toronto Star*** **August 9, 2003**
http://www.globalpolicy.org/ngos/advocacy/protest/iraq/2003/0809americans.htm
[229] http://www.democracynow.org/article.pl?sid=06/04/07/144219
[230] Weapons of Mass Deception, DVD
[231] INN World Report –Dish TV DeC. 1 2005 [INNWorldReport.net]
[232] **Fmr. Democratic Senator and Presidential Candidate Gary Hart: "Both Houses of Congress Belong to the President's Party"** *Tuesday, March 28th, 2006*
Democracynow.org
[233] The Party of Davos by Jeff Faux
[234] ibid
[235] Harry Belafonte on Bush, Iraq, Hurricane Katrina and Having His Conversations with Martin Luther King Wiretapped by the FBI, Democracynow.org *Monday, January 30th, 2006*
[236] INN World Report –Dish TV March. 8 2006 [INNWorldReport.net]
[237] *Egyptian Proverbs* by Muata Ashby
[238] http://www.usconstitution.net/consttop_ccon.html
[239] **The Strong Must Rule the Weak: A Philosopher for an Empire**
By Jim Lobe | May 12, 2003
[240] *Leo Strauss and the American Right* by Shadia Drury, author of 1999
[241] **The Strong Must Rule the Weak: A Philosopher for an Empire**
By Jim Lobe | May 12, 2003
[242] From Wikipedia encyclopedia, **The Strategist And The Philosopher** By Alain Frachon et Daniel Vernet **Le Monde**: Translated by Mark K. Jensen April 15, 2003
http://www.informationclearinghouse.info/article2978.htm,
http://www.lemonde.fr/article/0,5987,3230--316921-,00.html
[243] **U.S. Enters New Nuclear Age as Bush Seeks Funds for New Generation of Nukes**
Democracynow.org *Thursday, March 2nd, 2006*
[244] http://www.cbsnews.com/stories/2006/04/11/world/main1488619.shtml
[245] Want stability in the Middle East? Get out of Iraq! By William E. Odom | November 11, 2005
[246] Democracy Now, ***Overthrow: America's Century of Regime Change from Hawaii to Iraq,*** *Friday, April 21st, 2006*
[247] From Wikipedia Encyclopedia
[248] "75 years later that the Navy convened a board of inquiry, which turned up the fact that the *Maine* was actually blown up by an internal explosion." ibid
[249] From Wikipedia encyclopedia,
http://en.wikipedia.org/wiki/Gulf_of_Tonkin_%281964%29
[250] http://en.wikipedia.org/wiki/Spanish_American_War
[251] http://www.cooperativeresearch.org/project.jsp?project=911_project
[252] William Norman Grigg, "Did We Know What Was Coming?" The New American (www.thenewamerican.com) 18/5: March 11, 2002.

[253] *Rebuilding America's Defenses, The Project for the New American Century* The quote appears in Chapter V, of the document section entitled "Creating Tomorrow's Dominant Force",
[254] Federal Aviation Administration
[255] Major Mike Snyder, a NORAD spokesman, was quoted right after 9/11 as saying that interceptions are carried out "routinely"; see Glen Johnson, "Otis Fighter Jets Scrambled Too Late to Halt the Attacks," Boston Globe, Sept. 15, 2001 (http://nl.newsbank.com/nl-search/we/Archives?p_action=print). With regard to the figure of about 100 times a year, the FAA has reported that there were 67 interceptions between September 2000 and June 2001 (FAA News Release, August 9, 2002, cited in William Thomas, "Pentagon Says 9/11 Interceptors Flew: Too Far, Too Slow, Too Late," in Jim Marrs, Inside Job: Unmasking the 9/11 Conspiracies [San Rafael: Origin Press, 2004], 145-49).
[256] INN World Report –Dish TV March. 7 2006 [INNWorldReport.net]
[257] "Secretary Rumsfeld Interview with the New York Times," New York Times, October 12, 2001. Condoleezza Rice made a very similar comment, which is quoted in Chalmers Johnson, The Sorrows of Empire, 229. Also The National Security Strategy of the United States of America, published September 2002, frankly said on page 28: "The events of September 11, 2001 opened vast, new opportunities" (www.whitehouse.gov/nsc/nss.html).
[258]Zbigniew Brzezinski, The Grand Chessboard: American Primacy and Its Geostrategic Imperatives (New York: Basic Books, 1997), 24-25.
[259] Ibid., 212; cf. 35-36.
[260] *Wikipedia, the free encyclopedia © 2001-2006*
[261] **The Price of Loyalty: George W. Bush, the White House, and the Education of Paul O'Neill** by Ron Suskind
[262] Democracy Now *Monday,* **Headlines for April 24, 2006**
[263] Smith, Merritt Roe and Marx, Leo, edited (1996) *Does Technology Drive History,* Cambridge, Mass, The MIT Press , p. 228 *The Political and Feminist Dimensions of Technological Determinism* by Rosalind Williams
[264] http://www.innworldreport.net
[265] http://www.allheadlinenews.com/articles/7002872618
[266] Revisited - The Real Reasons for the Upcoming War With Iraq: A Macroeconomic and Geostrategic Analysis of the Unspoken Truth by William Clark -Original Essay January 2003 - http://www.ratical.org/ratville/CAH/RRiraqWar.html#p4a
[267] Wikipedia encyclopedia, http://en.wikipedia.org/wiki/Signing_statement
[268] http://www.democracynow.org/
[269] Democracy Now *Friday, March 31st, 2006* EXCLUSIVE...Noam Chomsky on Failed States: The Abuse of Power and the Assault on Democracy
[270] Human Rights Watch 2003 World Report http://www.hrw.org/wr2k3/us.html
[271] Apocalypse Soon By Robert S. McNamara May/June 2005
[272] *The Great Bust Ahead* by Daniel A. Arnold
[273] July 21, 2004 - America's Protestant majority is about to disappear, according to a new study by researchers at the University of Chicago. According to survey results from more than 43,000 Americans gathered over the last 30 years, the percentage of Protestants in the national population has shrunk from 63 percent in 1993 to 52 percent in 2002.
[274] From Wikipedia, the free encyclopedia.
[275] *Exploring Social Change* by Harper and Leicht pp 332
[276] *Exploring Social Change* by Harper and Leicht pp 335
[277] Glen "Rodney" King (born April 2, 1965 in Sacramento, California) was an African-American motorist who, while videotaped by a bystander (George Holliday), was forcibly subdued and arrested by Los Angeles police officers (LAPD) during a police traffic stop on

March 3, 1991. The incident raised an outcry in the African-American community, which believed the incident was racially motivated. The subsequent acquittal in a state court of four officers charged with using excessive force in subduing King led to the 1992 Los Angeles riots and mass protest around the country.

[278] Farenheight 911 by Michael Moore

[279] http://www.cbsnews.com/stories/2006/04/12/eveningnews/main1494758.shtml

[280] http://web.amnesty.org/library/index/engafr540762004

[281] From Wikipedia Encyclopedia

[282] ibid

[283] ibid

[284] government by corporations (industry)

[285] *Confessions of an Economic Hit Man* By John Perkins

[286] Pathological Consumption by Addison Wiggin. Addison Wiggin is editorial director and publisher of The Daily Reckoning. He is also the co-author, along with Bill Bonner, of the recently released New York Times bestseller, Empire of Debt: The Rise of an Epic Financial Crisis.

[287] 2005 China Revaluation. All rights reserved.
http://www.chinarevaluation.com/impact_on_other_markets_euro.shtml

[288] theconservativevoice.com http://www.theconservativevoice.com/article/13186.html

[289] http://www.innworldreport.net/#

[290] *Wikipedia, the free encyclopedia © 2001-2006*

[291] *Wikipedia, the free encyclopedia © 2001-2006*

[292] ibid

[293] *ibid*

[294] http://english.pravda.ru/world/americas/31-01-2006/75027-dollar-0

[295] The Standard and Poor's Corporation (S&P), a subsidiary of McGraw-Hill, is a company that performs financial research and analysis on stocks and debt instruments. It is one of the top three players in this business. The other two are Moody's and A. M. Best. It is best known for its US-based S&P 500 and the Australian S&P 200 stock market index.
Wikipedia, the free encyclopedia © 2001-2006

[296] Robinson, Joan Violet, 1903–83, British economist, b. Surrey, England. A socialist, she worked with Keynes and taught at Cambridge Univ. (1931–71). Her treatise, *The Economics of Imperfect Competition* (1933), analyzes the debates over monopolistic competition and microeconomic theory. Robinson was outspoken in her criticism of social and economic injustices against the developing nations; she came under fire from some Cambridge colleagues, particularly because of her criticism of neoclassical economic theory. Other works by Robinson include *An Essay on Marxian Economics* (1942), and *The Accumulation of Capital* (1956, 3d. ed. 1985). Source: The Columbia Electronic Encyclopedia Copyright © 2004, Columbia University Press.

[297] Why Invest in Gold Now? By Dr David Evans

[298] U.S. Trade Deficit Hits All-Time High February 10, 2006 7:25AM
http://www.newsfactor.com/story.xhtml?story_id=41546

[299] The U.S. Housing Market Collapse of 2005 By Dan Denning

[300] CNN money.com
http://money.cnn.com/2006/03/21/news/economy/bernanke.reut/index.htm

[301] Japan's PM sees end to deflation –BBC Friday, 3 March 2006,

[302] the central bank of the United States; incorporates 12 Federal Reserve branch banks and all national banks and state charted commercial banks and some trust companies; "the Fed seeks to control the United States economy by raising and lowering short-term interest rates and the money supply"

[303] The Undervalued Asset Looking For A Catalyst by Jim Puplava July 2, 2003
[304]The U.S. Housing Market Collapse of 2005 By Dan Denning
[305] Article: Why Invest in Gold Now? By Dr David Evans
[306] The U.S. Housing Market Collapse of 2005 By Dan Denning
[307] ibid
[308] Gretchen Morgenson is assistant business and financial editor and a columnist at the New York Times. She has covered the world financial markets for the Times since May 1998 and won the Pulitzer Prize in 2002 for her "trenchant and incisive" coverage of Wall Street.
[309] NEWS AND ANALYSIS; The Envelopes, Please, January 2, 2005, Sunday By GRETCHEN MORGENSON (NYT); SundayBusiness.
[310] SHAKE-UP AT FANNIE MAE: THE OVERVIEW; Assessing What Will Now Happen to Fannie Mae, December 17, 2004, Friday, By STEPHEN LABATON; GRETCHEN MORGENSON CONTRIBUTED, REPORTING FOR THIS ARTICLE. (NYT); Business/Financial Desk
Late Edition - Final, Section C, Page 1, Column 2, 1235 words
[311] Article: Why Invest in Gold Now? By Dr David Evans
[312] Third World is a term originally used to distinguish those nations that neither aligned with the West nor with the East during the Cold War. These countries are also known as the Global South, developing countries, and least developed countries in academic circles. Development workers also call them the two-thirds world and The South. Some dislike the term developing countries as it implies that industrialization is the only way forward, while they believe it is not necessarily the most beneficial. Many "third world" countries are located in Africa, Latin America, and Asia. They are often nations that were colonized by another nation in the past. The populations of third world countries are generally very poor but with high birth rates. In general they are not as industrialized or technologically advanced as the first world. The majority of the countries in the world fit this classification. *Wikipedia, the free encyclopedia © 2001-2006*
[313] From Wikipedia Encyclopedia
[314] "Baby Boomer" generation
[315] February 3, 2006, *Shared Responsibilities: Solving the Problem of Global Imbalances* University of California, Berkley
[316] Article: Why Invest in Gold Now? By Dr David Evans
http://www.certifiedgoldexchange.com/pdf/special_edition_why_now.pdf
[317] *Wikipedia, the free encyclopedia © 2001-2006*
[318] *De jure* (in Classical Latin *de iure*) is an expression that means "based on law", as contrasted with *de facto*, which means "in fact".
The terms *de jure* and *de facto* are used instead of "in principle" and "in practice", respectively, when one is describing political situations. *Wikipedia, the free encyclopedia © 2001-2006*
[319] *Wikipedia, the free encyclopedia © 2001-2006*
[320] The Columbia Electronic Encyclopedia Copyright © 2004, Columbia University Press.
[321] *Wikipedia, the free encyclopedia © 2001-2006*
[322] *ibid*
[323] Why Invest in Gold Now? By Dr David Evans
[324] *Wikipedia, the free encyclopedia © 2001-2006*
[325] INN World Report –Dish TV March. 8 2006 [INNWorldReport.net]
[326] http://www.washingtonpost.com/wp-dyn/content/article/2006/03/16/AR2006031602019_pf.html
[327] http://news.goldseek.com/JamesTurk/1142438460.php

---

[328] Democracy Now.org ***Fmr. GOP Strategist Kevin Phillips on American Theocracy: The Peril and Politics of Radical Religion, Oil, and Borrowed Money in the 21st Century* 3-21-06**
[329] Defunct Economists by William Greider *posted December 2, 2004 (December 20, 2004 issue)* The Nation
[330] *African Religion Vol 4: Asarian Theology* by Muata Ashby
[331] see the book *African Origins* by Muata Ashby
[332] see the book *Introduction to Maat Philosophy* by Muata Ashby
[333] *deben:* about 92 grammes, ten *kit* equalled one *deben.*
[334] *seniu*: or *shat*, was used until the New Kingdom, one twelfth of a deben, about 7.6 grammes, was replaced by the *kit.*
[335] Coins struck in Ancient Egypt exhibit the Athenian owl, but the Greek olive branch was substituted for a papyrus plant and the inscriptions were in Aramaic or Demotic.
[336] Wangstedt, Sten V. *Ausgewählte demotische Ostraka aus der Sammlung des Victoria-Museums zu Uppsala und der Staatlichen Papyrussammlung zu Berlin*
[337] Origins of Money and of Banking by Roy Davie
[338] a British financial system in which a bank or a post office transfers money from one account to another when they receive authorization to do so
[339] *Wikipedia, the free encyclopedia © 2001-2006*
[340] *source:*
http://www.nytimes.com/2006/01/29/science/earth/29climate.html?_r=3&oref=slogin&emc=eta1&pagewanted=print 30jan2006
[341] ibid
[342] International News Net World Report February 28, 2006
http://www.innworldreport.net/#
[343] **PM issues blunt warning on climate change Matt Weaver Monday January 30, 2006 http://politics.guardian.co.uk/green/story/0,,1698216,00.html**
[344] Thursday April 29, 2004 The Guardian,
http://www.guardian.co.uk/life/opinion/story/0,12981,1205166,00.html
[345] The Alliance for Healthy Homes was founded in 1990 as the Alliance To End Childhood Lead Poisoning. Our name change in July of 2003 reflects the expansion of our work on lead poisoning prevention to address other housing-related health hazards.
http://www.afhh.org/res/res_alert_archives_jul05.htm
[346] ***Divine Destruction : Dominion Theology and American Environmental Policy*** by Stephenie Hendricks see also: interview on Ring of Fire- *Air America Radio* March 4, 2006
[347] ibid
[348] Federal Emergency Management Agency
[349] Pro-Bush Demonstrators Mount "I Give a Sheet" Campaign Democracynow.org *Monday, August 22nd, 2005*
[350] Ring of Fire- *Air America Radio* interview Stephenie Hendricks March 4, 2006
[351] Debate on Climate Shifts to Issue of Irreparable Change
Some Experts on Global Warming Foresee 'Tipping Point' When It Is Too Late to Act
JULIET EILPERIN / Washington Post 29jan2006 *source:*
http://www.washingtonpost.com/wp-dyn/content/article/2006/01/28/AR2006012801021.html 30jan2006
[352] ibid
[353] http://www.washingtonpost.com/wp-dyn/content/article/2006/03/02/AR2006030201712.html
[354] Debate on Climate Shifts to Issue of Irreparable Change

---

Some Experts on Global Warming Foresee 'Tipping Point' When It Is Too Late to Act JULIET EILPERIN / Washington Post 29jan2006 *source: http://www.washingtonpost.com/wp-dyn/content/article/2006/01/28/AR2006012801021.html 30jan2006*

[355] ibid

[356] Sacks FM, Donner A, Castelli WP, Gronemeyer J, Pletka P, Margolius HS, Landsberg L, Kass EH.
Effect of ingestion of meat on plasma cholesterol of vegetarians. JAMA. 1981 Aug 7;246(6):640-4.

[357] The Comparative Anatomy of Eating by Dr Milton Mills, M.D., http://www.vegsource.com/veg_faq/comparative.htm

[358] Rave Diet

[359] Source: *WordNet ® 2.0, © 2003 Princeton University*

[360] Dictionary.com

[361] *Federalist Papers*

[362] Wikipedia Encyclopedia

[363] ibid

[364] *Exploring Social Change* by Charles Harper and Kevin Leight

[365] Wikipedia Encyclopedia

[366] ibid

[367] **Arundhati Roy Abriged version of speech given at the World Social Forum in Mumbai, 16. January 2004 INDIA: `We have to become the global resistance - January 16, author and activist Arundhati Roy**

[368] *Democracy Now* **Dubai Firm Pulls Out of U.S. Port Deal, Headlines for March 10, 2006**

[369] Religion & Ethics Newsweekly, Headlines **Week of March 10, 2006**

[370] The Party of Davos by Jeff Faux

[371] Paul Adolph Volcker (born September 5 in Cape May, New Jersey, 1927), economist, is best-known as the Chairman of the Federal Reserve under United States Presidents Jimmy Carter and Ronald Reagan (from August 1979 to August 1987). From Wikipedia ancyclopedia.

[372] *Daily Reckoning* Financial Newsletter http://www.dailyreckoning.com/LP/OutstandingInvestments.html

[373] Documentary: *Deadly Arrogance: Nuclear Nightmare*

[374] **Fmr. Democratic Senator and Presidential Candidate Gary Hart: "Both Houses of Congress Belong to the President's Party"** *Tuesday, March 28th, 2006* Democracynow.org

[375] *Egyptian Proverbs* by Muata Ashby

[376] Arundhati Roy Abriged version of speech given at the World Social Forum in Mumbai, 16. January 2004 INDIA: `We have to become the global resistance **-January 16, author and activist Arundhati Roy**

[377] ibid

[378] De-stressing: Tools for Living a Stress-Free Life By Dr. Karen Dja Clarke-Ashby

[379] *Democracy Now* with Amy Goodman, Newsmaker interview with Robert J. Lifton [Broadcast 01/05/04]

[380] estimates range from 1.5 to 3 million out of a population of nearly 8 million people. From Wikipedia, the free encyclopedia

[381] the economy of the country, as in *Starve-the-beast*

INDEX

Printed in the United States
49859LVS00006BA